LUCY STONE

LUCY STONE

AN UNAPOLOGETIC LIFE

SALLY G. McMILLEN

OXFORD
UNIVERSITY PRESS

OXFORD
UNIVERSITY PRESS

Oxford University Press is a department of the University of Oxford.
It furthers the University's objective of excellence in research, scholarship,
and education by publishing worldwide.

Oxford   New York
Auckland   Cape Town   Dar es Salaam   Hong Kong   Karachi
Kuala Lumpur   Madrid   Melbourne   Mexico City   Nairobi
New Delhi   Shanghai   Taipei   Toronto

With offices in
Argentina   Austria   Brazil   Chile   Czech Republic   France   Greece
Guatemala   Hungary   Italy   Japan   Poland   Portugal   Singapore
South Korea   Switzerland   Thailand   Turkey   Ukraine   Vietnam

Oxford is a registered trade mark of Oxford University Press
in the UK and certain other countries.

Published in the United States of America by
Oxford University Press
198 Madison Avenue, New York, NY 10016

© Sally G. McMillen 2015

Library of Congress Cataloging-in-Publication Data
McMillen, Sally G. (Sally Gregory), 1944-
Lucy Stone : an unapologetic life / Sally G. McMillen.
p.   cm.
Includes bibliographical references and index.
ISBN 978-0-19-977839-3 (hardback)
1. Stone, Lucy, 1818-1893. 2. Suffragists—United States—Biography.
3. Women's rights—United States—History—19th century. I. Title.
JK1899.S8M36 2015
324.6'23092—dc23
2014028027

1   3   5   7   9   8   6   4   2

Printed in the United States of America on acid-free paper

To Conor, Sarah, and Anna

Contents

Introduction

In the rotunda of the Capitol stand marble statues of a number of our nation's greatest figures, and among them is an eight-ton marble monument of three nineteenth-century suffragists—Elizabeth Cady Stanton, Lucretia Mott, and Susan B. Anthony.[1] The inscription on this group sculpture, which is known as the Memorial Sculpture, identifies the women as the "three great destiny characters of the world" and adds, "Historically these three stand unique and peerless." These women are, indeed, worthy of the honor and central both to American history and to the status of women in this country.

Figure 1. Portrait Monument to Lucretia Mott, Elizabeth Cady Stanton, and Susan B. Anthony (LC-DIG-hec-30,740, Library of Congress, Washington, DC)

There should be a fourth figure memorialized here, and her absence is nearly astonishing. Lucy Stone was every bit as involved as Stanton, Mott, and Anthony—however weighty and worthy their accomplishments— in the fight for human rights and equally worthy of enshrinement. Stone's pursuit of abolition and suffrage was no less relentless than that of the others mentioned above, and just as fully and fervently as they did, she recognized the inhumanity of slavery and the subordination of women as wrong, causing her to challenge the country's claim to democracy. Stone was a pathbreaker. On her own and counter to her parents' wishes, let alone that of the world in which she lived, she attended the only college in the nation that was open to women: Oberlin Collegiate Institute. Graduating with a bachelor's degree at the age of 29 in 1847, she became the first Massachusetts woman and one of the first women in the nation to earn a college degree.

Stone was determined to devote her life to her nation. She chose public speaking as her career at a time when few women dared even voice an opinion, much less address such controversial issues as antislavery and women's rights. In the spring of 1848, the Massachusetts Anti-Slavery Society hired her as a lecturer. By the early 1850s, she had become one of the most famous women in America, earning a substantial income and attracting widespread attention—respected and heralded by some and denounced by others. But everyone who heard Lucy Stone, whether critic or supporter, recognized her passionate commitment to her cause.

Stone played a pivotal role in the women's rights movement. Months before the first major organized women's rights convention met at Seneca Falls, New York, in 1848, she had spoken on women's suffrage. During the 1850s, she was instrumental in organizing and speaking at several annual national women's rights conventions, including the first one, held in Worcester, Massachusetts, in 1850. During the Civil War, she joined others in founding the Woman's Loyal National League, and after the war, was an active participant in the American Equal Rights Association. In 1869, Stone and a few others founded the American Woman Suffrage Association, one of two national women's rights organizations that fought for women's right to vote. The following year, she and husband Henry Blackwell founded and published the *Woman's Journal*. This weekly newspaper endured for a half century until the Nineteenth Amendment passed in 1920 and women gained the right to vote. Yet despite her leadership, significant contributions, and ceaseless efforts to abolish slavery and to win women the right to vote, today most Americans have never heard of Lucy Stone.

Figure 2. Lucy Stone (LC-USZ62–29,701, Library of Congress, Washington, DC)

That Stone was not chiseled alongside these three other suffragists is a singular omission in United States history and in American women's history.[2] Her absence in the rotunda is one that speaks volumes about the way we have represented our past, for she was one of the most influential figures in nineteenth-century American history. This volume seeks to chisel her in.

I became drawn to Lucy Stone when I first began teaching American women's history. I simply found it impossible not to admire her courage, passion, and dedication, her unyielding determination to devote her life to fighting for abolition and for women's rights, despite the many challenges and ardent opposition she faced. Although people flocked to hear her lecture, many did not welcome her message. Mobs sometimes tried to drown her out; men pelted her with books and rotten vegetables and doused her with cold water. Yet she continued her campaign because she knew her causes were just. I admired how she managed to develop a meaningful career in the public sphere at a time when nearly all American women spent their lives in the domestic sphere. For years, Stone rejected the idea of marriage because she abhorred the laws that subordinated women to their husbands. She finally relented, however, after a determined suitor,

Henry Browne Blackwell, convinced her that theirs would be a unique marriage of true equals. He kept his word. Lucy became a mother at the age of 37. I admired how she, like other mothers then and now, struggled to balance the joys and demands of childrearing with her lecturing career, temporarily sacrificing public speaking to devote herself to raising daughter Alice. I admired her for returning to campaign for justice that was her life's work.

Stone's absence from the Memorial Sculpture was no accident, for the other three knew her and she them. Her close friendship with Anthony in the 1850s began to fray after the Civil War, when both Stanton and Anthony rejected the passage of the Fifteenth Amendment giving black men the right to vote. In 1869, those two founded a women's rights organization. Stone, who supported the Fifteenth Amendment, founded a rival women's rights organization, the American Woman Suffrage Association. In 1870, she sensed the need for a voice to promote the women's suffrage movement and to publicize women's activities and accomplishments to a national audience. The *Woman's Journal* became the most successful women's newspaper in the country, perhaps even in the world, each week providing insights into women's lives and activities as they fought for equal rights and a claim to citizenship. Stone unapologetically forged her own path, driven by the cause of suffrage that bonded her with and alienated her from the other three but which never ceased to galvanize her and give her a profound sense of purpose. When women finally won the right to vote twenty-seven years after her death, it was in good part because of Lucy Stone, the fourth woman.

I owe many thanks to a number of historians, scholars, friends, and family members who have aided this project. Four biographies on Lucy Stone precede this one, and they have provided essential background for this book: Alice Stone Blackwell, *Lucy Stone: Pioneer of Woman's Rights*; Elinor Rice Hays, *Morning Star: A Biography of Lucy Stone, 1818—1893*; Andrea Moore Kerr, *Lucy Stone: Speaking Out for Equality*; and Joelle Million, *Woman's Voice, Woman's Place: Lucy Stone and the Birth of the Woman's Rights Movement.*[3] Tim Bent, my editor at Oxford University Press, provided the inspiration for this book by encouraging me to write a biography. The first person who came to mind was Lucy Stone, and I am ever grateful for this journey through the intimacies of her fascinating life. Tim has been a meticulous, demanding, and inspiring editor. I so appreciate the care with which Richard Newman and Carol Lesser read and commented on an earlier draft of this manuscript. I thank Barbara Campbell, Margaret Sprinkle, Justin Warren, and Joe Gutenkanst for aid in producing this work. Keely Latcham's assistance at Oxford has been invaluable in acquiring images and overseeing final details in publishing the book. Even though all scholars are becoming more dependent on the Internet, I could not have come to know Lucy Stone without actual archival work in libraries. For that I thank the assistance of librarians at the Schlesinger Library in the History of Women at the Radcliffe Research Institute; the Sophia Smith Collection at the Smith College Library; the archive room at Mudd Library, Oberlin College; the Massachusetts Historical Society in Boston; and the American Antiquarian Society in Worcester. I thank Carrie and Dave for hosting me during my several research trips to the Boston area. My husband Bruce has provided invaluable support and been an enthusiastic participant as we visited the places where Lucy spent various periods of her life—and death. Bruce has also been an exacting editor and so helpful in seeing Lucy through the eyes of a non-historian in order to make her come alive as a person. As always, I am thankful for the support of Mary Reynolds Babcock funds and the encouragement of friends and Davidson colleagues, especially former Davidson College Dean Clark Ross.

It is to our three grandchildren—Conor, Sarah, and Anna—that I dedicate this book. May they always pursue justice and seek to live inspired lives.

LUCY STONE

I

A Massachusetts Childhood

"Oh dear! I am sorry it is a girl. A woman's life is so hard." Thus, supposedly, complained Hannah Stone upon the birth of another daughter on August 13, 1818.[1] This was hardly an auspicious initiation into the world. Lucy Stone's mother may have shared her reaction years later when these words might have meant something to her daughter Lucy. Or the story may be apocryphal. In any case, Hannah Stone's reaction reflected how many American women felt in the early nineteenth century, knowing their daughters would likely experience a life as hard as their own—bearing and raising their many children, working long hours each day in the home and on the farm, and existing in a society in which they lacked political and economic rights.

Lucy was the eighth of nine children and the third of four daughters born to Hannah Bowman Matthews and Francis Stone.[2] She grew up near the farming community of West Brookfield, Massachusetts. Aside from paved streets and sidewalks and a few stores, the outline of the town today probably resembles the nineteenth-century village, located three miles from the Stone farm. An expansive, grassy town green marks the center of the community. The Female Classical Seminary, a private girls' school housed in a two-story cottage off the town green, features a plaque commemorating its founding in 1825. A historic marker notes the town's position as part of the Boston Post Road that connected Boston to Springfield, Massachusetts. Although no longer in its original building, West Brookfield's Congregational Church sits on the same site as the church the Stone family attended. Rolling farmland and forested hills stretch in all directions, as they did nearly two centuries ago.

Lucy Stone was born in the family's sprawling sixteen-room farmhouse. Located atop what is known as Coy's Hill, the house was situated on over 400 acres of land, among many trees that today are in their second or third generation of growth. At least one or two of the oaks across from the Stone farmhouse's ruins—it burned down in 1950—may have been there when Lucy was growing up.[3] A pond lies at the bottom of Coy's Hill. The house sat "on a romantic hillside commanding beautiful views of rolling, rocky pastures, woods, and vallies [sic]."[4]

Throughout her life, Lucy felt the pull of her family home and farm and yearned for them when she was away. She was very much a product of the environment where she grew up. As she wrote when she returned home after four years at college and absorbed the scene before her: "It reminds me of those early days, when I seemed to hold converse with the winds and find companions in the clouds."[5] As an adult, she visited home often to rest and to recuperate. In the final weeks of her life, Lucy returned to the region for several days, seeking tranquility, crisp air, fresh spring water, and a chance to reconnect with this place she loved.

West Brookfield was originally part of greater Brookfield, located on the southwestern border of Worcester County, about twenty miles from the town of Worcester in the central part of the state. Like the founders of many early New England communities, Puritan dissidents were its original settlers. They were mostly single men from Ipswich, Massachusetts, who received a land grant in 1660. Some were drawn by the fur trade; others by the opportunity

Lucy Stone's Home : West Brookfield, Mass.

Figure 3. Lucy Stone's Home, West Brookfield, MA (c. 1923) (Photograph by Ottilie Amend. Schlesinger Library, Radcliffe Institute, Harvard University)

to try to Christianize local Indians. Brookfield, or as it was originally called, Quaboag Plantation, was officially incorporated as a township in 1673. The first settlers built a structure they named Fort Gilbert to protect themselves from the Quaboag Indians, who attacked the settlement repeatedly, most viciously in 1675 during the King Phillip's War, 1675–78. This was a brutal and bloody struggle in which Indian tribes attacked some fifty New England communities and wiped out a tenth of the European population. Settlers in the Brookfield area immediately deserted the region. But they and others returned as the area stabilized after the Indians either died or departed. Initial growth was slow, with only thirty-eight inhabitants living there by 1706.[6] Over the years, however, more families moved to the area, drawn by rich farmland and a plentiful water supply from nearby ponds and rivers. Brookfield grew, with some 100 taxpayers by 1718. Families came to call Brookfield home and demonstrated their sense of community by constructing the village's first schoolhouse in 1733.[7]

Between 1775 and 1830 greater Brookfield thrived, reaching a population of 2,342 inhabitants, though by this time it had split into three separate communities, with West Brookfield becoming the largest and most prosperous. In 1848 when the town was officially incorporated, West Brookfield had a population of about 800. A decade later, the town boasted some 1,344 residents. The First Congregational Church of West Brookfield had been dedicated in 1795, though over the years, fires and hurricanes destroyed the structure, causing it to be rebuilt four times.[8] The town also had a printing office that opened in 1798, and from there Ebenezer Merriam and his brother Daniel printed the town's first newspaper, *Political Repository or Farmers' Journal*. Subscriptions never matched the two men's dreams, and within three years they turned to printing and binding textbooks, Bibles, and almanacs, which they sold throughout the region. Colonel Fisher's Store opened in 1800.[9] Methodists built a church in West Brookfield in 1823 to rival the well-established First Congregational Church. Religious revivals, a product of the Second Great Awakening that erupted in the early years of the nineteenth century, became a common sight during the first quarter of the nineteenth century and had a profound impact on many area residents. During Lucy's childhood, itinerant ministers visited the community and tried to intensify religious sentiments and convert the local population.

Farming remained the principal occupation of the region. By the early nineteenth century, the area was home to a number of prosperous farmers, including Francis Stone, who grew hay, grasses for their cattle and sheep, and grains and potatoes to sell to local markets. Farmers also produced wool, hides, meat, cheese, and butter. Much of Francis's plowed land was given over to pasture for cattle.

Improved transportation contributed to the area's growth. The Boston Post Road was laid out in 1753, facilitating travel to (and commerce with) Worcester and Boston to the east and Springfield and Albany to the west. Of greater importance was the completion of the Western Railroad's connection to West Brookfield in 1839. Train tracks ran along the Quaboag River corridor, with West Brookfield's train depot situated a few blocks from the town green. In 1849, a town hall was erected to display the community's growing sense of importance.

Francis Stone, born in 1779, was raised in his father's tannery yard. Upon his father's death in 1802, he and his brother Calvin took over the business and produced fine leather, which always found a ready market to be made into shoes, saddles, and book covers. For a number of years, Francis was also a schoolmaster in North Brookfield. Apparently he was an effective teacher, for he received several job offers from various schools. The year before Lucy was born, however, Hannah was somehow able to influence Francis to give up the tannery, a rare moment when he acceded to her wishes. Hannah, a woman of piety and strong morals, found the tannery a place of "loose habits

Figure 4. West Brookfield, MA (Lithograph by Charles Volkmar, American Antiquarian Society, Worcester, MA)

and games of cards and dominoes," in short, a bad place to raise their children.[10] Francis acquired land and turned to farming and raising cattle. Well-respected by friends and neighbors, Francis and Hannah worked hard, and they expected the same of their children.

Only a few details are known about Lucy's early years. Throughout her life, she was more a person of action rather than of self-reflection and did not keep a diary. Like most families at this time, the Stones rarely strayed far from home and community, so there was little reason to write one another. In her teens, Lucy wrote a handful of letters to brothers Frank and Bo (short for William Bowman) when they attended colleges in Bangor, Maine, and Amherst, Massachusetts, respectively. Other details come from childhood stories that Lucy occasionally later incorporated into her speeches and in old age, shared with daughter Alice.

Remaining close to home typified women's lives in the early nineteenth century, for society professed—at times celebrated—the idea that a woman's sphere was the home. Here a woman would bear and raise her many children, ensure her husband's and family's well-being, and oversee the myriad tasks of running a household. Hannah Stone's life resembled that of most farm women who engaged in essential but demanding domestic chores, whether weaving cloth for the family, nursing ill children, making and mending the family's clothing, cooking over an open fire or wood-burning stove, gardening, washing clothes and linens, and, in Hannah's case, making butter and cheese. One of Lucy's most vivid childhood memories was of how hard her mother had worked—tirelessly and thanklessly. Only at night after all the work was done did Hannah finally sit down to sew or read. One year when Lucy experienced periodic ill health, she continued to perform her household chores, not wanting her mother to know how poorly she felt and burden her with additional work. By the time she was approaching her teens, Lucy did everything possible to try to lighten her mother's load. Beginning when she was 12, every Monday morning Lucy rose early to wash the family's clothes before she walked the mile to school. She then returned at noon to hang out the wash so it could dry.[11] As Lucy recalled years later, she believed her mother always worried about her children and never had a night of undisturbed sleep for over twenty years.

Hannah lived under her stern, tradition-bound husband, for Francis believed men should rule their households and over their dependents. As Lucy later commented, "There was only one will in our home, and that was my father's."[12] Francis's major fault was that he drank a good deal of liquor, at

least during the years when his children were growing up. Lucy recalled her
father becoming belligerent when he had imbibed too much "cider." But
when he was sober, she recalled his being "bright and witty."[13]

All the Stone children had daily chores to perform. Working hard was
expected of children, for their labor contributed considerably to farm pro-
ductivity. Beginning when she was 5 or 6 years old, Lucy walked behind her
father, dropping corn and pumpkin seeds into the furrows made by his plow.
She later said she felt proud to be given such responsibility. Often Lucy and
her brother Luther drove the cows out to pasture before the sun rose and
then back again in the evening. As a young girl, she helped her mother
weave cloth for the family, sitting under the loom and handing threads in
their proper order to her mother as she wove. At night, Lucy and Luther had
to bring in wood, enough for the fire to burn all evening. At a young age,
Lucy learned to sew, and when she was 11, completed an embroidered sampler that displayed her skill in needlework.[14]

Along with farming, manufacturing and a burgeoning market economy
were having an impact on the Brookfield area. By the early nineteenth century, a third of the local residents engaged in simple manufacturing. In 1830
the area claimed three sawmills and a gristmill, as well as a blacksmith, a
leather-maker, a woodworker, and a dressmaker. Because the Brookfield area
had a number of tanneries—such as the one Francis had sold—shoe production became a common economic activity in the region. Shoemaking was
introduced in the early nineteenth century and became the region's main
light industry, carried on in small shops and in homes. At its peak in 1855,
shoemaking employed 131 men and 17 women in the area, with a number of
small companies producing boots and shoes.[15]

Shoe manufacturing in West Brookfield took place not in large factories
as was happening in New England towns like Lynn, Massachusetts, but
through what was called the "putting out system." In this rudimentary form
of production, tanners distributed leather and other raw products to individual households, and family members then crafted raw materials into
shoes. In addition to their farm chores and domestic tasks, Lucy and her
sisters Rhoda and Sarah were among several local girls who sewed the up-
pers of coarse shoes that were sold to local farmers and to meet the growing
demand for shoes in southern slave states. The girls earned four cents for
each pair they sewed, and Lucy was expected to complete nine pairs a day.[16]
All these responsibilities taught her the meaning of hard work, a lesson she
carried with her through life. The Stone children did not resent what was

asked of them. As Lucy later recalled, "We all worked hard, but we all worked together; and we had the feeling that everything was ours—the calves, the stock, the butter and cheese."[17]

Although she had many chores to perform under the stern eye of her father, Lucy's memories of childhood generally were happy ones. Being the second youngest child, she looked up to her older brothers and sisters, and from all accounts, they adored her. Lucy exhibited strong affection for her siblings—Frank (Francis), Bo, Eliza (Elizabeth), Rhoda, Luther, and Sarah. Her relationship with each one varied by age and gender. Frank, who was twelve years Lucy's senior and her favorite brother, often pinched and tormented her but also felt responsible for his younger siblings' behavior. At one point, Lucy began to sneak sips of hard cider from her father's mug, with the "greatest eagerness and enjoyment." Frank saw her doing this and gave her a stern lecture on the evils of alcohol. She was a quick learner, for apparently that was the last time Lucy ever touched alcohol. In another instance, mimicking her father's salty language when he handled the cows, Lucy did the same when she drove the cows home, shouting out, "You old strumpet!" She had no idea what the word meant, but Frank told her she should never use such language.[18]

Luther was the brother who constantly teased her, but Sarah, the younger sister who followed her everywhere, proved the most annoying. With Rhoda she shared a love of reading. Eliza, who apparently was not as clever as her siblings but had a kind, sweet nature, once saved Lucy from a whipping when Lucy accidentally tore her dress on a fence post. Upset because she had ruined her dress, Lucy crept into the house and showed Eliza, who mended the long tear that evening before their mother discovered the mishap.[19]

Lucy especially admired her older brothers Frank and Bo. As she wrote Frank in May 1844 when she learned of his intended marriage, "At first I shed some tears about it for I thought the love you had cherished for me, would be given to another; and a kind of feeling came over me, that now I have no brother." But she quickly amended those feelings, realizing they were selfish, and she expressed profound happiness for his future. "I think my dear brother that you deserve a good wife. I hope you have one, every way worthy of your love, and that she will always deserve, and have the warmest place in your heart." She ended, "Whatever adds to your happiness adds to mine."[20]

Her letters to Frank and Bo while they were attending college reveal her high regard for them but also that she could hold her own with them. To Frank, she expressed her "undying love and unchanging confidence."[21]

Although younger than both by several years, Lucy freely dispensed advice and opinions. For instance, when Frank was at Bangor College, she chided him repeatedly for misspelling "babby" [*sic*] and urged him to correct it as well as his many other mistakes, for "when you wrote home from Marietta, almost every letter was half spelt wrong."[22] Lucy's close relationships with her brothers had a profound impact on her and later fostered in her a unique sense of the significant role that men could play in the women's movement. Rather than blaming men for women's oppression, as a number of other women reformers would do, she explained in 1893, "I grew up with four [*sic*] brothers and have all my life had more or less to do with men."[23]

Some of Lucy's happiest childhood memories drew upon the world around her. Strong connections with the natural environment were a part of her character and remained so throughout her life. When their chores were completed, she recalled, the Stone children "were left perfectly free" to "run like spiders" around the farm.[24] She loved the farmland, the lush forests, the splendid view from atop Coy's Hill, the cold spring water, and the profusion of fresh fruits and vegetables the family grew and consumed every summer. Weather permitting, Lucy and her siblings ran barefoot and explored the surrounding countryside, memorizing every tree, rock outcropping, stream, and pond that populated farm and woods. Living far from town, childhood friends most likely were those whom she met at school. One classmate, Emily Pierce, wrote Lucy when she was at Oberlin, recalling the "good times" they shared when playing at Lucy's home, and also remembering school days when during recess, Lucy jumped out of the window.[25] Lucy was energetic and enjoyed skipping rope while her pet sheep, Top, jumped beside her. She loved to run across the fields "as light as thistle down." The Stone children also had a dog, Old Bogue, that helped them herd cows.[26] Years later while visiting the family home, her daughter Alice commented: "I don't wonder Mama is brave, having grown up in this glorious hill country."[27] Looking back at her childhood only days before she died, Lucy commented wistfully, "It seems as if nothing could ever happen to a little girl so full of life—as if she must overcome everything."[28]

Years later when she was at Oberlin and dining on the college's Spartan diet, Lucy longed for the food her family enjoyed. The Stone household was "opulent" in terms of what the family ate—"barrels of meat . . . plenty of fresh milk, cream . . . cheese and eggs, peaches, quinces . . . berries . . . plums," honey, "a wagon-load of salted shad to eat throughout the winter, an abundance of apples," wild game that Lucy's brothers killed, and "the very best butter."[29] The family never drank tea or coffee. Francis had his mug of hard cider with his meals while Hannah and the children drank milk or water. Food was plentiful, if plain, with most of it produced on the farm.

By all accounts, including her own, Lucy was a fearless child, a characteristic that was so evident as an adult when she became the target of attacks. She was also willful and possessed a strong temper, traits which she sought to curb. In one instance when she was about 12 and Sarah had angered her, Lucy chased her younger sister around the house until she suddenly caught sight of her own face in a mirror. As Lucy related the story, she was shocked because her look resembled that "of a murderer." Indeed, she thought she might become one if she did not learn to control her temper. Lucy went outside behind the woodshed and rocked herself to and fro on a rock, thinking how she could learn to control her rage. She remained there until long after sunset when her mother finally found her.[30] On another occasion when Sarah made her angry, Lucy was able to resist reacting by counting to 100 and squeezing her hands tightly so she would not strike her sister. Realizing how easily she responded to his taunts, Luther teased Lucy constantly, especially about her upturned nose and her beet-red face when she became angry. Once when she could hardly contain her fury at Luther, Lucy went out to sit on Hemlock Hill and listened to a trickling stream, which eventually calmed her.[31]

Lucy was proud and usually scrupulously honest. She recalled the time her father offered each of his children six cents for any horseshoe or ox shoe they found and brought home. Lucy found a pair in the dirt and in great excitement took them to her father. He did not believe that she had actually found them and proceeded to visit the local blacksmith to ask if the horseshoes were his. The man affirmed that they were not and thought they probably came from Canada because of their small size. Only then did Francis offer Lucy her reward, but she refused the twelve cents, upset that her father thought she had lied.[32] Lucy also had an "extreme" sense of order and tidiness, according to Sarah. Each sister had a single drawer for her clothes, and every item of Lucy's was always folded perfectly, an "exactness" that eluded Sarah.[33]

On winter evenings, the family often gathered around the huge open stone fireplace where Francis built "magnificent fires," and the children roasted apples or popped popcorn. They studied their school lessons by lantern light, sitting at the single square table in the main room while Hannah sewed. Sometimes one or more of Francis's male friends visited, some of whom he had known since childhood. None of the men was apparently ever turned away. They showed up to enjoy Francis's supply of cider, to swap stories, and often to spend the night. Hannah and the Stone children disliked these sometimes coarse, hard-drinking men and the additional work entailed in feeding and housing them. They also resented the men's bad manners and drunken behavior. On one occasion, Lucy and Luther found a rum jug that belonged to Jim Clark, one of the men, which was hidden outside behind a stone wall. The two children smashed it with a rock. Being three miles from town, there was no way Clark could purchase more rum and make it back that evening. Francis questioned Lucy and Luther about the broken jug; they denied ever having seen it, blaming the accident on a sheep.[34] In this case, Lucy probably realized total honesty did not serve her well, for if discovered, the two would have received a spanking.[35]

Physical punishment was the norm in nineteenth-century childrearing practices. In the local schools the Stone children attended, spanking was common. Lucy recalled one teacher, a neighbor, Tom Coney, as a "cross teacher" who hit Lucy's ear with his ruler and "struck her the hardest blow she ever received except from her father."[36] Lucy never forgot the spanking her father gave her when she refused to go to the cellar with Luther after their father asked him to retrieve more cider. Luther was afraid of the dark and wanted Lucy to come with him to hold the candle. She did not move, for she saw no reason why Luther could not hold the candle, put it on the floor while he poured the cider, and return upstairs. After Luther complained, Francis took Lucy over his knees and spanked her as hard as he could. Bo watched his little sister being so severely punished and later attributed their father's abusive action to his drinking too much cider.[37]

Perhaps inevitably, Lucy's childhood affection and sympathy lay with her mother rather than with her father, though as Francis mellowed over the years, she became closer to him. She admitted loving her mother more than she did her father because Hannah was kind to all her children and took a greater interest in them. In writing her mother shortly after her wedding, Lucy conveyed her "love and gratitude": "You gave me birth, watched my infancy . . . guarded my earlier youth, and have lived and sympathized with all my varied and vagrant life."[38] She recalled that when she was little, her mother often reached down to touch her in her trundle bed to be sure she was well covered. At night, Hannah often got out of bed to soothe one of her crying children. "No soldier ever held such long and patient watch!" Lucy wrote.[39] One night when Hannah had to leave home to assist a neighbor,

Lucy woke up, wrapped a blanket around her, went out to sit on the hearth, and began to cry. Francis had no patience with such behavior and threatened her with a spanking if she did not stop. Lucy, who was afraid of him and of "his slaps," went back to bed and cried herself to sleep.[40]

Lucy also felt her father favored younger sister Sarah over her as she watched him play with Sarah on his knees. It must have been crushing when her father told Lucy that she was no beauty, that her face was like a black-smith's leather apron—"It keeps off the sparks," he said. She blurted out she had no intention of ever marrying and wished she were even plainer so her looks would drive away all possible suitors.[41]

Although Lucy was never described as a natural beauty, she was far more attractive than her father's assessment. The few early photos and descriptions of Lucy reveal a round-faced young woman, with bright gray eyes, thick brown hair often worn short and parted in the middle, and by all accounts, a rosy complexion. She had a mole above her lip on one cheek. When she began her career as a public lecturer, most people in the audience were surprised by her slight figure, youthful appearance, and personal appeal. Newspaper accounts of her described her as diminutive, rosy-cheeked, and attractive.

Figure 5. Lucy Stone (LC-USZ62–77,000, Library of Congress, Washington, DC)

Lucy was generally blessed with good health and a strong constitution. Far ahead of the thinking of the time in how women should take care of themselves, she loved to exercise and regarded both planned and spontaneous exercise as important to good health. Writing to Frank when he was in college, she chided him when she learned he was studying too much. Exercise at least two hours twice a week, she urged him. When he woke each morning, instead of studying immediately, he should take a walk of a half mile or mile and run part of the way. "I consider it just as much a suicide to kill yourself studying, as if you should take a knife and cut your throat," she wrote rather dramatically. Studying all the time was not good for anyone, she insisted. "Be out occasionally to get fresh air," she urged. "Too much of one thing is good for nothing, and it may prove so with regard to your studying, it may make you crazy, and what will you be good for then?"[42] When Lucy later attended Wesleyan Academy, she wrote home that she and a friend had walked to the village of Springfield and back, a total distance of nearly twenty-five miles. "We do not feel any inconvenience from it," she added.[43]

The Stones, like most New Englanders, were churchgoers. Each Sunday, those who could fit piled into their wagon while other family members walked to West Brookfield's Congregational Church. The next Sunday, those who had walked got to ride. Hannah set the standard as the most pious member of the Stone family. She joined the local Congregational Church in 1819 and remained a member until she died. Hannah tried, but with only partial success, to pass on her faith to her children. She insisted they all learn hymns and Bible verses. In the evenings as Lucy and Luther carried armloads of wood to stoke the stove and fireplace, Hannah read them hymns and scripture, which they then memorized and recited back to her. Lucy was proud that she could learn her verses twice as rapidly as her brother. Hannah had more success instilling her strong sense of morality in her children, warning them about the evils of dancing, novel reading, card playing, and attending the theatre, and wanting them to become responsible, principled individuals.[44] Throughout her life, Lucy held herself—and often others—to these high moral standards.

The few letters Hannah wrote her children in her scratchy script and phonetic spelling expressed her strong faith, urging them always to depend on God to guide them through life. All the Stone children joined the local Congregational Church.[45] Although Lucy's faith never matched her mother's or that of her brother Bo, she joined the church in 1839 when she was 21 years old. Until then, Lucy grappled with her faith. Perhaps she viewed her mother's piety as an unattainable ideal. Like her father, she struggled to become a true believer. Lucy wrote Bo when she was attending Wesleyan Academy, commenting on a revival in nearby Warren, "My own heart is cold as clay. I often think that I have never been a Christian, for how can one who has ever known the love of God go so far away?" She asked Bo to pray for her.[46]

Although Lucy joined the church, she sometimes questioned what she read in the Bible. Certain passages in it upset her, especially those noting women's inferior status and insisting that women should remain silent and submissive. While she remained a person of faith, failing to become a true believer bothered her. When Lucy began to teach school, she worried that without a strong sense of piety, she might have a negative impact on her pupils. When teaching in the nearby town of Paxton, she characterized three of her students as "hopeful and pious." Instead of rejoicing, though, Lucy found this a "fearful" situation. "My influence and example all tell upon their eternal destiny and if this should be lost through my unfaithfulness, how could I stand acquitted at the day of Judgment?" Still, she recognized she was probably in good company. "The state of religious feeling in this place is very far from what it should be," she added.[47]

Education in the Stone family was also prized, as it was throughout Massachusetts. Since its earliest days, Massachusetts had been a leader in public education. In 1647, the colony enacted what was called the Old Deluder Satan Act which required towns with fifty or more families to hire a schoolmaster to teach children to read and write. That commitment to education carried down through the decades. All the Stone children received a solid education at local common schools. By the second quarter of the nineteenth century, ideas about women's education had begun to shift. Having once regarded schooling for girls as of limited usefulness, Americans now reasoned that education made women better wives, companions, and mothers. An educated mother could be more effective at teaching her children, especially her sons, to become model citizens of the republic.[48] Higher education, however, was a different matter. When Bo and Frank expressed a desire to attend college, their father sent them. But at least until 1833, no college admitted women. Francis was not the type of man who would have supported college education for his daughters, even had women been allowed to attend. Most people saw no need for women to attend college since their adult lives were confined to home and family. The image of over-educated women was, if anything, a threat to the common order and ran counter to the prevailing idea that women could not withstand the rigors of higher education.

To Lucy, from the time she was young, education meant as much to her as nature, and she always craved more. When she was 3 years old she ran after her brothers and sisters as they set off for school. In a couple of years, Lucy was able to join them. She came to realize that schooling was key to women's advancement and to leading a purposeful life. As she explained to Bo in 1840, "Only let females be educated in the same manner and with the same advantages that males have, and, as everything in nature seeks its own level, I would risk that we would find out our 'appropriate sphere.'"[49]

Lucy also was a voracious reader and read everything she could get her hands on, including newspapers the family subscribed to—the *Massachusetts Spy*, published in Worcester by Isaiah Thomas; William Lloyd Garrison's the *Liberator*; and the *Anti-Slavery Standard*, the paper of the American Anti-Slavery Society.[50] Other papers the family was able to borrow, including *Youth's Companion* and the *Advocate of Moral Reform*. Lucy and Rhoda subscribed to the *New England Spectator*, which Lucy described as a "family paper" covering "the study of the Bible, family religion, active piety, the abolition of war, slavery, and licentiousness and to promote the circulation of useful intelligence."[51] Lucy devoured books though did not read her first novel until she was in her teens, for Hannah, no doubt influenced by Puritan New Englanders' misgivings regarding novels, considered reading fiction a useless pastime. That first novel Lucy read was either *The Children of the Abbey* or *The Lady of the Manor* (she could not remember which one), which Rhoda lent her. Since she knew her mother would disapprove, Lucy locked herself in her bedroom to read the book in secret, but Sarah peeked through the keyhole and tattled. Hannah was horrified, having taught her children that novels were "wicked." Only after Rhoda assured her mother the book was acceptable did Hannah allow Lucy to finish it. Years passed before Lucy read another novel.[52]

Through sheer and stubborn determination, Lucy received an exceptional education, far more schooling than nearly all women of her day. This she did on her own, for her father would not pay her tuition. Initially, she carried out her resolve to pursue more schooling when Mt. Holyoke Female Seminary opened in November 1837 in nearby South Hadley, Massachusetts. Its founder, Mary Lyon, born in 1797, was well educated and began teaching school at the age of 17. After twenty years of teaching in various schools, Lyon decided to establish an academy of higher education for women, with an academic curriculum and rigorous entrance requirements. Having seen a number of institutions fail due to a lack of financial support, Lyon was determined to put her school on a solid footing. She spent four years raising money and then seeking a suitable location.[53] One of her many fundraising stops was in West Brookfield, where she spoke to Lucy's sewing circle, a group of young women who made shirts and socks for young men studying for the ministry. Lyon explained that women needed and deserved greater educational opportunities. Her desire was to train the best women to become teachers or missionary wives by creating a seminary that would attract women from varied backgrounds. Lyon's talk profoundly affected Lucy. Apparently she put down her sewing on a table, leaving it unfinished, thinking to herself that the man who would wear that shirt could earn a dollar a day while she could only earn a dollar a week.[54]

Mary Lyon's campaign paid off. Town fathers in South Hadley found her appeal persuasive, recognizing the positive benefits of having a girls' school in their community. They offered Lyon $8,000 toward building her seminary, and construction on the main building began. Once Lucy heard about the new school, she asked her parents' permission to attend. They told her she had already acquired more than enough education to find a good husband. Ignoring their objections, Lucy used the money she earned from teaching school to enroll at Mt. Holyoke in April 1839.[55] In order to prepare for the rigors ahead, she received tutoring from Alfred Bartlett, a classmate of Bo's from Amherst College, perhaps the most prestigious college west of Boston. She studied Latin, grammar, mathematics, and algebra, subjects she had not learned all that well in local schools.[56]

Lucy's experiences at Mt. Holyoke were not as positive as she had hoped. Mary Lyon was a devout Christian who had undergone a transformative conversion years earlier. That experience convinced her to base her school on Christian principles. While Lyon's views on women's educational needs were advanced for the time, she still embraced traditional ideas about women's proper role. Lyon wished to provide all her students with the skills and morals they needed to become good wives, mothers, and missionary wives, or as she put it, "man's helper, not his equal." In contrast, Lucy already believed that "for herself alone, woman should receive the highest mental cultivation of which she is capable."[57]

In addition, Lucy's reform interests did not mesh with Lyon's. By 1839 Lucy was a confirmed abolitionist. Every student at the school was encouraged to keep a mite box to fill with pennies to help fund missionary work overseas. Lucy had a mite box, but her few pennies went to support the American Anti-Slavery Society. On her box was the famous picture of a kneeling slave, arms extended, pleading, "Am I not a man and a brother"? Lucy also received copies of the *Liberator* sent by Bo, and she laid these out in the reading room after she finished them. At first, no one knew how the newspapers got there. Finally someone asked Lucy if she was responsible, and she admitted she was. Lyon admonished Lucy, reminding her that the anti-slavery movement was extremely controversial, not a cause in which the new school should become embroiled.[58] After one term at Mt. Holyoke, Lucy left, perhaps somewhat disenchanted with her experience. Far more important in drawing her home, though, was the death of her beloved sister Rhoda, who had been ill for some time. She died July 31, 1839. Hannah was distraught, and Lucy needed to be home to help care for Rhoda's children and her mother.[59]

Lucy's disappointing experience at Mt. Holyoke did not lessen her determination to pursue additional schooling. For the next few years, she taught intermittently at common schools in order to earn enough money to spend a semester at several private schools. In 1840–41, she attended Wesleyan Academy in Wilbraham near Springfield, and the following year, she and Sarah spent a term at Monson Academy in Monson, east of Springfield.[60] In 1842, the two attended fall term at Quaboag Seminary in Warren, a new co-educational school founded by Methodists which promised to drill students in Greek and Latin.[61] Lucy was able to borrow ten dollars from her father to pay her tuition and wrote him a promissory note to repay him "when convenient." She thought—and hoped—her father would not demand repayment, but he did.[62]

Perhaps at this point Lucy's focus on schooling and a determination to improve her mind dampened any interest in marriage. But according to a couple accounts and another by her father, Lucy had several suitors, including tutor Alfred Bartlett. He fell in love with her, and she was "smitten" with him, though none of Lucy's written words confirm any depth of feeling on her part. In 1838, Bartlett lived with the Stone family, tutored Lucy, and taught school as he prepared for missionary work. Lucy's daughter Alice later recounted that Bartlett fell for her mother, and in Lucy he awakened "the first stirrings of the tender passion." He bought or loaned her a copy of Sarah Grimké's recently published essays, *Letters on the Equality of the Sexes*, in which Grimké claimed that God ordained the equality of the sexes, and it was man, not God, who confined women to their homes. Lucy must have found this book inspiring, and likely Bartlett's gesture strengthened her feelings for him. How or why this relationship dissolved is unclear; perhaps it was never intense on her side. Lucy enjoyed Bartlett's company, and he admired her spirit and strong work ethic, telling her at one point that she would make a great missionary wife working in the Rocky Mountains. By this point, Lucy may have resolved never to marry—as she had once told her father—or the relationship may have floundered for other reasons.[63]

Independence of self, education, and paid work attracted Lucy rather than marriage. Teaching had become a popular and acceptable profession for educated young men and women. Bo, Rhoda, and Sarah all taught after they completed their schooling. Demand was high, for teachers were needed to staff the growing number of academies and common schools throughout New England. A significant change from the past was the number of young women now entering the profession. Teaching was one of the few acceptable jobs for middle-class women to pursue before they married, though once wed, it was assumed they would retire to the domestic sphere. Teaching seemed most appropriate for women since it was seen as a natural extension of their maternal nature. On a pragmatic level, hiring female teachers made sense since school districts paid them a third to half of what they paid men.[64] Lucy learned about inequitable pay firsthand when her brother became ill and she substituted for him at West Brookfield's school. She taught all the same subjects he did yet was paid a much lower wage.[65]

Lucy took her first teaching position at a school in North Braintree, boarding with her sister and brother-in-law, Eliza and Ira Barlow, and earning $1 per week. She was 16. Her weekly salary rose to $1.50 as she gained more experience and began to teach in larger schools. Eventually Lucy was earning $16 a month, considered good pay for a woman, even though well below what male teachers could make. In village schools a single teacher typically was responsible for all pupils of wide-ranging ages and abilities. In 1836, Lucy described her situation at what she called a "large" one-room school with seventeen pupils and between eight and fourteen attending on any one day. Because of the pupils' different ages, she taught six classes in geography, two in grammar, two in spelling, two in arithmetic, and one in writing. She found her greatest trial early on was exhibiting patience, especially when pupils recited their lessons and said something that contradicted what she had just drilled into them. Some students seemed to remember nothing, even after she repeated a lesson three times. This puzzled her deeply, given how quick she was to pick up and retain information. But gradually, Lucy admitted the children were beginning to learn a "considerable" amount, and if they did not, "I should give up all hopes of ever teaching school again."[66]

Lucy persevered and became an outstanding teacher despite the challenges and pay inequity. She possessed an innate ability to teach and earned the devotion and respect of her pupils wherever she worked. She seemed to possess a true sense of how to reach her students, understand their needs, and inspire them. In one instance when she needed to earn extra money before leaving for Oberlin, Lucy agreed to finish teaching the winter term at a school in Paxton, accepting the position after the school district fired a young male teacher because he could not control his pupils. Winter school terms typically attracted older boys because they had fewer farm chores to perform than they did in the fall and spring and thus had time to attend school. These older boys tended to show no patience with ineffectual schoolmasters. One day, a group of them pitched the teacher out of the window into a snow drift. Lucy was told nothing about such troubles in the school. The day she took over, the ringleader of the gang, a young man of 17 or 18, confronted her on the school steps. "Are you going to lick me?" he challenged as she walked into the school house. Lucy calmly took roll and made a personal comment to each pupil. She then asked the ringleader what subject he liked best and urged him to come see her when he had trouble with arithmetic. From that point forward, Lucy never had a problem with him or with any of the other boys. In fact, each morning the ringleader built a fire in the schoolhouse, and when one of the girls fell on ice and broke her wrist, he ran for the doctor. Lucy's gentle manner—though no push-over—and calm, personal approach turned her students into an orderly, obedient class, with the older boys offering to do anything to help "Miss Stone."[67]

Reaching out to help others and self-improvement seemed ingrained in her, yet in reading about Lucy's upbringing, one can't help but wonder what instilled in this Massachusetts farm girl so intense a desire to devote her adult life to fighting for two causes—antislavery and women's rights. Much of Lucy's childhood resembled what other farm girls experienced in the early nineteenth century, yet they never considered the bold path that Lucy pursued. Certainly she grew up during a time of reform and ferment in our nation's history. As historians Ronald Walters and Daniel Walker Howe have observed, the nation was undergoing a "broad transformation."

Americans exhibited a "confidence in progress and human will," much of it motivated by religious excitement generated by the Second Great Awakening; by economic changes including revolutions in technology, communications, and transportation; and by a belief in the millennium.[68] Like Lucy, a number of Americans at the time shared a commitment to reform. But it also could have been in her DNA; some of her ancestors had believed in and fought for various causes. Maybe it was the spoken and unspoken lessons her parents and siblings conveyed. Or perhaps it was early life experiences, reading and hearing about the horrors of slavery and witnessing women's subordination, leading Lucy to link them—which not all advocates of women's rights or abolitionists did. Likely, it was a combination of all of these.

Lucy's ancestors were tied to significant events in the nation's past. One acquaintance called her ancestors "good sober, earnest New England stock."[69] Some of them had been committed patriots; a few even were apparent rabble rousers—with strong passions and a fearlessness in challenging authority, traits that seemed ingrained in Lucy's character. Hannah's mother descended from the Bowman family, which was well regarded socially and included a number of Harvard graduates. As Alice later observed, they were "educated and public-spirited." Francis was a descendent of Gregory Stone, who immigrated to the American colonies in 1635, seeking religious freedom. He settled in Cambridge, Massachusetts, and held various public offices. He and his wife defended a woman accused of witchcraft. In 1664 Stone and three other men formed a committee that collected signatures to protest Great Britain's intention to govern the Massachusetts Bay Colony by Royal Commission. They publicly denounced the plan because colonists were not represented in Parliament.[70]

Francis's father, Lucy's grandfather, also named Francis Stone, was 17 when he joined his father who was fighting for the British in the French and Indian Wars. When the senior Stone was killed at the Battle of Quebec in 1759, General James Wolfe sent young Francis home since he was his family's sole surviving son and needed to support his mother. Lucy's grandfather later became a captain and fought in the American Revolution and then was one of the leaders of Shays's Rebellion. There, in 1786-1787, thousands of men in western Massachusetts protested against high taxes and, in their eyes, against the ineffective new national government framed under the Articles of Confederation. Thus, on her father's side of the family were traits of courage, determination, and a belief in principle.[71]

Lucy's family became strong supporters of the antislavery movement. The abolition cause was part of her upbringing and a frequent topic of conversation. By the second quarter of the nineteenth century, the antislavery movement had become one of the most radical political reform efforts of the time. By the 1830s, antislavery had an impact in the Northeast as abolitionists traversed the countryside and visited towns and cities to recruit new converts to the cause, including many women. It was hardly a popular cause, with perhaps no more than 1 percent of all northerners joining an antislavery society by 1850. Over time, however, more people came to embrace abolition, though many northerners and nearly all southerners regarded abolitionists as dangerous extremists, stirring up trouble and openly challenging religious, political, and civil authorities for failing to take a strong stand against slavery.

The abolition movement's radical spokesman, William Lloyd Garrison, became Lucy's hero. Throughout much of her adult life, she hung an engraved portrait of Garrison in her bedroom. Born in 1805 and raised in Newburyport, Massachusetts, by a single mother after his father had abandoned the family, Garrison apprenticed to a local printer and newspaper editor while in his teens. There he found his life's work. After publicly accusing a prominent merchant of robbery and murder because the man engaged in the domestic slave trade, Garrison was arrested for libel. While in jail, he wrote about his situation and attracted the attention of abolitionists Lewis and Arthur Tappan of New York. They posted his bail and began to support Garrison's extreme antislavery convictions. In 1831, Garrison began publishing a newspaper, the *Liberator*, in which he boldly declared, "I do not wish to think, or speak, or write, with moderation."[72] Garrison saw no reason to compromise on an issue that undermined the democratic ideals of the nation. He had no use for politicians or for the political process. His demand was for an immediate end to slavery. He was one of the founders of the American Anti-Slavery Society, organized in 1833. Although Garrison decried the use of violence to end slavery, his writings and lectures often generated violent responses. So uncompromising was his insistence on an immediate end to slavery that at one point he denounced and then burned a copy of the US Constitution because several of its clauses condoned slavery.[73]

Not all abolitionists were of one mind, however, and many did not embrace Garrison's extreme views. To their thinking, it was better to end slavery by working through the political system.[74] Another issue that put Garrison at odds with some abolitionists was his encouraging women's participation in the antislavery movement. He became a supporter of women's rights, which, for Lucy, was another major factor in his favor.

Wm. Lloyd Garrison.

Figure 6. William Lloyd Garrison (LC-USZ62–10,320, Library of Congress, Washington, DC)

No evidence indicates that any Stone family members joined an antislavery organization while Lucy was growing up, but all of them, except Rhoda, were committed abolitionists.[75] The Stones subscribed to and read the *Liberator* and, as Bo did for Lucy, often shared copies with family members who were away from home. Yet Lucy had no recollection of when or why the family came to embrace the antislavery cause with such fervor. In a letter to brother Frank in 1837, she explained, "we are all of us well and abolitionists the same as ever" and called it "the cause which lies nearest my heart." Antislavery also attracted support among some West Brookfield residents. As Lucy commented in the same letter, "The abolition cause is gaining ground rapidly among us" and mentioned a few men in the area who were lecturing on the issue.[76]

One can only imagine what conversations took place among the Stones as the slavery issue came to dominate American politics. In that same letter, Lucy shared her reactions to the killing of Elijah P. Lovejoy, a minister and newspaper editor in Alton, Illinois, who was murdered by a mob in November 1837 for publishing incendiary comments denouncing slavery.[77] The next year, Lucy wrote Frank that she hoped he was "the same as ever" and had not given up his antislavery beliefs while attending Bangor College. At another point, Lucy wrote that the family had read "some beautiful pieces" by "Miss Grimké" and others by Garrison, which she claimed "does us lots of good." The family heard a Mr. Norton deliver an antislavery lecture in West Brookfield. When Frank informed Lucy of his forthcoming marriage, she commented on his fiancé, "I had an impression that she was not an abolitionist but I think it must be erroneous, for I don't believe you would marry a wife who was not antislavery." Later, Lucy was appalled to learn that a family friend was making a living by selling books in the South, "sharing too largely in the advantage of slave labor."[78]

Although her family shared similar views on abolition, a belief in women's equality was a cause unique to Lucy. From a young age, instances of women's inferior status and unjust treatment made indelible impressions on her. Women's confinement to the home simply did not sit well with Lucy. She could not fathom why half of the population did not deserve and enjoy the same treatment and opportunities as the other half. Lucy became aware of gender inequality from observing relationships around her. She saw how her father controlled and mistreated her mother and how badly many other husbands treated their wives, images that had an indelible impact on her later.

In most cases, women had no right to protest, much less to alter their situation. Divorce was extremely difficult, expensive, and time-consuming, and in rare instances when a woman did win one, what could she do? Most jobs and professions were closed to them. According to the laws of the time, a wife could not claim property she brought to her marriage or any money she might earn. She could not sign contracts, engage in independent business or legal transactions, and, of course, had no right to vote, to hold office, or to serve on juries. A mother typically lost custody of her children in a rare case of divorce. According to Blackstone's Law, which at the time was the basis for most statues in America, a married woman was deemed a *feme covert*, meaning she and her husband were one—with husbands wielding the power. On the other hand, single women or widows, legally known as *feme soles*, could claim rights that married women could not, such as the right to own property, to keep the money they earned, to conduct their own businesses, and to sign contracts. Yet despite these legal differences in status, at this time in our history, most women wanted to marry and did so.

As Lucy understood the degree of wives' dependence on their husbands' authority, she became determined that laws must be changed. One day while reading the Bible, she read Genesis 3:16, "Thy desire shall be to thy husband, and he shall rule over thee." Agitated, she sought comfort from her mother and asked what the passage meant and why God insisted on women's subordination. Her mother affirmed the scriptural passage, telling Lucy that a woman's duty was to obey her husband. "My mother always tried to submit. I never could," she later admitted to Alice. In vowing she would never do so, Lucy decided to learn Greek and Hebrew to see if the Bible had been translated correctly.[79]

She had living examples of women's subordination all around her. She observed the situation of her Aunt Sally, her father's half-sister, who lived with the Stone family. A single woman dependent on her extended family, Sally spent most of her time knitting stockings. Like many women at the time who were widows, abandoned wives, or "spinsters," Sally lived with extended family and helped with household chores. In a more telling instance, in December 1843 when Lucy was teaching near Worcester, she attended the wedding of Sarah Adams, who was marrying Bo's wife's brother, Charles L. Robinson. The bride's father had settled a substantial monetary gift on his daughter. No sooner had the couple said their vows than Robinson's creditor appeared and demanded the money owed him—from Sarah's dowry, which now belonged to Robinson. According to one account, this event led Lucy to swear that she would fight for the rest of her life to ensure that married women could retain their own property.[80]

Upsetting to Lucy—and to her mother—was the fact that Francis Stone was incredibly stingy, or as Lucy described him, "very ugly" about money. He rarely let Hannah have any, despite her working as hard as he did. Hannah finally gave up asking. But she found devious ways to deal with his stinginess and get some of what she felt she deserved. Frequently she secretly stole small amounts of change from his pocketbook, which he had hidden under his pillow, taking only a 6½ cent piece each time so he would not miss it. Sometimes Hannah hid from Francis a small portion of the money she made from selling cheese. Typically a few hundred pieces of cheese were stored in the farm's cheese room, so he never knew what was missing or how much had been sold. After all, Hannah had made the cheese. Once, when Francis refused to give Hannah any money, Lucy started out for the town of Ware to sell a twenty-pound cheese for her mother, which she had hidden under her cloak. Just as she was pulling the horse out of the barn, her father appeared, but Lucy kept moving, with the cheese hidden from sight and her father none the wiser. Although

Hannah realized technically she was "stealing," at least according to the law that gave husbands control over all family assets, she told Lucy, "I have a right to it."[81]

Later, when Francis first made out his will, he left Hannah only the use of one room in the large farmhouse and enough milk for her to sell and to make cheese. The majority of his estate was to go to his sons. When the Stone children learned of this, they united and objected vehemently. Francis gave in and changed his will, leaving Hannah everything. As it turned out, Hannah died before he did, but at the time, "she felt the justice of it."[82]

The worst times for the family were when Francis's bad temper and abusive behavior took over, typically when he had too much to drink. His drinking habit was not unusual; in the early nineteenth century according to Daniel Howe, men "quaffed alcohol in prodigious quantities." All too often the result was domestic abuse and violence.[83] On one occasion, Lucy's mother wanted to purchase a pretty tablecloth to use when company came. She feared asking Francis for money and used Lucy as her intermediary. When he heard the request, Francis was furious, responding that any tablecloth good enough for him was good enough for company—a response Lucy blamed on "cider."

As she matured, Lucy continued to recoil—first instinctively and then with deep understanding of why—against the restrictions society placed on her due to her gender, especially as she read and heard about a handful of women now speaking out publically and demanding racial and gender equality. Perhaps in a local newspaper Lucy read about the radical Scotswoman, Frances Wright, who came to the United States in 1828 and lectured on abolition, more liberal divorce laws, birth control, and opposition to capital punishment. One of Wright's stops was in nearby Worcester.[84]

In 1837, while Lucy was teaching in West Brookfield, another incident took place that had an enormous impact on her. In the late 1830s, Sarah and Angelina Grimké, sisters from a privileged Charleston, South Carolina, family, had begun to lecture and to write about the evils of slavery. Although having grown up in a slave-holding family, they recoiled against the horrors of slavery and southern white families' dependency on slaves, to say nothing of how the enslaved were forced to live. In 1819, Sarah accompanied her ailing father to Philadelphia where he sought medical treatment, and she was drawn to the city's large Quaker population and to its strong antislavery sentiment. Two years later, at the age of 28, she moved there. Several years later, younger sister Angelina followed.

Figure 7. Sarah Moore Grimké (LC-USZ61–1608, Library of Congress, Washington, DC)

Figure 8. Angelina Emily Grimké Weld (LC-USZ61–1609, Library of Congress, Washington, DC)

The Grimké sisters joined a Quaker Meeting and the Philadelphia Anti-Slavery Society. In 1835 Angelina wrote a letter to Garrison's *Liberator*, sympathizing with his cause and decrying the evils of slavery. Her thoughts offered a unique perspective on slavery, given that she had grown up in a southern home surrounded by slaves. Garrison published her letter and urged her to write more. Sarah became involved in the abolitionist cause as well and began to write. In 1836, Garrison encouraged the sisters to become lecturers for the American Anti-Slavery Society, and they began speaking to gatherings of women. By the following year, as they lectured in various venues across New England, men also showed up to listen. The Grimkés' lecturing was now deemed totally inappropriate since women were not supposed to speak in public, especially to mixed audiences.

Massachusetts Congregational ministers reacted in horror to the Grimkés' lecturing, and from June 27 to 29, 1838, they gathered in North Brookfield to compose a "Pastoral Letter" denouncing the sisters for their behavior.[85] To orthodox ministers, women's alleged authority came from their dependence and weakness. As Lucy later commented, the idea of a woman being confined to the domestic sphere was like "a band of steel on society" and thus, the "church was moved to its very foundation in opposition" to women's right to speak in public.[86] That was a job for male ministers—to engage in moral discourse as heads of the church. Ministers were already troubled by the public lecturing of abolitionist Abby Kelley. It was essential to silence all these women. After all, as Paul proclaimed in 1 Corinthians 14:34: "Let your women keep silent in the churches, for it is not permitted unto them to speak." Women should understand that their rightful place was in the home, not on a dais and certainly not presenting themselves to mixed audiences as experts on a controversial, moral issue.

The public reading of the "Pastoral Letter" in churches across New England occurred while Lucy was teaching in North Brookfield and boarding in the home of her cousin, Delindy Edmonds Johnson. The two young women attended the quadrennial meeting of the General Association of Massachusetts Congregational Churches where a minister read the letter. Ministers packed the church pews; laymen and women sat in the balcony. The letter denounced the Grimké sisters for speaking on slavery to mixed, or "promiscuous," audiences. Ministers warned the public of "the dangers which at present seem to threaten the FEMALE CHARACTER with wide-spread and permanent injury" by leading women away from their assigned sphere. "The power of woman is her dependence. God had ordained her weakness and need of protection," proclaimed the ministers, and any woman who lectured in public lost the right of male protection, for "her character becomes unnatural."[87]

With Lucy and some others, the ministers' message backfired. She was furious that anyone would try to silence these inspiring sisters from South Carolina. Each time the pastor read a portion that Lucy found appalling, she poked her cousin, who was sitting next to her. Years later, Lucy recalled, "I was young enough then so that my indignation blazed." Her cousin's side apparently turned black and blue because of Lucy's sharp nudging with her elbow each time she heard a maddening sentence. She told Johnson, "if I ever had anything to say in public, I should say it, and all the more because of the Pastoral Letter." There is little question that this was a turning point in Lucy's life. "If I had ever felt bound to silence by interpretations of Scripture texts or believed that equal rights did not belong to women, that pastoral letter broke my bonds," she recalled years later.[88]

"Breaking bonds" was the key phrase. A few women abolitionists, including the Grimké sisters and Anne Warren Weston, a leader of the Boston Female Anti-Slavery Society, who heard or read "The Pastoral Letter," now argued that women were enslaved, as were the slaves they were trying to free. Ministers who used the Bible to justify slavery were using the same passages to justify women's subordination. Even a few men found the minsters' message appalling. The popular poet John Greenleaf Whittier wrote the Grimké sisters in sympathy and composed a fifteen-verse satirical poem in response to the "Pastoral Letter," denouncing Congregational ministers for their insistence on women's silence.[89]

During this controversy, Sarah Grimké wrote a series of essays for the *New England Spectator* on "The Province of Woman." She articulated her many concerns, including that women lived under laws that kept them silent and submissive. She insisted that women be given equal educational opportunities. Grimké recalled that her father would not let her study Latin alongside her brothers merely because she was female, though he admitted she had a great mind to become a lawyer—if she were male. The sexual abuse of slave women by white men was unspeakable and all too apparent, and she urged white women to empathize with black women's plight. Grimké criticized the nation's laws that gave husbands control over their wives, claiming wives' relationships to their husbands were like slaves to their masters. She defended women's right to express themselves in public. Women who relished their dependence and enjoyed leading lives of leisure also upset her. "If women felt their responsibility, for the support of themselves, or their families, it would add strength and dignity to their characters," she insisted.[90] Grimké's essays were collected into one of the nation's first feminist treatises, *Letters on the Equality of the Sexes, and the Condition of Woman*, the same book that Alfred Bartlett gave Lucy in 1838.[91] Throughout her life, Lucy often mentioned these essays that so clearly articulated the injustices women suffered.

It would be impossible to overstate the significance of the Grimkés in Lucy's development. As she explained to Bo, if he read Sarah Grimké's essays, "I guess you would not think that I was too 'obstreperous.' I tell you, they are first-rate and only help to confirm the resolution I had made before, to call no man master."[92] But while male abolitionists like Whittier and Garrison applauded the Grimké sisters' writings, these essays stirred uneasiness among many abolitionists who did not want to conflate two radical issues— antislavery and women's rights—for fear of mitigating the primacy of abolition. Also, most Americans, in both the North and South, opposed women's demands for equality and were upset by these assertive sisters trying to upend women's traditional roles.

But the Grimkés had more to say. On February 21 and 23, 1838, Angelina Grimké became the first woman in the nation to address a state legislature. Hearing advance notice of her appearance before the Massachusetts State Legislature, spectators—men and women—packed the State House for this most unusual event. Massachusetts women had circulated antislavery petitions, collecting some 20,000 signatures and demanding that legislators act on the issue. Angelina Grimké's task was to present the petitions and then demand that elected representatives take a stand and condemn slavery. She argued for the cause of antislavery but also denounced women's oppression, claiming women were equally concerned about abolition and their own inferior status and needed to be heard: "This dominion of woman must be resigned—the sooner the better; in the age which is approaching she should be something more—she should be a citizen." This was a major step toward allowing a woman to speak in a political setting.[93] The event had a profound impact on Lucy. She often cited Angelina Grimké's appearance before the legislature where she, "with eloquence rare and wonderful," pleaded with male officials and insisted the government work to abolish slavery.

The other early spokeswoman who inspired Lucy's decision to devote her life to abolition and to women's rights was the aforementioned Abby Kelley (later Foster). Kelley was a passionate reformer with strong views who gave much of her life to the antislavery movement. She was born in Pelham,

Massachusetts, in 1811, into a Quaker family of modest means. She grew up in Worcester, was educated at common schools, and attended a Friends' boarding school in Providence, Rhode Island. For several years Kelley taught school, but in the mid-1830s, was drawn to the antislavery movement and decided to dedicate her life to this cause. She became a follower of Garrison and much admired the Grimké sisters, officially beginning her work in 1838. She was the first woman in New England to try to support herself as an antislavery lecturer. So strong were her beliefs and so unfiltered were her words that Kelley aroused much opposition, especially among clergymen. She ignored the opposition, for she knew her cause was just, and she continued to speak out.[94]

In 1840, Kelley created a split in the New England abolitionist movement. Garrison and some of his followers supported her appointment to the business committee of the American Anti-Slavery Society. A number of members were appalled that a woman might serve in this important position, and they demanded Kelley's resignation. She refused. Several more conservative members, including brothers Lewis and Arthur Tappan and Henry Stanton

Figure 9. Abby Kelley Foster (American Antiquarian Society, Worcester, MA)

(future husband of Elizabeth Cady Stanton), walked out of the meeting in protest and formed a new antislavery association devoid of women: the American and Foreign Anti-Slavery Society. While attending Wesleyan Academy, Lucy followed this controversy closely and was incensed. She complained to Bo, "There seems to be no feeling of Liberty about it. Its great object seems to be to crush Garrison and women. While it pretends to en-deavor to remove the yoke of bondage on account of color, it is actually summoning all its energies to rivet more firmly the chains that have always been fastened upon the neck of women." She mentioned H. G. Ludlow, who apparently ran the New Haven Anti-Slavery Society and who refused to let any woman speak in that Society's meetings. In her letter, Lucy denounced Ludlow for "the inalienable right that God had given is wrested from her."[95]

Kelley first spoke at an antislavery convention in 1837 and two years later began addressing the public in her bold, inimitable style. Her approach was confrontational; her intent was to stir a response in her audiences. That she did. Lucy recognized the barriers Kelley eventually eliminated for women, remarking years later, "The great service Abby Kelley rendered the slave is less than that by which, at such a price, she earned for us all the right of free speech." For years Kelley stood "in the thick of the fight" as ministers and critics "poured upon her vials of bitterness and wrath."[96] Had Kelley been weaker or less noble, Lucy believed, she might have given up, but she did not.

Although Lucy followed Kelley's lectures and activities in articles that were carried in the *Liberator*, their first physical encounter occurred in 1842 when Kelley spoke in West Brookfield. All the Stone family went to hear her. When they arrived at the meeting, Lucy went forward to welcome her. Kelley, who was always seeking new converts to the antislavery movement, asked Lucy to join her at the front. Lucy refused, explaining that her hair was "all blown about" from the wagon ride. Kelley laughed and told her, "Oh Lucy Stone, you are not half emancipated!"[97]

Riding home that night, Lucy sensed something extraordinary had happened—she had witnessed a woman speaking in public to a mixed audi-ence on the radical topic of abolition. Her father, however, was not impressed, muttering to Lucy after he heard some dogs barking in the distance, "When the sluts are out, the dogs will bark." If anything, her father's rude remark sealed Lucy's convictions. She never forgot how inspired she had been when hearing Kelley speak.[98] As she recalled years later, "Abby Kelley earned for us all the right of free speech. The movement for equal rights of women began directly and emphatically with her."[99]

These three women influenced Lucy's decision to devote her life to anti-slavery and to women's rights. They had broken barriers for women's right to speak in public. When the Grimké sisters and Kelley began to lecture, people viewed them as "something monstrous," Lucy commented. "All the cyclones and blizzards which prejudice, bigotry and custom could raise, were let loose upon these three peerless women." But they ignored "the howling" mobs, the negative press, and "thunders from the pulpit" as they "literally put their lives in their hands."[100]

Two years before Kelley's West Brookfield appearance, an event sharpened Lucy's views on antislavery and women's inferior role in the church and their connection. The issue involved Deacon Josiah Henshaw of West Brookfield's Congregational Church. On March 14, 1838, Henshaw was brought before church elders because of his antislavery views and activities, including his hosting Abby Kelley in his home, attending antislavery meetings, distributing abolitionist literature, and serving as president of the Worcester County Anti-Slavery Society. Lucy and a few other women sat in on the church meeting to hear the charges brought against Henshaw and to determine if the church should expel him. When the first charge was read, Lucy, either not realizing or ignoring the fact that women were not allowed to vote on church matters, raised her hand to oppose his expulsion. Lucy recalled decades later that the minister, with "an accent of scorn," told the vote-counter to ignore her raised hand, reminding everyone present that Lucy had no voice in the matter. According to Saint Paul, women were to be silent. Lucy persevered, for as a church member who had opinions on the issue, she felt she should be allowed to vote. In each of the subsequent five votes, Lucy raised her hand to oppose Henshaw's removal and was ignored each time. The church expelled him. So deeply embedded in her consciousness was this event that when Lucy was on her deathbed and relating the story to daughter Alice, she dramatized the moment by raising her arm "with a flash in her eye."[101]

Lucy was also deeply troubled by a neighbor woman whose husband mistreated her and beat her repeatedly. Mrs. Lamberton was apparently an "excellent woman." By contrast, her husband, a blacksmith, drank excessively, was an adulterer, and often abandoned the family for days or weeks at a time, leaving his wife and children dependent on kind neighbors, including the Stones, for food and assistance. Once when Mrs. Lamberton was about to bear another baby and her husband had been absent for weeks, Mrs. Lamberton's father, who lived in nearby Ware and knew of his daughter's domestic troubles, drove over to bring his daughter and grandchildren home with him. Mr. Lamberton got wind of this and was waiting at the door when his father-in-law arrived. Claiming his right as a husband, he forbade his father-in-law from taking his family. Mrs. Lamberton's father had to back down.

When Lucy learned about this, she was outraged. Why on earth could Mrs. Lamberton's father not intercede to rescue his own daughter? This entire scene—the pitiless and heartless drama, the profound injustice, the deeply human unfairness of it all—had a huge impact on Lucy, so much so that it later became one of several reasons she cited to explain why she would never marry. "Lamberton" spoke volumes. He was the maddening embodiment of laws that allowed husbands to wield such power over their wives. This time it did not work for Lucy to count to one hundred and wait for her rage to pass. This episode did not pass.[102]

So it was with Lucy's growing resolve to gain for women the same rights that men had, her commitment to antislavery, and her yearning for more education that she was determined to attend the first college in the country that had opened its doors to women—Oberlin Collegiate Institute in Ohio, which was founded in 1833 and admitted women to its college program in 1837. How she heard about Oberlin and its unique co-educational identity is not clear, but in a few short years since its founding, the school had certainly attracted local and even national attention. According to one account, Amasa Walker, living near West Brookfield and who had taught as an adjunct professor at Oberlin, told Lucy about the school and urged her to apply.[103] Oberlin was mentioned in articles in newspapers in Connecticut, Ohio, New York, Massachusetts, and elsewhere. Papers carried both brief notices and longer accounts of this "flourishing" and "celebrated" school. For instance, appearing in a Philadelphia newspaper was a report on the May 1837 Anti-Slavery Convention of American Women held in New York City. There, Angelina Grimké praised Oberlin for its "noble stand" in not only admitting women but also African Americans. Grimké heralded the fact that "our oppressed sisters may find at least one seminary in our republican despotism, where they may enjoy the benefits of a liberal education." Two years later, the *Liberator* celebrated the school, claiming "the day is coming when woman shall take her appropriate place as a moral being and she is no longer regarded as an instrument to pamper." The first women to graduate from Oberlin with bachelor's degrees did so in 1841.[104]

Lucy saw Oberlin as her opportunity to fulfill her dream of earning a college degree. But when she approached her father about it, Francis turned to Hannah. "Is the child crazy?" he asked.[105] Since Francis was unwilling to pay her college costs, Lucy did. It took a few years to save enough money from various teaching jobs to pay her tuition and fees and to study for the college's qualifying exams. Despite parental apprehension and opposition, and perhaps with some nervousness at going so far from home for the first time in her life, yet with the determination that had always guided her—as a child, a teacher, a "half-emancipated" young woman—in August 1843 Lucy set off to attend college.

2

Oberlin Collegiate Institute

Oberlin Collegiate Institute opened in December 1833, the first college in the country to admit both men and women. When Lucy arrived there ten years later, she announced to her family that she had at last reached the "long talked of, and to mother, <u>long dreaded</u> Oberlin."[1] For Lucy, this was anything but a "dreaded" place; it was the fulfillment of a dream come true. When she graduated four years later, Lucy Stone became the first woman from Massachusetts and one of the first women in the country to earn a bachelor's degree. It was not just a notable achievement but a groundbreaking one, and Oberlin's influence on her was lifelong.

By the second quarter of the nineteenth century, scores of colleges had been founded to offer higher education to young men. A number of denominations established many of these schools, initially hoping to train young men for the ministry. Other institutions had the financial backing of an individual or a group who recognized the value of a college degree and of a liberal education. Some offered both. The first college in the nation, Harvard College, had been founded in 1636 by benefactor John Harvard who donated money and his entire library to establish an institution to train Puritan men for the ministry. Other schools, including William and Mary, Yale, The College of New Jersey (Princeton), Columbia College, Brown, Dartmouth, and others followed over the course of the next century.

Oberlin, however, was entirely different from them all. It was the brainchild of two New England ministers, John Jay Shipherd and Philo Penfield Stewart. Shipherd, born in 1802 near Granville, New York, grew up in Vermont in a prominent family. As a young man, he was profoundly influenced by the Second Great Awakening as he and other Protestant Americans sought to renew or affirm their faith and prepare for the millennium. Shipherd's personal revelation apparently came after recovering from injuries he sustained after falling from a horse and from accidentally imbibing a dose of poison that affected his eyesight. Having achieved little success in several business ventures, he decided to turn his life to God. Shipherd attended theology school and began to preach. His religious awakening impressed upon him the sense that he had to do more than attend church, pray, and read the Bible. He also needed to engage in good works by reaching out to help the needy and by addressing the numerous ills that seemed to be afflicting the nation's spiritual health. By the second quarter of the nineteenth century, reform was in the air, partly driven by a profound religious sense. Men like Shipherd sought to tackle such problems as drunkenness, illiteracy, prostitution, immorality, and, of course, slavery. Shipherd felt his faith obliged him to engage in good works, not only to uplift the nation but to reflect positively on his Christian character. He had a calling.[2]

After receiving ordination by the Congregational Council, in 1830 Shipherd left Vermont to serve as a home missionary. He headed west to spread the faith. He made a special point to visit Rochester, New York, where he met the nation's most famous evangelical minister, Charles Grandison Finney. Historian Nathan Hatch describes Finney as "blunt, self taught, and immensely persuasive."[3] The man's fiery sermons, charismatic personality, and rousing revivals led to the conversion of hundreds of people across upstate New York, so many, in fact, that the central and western portions of the region came to be known as the "Burned Over District." Its name derived from the number of religious revivals and resulting agitation that took place there. The area was a hotbed of radical religious thought. By the mid-1820s, Finney had gained a national reputation. But Shipherd's assignment directed him farther west. Traveling on, he arrived in Cleveland, Ohio, a town of some 1,000 people, located on the shores of Lake Erie. Here was the region where he was to carry out his duties.[4]

In response to a request from residents of Elyria, a town several miles west of Cleveland, his denomination assigned him to move there. It was a fairly rough frontier town, consisting of two taverns, two mills, several stores, a school, and a newspaper. Shipherd found its residents, whose moral condition he deemed "deplorable," desperately in need of his inspired preaching. He settled in as a missionary pastor, joined the local temperance crusade, and held a revival in the spring of 1831. But Elyrians proved stubbornly impious, and when a former Vermont schoolmate, Philo Penfield Stewart, visited Shipherd, the two conceived the idea of founding a colony and a school in the area.[5] To Shipherd, education was the "handmaid of religion," and he now envisioned this new project as his life's mission.[6] Believing in the possibility of human perfection and exhibiting a sense of "perfectionist enthusiasm" that characterized the founding of several utopian communities, such as the Shakers in the East and New Harmony in Indiana, Shipherd and Stewart began to plan their colony and its center, their school.[7]

The two men found the perfect setting in an area called Russia Township, a few miles west of Elyria, which at the time was a virtual wilderness, or, as one newspaper later described it, "a clay morass, covered with dense forest."[8] But Shipherd and Stewart recognized that the area offered great potential, once cleared, to become productive farmland. As they commented a few years later, the setting was ideal because it was fertile, easily approached via western lakes and canals, and "sufficiently remote from the vices and temptations of large towns."[9] The township, one of eighteen in Lorain County, had available 5,000 acres of woods in a tranquil setting, far removed—or at least a few miles—from worldly distractions. Here they could undertake their experiment: creating a school "of the first order" and a village to sustain it. "Pious Eastern families," they felt sure, would settle there "for the purpose of glorifying God, and doing good." Shipherd traveled east to New Haven, Connecticut, to negotiate a price with the two businessmen who owned the land. He purchased several hundred acres at $1.50 an acre, hoping to entice families to move west, purchase plots of land, and join this great experiment of spiritual re-education. He and Stewart also visited wealthy individuals who might support their idealistic venture, seeking to raise $15,000 for the school and colony.[10]

Almost from the beginning, the two men conceived of something quite radical—an educational institution open to both men and women and that would offer a college degree to those for whom one had been financially out of reach. Oberlin was not designed as a school for the elite but for young men and women from varied backgrounds who could interact with one another as equals. In the process of learning and preparing for the millennium, students would be restored to "gospel simplicity & devotion." As Shipherd described the school to his brother, "Every one regardless of worldly maxims, shall return to Gospel simplicity of dress, diet, hours & furniture & all appertaining to him, & be industrious & economical with the view of earning & saving as much as possible." The school was named after Jean Frederic Oberlin, a French minister and philanthropist working in the Alsace region whose inspired teaching and good deeds among the poor motivated the two men. Their school would give those in the West a rigorous college education on a par with that offered by institutions in the East, such as Middlebury, where Shipherd had hoped at one point to matriculate, or Amherst. Oberlin students would be able to compete with the very best of them. [11]

Surprisingly, the radical notion of creating a co-educational institution seemed to raise little fuss. Oberlin had been designed to admit women, and it did so from the very beginning with the creation of a Female Department. An 1845 report on the school conveyed the founders' initial belief that since men could "be initiated into all the mysteries of science," women should not be denied that same opportunity. The ignorance of one sex was a "millstone about the necks of the others." [12] Only four years after the school opened, when a few female students expressed a desire to obtain a college degree, Oberlin administrators and faculty apparently agreed. From then on, the school offered women the opportunity to enroll in the Ladies Department or in the college degree-conferring program, "bringing within the reach of the misjudged and neglected sex, all the instruction privileges which hitherto have unreasonably distinguished the leading sex from theirs." [13]

The main differences between the two programs offered to women were the level of rigor, the length of study, and the requirement of learning classical languages to earn a bachelor's degree. Only men taught in the College Department, earning $450 to $600 annually. Women taught in the Ladies Department and were paid $150 per year. The majority of young women attending Oberlin were enrolled in the Ladies Department. Shipherd and Stewart also set up a Preparatory Department that offered basic education to children 8 years and older; within a few years it attracted several hundred students from the surrounding area.

Annual college tuition was set at $15 a term for men and $12 for women. Boarding in the dining hall cost $1 per week, and room rental was $4 to $6 a year. The college provided a bed frame and stove. Wood was free so long as students chopped their own and carried logs to their rooms—or paid someone else to do it. [14] Lodging with families in the village typically cost $.75 to $1.25 per week.

Another significant feature of an Oberlin education was required manual labor. To Shipherd and Stewart, the benefits were obvious. Students would build strong bodies, develop "clear and strong thought, with a happy moral temperament," and "aid in forming habits of industry and economy." The manual labor requirement also offered financial benefits to Oberlin by keeping maintenance costs low. Making all students work and earn money to cover their expenses also meant the college could attract young men and women of limited means. Shipherd envisioned young women engaged not only in housekeeping, sewing, gardening, cooking, and growing and packaging seeds but also in wool manufacturing and in silk culture. Their jobs would be "suited to their sex, and conducive to their health, good habits, and support," he proclaimed.[15] Underlying this was more conventional thinking and the founders' sense that "in every mother should be inculcated knowledge of domestic affairs."[16] Young men were to engage in more physically demanding chores, such as chopping down trees to clear forests, constructing roads, planting and harvesting crops, and tending the college's cows, sheep, and pigs.

Shipherd's and Stewart's initial expectations were high. When the college opened, they demanded that every student work four hours a day in addition to attending classes and studying. Within a year or two, compulsory work hours were reduced to three per day; by the time Lucy arrived in 1843, nearly a decade after Oberlin's founding, students performed two hours of manual labor each day. Wages paid by the college were standard: three cents per hour paid to women and five cents to men. Within a few years, the number of students outpaced the number of jobs available at the college and in the village, though administrators still anticipated that students could earn at least a portion, if not all, of their expenses through this work plan. They also expected students to use their winter vacations to earn additional money. The school year divided into two semesters, one starting in early August and ending in December, and the second starting in February. Oberlin's three-month winter break coincided with winter term in nearby public schools, and Shipherd and Stewart urged Oberlin students to spend those months earning part of their tuition by teaching there. Women teachers from Oberlin were paid a standard fee of $10 a month while men earned $16.[17]

Religion influenced nearly every part of life at Oberlin. The First Church Meeting House was completed in 1844 while Lucy was a student, and within a few years it boasted a congregation second in size only to Plymouth Church in Brooklyn, New York.[18] The school required students' attendance at daily public prayers both morning and evening. Among the many rules was one that forbade students from traveling to or from Oberlin on the Sabbath. On Sundays, they had to attend public worship at a Congregational service, though if of a different denomination, they could seek faculty permission to attend another church in the village. All students were expected to exhibit strong moral character. The school explicitly prohibited "all vulgar and profane words, writings, and actions," as well as "quarreling," gambling, and "games of chance"—meaning card-playing. Alcohol was strictly forbidden.

According to the school catalogue, proper behavior required that "The Ladies shall not receive at their rooms the visits of gentlemen," and men had to vacate their rooms when female students were "engaged in domestic chores" (i.e., cleaning them).[19]

Austerity also characterized Oberlin. One female student, Charlotte Hickox, who attended Oberlin before Lucy arrived, described it both as a "celebrated place" and a "manual labor institution." She found the faculty and students extremely pious. Food was simple fare, and she teasingly identified the breakfast meal as hash and cold water, lunch as "kitten fried in bran," and supper, mush and milk.[20] As the college catalogue noted, no tea, coffee, highly seasoned meats, rich pastries, or foods deemed unwholesome or expensive would be served. Students who wanted to eat meat once a day had to pay extra. Typically—Hickox was not far off—everyone dined on pudding, milk, and thin cakes for breakfast and brown bread and milk for supper. Much of the college diet was based on the so-called Graham system, a quasi-vegetarian diet that had been recently popularized by Sylvester Graham, a diet reformer and evangelist who also created a wheat cracker later associated with his name.[21] Lucy must have found the food palatable, for by sophomore year, she admitted to her family that she had gained nine pounds. Generally Lucy was healthy during all four years at Oberlin except for periodic migraines, usually brought on by stress, overwork, and her menstrual cycle.

Figure 10. The Meeting House, Tappan Square and Oberlin Collegiate Institute, 1846 (Oberlin College Archives)

Oberlin Collegiate Institute officially opened with thirty pupils present, the majority of them the sons and daughters of town residents and faculty members. As students started attending classes, Shipherd and Stewart worked to hire an "able and morally purposeful" faculty. Oberlin enjoyed a major boost in its hiring as it struggled through its first year, thanks to an event at a school nearby. In February 1834 a controversy erupted at Lane Seminary in Cincinnati, a school founded in 1830 and headed by the Rev. Lyman Beecher. Led by Theodore Dwight Weld, a group of Lane students held an eighteen-day-long debate to convince others to reject colonization as the appropriate means to deal with slavery. This idea, promoted by the American Colonization Society, which had been founded in Maryland in 1816, sought to raise money to send slaves and free blacks to Liberia in Africa. Instead, these young men at Lane insisted that people follow Garrison and call for an immediate end to slavery. Lane trustees demanded this open discussion of slavery be silenced. In protest, a few dozen students and several faculty members left the seminary. Getting wind of the controversy, Shipherd, a member of the Western Reserve Anti-Slavery Society, made a well-timed journey to the school and visited with minister and Lane trustee Asa Mahan. Shipherd was able to convince Mahan as well as mathematics professor John Morgan and several Lane students to come to Oberlin. Shipherd and Stewart appointed Mahan as Oberlin's first President and Professor of Intellectual and Moral Philosophy and Professor of Theology, a man widely known for his intellect, but also for his aggressive, imperious manner.[22]

At the same time as this hiring boon, Oberlin received the promise of a generous contribution from wealthy New York businessman Arthur Tappan, one of the future founders of the American and Foreign Anti-Slavery Society. He pledged to Oberlin Collegiate Institute $10,000, with $5,000 to be paid at once and the remainder to come in five annual installments. Tappan well understood that money buys favors, and he insisted that the school hire the Rev. Charles Grandison Finney as a professor and establish a Theology Department. With such generous support offered to a new, struggling school, who could say no? The idea of hiring Finney, one of the leaders of the Second Great Awakening, obviously pleased Shipherd, for when he had first come to Elyria, he had written Finney, urging him to come west, where people desperately needed his ministrations and where "indigent youth" deserved "an opportunity to be educated." "The churches on almost this whole western reserve are dead, & iniquity lives most fearfully," he had written despairingly.[23] With a founding grant and Finney's likely presence, the future seemed assured.

Figure 11. Charles Grandison Finney (Oberlin College Archives)

In January 1835, Oberlin made Finney a generous offer: an annual salary of $800, which was more than that paid to any teacher or even to the school's president. Oberlin also promised him a new home and three to four months off each year to preach elsewhere. Finney accepted. Students, however, did not seem to be as enamored with him as were Shipherd and Tappan. Lucy described Finney as "the crossest looking man I ever saw" after she heard his preaching. Charlotte Hickox characterized him as "a harum scarum fellow," perhaps referring to his fire and brimstone when making a point.[24] Despite Lucy's and Charlotte's negative impressions, Finney must have found the position appealing. He spent the rest of his life on the Oberlin faculty and served as president, and his presence did much to enhance the reputation of the young college.

Even with Tappan's financial backing, during the school's early years Oberlin struggled to sustain itself on limited resources. Students sometimes were paid for manual labor in what Lucy called "institution orders," a scrip system in which they earned credit for their work against institutional expenses. Fundraising by trustees and administrators was ongoing. When she was at Oberlin, Lucy wrote her father, mentioning the school's plan to send a Mr. Bristol to the East Coast to solicit donations. She warned him that Bristol might visit West Brookfield. In advance of that trip, Bristol had written an article that appeared in the June 1845 *Evangelist*, a weekly New York antislavery newspaper, that described impoverished Oberlin faculty members whose children wore threadbare clothes. Lucy countered that the report exaggerated matters. Both Mahan and Finney owned handsome carriages and teams of horses; another professor wore a gold watch; and faculty children were attired in fashionable clothing and lived in homes with carpets. As Lucy concluded, "I thought Father might give, and I wanted he should know to what kind of poor he gave."[25]

Tappan's financial support and Finney's professorship provoked another debate: whether to admit black students to the school. In December 1834, several townspeople and faculty members petitioned Oberlin's trustees, asking for guidance on the issue. "God assisting us we will lay aside every prejudice and do as we shall be led to believe God would have us do," signers asserted. The issue fostered loud debate. Some town residents opposed the idea, fearing an influx of freed blacks would threaten their community. Students took a poll that same month; thirty-two opposed the admission of blacks while twenty-six favored the idea. But Finney countered that he would not teach at a school that did not admit students of African descent, and President Mahan supported the idea as well. The proposal then went before the faculty, who discussed it at three gatherings in early 1835. Trustee meetings on the issue were contentious, or as one observer commented, filled with "rancor and malevolence." Benjamin Woodbury, the school's financial agent, warned Shipherd that admitting black students might cause the demise of Oberlin, for "the whites will begin to leave." Some trustees feared the possibility of "amalgamation," the term used for the sexual mixing of the races.[26]

But Shipherd held firm, claiming the school would lose Tappan's financial backing as well as the presence of Finney and Mahan if it did not accept blacks. Shipherd even threatened to quit over the issue. As he explained to some Oberlin trustees, "I did not desire you to hand out an abolition flag or fill up [the school] with filthy negroes," but the school should not "reject promising youth." When speaking to trustees, he concluded, "We do injury to blacks by not accepting them."[27] Nonetheless, questions remained. Two major concerns were determining where black students would eat and sleep and whether or not white students would accept them.

After much debate, the faculty and trustees agreed by a single vote to admit them, noting that Dartmouth College enrolled Indians, Lane Seminary had graduated a student from Africa, and Princeton had a black student. It was "resolved that the education of the people of color is a matter of great interest and should be encouraged in every proper way & measure & sustained in this institution."[28] In 1835, the first African Americans arrived on campus.[29] By the Civil War, a few hundred black students had attended Oberlin, though they never comprised more than 5 percent of the student population. Most of them enrolled in the Preparatory Department, though the first black male earned a bachelor's degree in 1844; the first black female in 1862.[30] No doubt the biracial student body was another factor in the school's appeal to Lucy.

Admission requirements in the mid-nineteenth century shared little in common with what Oberlin College requires today. Lucy and other students had to bring "trustworthy testimonials" of their moral character as a condition of admittance. Oberlin's first catalogue stated that students had to be "of good intellectual and moral character," have "an ability to work four hours per day," and practice "total abstinence from ardent spirits as an article of drink or refreshment, and tobacco except as a medicine."[31] Lucy had a letter of commendation from her brother Bo, who had hosted President Mahan a few years earlier when he preached at Bo's Congregational Church in Gardner, Massachusetts. Incoming students had to take placement tests, and shortly after she arrived, Lucy happily reported to her parents that she had passed Latin, Greek, and mathematics. No matter how well qualified students were, however, each of them had to "honorably" pass a six-month probation period to ensure they could handle both the academic and manual labor requirements.

Since childhood, Lucy had yearned to become as well educated as her brothers. She had often resented the fact that they earned her parents' praise when they performed well in school while she garnered none, even though she performed as well as or better than they did. It was unfair that her father paid college tuition for Frank and Bo but—at least initially, since eventually he did relent—refused to assist her. Already Lucy viewed education as vital to a meaningful life. The only way she could continue her education, she knew, was to do what she had done before and earn money to pay her own way. That is exactly what she did, leaving for "dreaded Oberlin" with great anticipation and some $90 in hand.

Traveling alone across the country for more than 650 miles in August 1843, at 25 years of age, Lucy encountered new sights and experiences, for she had never ventured beyond her home state. This trip would have been challenging and thrilling for almost any single woman in mid-nineteenth-century America since few women ever traveled far, much less on their own. No doubt Lucy raised a few eyebrows among those whom she met en route, for they were likely encountering for the first time a young, single woman setting out for, of all places, college. On leaving home, Lucy admitted she had "an anxious heart," but it had less to do with what she was leaving behind than what lay ahead. Her main concern was her fear she might not pass the college's entrance examinations.

Lucy set off from West Brookfield by train. Although she could only afford a second class ticket, she found herself placed in a first class car. Her conscience finally got the best of her, however, and when she explained the error, porters placed her in the immigrants' car, which was more crowded. There she concentrated on studying her Greek grammar.[32] On the train from Albany to Utica, she sat next to General Francis Spinner. The two struck up a conversation, and he asked why she was studying Greek. Why not study physiology instead? Lucy responded that she already had done so. He then quizzed her on the number of bones in her arm, which she answered correctly. He bought her ice cream in the dining car and later invited Lucy to visit him at his home in Henniker, New Hampshire, if she ever were in the area. In later years, Spinner, an upstate New York banker and politician (his military title was due to his service in the militia) served as Treasurer of the United States under Abraham Lincoln. After Lucy had become a famous lecturer, Spinner occasionally sent her official documents and items of interest from Washington, DC.[33]

From Buffalo, an overnight steamboat took Lucy across Lake Erie to Cleveland. She could not afford a sleeping room so, along with a few other women, slept on grain sacks piled on the open deck among the horses and freight. Several men did the same on the other side of the boat. Lucy wrote home that the lake was as smooth as glass, and she did not get seasick. In Cleveland, she picked up pretty stones along the lake shore to give to her two nieces. From Elyria, she traveled the last few miles by stage over a bumpy corduroy, or log, road to Oberlin. Writing to her family shortly after she arrived, Lucy detailed every aspect of her trip. Her mother had fretted about problems she might encounter, but Lucy claimed she had made the trip "without having had a <u>particle</u> of trouble." The only casualty was a lost pair of gloves. She accounted for every penny of the $16.65 she spent on her travels and described the many people she met, most of whom had been kind and helpful.[34]

Lucy arrived on Oberlin's campus as one of seven women, along with thirty-four men, who enrolled in the college department that year. In these early years, the campus was situated on a large, grassy, tree-less square with muddy paths. Woods surrounded the few college buildings and professors' homes. Lucy was assigned a room in the Ladies' Boarding Hall and a roommate, a "good-natured," 16-year-old girl from South Carolina who had enrolled in the Ladies' Department. Lucy wrote very little about their relationship. One can only wonder whether or not Lucy had any impact on her young roommate's worldview. The girl's father, a slaveholder, had warned his daughter not to discuss slavery "for fear she will become an Abolitionist," and she confessed to Lucy that "it would kill her mother if she should be one." As Lucy later explained to her family, no one could choose a roommate—the school placed older students with younger girls, hoping older students would set a good example.[35]

One of Lucy's first tasks after settling in was to find a way to earn additional money beyond what she was paid to perform required chores for the college. With no other means of financial support, money remained a constant worry. Shortly after she arrived on campus, Lucy visited President Mahan to seek a teaching position, describing her past experiences in a number of Massachusetts schools. Mahan told her that Oberlin did not let students teach until they had been there at least a year so that the faculty could ascertain their morals, trustworthiness, and ability. Lucy must have convinced Mahan otherwise, for she soon was teaching two sessions of mathematics in the Preparatory Department, earning 25 cents a day toward her weekly boarding fee of $1. For her required chores, Lucy performed housework in the Ladies' Boarding Hall, worked in the kitchen where she dried dishes, a book propped up in front of her so she could study at the same time, and mended clothes for other students.[36]

Lucy found other means to earn money during her college years. As a sophomore, she earned additional income by teaching at the town's school for free blacks, called Liberty School. Because Oberlin served as a stop on the Underground Railroad and quickly had gained a reputation as a progressive community, the village attracted a number of blacks, including some fugitive slaves. In the early 1840s, the community established Liberty School, designed to educate adult African Americans. Several other Oberlin students taught there in addition to Lucy. Her parents were proud when Lucy told them about working at the school. Her students, however, were initially wary. Some of the older male students complained about having a female instructor. Lucy described her past teaching experiences to them and then proceeded to conduct her class. As had happened when she taught at the Paxton school years earlier, it took little time for her to gain the students' devotion. Weeks later when a fire broke out in Oberlin's Ladies' Boarding Hall, some of Lucy's students rushed to the scene to assist. They asked, "Where is Miss Stone's trunk?" Their first thought was of her.[37]

Lucy began by teaching several hours a week, but that schedule proved impossible to maintain, and she reduced her weekly teaching to three hours. In addition to her classroom duties, Lucy wrote letters for her pupils and listened to their accounts of their former lives as slaves, gaining a deeper and more personal understanding of the horrors of slavery.[38] By her junior year, Lucy found that teaching even that much, in addition to attending class, studying, and laboring for the college, was more than she could handle, and she resigned. As she told Sarah, "I was completely worn out. I was never so tired, or so poor in flesh in my life."[39]

Lucy's other source of income was teaching in common schools during the school's winter breaks, just as Oberlin's founders had envisioned. She developed close relationships with her students and their parents in nearby Wellington. Families with little cash sometimes paid her in apples, lemons, soap, candles, lumps of maple sugar, and even a new broom. Townspeople grew fond of her. One woman told Lucy that she always had a home in Wellington, and that if she ever became ill, she would take care of her.[40]

During her sophomore year, Lucy received an unexpected offer. Despite his negative feelings about Lucy's pursuing a college degree, her father wrote her in January 1845. Having learned that Lucy was waking up at 2:00 a.m. to study, he offered to lend her the money she needed to pay tuition, room, and board. In his letter, one of the most poignant and self-revelatory he ever wrote, he recalled his younger years when he labored in his father's tannery, waking up long before dawn in order to start work. "I little thought then that I should have children or a child that would have to do the same, not the same work, but perhaps as hard. . . . There will be no trouble about money. You can have what you need without studying nights or working for 8 cents an hour." Francis had given his family financial security, and he did not want his children to suffer by working as hard as he had. Hannah added her thoughts to her husband's letter. "I felt bad when I heard how hard you have studied. Take good care of your soul and body," she urged.[41] Not until senior year, however, did Lucy accept a loan from her father, borrowing instead from her sister Sarah and her brothers.

Life at Oberlin was tightly scheduled, with limited time for students to do more than work, study, and attend class. In her second year, Lucy detailed her typical weekday. She rose at 5:00 a.m. and spent an hour tending to dressing, grooming, and straightening her room for inspection later in the day. Breakfast and morning worship were at 6:00 a.m. An hour later, she recited Latin and Greek, and from 9:00 to 10:00, studied algebra. Her first teaching assignment in the Preparatory Department met from 10:00 to 11:00. From 11:00 to noon, she recited algebra. Dinner—as the midday meal was called—and exercise for women took place from noon to 1:00 p.m. She then taught her other Preparatory math class. From 2:00 until 5:00 p.m., Lucy studied. Prayers and supper were from 5:00 to 6:00 p.m., and in the evenings, she studied until lights were out at 10:00. There were few alterations to the daily schedule. She set aside time on Monday afternoons for washing her clothes. On Tuesday afternoons, female students met with the Ladies Board of Managers for an hour, and on Thursdays, they attended an hour-long prayer meeting and heard an hour-long lecture presented by a faculty member. The Sabbath was reserved for religious worship.[42] It was a demanding schedule, but Lucy was able to accomplish everything, for, as her childhood friend Sarah Pellet later observed of her, "She was always in a hurry. She is like her father; he was always in a hurry & pushing things through."[43] Throughout her life, Lucy was conscious of time and invariably showed up early for every event.

Because money was tight, Lucy spent all four years at Oberlin, never returning home, not even to attend Frank's and Sarah's weddings. Nor did immediate family members visit her, though cousins living in Michigan came to see her, and another cousin, John Locke, brought Lucy a supply of candles and welcomed her to his home. She was excited when an acquaintance from the Brookfield area, James Monroe, enrolled in Oberlin's junior class.[44] In addition to limited financial means, Lucy's determination to succeed in all her studies also may have been a factor in her remaining at school. As she did throughout her life, she kept her focus on the task at hand.

This cannot have been an easy time for Lucy, despite her determination to earn a degree. She missed her family and retained a strong attachment to home. Letters from family members were infrequent. One impediment was the high cost of postage, which letter recipients typically paid. Lucy sometimes found someone traveling near or to West Brookfield who could hand deliver her letters. In May 1845, when Congress passed a Postal Act that promised better service and lower postal fees, she expressed hope for more letters from her family.[45] She wished Sarah could attend Oberlin and asked Frank to beg their parents to let her come. But at times, she was desperately lonely. At the start of her junior year, Lucy wrote a plaintive letter to her parents about how she had not received a letter from them in six months. She hoped her mother and father could write during the winter when farm chores were minimal. "I waited in vain" for a letter, she admitted.[46]

Her own letters were more frequent and detailed, always containing inquiries about family members, friends, and neighbors, the number of cows the family owned, the price they could get for their butter and cheese, and what crops were thriving. Her hope was for a similar response. She urged Frank to describe all the events at home, stressing that she was "not any less interested in things because I have been gone three years." She encouraged him to give her parents her love. "You can't tell how much I want to see you and know all how you are doing." But, she reassured him, in only two more years she would be home. "I am well and succeed well with my studies," she added.[47] She also expressed constant concern about how hard her parents worked, especially with no grown children now at home. "When I go home Mother shall have a long resting spell, and if I were Father, I would quit hard work altogether," she wrote. She hoped her mother would hire someone to help out, "so that your ankles won't ache so when night comes." She urged her father to wash his lame shoulder in warm salt water and vinegar, but added that the best way to cure it would be if he did not work so hard.[48] To deal with her loneliness, she followed Frank's advice when he had been away at college—to look up at the moon and imagine family members doing the same. Lucy insisted that she was not homesick, though she wished her parents would visit, assuring them the trip to Ohio was an easy one.

Her letters home reflected her observations on a number of issues, including race. Although a confirmed abolitionist when she arrived on campus, Lucy's experiences with black students at Oberlin and teaching at the Liberty School were her first sustained interactions with them. She expressed surprise that black male and female students were fully integrated into Oberlin life. "They sit, some at each table in the dining hall and nobody cares, or whines about it either. . . . In church they are on terms of perfect equality; there is no negro pew."[49]

Indeed, the problems the school had anticipated in admitting black students had failed to materialize, though administrators nonetheless discouraged interracial relationships among students and tried to quiet any ugly rumors. Yet, on occasion, relationships between black and white students did happen. In one situation, a black student threatened to commit suicide after a white female student with whom he had fallen in love refused to marry him. He would, he announced despairingly to Lucy, drown himself in the college well. Lucy replied that he would spoil the college's water supply by throwing himself into the well; it would be better if he slashed his throat instead. Her wry comment seemed to have dissuaded him from doing anything at all.[50]

Lucy also reached out to help John Mercer Langston, a "clever colored boy" who was two years behind her, with his studies. For the rest of his life, Mercer expressed gratitude to Lucy for her friendship and assistance, and he became a supporter of women's suffrage before he graduated. After Oberlin, he went on to become a prominent lawyer in Ohio and an ardent abolitionist and reformer, eventually founding the law department at Howard University and becoming the first black elected to Congress from Virginia. He later called Lucy a "first class woman" who "nobly worked" for black equality and a skillful speaker who was the equal of any man.[51]

Despite homesickness, hard work, and sometimes an overwhelming sense of isolation at Oberlin, Lucy thrived. She was a born scholar. She loved to borrow books from the college library, checking out one at a time, a privilege that cost her twenty-five cents a year. During sophomore year, at least for one class, she wrote her compositions in the form of a small newspaper, "The Plain Speaker," and submitted them on narrow sheets of paper.[52] She craved learning and spent a great deal of time preparing for each class. "I want to learn a <u>great deal faster</u> and a <u>great deal more</u>," she confessed to Frank. Sophomore year, in addition to studying Cicero, rhetoric, and trigonometry, she read—for pleasure—British author Harriet Martineau's *Illustrations of Political Economy* (1832), nine volumes of essays that explained political and economic issues. Lucy described the work as "very interesting."[53] She also read Frederick Douglass's *Narrative of the Life of a Slave*, telling Sarah that she "had never read a more thrilling tale; I hate slavery . . . worse than war."[54] Oberlin's Ladies' Literary Society subscribed to thirty-two magazines, which offered her plenty to read. But mostly she studied and studied. At the end of junior year she wrote that she faced twelve hours of exams, "but I don't dread it at all, for I am very well prepared for it." Lucy told her parents she wished they could witness her oral exams to "see whether it is profitable to keep me at college.... I can honestly tell you I think it is."[55]

During senior year and now dependent on her father's loan for tuition and expenses, Lucy asked her parents if they thought it was a good idea for her to stay at Oberlin for her final year. Acting the part of a dutiful daughter, she wrote, "as long as you furnish me the means, I want to do the way you think best." She herself had determined to stay, whatever the cost. She promised to pay her father back his loans and sent a note home, specifying how much she owed him. Estimating future needs, Lucy concluded that $15 for the winter term at $1.25 per week would cover basic expenses, but she hoped to do some teaching and sewing to earn extra money beyond what her father loaned her.[56]

She did stay, of course. In her senior year she studied the Hebrew Bible, Prometheus's *Vinctus of Aeschylus*, Joseph Butler's *Analogy of Religion*, Lord Henry Holmes Kames's *Elements of Criticism*, Hebrew poetry, intellectual and moral philosophy, political economy, and chemistry. She also wrote compositions and presented monthly declamations—much of education was still based on oral presentation. This suited her, as writing essays was an academic pursuit she claimed she did not enjoy, an interesting comment from someone who would later write for and publish a newspaper.[57] By the spring of senior year, Lucy wanted nothing more than to study hard, "for it is my last term, and I must make the most of it."[58] That she did, for fellow students called her the most "brilliant" woman of her age.[59]

Amidst the demands of college life, Lucy still was able to keep abreast of national events. She was elated when she learned that Cassius Marcellus Clay, one of Kentucky's most prominent planters and politicians (whom later Lincoln appointed as US minister to Russia), had freed his slaves. While at Yale, Clay had heard Garrison speak and been converted to the abolitionist cause. He then wrote a searing critique of slavery which he claimed was an inefficient labor system and impeded the growth of southern industry.[60] In 1846, as the situation in the Texas Republic grew increasingly tense, Lucy wrote Frank, worried that the United States might annex Texas as a slave state: "What shall we do then"? she asked.[61] She mentioned problems that a visionary religious sect, the Millerites, one of the oddest expressions of the Second Great Awakening, was causing a number of churches, including Bo's congregation, as several of his parishioners prepared for Christ's anticipated second coming.[62] She questioned Frank's interest in the Liberty Party, which had formed in 1840. Its followers regarded the political process as the best means to eradicate slavery, in opposition to Garrisonians like Lucy who had little use for politics and sought an immediate end to slavery. The Liberty Party ran James G. Birney, a former Alabama and Kentucky slaveholder, as its presidential candidate in 1840 and again in 1844. "I believe that there are men in it, of sterling worth, of unbending integrity, but in its leaders at the East I have no confidence," Lucy opined. She felt the party's leaders were "destitute of moral principles and are pushing this enterprise out of spite." While she endorsed enthusiastically its antislavery stance, she recognized that the Liberty Party was causing a fissure in the antislavery movement.[63]

Isolated though Oberlin was, the nature of its founders, faculty, and students involved it in events in the greater world. Most of all, this meant the antislavery movement. Lucy remained a committed Garrisonian throughout her college years, though she was only one among a handful of students, faculty, and administrators, who supported his radical views.[64] Despite Oberlin's progressive reputation—its acceptance of blacks and women still made it unique in the entire country—Lucy was surprised to discover that no one subscribed to the *Liberator*. "At the table where I sit they hate Garrison, but they all acknowledge him a talented man, and they don't know but he may be a Christian," she observed with dry sarcasm. Most students and even faculty regarded Garrison's call for an immediate end to slavery as far too extreme, in part because he also demanded that everyone involved in the movement sever ties with any institution that had any association with the inhumane institution. Arthur Tappan's more moderate approach to abolition influenced the school community as well, given the significance of his financial support. Most, in fact, did not embrace Garrison's belief in female equality. About the Oberlin faculty, Lucy commented, "They hate Garrison and women's rights. I love both, and often find myself at swords' points with them."[65] The family she boarded with in town during senior year likewise hated Garrison and Abby Kelley and Stephen Foster "most unmercifully," but Lucy tried "to bear it patiently."[66] She mentioned to Frank that "President Mahan asks once in a while if I retain my Garrison views yet."[67] Her answer was always that she did, putting her in the minority at Oberlin with her unshakeable belief in human equality.

Thus, it is understandable that Lucy was one of the few students who publicized and welcomed the appearance of Abby Kelley and Stephen Foster (who had married in December 1845) when they spoke in the village of Oberlin in February 1846. A religious revival was occurring at the same moment and drew huge crowds, depleting the number of those who might have otherwise come to hear them. Nevertheless, the two delivered a series of antislavery speeches attacking everyone and everything—preachers, politicians, the US government, and the US Constitution—for justifying slavery. Many local residents were shocked by Abby Kelley Foster's strident tone and "the specimen of what woman becomes when out of her place."[68] Some people labeled the couple as "infidels." However, their words thrilled Lucy. After their visit, she was positively ebullient and wrote Kelley Foster: "I wish I could tell you how much good I received from your visit here. My heart dances gaily at the remembrance—it will be long before I shall be so cheered again." Although most were offended by hearing a woman speak in public, Lucy felt her words "set the people to thinking, and I hope great good will result."[69]

After much campus debate over extending the Fosters a second invitation—with Lucy heavily involved in it—the couple came the following September and spent four days lecturing in the village, including a raucous, twelve-hour debate between Stephen Foster and President Asa Mahan.[70] Again, not everyone was pleased with their appearance. Professor James Fairchild, delivering one of the monthly lectures to students, decried Abby Kelley Foster's lecturing "in angry debate." As he reminded students, a woman's soft voice "was made for the fireside and not for the forum."[71] Bo later wrote Lucy that he had heard Abby Kelley Foster and met her when she had lectured near Gardner. Foster spoke to him about her trip to Oberlin and complimented Lucy. Ever the proud brother, Bo added, "Her commendations, however, did not raise you at all in my estimation. . . . The good opinion which I have formed of my sister Lucy is not likely to be surpassed by others."[72]

In addition to hard work, long hours of studying, and stirring debates on abolition, Lucy's college life included a few lighter moments. In 1845, she joined the school's Ladies' Moral Reform Society—a natural interest—and served as its secretary/treasurer. She described a day spent off campus when she and several students rode a hay wagon to Vermillion on Lake Erie. They brought their bathing outfits to swim, and "all felt gay."[73] At graduation, a classmate, Edward Henry, wrote her a poem, including the rather provocative line, "'Tis known to thee that we must part, But we will still be joined in heart." Later, Lucy corresponded with several Oberlin classmates, suggesting that despite her commitment to the life of the mind and the betterment of humankind, she found time to make friends. Interestingly, more were male than female.[74]

Lucy's closest college friend, nonetheless, became Antoinette Brown, who arrived on campus in February 1846 during Lucy's junior year. Nette, as Lucy called her, was born in 1825 to a privileged family living in Henrietta, New York. Even before she arrived at Oberlin, Nette had heard about Lucy Stone. While traveling by stagecoach to campus, she sat next to an Oberlin trustee who warned her about Lucy—a student "who held wild and radical ideas on religion and other subjects." He advised Brown not to befriend this "very bright girl, but eccentric, a Garrisonian, and much too talkative on the subject of woman's rights."[75] That comment made her very eager to meet Lucy. The first time Nette saw her, Lucy was seated at a long table in the college dining hall, men on one side, women on the other. She was engaged in a vigorous debate with two men, speaking nonstop "with much earnestness and with very positive convictions." Seeing a "small, fresh, round-faced girl in a neat calico frock with short hair," Nette imagined Lucy to be no more than 18 and was therefore surprised by her audacity in debating with such confidence and intensity older men, one of whom was superintendent of the dining hall, a college graduate, and a clergyman. As Nette recalled years later, "I promptly decided that she talked altogether too much and with an unfitting absoluteness of conviction and of authority for any young girl." Only later did she discover Lucy was 27.[76]

Figure 12. Antoinette Brown (Oberlin College Archives)

Although Nette enrolled in the Ladies Department while Lucy was in the college program, many of their classes overlapped. The two became fast friends, enjoying a relationship that was close emotionally and physically. They formed a bond that only strengthened later as they became public lecturers on women's rights and eventually sisters-in-law. They did not always see eye to eye, however, especially on issues related to religion. Antoinette, who was deeply religious, came to Oberlin to earn a degree in theology and become a minister, even though that profession was generally closed to women.[77] Nette disapproved of Garrison's attacks on the clergy while Lucy defended them. Lucy feared her friend's interest in theological studies would curb her independent spirit and was especially upset when Nette later returned to Oberlin to study what Lucy dubbed "that old musty theology," wasting, in Lucy's thinking, three years of her life "wading through that deep slough."[78]

Wading through slough or not, Nette loved fine fashion and nice things. When Lucy once saw Nette on her way to church wearing a straw hat covered with artificial flowers, she asked why she had put a flower pot on her head. Lucy, who never drank alcohol—her father's example and Frank's reprimand never left her—had little tolerance for others who did. She admonished Nette when she occasionally sipped wine. She also fussed at her because Nette was absent-minded and untidy.[79]

Despite their differences, the bond between the two young women expressed in both conversation and correspondence while in college lasted for the rest of their lives. At night, Nette often sneaked out of the girls' boarding hall, walked through Tappan Hall, and joined Lucy in her room to talk "about all sorts of things" and to snuggle in bed together well into the night.[80] As Nette later related, "Mine was the intense admiration of a younger girl for one much more experienced and influential."[81]

One part of their bond was a shared passion about the role of women and objections to restrictions the school (and the nation) imposed on them. Both pledged never to marry because of the laws that made a wife dependent on her husband and that removed nearly all her rights. Marriage, they agreed, would curtail their ability to function as independent women, Lucy as a public lecturer and Nette as a preacher. As Nette wrote Lucy in 1847, "Let us stand alone in the great moral battlefield with none but God for a supporter.... Let them see that woman can take care of herself & act independently without the encouragement & sympathy of his 'lord & master,' that she can think & talk as a moral agent is privileged to. O no don't let us get married." After graduation, Lucy urged Nette to read Edward D. Mansfield's *Legal Rights, Liabilities and Duties of Women* (1845), likely the first lay guide in this country that explained, in clear language, the legal and civil rights and laws on domestic relations.[82]

Still, Lucy's views on marriage were conflicted, torn between traditional views and a more radical perspective of how an independent woman ought to think and behave. Although she resolved to remain single, she admitted to Nette that it would be "horrid" to live without the "intimate companionship and gentle loving influences" of a husband. "But nothing is so bad as to be made a thing, as every married woman now is, in the eyes of the Law." Lucy hoped the laws regarding wives' dependence on their husbands would change, though she doubted this would happen in her lifetime.[83]

In July 1845, her sister Sarah married Henry Lawrence, a schoolteacher. Although Lucy rejected marriage for herself and encouraged women's independence, she had plenty of advice to offer Sarah on how to sustain a strong marital relationship. Her list reflected some of the most traditional ideas of the day. Sarah should always confide in her husband; never conceal anything from him or spend money without telling him; always take an interest in his family; keep his wardrobe in order; organize a plan for her days so she could determine when she would mend, bake, and perform certain chores; maintain a well-ordered home and separate drawers for his clothes so she could readily find them; mend clothing as quickly as possible; not let bread go dry; and be good company so he would not be tempted to seek companionship elsewhere. In closing, Lucy urged Sarah to "be a commonsense wife and a Christian one."[84]

Sarah responded to Lucy's letter, neglecting to comment on her advice but upset because she had learned that their father's will stipulated his plan to give his two surviving daughters $200 apiece but divide his $4,000 estate among his three living sons. Lucy responded that she did not "care a particle about it, for I know that Father has not done it because he loves his sons more than he does his daughters." Although there was no justice in it, she did not feel it was their father's fault so much as "the time when his impressions of what is right in such a case were formed." To Lucy, the central issue was changing society's ideas and laws regarding men and women; only then would individual behavior, like their father's, change. "When he was young," she continued, "it was the universal custom to give the property principally to the sons, and he possibly is only acting in accordance with what he thinks is right. It is only an additional proof of the tyranny of custom, and shows the necessity of making custom right."[85] Lucy offered to give Sarah her share of their inheritance, feeling she would need it more than Lucy might.

Lucy, indeed, imagined little need for personal wealth, for she lived simply. Oberlin's frugality paralleled and likely solidified Lucy's own values. She dressed plainly and neatly in her homemade calico dresses, mending and re-mending her clothes, always appearing clean and fresh despite a limited wardrobe. Ever concerned about money, she boarded off campus for fifty cents a week during her last two years at Oberlin, and she often cooked meals in her room rather than pay for board. She watched every penny and pur-chased material for only one new dress during her Oberlin years (though she did indulge in black silk to make into a dress to wear at graduation).[86] She also asked her mother to send cotton cloth so she could make more chemises, and her mother, Sarah, and her sisters-in-law quilted her a warm cloak to wear in winter. Lucy's major indulgence during college was a $4 rocking chair in which she could read, study, and gain relief from her migraines.[87] She expressed these same values in writing home. When Sarah married, Lucy commended her for a ceremony "that was entirely destitute of ostentation." But she fretted over Sarah's moving to a home near Albany, New York, where Lucy imagined her sister might be "surrounded by such votaries of fashion." She urged Sarah not to be tempted by fashion or to "forget what the adorn-ing of a Christian should be," and not to succumb to any display of finery.[88]

While in college Lucy must have spent time pondering her faith, though there is little evidence of this in her letters home. Hannah had tried her best to impose her strong Christian values on family members, but in Lucy's case, her efforts had limited success. Yet even after she became disenchanted with the Congregational Church, Lucy professed a basic sense of faith throughout her adult life and on rare occasions, attended church. In writing Frank in May 1844 during her first year at Oberlin, she commented on his forthcom-ing marriage to Harriet Blake and shared thoughts about her own faith, prompted by an essay she read in the *Evangelist*. She admitted that she had always felt the presence of a higher power and a connection to God, "I have always known it, but now I think I feel it more than I ever did before. We can cast all our care, on Him and feel that He will care for us for he says he will, and we should let God be true." Sounding very much like her pious mother, she closed, "If thou believest, all things are possible to him that believeth."[89]

By junior year, Lucy had come to question Oberlin's religious conserva-tism, which she felt often created sinners rather than converted them. "There is so much truth preached, which the students are obliged to hear, that they do not yield to it, they grow hardened under it. You never heard such scorching, plain, personal, practical preaching as we get here," she explained to Sarah, perhaps a reference to Finney's impassioned sermons. In church, ministers were wont to publicly announce a sin they believed someone in the congregation had committed, using the incident to create an example and to pressure the guilty party to confess. Eventually the perpetrator usually did so. Lucy described one situation in which someone had stolen honey from the college's bee-hives. Finney mentioned the theft every Sunday until a young man finally broke down and confessed.[90]

So it was that Lucy's outward expression of faith ebbed during college. Years later, looking back at Oberlin, she admitted Finney's lectures and his discussions of the Trinity profoundly affected her faith, but not in the manner Finney might have hoped. According to Lucy's daughter Alice, this "left her a Unitarian." By spring of junior year, Lucy's views were set. She explained to Frank that she had little use for churchgoing or marriage: "I have not changed my views of church, ministry, sabbath or matrimony in the least."[91]

But where Lucy found herself most at odds with the Oberlin community was in its treatment of women. As we have seen, though the school was far ahead of its time as a co-educational and biracial institution, its administration and faculty expressed conservative views on women, often citing scriptural passages to keep women in their place. Two years after Lucy graduated, Professor James Harris Fairchild published *Woman's Rights and Duties* in which he claimed, "It is a thing positively disagreeable to both sexes to see a woman a public character." Women were to be educated for "intelligent motherhood" and tend to their domestic duties. The idea of women holding public office was "too unnatural to be dreamed of."[92]

Some of this conservatism about female behavior made sense, for Oberlin's administrators, teachers, and staff were responsible for monitoring the behavior of men and women. Rules were strict because they had to be. To protect and oversee female students, one of the first buildings erected on campus was the Ladies' Boarding Hall, a substantial brick structure three stories tall, completed in 1835. Here resided a majority of female students under a matron's supervision. Lucy lived in the Ladies' Boarding Hall during her first two years. As the nation's first co-educational college, Oberlin felt constrained to hold men and women to the highest moral standards and sometimes struggled over how to control their frequent and inevitable interaction. School administrators clearly understood that that they were *in loco parentis*; that parents were entrusting their daughters' education to others in a co-ed setting, far from parental supervision. The school closely monitored contact between the sexes, allowing men and women to sit next to one another in class but on opposite sides of the table at mealtime.[93] The school even worried about the content of some textbooks. Concerned about offensive passages in required course readings, the faculty in 1845 voted to "expunge from the list" of books "all portions of the heathen classics as pollute and debase the mind."[94]

The school set up a Ladies' Board of Managers, initially comprised of Mrs. Mahan and five faculty wives, whose responsibility it was to dictate proper female behavior. Young women were required to attend a lecture every Thursday afternoon, presented by a Board member on a topic relevant to women's lives and usually laced with Christian overtones. The Board scrutinized female deportment and manners and, according to one student, insisted that all young women walk around campus with perfect posture. Any female student who broke a rule or engaged in inappropriate behavior had to appear before the Ladies' Board—a familiar occurrence for Lucy and Nette who often challenged the school's strict rules.[95] Nette later admitted that she enjoyed going before the Board, since it gave her an opportunity to air her views.

Even with these rules in place, faculty and trustees began to sense growing problems with their co-educational campus, and in August 1845, at the start of Lucy's junior year, a committee presented a report detailing its concerns, containing suggestions on how to handle interactions between male and female students. As the report noted, young men and women had "a tendency to spend too much time and to be too engrossed in each other's society." It suggested instituting tighter rules though reluctantly conceded that getting students to obey them posed "great difficulty." Also troubling was what the report called the "evil" of "matrimonial engagements." These were causing a "decline in piety, a distaste for study, and impaired usefulness." The committee concluded that female students needed to attend more lectures on proper deportment and that more young women should board in the Ladies' Hall rather than in the village so they could be watched.[96]

Men were not the only distraction challenging female students. The college catalogue warned parents not to encourage their daughters to visit home during the school term "since it essentially hinders their progress to study." It also urged female students to work but not to overexert themselves, earning only enough money to cover half their expenses in order to promote their "physical, mental, and moral" well-being and the "highest good."[97]

Lucy challenged school rules, whether consciously or instinctively. At the start of her junior year, her migraines sometimes lasted three weeks and were especially painful on Sunday afternoons after she sat through lengthy church services. Wearing her bonnet made the headaches worse, so she removed it. The Ladies' Board reprimanded Lucy and insisted she wear it. St. Paul said it was shameful for a woman to uncover her head in the presence of God. Lucy explained that her headaches made her spend Sunday afternoons in bed rather than engaged in useful Christian activities. The Board relented, allowing her to remove her bonnet but making her sit at the back of the church.[98] On another occasion, Lucy apparently told a group of students that it was wrong for husbands and wives to have too many children if they could not afford them. The Ladies' Board told her she was meddling in matters "too high for her." Lucy defended her position, claiming that children often placed an unfair burden on women and on the public. The health of the nation was hurt by such "excesses." The outcome of the Board's internal discussions is unknown, but one can imagine how shocked the women were at Lucy's airing such a delicate subject.[99]

Lucy challenged Oberlin's conservative views on the proper role of women. While reading a textbook for one class, she came across the sentence: "Women are more sunk by marriage than men." She asked her professor what that statement meant. According to Nette, who was in the class, the professor found himself in a difficult situation. As Nette recalled, he responded: "Well . . . a married woman loses her maiden name for one thing; her family are not as readily traceable in history as her husband's; the law gives her property into her husband's keeping, and she is little known to the business world. The expression is not a happy one, but of course it doesn't refer to any moral loss or degradation." Much like what Lucy felt when she heard the "Pastoral Letter" years earlier, this response strengthened her resolve to fight against women's assumed inferiority and their loss of self when they married. Nette was convinced that this moment had an indelible impact on Lucy and likely planted in her head the idea of not changing her surname if she ever married.[100]

While teaching in Oberlin's Preparatory Department, Lucy discovered that women students who were hired to teach were paid only half of what young men received for the same job. In protest, she threatened to stop hearing her pupils recite and then took her complaint to the Faculty Board to demand equal pay for equal work. She presented her case, showing "there was no reason, based on justice, or common sense, to pay different wages for the same work if well performed." Oberlin was not living up to its professed ideals, similar to those of the founding fathers when they "wrote great truths in their Declaration of Independence, which neither they, nor their children, have been willing to practice." After much discussion over several weeks, the Board agreed to pay men and women student teachers the same wages. For years after she graduated, Oberlin students, women in particular, heralded Lucy for her principled stance.[101]

By senior year, Lucy had decided to pursue a career as a public lecturer on behalf of antislavery and women's rights. She ignored the fact that nearly all public speakers were men, and instead she focused on the inspired work of the Grimké sisters and, of course, Abby Kelley Foster. Lucy's experiences at Oberlin had helped her understand the challenges she would face in pursuing this career. As she later reflected back on her college years, she wrote, "I was never in a place where women are so rigidly taught that they must not speak in public."[102] Female students were not allowed to lecture in public, debate in class, or join the college debating society. The school found no scriptural support for women engaging in such public displays; indeed, just the opposite. Public speaking did not conform to society's view of the ideal woman as pious, submissive, and modest. Lucy took it upon herself to study rhetoric on her own by checking out of Oberlin's library Hugh Blair's three-volume classic, *Lectures on Rhetoric and Belles Lettres*.[103]

To prepare for a career in public speaking, Lucy and Nette enrolled in Professor James Thome's rhetoric class during their senior year. There they were allowed to listen to male students read their essays and debate one another though not participate in these activities themselves. Feeling emboldened, they asked Thome to let them hold a debate in class. Thome agreed, even allowing the two young women to choose a subject to debate. Word spread quickly, and on the appointed day, the classroom was packed with students and outsiders who had come to listen to this "novel entertainment." Afterward, Thome critiqued their presentation, and according to Nette, offered not a "word of sympathy or approval."[104] When the Ladies' Board of Managers learned about the debate, the women condemned the activity as unfeminine, and the school banned future public debates involving female students.

This, of course, did not stop Lucy and Nette. In secret, they formed a female debating society. The young women, six or eight in all, sometimes met in the woods; at other times, members met at the home of a black woman in the village whom Lucy had taught to read. They must have enjoyed to some degree the risks and subterfuge, sneaking away from campus one at a time or in pairs in order not to attract attention and then debated various topics, including "Egotism" and "The Qualifications of a Minister's Wife."[105] Lucy and Nette later claimed theirs was the first college female debating society in the nation.

Lucy took an even bolder step on August 1, 1846, when she delivered her first public address, "Why Do We Rejoice Today?," to the village of Oberlin's black population as they celebrated West Indian Independence Day, an event held in many black communities across the nation. Two other female students also wrote essays for the celebration but elected to have men read them aloud, as was expected. Not Lucy. As she explained to her parents, "it is not considered proper here for women to do anything of the kind, but I thought it was right, so I read it." Lucy gave little thought as to whether it was considered right or wrong for her to speak in public before an audience of men and women; she just knew she had to do it. "Father told me once, 'So long as you have a good reason, stick to it,' and it has often helped me to stick to, since I came here, where I differ entirely on many questions from the people." She believed that even her detractors saw her as principled and honest, even if "they are sorry I believe as I do."[106]

As Lucy anticipated, the Ladies' Board eventually summoned her for delivering her address. Mrs. Mahan asked Lucy if she had felt uncomfortable, frightened, or embarrassed to be the only woman on stage among so many male speakers, including President Mahan and Professor Thome. Lucy responded that the men were her professors and that she saw the college president every day, so she had not been in the least bit afraid. The Ladies' Board dismissed her with an admonition.[107] Lucy shared with her parents the comments that appeared in a Cleveland newspaper following that speech. The reporter observed that a speech "was read by one of New England's white girls" who "gave evidence that a mind naturally brilliant had not been dimmed, but polished rather, by classical studies and the higher mathematics. . . . She is one of those who believes that neither color nor sex should deprive [anyone] of equal rights."[108]

Oberlin's graduation gave Lucy one final opportunity to speak in public. Commencement was held the fourth Thursday of August 1847 for the seven women and sixteen men in Lucy's graduating class, a group which Nette later described as "one of the most eclectic that Oberlin has ever known."[109] At the graduation ceremony, Oberlin allowed its most accomplished seniors to read an essay they had written. Lucy was one of those chosen by the faculty to do this, and she anticipated that she and other female students would be allowed to read their own essays. "They have never been allowed to do it, but we expect to read for ourselves, or not to write," she wrote hopefully. But school administrators and faculty insisted her essay be read by a man. To Lucy, having a man read what she had written was an affront to everything she believed in regarding women's rights, and she refused to submit an essay.[110] When Lucy wrote her family about this, a proud Sarah replied, "I think you did perfectly right in refusing to write for Commencement. I am so glad you did so."[111]

No immediate family member was present at Lucy's graduation, although William Lloyd Garrison, Frederick Douglass, and Stephen Foster all happened to be in Oberlin that day to attend antislavery meetings being held in town. Their presence on that particular day was an amazing coincidence, considering Lucy's eventual career in the antislavery movement. These men and hundreds of other spectators witnessed the ceremony honoring the graduates. Lucy met all three men and made an impression, even without reading her essay. "Among others with whom I have become acquainted is Miss Lucy Stone, who has just graduated," wrote Garrison. "She is a very superior young woman, and has a soul as free as the air, and is preparing to go forth as a lecturer, particularly in vindication of the rights of woman. Her course here has been very firm and independent, and has caused no small uneasiness to the spirit of sectarianism in the institution."[112] Garrison summed up perfectly Lucy's (and Oberlin's) character and her future. Having successfully earned the bachelor's degree she had long dreamed of, she was now ready, at the age of 29, to embark on an independent course.

3

"Well, Whether We Like It or Not, Little Woman, God Has Made You an Orator!"

Lucy's decision to become a public lecturer was, to say the least, a brave one. It went against all odds. She had no financial resources and no name-recognition beyond her home and the Oberlin community. Most of all, she was a woman preparing to step onto a public stage literally dominated by men. To say that most mid-nineteenth-century Americans deemed this occupation wholly inappropriate for women was a truism. Women were not supposed to have a public persona; they were supposed to marry and spend their lives in the quiet of home. And the two causes that Lucy espoused on which she intended to speak were radical ones. Not only would she attract public ire, Lucy faced immediate opposition from several members of her family. Her mother urged Lucy to consider teaching and marriage instead. Frank conveyed the family's worry that lecturing "will make much talk in our quarters of the World." He explained that their mother found no biblical justification for women preachers or women lectures and therefore "thinks it is a wrong course for you to take." But he also knew his sister well and realized that Lucy would do what she knew she must.[1]

To try to alleviate her mother's concerns, Lucy wrote her another letter the following March:

I know you feel badly about the plan I have proposed to myself, and that you would prefer to have me take some other course, if I could in conscience. Yet, Mother, I know you too well to suppose that you would wish me to turn away from what I think is my duty, and go all my days in opposition to my convictions of right, lashed by a reproaching conscience. I surely would not be a speaker if I sought a life of ease for it will be a most laborious one; nor would

I do it for the sake of honor for I know that I shall be dis-esteemed, nay even hated by some who are now my friends, or who profess to be. Neither would I do it if I sought for wealth, because I could secure it with far more ease and worldly honor by being a teacher. But Mother, the gold that perished with the using, the honor that comes from men; the ease, or indolence which eats out the energy of the soul are not the objects at which I aim. If I would be true to myself, true to my Heavenly Father, I must be activated by high and holy principles and pursue that course of conduct which, to me, appears, best calculated to promote the highest good of the world.

Appealing to her mother's piety and antislavery sentiments, Lucy argued that if she did not pursue this calling, she would have "no right to think myself a Christian, and I should forever despise Lucy Stone." Her appeal contained a fair share of melodrama. "If, while I hear the wild shriek of the slave mother robbed of her little ones, or the muffled groan of the daughter spoiled of her virtue, I do not open my mouth for the dumb am I not guilty?" She would take on the cause of "suffering humanity everywhere," both on behalf of slavery and for "the elevation of my sex." To Lucy, the union of those two was indissoluble. She had not yet told her father, asking her mother to support her in what she knew was her duty.[2]

Sarah also opposed Lucy's plan, warning her sister that she would forgo future happiness as a wife and mother and her proven talents as a teacher. "Not that I think it wrong in itself, but because I think it an employment a great many grades below what I believe my only and dearly loved sister is qualified to engage in," Sarah explained. She saw no reason why women needed to be freed from "some thralldom imposed by man." Sarah, who had now been married for well over a year, felt women were not "groaning under half so heavy a yoke of bondage as you imagine." Not being able to vote was no loss to women, she contended, for "I would not if I could." She believed men who had been properly raised and instilled with a sense of duty were well qualified to vote in women's stead. Sarah did agree that the lower wages paid to women were unjust, but she partially blamed women. If they prepared themselves the same as men did, they would earn the same amount. She urged Lucy to "spend the remainder of your life in educating our sex," for that would do far more good than "hurling back 'the insults and indignities that men heap upon us.'"[3]

Four months later, however, Sarah became somewhat reconciled to Lucy's decision. She realized her sister's determination and sense of duty, even though she did not feel God had consigned to women Lucy's chosen career.

Sarah accepted the concept of separate spheres for men and women. While public speakers could influence people with their eloquence, she felt their truths never "sink into the heart with such deep abiding power as when dropped from the lips of the mother" to a child. To Sarah, a woman's greatest contribution was to bear, raise, and educate her children. "But my sister," Sarah concluded, "pursue that course which an enlightened God directed conscience dictates and I shall have no fear of your doing wrong."[4]

Lucy responded to Sarah by sending her a copy of Unitarian minister and abolitionist Samuel J. May's 1845 sermon, "The Rights and Condition of Women." His thoughts paralleled Lucy's own. May countered all the traditional arguments used to deny women suffrage—fears that they were too delicate, that the voting process was too contentious, that women were ill-informed about political matters, and that female voters would neglect their families when they cast ballots. May insisted women should have the right to vote in order to help determine the form of government under which they lived—just as men did.[5]

Bo, now a minister in Gardner, Massachusetts, was more supportive of Lucy's decision than were his mother and sister. He assured Lucy she was fully justified in becoming an antislavery lecturer and addressing women's rights, though he hoped she would teach school as her primary vocation and then lecture part-time. He felt Lucy could do more good lecturing on antislavery than on women's rights, since slaves were in a far worse situation than were women. Bo offered to listen to her lecture before she embarked on her career and suggested she model herself after three abolitionists: Garrison; Wendell Phillips, a wealthy, Harvard-educated lawyer and one of the most eloquent and effective speakers of the day; and the well-known Quaker minister Lucretia Mott. Although other family members opposed Lucy's chosen career, he reassured her that "for my part, I wish you to do what you think is duty."[6] Lucy followed Bo's advice and before she began her official duties, traveled to Gardner and delivered her first speech on women's rights to his congregation.[7] One can only imagine the surprised reaction of many of Bo's parishioners when they heard her speak.

Lucy understood the challenges of her chosen profession, or believed she did, but several events and individuals had given her the inspiration to overcome them. By the early 1830s, the antislavery movement had attracted a number of women throughout the Northeast and Midwest. These activists founded and led their own local abolitionist organizations, wrote and distributed essays and pamphlets, and organized bazaars and fairs to raise money for the cause.[8] They also engaged in petition campaigns. Critics deemed this action as political meddling and a totally inappropriate activity for women. In going door-to-door collecting signatures, women often were rudely reminded that such behavior undermined the idea of their being "ladies."[9] Female abolitionists felt every bit as committed as did men, and they defended their actions, noting the impact that British women's petitioning had in hastening Parliament's decision to emancipate slaves in the British colonies in 1833. To advance their agenda, in the late 1830s, women held three large antislavery conventions in the Northeast. Opposition to these meetings, however, was fierce, especially the May 1838 meeting that convened in Philadelphia. There, angry mobs gathered outside the auditorium, upset by the biracial and mixed gender composition of the gathering as well as by women's brazen efforts to discuss such a radical issue. Eventually the men rushed inside, disrupted the proceedings, and set fire to the city's beautiful, new Pennsylvania Hall for Free Discussion, completely destroying the building.[10]

No doubt Lucy read about that event as well as the treatment that eight American women delegates received when they attended the 1840 World Anti-Slavery Convention in London. Encouraged by Garrison to attend the meeting, these women, who represented three female antislavery societies, sailed across the Atlantic to take part in the event. During the entire first day of the convention, male delegates debated whether or not to allow the women to participate. Despite the passionate support of a few defenders led by Wendell Phillips, at day's end, the men voted overwhelmingly to prohibit women's participation. In what male delegates likely regarded as a magnanimous gesture, they did allow the eight women to sit at the back of the hall, cordoned off behind a curtain where they could listen but not speak. Here Lucretia Mott, a convention delegate, and Elizabeth Cady Stanton, who was on her honeymoon, met and shared their outrage at women's exclusion. According to Stanton's later account, it was there where she and Mott decided to organize a meeting to address women's rights when they returned home.[11] That meeting would become the Seneca Falls Convention of 1848.

While Lucy's career path was most unusual for a woman, she, a handful of women, and scores of men were responding to the growing popularity of public lectures as forms of entertainment. Across the country, speakers were in demand to address the public on almost any topic and fad: phrenology, mesmerism, Millerism, Mormonism, spiritualism, Sabbatarianism, temperance, public education, prostitution, moral reform, capital punishment, as well as antislavery and women's rights. Beginning in the 1820s, a number of communities established "lyceums," or nonprofit civic organizations, whose purpose was to educate local citizens by exposing them to various issues. Initially, speakers tended to be volunteers who spoke on whatever topic they happened to know well. Many, such as Bronson Alcott and Nathaniel Hawthorne, focused on intellectual and cultural uplift; others delivered stronger and more controversial messages. Reformers organized conventions to discuss their particular concern, inviting speakers to try to convince the public about the worthiness of their cause and to gain additional support.

In true American fashion, at least for a few, lecturing soon became a lucrative career. Lyceums set up lecture series and invited famous individuals to speak—such as Frederick Douglass, Wendell Phillips, and Ralph Waldo Emerson—and paid them well, typically between $50 and $100 an evening. Agencies represented lecturers and lined up engagements for them.[12] At a time when people yearned for entertainment beyond church and community activities, public lecturers could attract hundreds, sometimes even a couple thousand people—as did the Rev. Parker Pillsbury and even Lucy on occasion—who welcomed a discussion on almost any subject.[13]

Oberlin had taught Lucy well about the prevailing prejudice against women speaking in public, especially on sensitive issues. But this did not cause her to question her career choice; rather, it emboldened her. Before Lucy left Oberlin, she was presented with the opportunity to lecture for two antislavery societies. When Abby Kelley Foster had visited Oberlin during Lucy's senior year, she suggested to Lucy that she speak on behalf of the Massachusetts Anti-Slavery Society (MASS). The organization was trying to rally more supporters and to have its lecturers reach more communities. Lucy was intrigued by the idea. Several months later, Elizabeth Jones, representing the Western Anti-Slavery Society headquartered in Salem, Ohio, having heard of Lucy's desire to lecture, wrote her a lengthy letter. Jones invited Lucy to come to Ohio immediately and assured her that on-the-job training would suffice. Still, she also recommended that Lucy confine her speaking to antislavery and avoid women's rights, for the latter would only stir up the "womanly miscreants that would trample us down." "Better for women to occupy positions they deserved rather than beg for them," she added.[14] This idea was likely not tempting to Lucy since she had already determined that the whole point of her public lecturing was to fight for— and link together—the two causes.

But in August 1847, Lucy was more immediately focused on her family and Coy's Hill. She had not been home in four years. Following graduation, she returned to West Brookfield. Her first responsibility was to earn enough money to repay what she owed her father. She taught school for a few months and waited for a call to lecture. Hearing nothing, in the spring of 1848 she went to Worcester to visit Abby Kelley Foster, who contacted Samuel May Jr., corresponding secretary of the MASS. Early that summer, the Society hired Lucy as a lecturer at a salary of $6 a week.[15]

Lucy moved to Boston in early summer of 1848, lodging with a family in its boarding house on Hanover Street, paying 12.5 cents a week for meals and 6 ¼ cents for board by agreeing to sleep in a single bed in the attic with the family's two daughters.[16] She scrimped to pay for food and lodging as she traveled and lectured for the MASS. In her first year the work took her to dozens of communities across the state, from Pittsfield to Fall River, often sharing the stage with Wendell Phillips, Stephen Foster, and the Rev. Parker Pillsbury, all of them stars on the podium. Her schedule was relentlessly demanding and meant she often spoke in five or six different towns each week. But the work seemed to have paid off. Lucy was an immediate hit with audiences, for in its annual report for 1848, the MASS boasted of her "thoroughness of preparation, the intrepidity of utterance and the gentleness of demeanor." The Society acknowledged that her services were "of very high value" to the antislavery cause.[17]

That year was an exciting but particularly challenging time for the antislavery movement. Slavery and the internal slave trade were thriving in the South with a growing demand for raw cotton in the United States and abroad. Southern planters defended slavery as basic to their profitable cash-crop economy and to their way of life. They touted the alleged benefits they provided slaves by claiming to civilize slaves through a paternalistic system, teaching them valuable work skills, providing them food, shelter, clothing, and medical care, and exposing them to Christianity. Exported raw cotton comprised a huge part of the nation's economy.

By the late 1840s, the possibility that slavery might spread beyond the South had become a focus of intense national debate everywhere. With the end of the Mexican-American War in September 1847 and the signing of the Treaty of Guadalupe Hidalgo five months later, a victorious United States gained extensive land holdings in the West and Southwest, including Upper California and the New Mexico territory (currently Arizona, New Mexico, and parts of Nevada, Utah, and Colorado).

Figure 13. Lucy Stone (LC-USZ62–77,001, Library of Congress, Washington, DC)

California, with its burgeoning population due to the discovery of gold in January 1848, sought entrance to the United States as a free state. Congress considered the question of whether or not other western lands acquired from Mexico would be open or closed to slavery. Acrimonious and lengthy debates arose over the possible westward expansion of slavery. What seemed at stake was the very identity of the nation. Southerners demanded their right to take their slave property anywhere in the country, while most northerners wanted to limit slavery to the South and to preserve western lands for free labor. Abolitionists like Lucy, of course, wanted to eliminate slavery everywhere.

All these arguments and debates led to the Compromise of 1850, an omnibus bill negotiated by Henry Clay, John C. Calhoun, and Daniel Webster, which allowed California to come in as a free state but required the use of popular sovereignty to determine the future of slavery in new territories. First proposed by Michigan Congressman Lewis Cass during the Mexican War, popular sovereignty allowed male residents at some future date to vote on whether their territory would be open or closed to slavery, thus giving northerners and southerners equal opportunity through the ballot box to determine the outcome.

The issue in the Compromise that most upset abolitionists (and the one section that gave the South something of substance) was the strengthening of the nation's Fugitive Slave Law. This clause, first articulated in the US Constitution, expanded the role of the federal government in capturing runaway slaves and sending them back to the South. People living in free states were required to inform authorities if they sighted or knew of any escaped slaves. Abolitionists found this clause abhorrent because it strengthened slavery's hold on the nation and on the federal government's commitment to support it. In their view, the Compromise was no compromise at all but a moral sellout.

While slavery obsessed abolitionists and a number of politicians, most northerners showed limited, if any, interest in these disputes. In fact, many, and particularly northern bankers, shippers, investors, and textile manufacturers, benefited from the products produced by slave labor. Others felt that abolitionists were stirring social unrest and intensifying the divide between northern and southern states. Most Americans were content to allow slavery to remain in the South as long as it did not expand westward and compete with free labor. To Lucy and other abolitionists, it felt as if their moment had come. "What an excitement the Fugitive Slave Bill is making," she wrote Samuel May in October 1850. "There has never been a time when antislavery effort could be more immediately effective than now."[18]

Despite the growing popularity of public lectures and conventions, Lucy was still a pioneer, one of a handful to pursue lecturing as a career. It is hard to impress upon readers today what a stir she created simply by being up on stage and opening her mouth. It could not help but have been a novelty to many. Not only was she a woman but a woman challenging conventions and institutions that very few sought to challenge and doing so before mixed audiences of men and women. But her initial foray into public speaking was anything but a triumph. Called upon unexpectedly at an antislavery meeting to respond to a speaker's comments, Lucy stepped forward, "but the crowd of faces . . . and everything about it drove all thoughts from my mind." Embarrassed, Lucy turned to the audience and uttered, "I have forgotten what occurred to me to say" and sat down.[19] This was a singular occurrence, however, as Lucy quickly gained confidence in front of audiences.

In her first year of lecturing, Lucy experienced an awakening when she visited the exhibit of American sculptor Hiram Powers's statue, "The Greek

Slave," while it was on its 1847–1848 tour of the United States. It created a sensation, as it was intended to do. Powers had completed the sculpture three years earlier in Florence, and he modeled it after the Uffizi Gallery's Medici Venus.[20] The statue was a total revelation to Lucy. Carved from white marble, it depicted a life-size nude woman standing erect, head cast down, shackled, positioned in front of dark green canvas. "There it stood, in the silence, with fettered hands and half-averted face. So emblematic of Woman!"

Lucy broke into tears when she saw it, deeply affected by this symbol of female oppression and the situation of millions of women nationwide. During her speech that night at an antislavery meeting, Lucy spoke as she had not done before, pouring out her heart on the subjugation of women. A concerned

Figure 14. Hiram Powers, *The Greek Slave* (Corcoran Gallery of Art, Washington, DC. Gift of William Wilson Corcoran)

Samuel May complimented Lucy afterwards but questioned the wisdom of introducing such a controversial subject into her antislavery lectures. "I was a woman before I was an abolitionist" was Lucy's response.[21]

May was not the only one who was apprehensive. Wendell Phillips was also concerned that by addressing women's issues, Lucy might lose her focus on abolition. When he mentioned this to his wife Ann, she told him to leave Lucy alone; she knew what she was doing.[22] Lucy was then able to negotiate an arrangement with the MASS that allowed her to lecture on antislavery themes on weekends, but on weekdays she spoke on women's rights. Her speaking fees were reduced from $6 to $4 per week. This mattered little to Lucy, who was committed to both issues.[23]

But money did become an issue. During her first months of traveling and lecturing, Lucy charged nothing for people to hear her speak. The MASS paid her a salary, though it was barely enough to live on. Abolitionists believed free events would bring larger crowds, and the issue of whether to profit from the popularity of lectures was a sensitive one. Many abolitionists were Quakers who felt that it was wrong for people to pay to hear the truth. But that thinking soon changed. At a meeting in Salem, Massachusetts, Lucy showed up wearing a decidedly shabby cloak and gown, unable to afford anything better. The Hutchinson Family Singers, a popular group that often entertained at antislavery meetings, was also in town that evening and apparently took note of Lucy's appearance. One of its members suggested to Lucy that they combine their efforts—they would sing first and then Lucy could lecture. They would charge for the event and would share what they collected. The singer told Lucy she was a "fool" not to charge money for her lectures, since people would come even if they had to pay. Lucy sensed that he was right and agreed to do so, deciding the money collected at lectures would go toward the cause—and toward a new cloak and dress. Shortly thereafter, Clarina Irene Howard Nichols, the editor of the *Windham County Democrat*, invited Lucy to speak in Brattleboro, Vermont. Nichols insisted they charge a fee for her lecture. From that point forward, Lucy passed a collection hat or charged a flat fee that typically varied between 12 ½ and 25 cents a person.[24]

Just as Lucy was completing several weeks of lecturing, the first organized women's rights convention met on July 19 and 20, 1848, in Seneca Falls, New York. Born from the anger at women's exclusion from the London Anti-Slavery Convention, the Seneca Falls meeting offered women long-oppressed and shut out of the political process a chance to express their discontent and deal with their frustrations as well as issues and aspirations that were truly their own. As historian Nancy Isenberg writes, women's rights activists regarded conventions "as perhaps the best stage for fashioning women into political actors."[25] Seneca Falls did just that. Organized by Lucretia Mott, Elizabeth Cady Stanton, Mary Ann M'Clintock, Jane C. Hunt, and Martha Coffin Wright, the meeting attracted some 300 people from across the region.

The basis for discussion and debate at Seneca Falls was the "Declaration of Rights and Sentiments," modeled after the Declaration of Independence and most likely composed by Stanton. The document proclaimed a radically new concept, asserting that "all men and women are created equal" and blaming men for women's subordination. The Declaration laid out sixteen injustices that fostered women's secondary status and offered resolutions for change, including access to higher education and to the professions, easier divorce laws, equal wages for men and women, marital property rights, and most radical of all, the right to vote.

No doubt Lucy read about the Seneca Falls Convention, since several newspapers, including Frederick Douglass's *North Star* and William Lloyd Garrison's *Liberator*, covered the meeting. Two months after the convention, Stanton suggested they keep the spirit alive by hiring someone to travel around the country addressing women's rights. "Lucy Stone I think might be engaged for that purpose," Stanton wrote abolitionist and women's rights activist Amy Kirby Post, obviously aware of Lucy's public speaking. Lucy's commitment to the MASS was to end soon, and "she said she wished to devote herself to the cause of woman." Lucy, of course, was already doing just that, but she responded to Stanton, requested details, and asked where she might be needed.[26]

Two of the women organizers of Seneca Falls who became leaders in the women's movement—Mott and Stanton—were among those whom Lucy most admired. Mott was born on Nantucket in 1793 into a Quaker family. From childhood, she was well aware of the strength of women. Her father, a whaling captain, was often absent from home, meaning her mother ran the household as well as a small shop. Through her faith, Mott grew up to believe that all humans, whatever their race or gender, were created equal. When the family moved to Boston in 1804, she attended common schools and then went to Nine Partners, a co-educational boarding school in Duchess County, New York. There she met James Mott, whom she married in 1811. They settled in Philadelphia and had six children, five of whom survived. In 1818 she began to speak in Quaker meetings and soon became an influential Quaker minister as well as a major force in the antislavery movement, helping to organize the Philadelphia Female Anti-Slavery Society. So dedicated were the Motts to the antislavery movement that they joined the Free Produce Movement, a group of individuals who refused to consume any products produced by slave labor. Because of her strong views expressed through her preaching and lecturing, by the late 1830s Lucretia Mott had become a household name.[27]

Elizabeth Cady Stanton was born in 1815 into a privileged family in Johnstown, New York. Her only surviving brother died when she was 11, and she vowed to fill the void in the family by becoming the son her father no longer had. Her determination was evident as a young girl. She could not tolerate the idea that women were inferior to men. Educated at Emma Willard's renowned Troy Female Seminary in Troy, New York, Stanton, like Lucy, was exasperated by restrictions that constrained her merely because she was female and by statements in the Bible and in literature that perpetuated myths about women's inferiority. Poring through her father's law books, she

Figure 15. Lucretia Mott (LC-USZ62–42,559, Library of Congress, Washington, DC)

became outraged by statutes that were little more than a means of oppressing wives. She sought to excel at many activities men could do, becoming an accomplished horseback rider and chess player. In her mind, any challenge could be overcome. Assertive and strong-willed, in 1840, against her father's wishes, she married abolitionist Henry Stanton and ultimately bore seven children. When the family moved from Boston to Seneca Falls in 1847, Stanton found the region too tame for her restless mind and spirit. The Seneca Falls Convention gave her a cause into which she could pour her intellectual energy, and ultimately she became one of the powers behind the women's movement.

Until 1851, the MASS arranged most of Lucy's appearances, the majority of them in New England. But as her fame grew—and by 1851, it indeed had—Lucy received invitations from towns and lyceums across the Northeast and Midwest, from Canada, and even from a couple of southern states.

Figure 16. Elizabeth Cady Stanton and daughter Harriot, 1856 (LC-USZ62–48,965, Library of Congress, Washington, DC)

She was now mostly operating on her own, responding to various invitations and speaking tours. She also spoke to various abolitionist organizations, such as the Philadelphia Female Anti-Slavery Society where she lectured in the spring of 1849.[28] Within three or four years, Lucy became one of the most recognized names in America. Her personal appeal and lecturing style were widely celebrated. Frederick Douglass later noted that she became "one of the most attractive and effective advocates" for the antislavery cause. No one involved in the movement "arrested more attention than did Lucy Stone," he attested. Stanton remarked, with admiration but perhaps a hint of jealousy, that no lecturer in the women's movement received more favorable press than did Lucy. "Her sweet voice and simple girlish manner made her first appearance on the platform irresistible," she observed years later.[29] Unitarian minister Thomas Wentworth Higginson, who became a well-known lecturer for both the antislavery and women's rights movements, wrote a friend, "Lucy is queen of us all. . . . You have no idea of the eloquence and power which have been developed in her; she is one of the great Providences of History."[30] Besides conveying the passion of her convictions, Lucy had a natural sparkle and a musical voice that few who heard her ever forgot.

One witness to her lecturing style was Maria S. Porter, who was present when Lucy spoke in Boston's Faneuil Hall. Lucy's lecture was a plea to northerners not to return fugitive slaves to the South. Phillips and Garrison spoke first, and then Lucy came to the stage, "a young woman in a simple white gown, whose fair round face, shaded with light brown hair, was aglow with feeling," Porter recounted. A "profound stillness" fell over the hall as Lucy brought forward a slave woman, and in a "voice full of eloquence, tenderness, and sweetness," Lucy shared the woman's story of her escape. At the end of her speech, Lucy placed her hands on the woman and uttered, "God bless you my sister." Massachusetts Senator Charles Sumner was in the audience with Porter, and the two of them came forward to meet Lucy and compliment her on her speech. The lecture also profoundly affected Phillips who commented that Lucy "spoke words replete with rare eloquence" that swept over her audience "with a power that has never been surpassed, and rarely equaled."[31]

As she became better known, Lucy set out on her own, no longer under the auspices of the MASS, and now posting her own handbills. On more than one occasion, young boys followed her and taunted her, tearing down the posters. Just as she had done with her trouble-making students years before, she spoke quietly to them, described the evils of slavery, and won at least some of them over.[32] Lucy often did her own advance work, sending notices to local newspapers to announce her talks. Speaking in a large hall or auditorium and making oneself heard by several hundred people was a concern for all lecturers, since at this time there were no amplification systems to project their voices. Lecturers often had to shout over noisy crowds, night after night. Apparently Lucy had a manner and a voice that was especially effective in making herself heard above the din. A number of observers commented that something unique happened when she began talking: people immediately quieted, even those who rarely did so for others.

By all accounts, Lucy was a compelling speaker. While some people initially were shocked to see her on stage, they later admitted that they never forgot her voice, which was variously described as sweet, musical, girlish, and compelling, not because of volume but pitch and tone. She used it to disarm those who came to jeer and hiss. Abolitionist and women's rights advocate Ednah Cheney recalled that people who heard Lucy speak likened her voice to a "silver flute" or called it "birdlike."[33] The *Springfield Republican* contrasted Lucy with Abby Kelley Foster, noting that while Foster was an "excellent" woman, she "rasped every nerve by her merciless denunciations of the tyrant man in high-keyed tones." Lucy, on the other hand, could utter similar points "but the same man who Mrs. Foster irritated would find himself absolutely agreeing with Lucy Stone." The paper concluded, "Never was [a] reformer gifted with a more persuasive voice than hers."[34] At times, journalists noted, you could have heard a pin drop when she paused before arguing a point.

Lucy had, in short, an innocence and seductive appeal, and she used them. Her physical presence was part of it. Mary Livermore, a women's rights activist, recalled years later that she first saw Lucy at an antislavery bazaar in Boston early in her career. Lucy could not have weighed more than 100 pounds, "a tiny creature with the prettiest pink color, and her girl look was just as sweet as the look of her later years."[35] Her looks and voice might have drawn them, but she was capable of delivering a spell-binding speech, marshaling all manner of rhetorical arguments to win converts. She was also an expert at extemporaneous delivery, and nearly all her early speeches and responses were spoken without notes—a mark of her speaking ability, though a tragedy for historians.

Lucy's success lay in her sincerity. She presented her messages with a sense of humility, not pretending to know more than she did, but with the passion of her convictions when they were well grounded. Julia Ward Howe, author to the words of the Union anthem, "Battle Hymn of the Republic," later identified Lucy's unique appeal as due to a "grace of self-possession," a logical mind, a winning smile, and a "gift of persuasiveness." To her audiences, she "had a deep and abiding faith in divine justice," observed Howe.[36] Usually she deftly handled detractors, even when they tried to drown out her words by booing and hissing. She was quick to respond to any interruption. At the 1853 Woman's Rights Convention in New York City, men hissed after she mentioned Antoinette Brown's call to the ministry, and she instantly shamed them for their rudeness: "Some men hiss who had no mothers to teach them better," she declared.[37] A fearlessness in speaking her mind gave Lucy's audiences little doubt about the strength of her convictions. She could shame without also humiliating.

Adding to Lucy's effectiveness was her use of storytelling to deliver her message, drawing in listeners and making it easy to understand her points. In a speech she first delivered at the 1853 American Anti-Slavery convention in New York City, for example, she related the tale of a slave woman and her infant who fled to Indiana, thinking that in a free state they would be safe. A slave catcher found them and threatened to kill them. The woman held her baby tighter, Lucy told the rapt audience, and she continued to flee. The man chased her and fired his pistol, the bullet shattering the baby's head, a graphic image that no doubt evoked gasps from the audience. The distraught mother could only hope her infant now would be free in heaven. Somehow the woman escaped and reached Canada and freedom.[38] This story aroused strong sympathies and became an oft-told tale at abolitionist meetings.

At a convention in September 1853 in New York's Metropolitan Hall, Lucy provided a brief history of the women's movement, beginning with Seneca Falls. She highlighted the accomplishments of many successful women, including Harriot Hunt, a doctor practicing in Boston; Antoinette Brown who had just become the nation's first female ordained minister, at a small church in Butler, New York; the many women who ran their own businesses or edited newspapers; and a woman who was a registrar of deeds.[39] At the 1855 National Woman's Rights Convention in Cincinnati, Lucy attacked the concept of separate spheres, arguing that the idea limited and blighted women's lives. "They will be found to have no basis except in the usages and prejudices of the age," she intoned. Every individual ought to determine his or her own sphere, she insisted, and not fall victim to the dictates of others. Lucy often cited the story of Sarah Grimké and Angelina Grimké Weld, showing how they had been actively engaged in the public sphere but were now enjoying quieter lives at home, focused on family and the three Weld children—a choice they made, not one made for them. Another of Lucy's stories involved a 16-year-old slave girl who had approached her when she was lecturing in Missouri, asking if she were Lucy Stone and could she help her flee the state. The girl had a young child in her arms. The mother and child created a powerful image in Lucy's mind as an example of how slavery could threaten the most basic of human relationships. "I never felt so deeply the necessity of dissolution of this Union, as when I stood there and heard that poor girl's imploring words, 'Am I not a woman and a sister? and can you not help me to freedom'"? Sorrowfully, Lucy told her audience, she could not.[40] Such stories gave audiences a powerful sense of the horrors and inhumanity of slavery.

The sheer volume of invitations and personal appeals she began to receive showed that people were eager to hear Lucy Stone. In 1854, the showman Phineas T. Barnum invited her to speak on women's rights at a benefit for the Methodist Church in Bridgeport, Connecticut.[41] The Rev. Horatio Alger asked Lucy to participate in a series of lyceum lectures in Marlborough, Massachusetts, arranged by young men in his parish. The usual stars including Emerson, Phillips, Theodore Parker, and Douglass were among the list of featured speakers. Alger wanted at least one woman, "and our first application to a female lecturer is to you," he wrote her.[42]

By the early 1850s, Lucy was earning hundreds of dollars a year, a considerable income, particularly for a woman.[43] But it was not money that lifted her spirits and justified to Lucy her career choice. Positive responses from receptive audiences and new converts to her causes, she felt, were far more fulfilling and were, without question, vindicating. At the aforementioned New York Anti-Slavery Convention in September 1853, she stepped up to the platform and was received in a "most enthusiastic manner." According to the National Anti-Slavery Standard, "Several minutes elapsed ere she could proceed, in consequence of the plaudits with which she was greeted. She never delivered a more eloquent address."[44] The Frederick Douglass Paper declared that she "thrilled" her audience by carrying listeners "above the earth . . . and made herself their favorite." In 1854, Lucy revealed that local newspapers called her lectures "the best that have been delivered this season."[45]

And the converts were especially gratifying. On more than one occasion, her speech changed someone's thinking. A reporter for the Syracuse Weekly Chronicle, who was covering the 1852 National Woman's Rights Convention there, had been initially reluctant to attend. The idea of a woman appearing "on public rostrums" horrified him, he confessed. Then Lucy appeared on stage. "Not long, however, had her low, sweet searching tone (that 'excellent thing in a woman') fallen on our ear, and into our heart, before every particle of hostility was melted away, at least for the time, and her supremacy was complete. When she ended and sat down, after having held an immense audience, for more than an hour, in breathless attention, we turned away, in a state of subdued perplexity, saying softly to ourselves: 'Well, whether we like it or not, little woman, God has made you an Orator.'"[46]

Lucy began to appear alone on stage rather than in the company of other speakers, a situation she preferred. When Boston minister and abolitionist the Rev. Parker Pillsbury had to leave the antislavery movement, likely because of exhaustion or poor health, Lucy reassured Samuel May that she could succeed on her own. Now when Lucy spoke in a church or municipal hall, she often stood beside an open window so that those who could not find room inside could hear her. An appearance on succeeding nights at New York's Anti-Slavery Convention in September 1853 was among her most successful solo performances. Later Wendell Phillips effused: "Let me congratulate you on the pre-eminent success of your meetings in New York, that eventful week, for they were all most emphatically yours.... They did noble work."[47] Susan B. Anthony, who had been inspired by Lucy's speech at the 1850 Worcester Convention and was just becoming involved in the women's movement, read about Lucy's two speeches in the spring of 1853, excited that they deeply affected listeners. Anthony predicted that the talks would soon be published and "carried to the remotest parts of this nation" and "be wafted across the Atlantic," to be read by people in Europe.[48] Whether Lucy stood solo on stage or shared it with others, she was a star.

But such fame was not achieved without sacrifices and a demanding life. In the late 1840s and early 1850s during the early years of her career, Lucy maintained an exhausting schedule, made more difficult by inclement weather and the challenges of mid-nineteenth-century travel. Rail was the fastest and easiest mode of transportation, but trains did not yet reach many communities, which meant the need of additional transit by stage coach, wagon, on horseback, or on foot. Large cities usually had several decent hotels, but in villages and towns, Lucy often spent the night in a small inn or boarding house; sometimes she stayed with her host family or with a friend. It was not unusual for her to share a bedroom with a complete stranger or to sleep next to a room full of men, separated from them only by a hanging blanket.[49] Some farm homes did not even have wash bowls. Weather was a constant worry, especially in winter with rain, snow, or sleet, making travel difficult and attendance low.

While the work was exciting, it was also, at times, discouraging. The hostility many northerners still felt toward the antislavery movement, abolitionists, and especially women's rights could be disheartening. Early on in her career, Lucy traveled to Hinsdale, Massachusetts, where Samuel May had contacted the local Unitarian minister to arrange her lecture. The minister was anything but pleased when Lucy showed up, upset by this radical woman lecturing on antislavery, and he said he would do nothing to advertise her speech. Lucy worked all day putting up notices and knocking on doors to announce the event. Late in the afternoon she went to her hotel where the exhausted hotel-keeper's wife reluctantly agreed to fix Lucy supper on condition that Lucy watch her children. The woman was so distracted that while chopping vegetables and meat for the hash, she also chopped up the dish rag. Lucy took her first bite of hash, chewed on a piece of rag, and that ended her meal. That night she lectured on an empty stomach.[50] Another time when visiting Georgetown, Massachusetts, with May, the two stayed in a home with an abolitionist and his pro-slavery wife. Although the house had several bedrooms, the woman assigned Lucy to a tiny room under the stairs, so small she had to dress elsewhere.

In the winter and spring of 1854 Lucy and Parker Pillsbury toured Long Island, speaking to a small but attentive audience in South Hampton and then in East Hampton's "well filled" hall. In Westfield, New Jersey, only twelve people came out in a snowstorm to hear them. The two cancelled the next day's event when only seven "half grown" children showed up. During their travels, one hotel owner refused to let them spend the night because of their radical views.[51] After a lengthy fall and winter tour of the Midwest in 1853–1854, Lucy finally could take a much needed rest, admitting, "I have dreaded these lectures more than I can tell. But they are past and very well too."[52]

Public speaking could also prove dangerous. During the first summer of her lecturing, while in East Bridgewater, Connecticut, Lucy was sitting on a bench waiting to speak when a man hurled a large prayer book at her, stunning her and bruising her neck and shoulder. As Parker Pillsbury reported, had her shoulder not blunted the volume's impact, she would have fallen to the floor. One winter when she was lecturing on stage, someone removed a pane of glass in the window behind her. Suddenly she found herself deluged by ice-cold water from a fire hose that had been stuck through the opening. Refusing to be intimidated, Lucy pulled a shawl around her shoulders and kept talking.[53] On another occasion when someone threw a raw egg at her, Lucy calmly wiped it off and told her audience she was certain the "seeds of truth" she had uttered would not be as easily removed from their minds as the stain from her dress. Another time, Lucy, Stephen Foster, Pillsbury, and former slave and abolitionist William Wells Brown were lecturing on Cape Cod when an angry crowd rushed the stage crying "Down with them," "Tar and feather him," and "Pass out that nigger." The mob became increasingly violent. Lucy managed to escape from the auditorium by turning to one of their attackers, asking the man to escort her outside to safety. He did so, and perhaps shamed by his previous mob action, then stood beside her to protect her as she continued lecturing on a tree stump.[54]

Anger and derision sometimes prevented even Lucy from speaking. At the 1853 New York State Anti-Slavery Convention in Metropolitan Hall, she asserted that this alleged democratic republic held a sixth of its population in slavery. When she said Americans should "crush this monstrous inequality," a voice shouted, "Your remarks excite ridicule," followed by loud hisses from the audience. Lucy continued to talk, but mocking laughter drowned her out. According to a reporter, she stood "immovable as though she were made of stone," eventually crying out, "not one of you would stop to hiss if it were a question of the liberty of your own individual brothers be abolished, or slavery be abolished." This statement led to a huge "storm" of groans, more hisses, and rude comments—and at that point, Lucy left the stage.[55] It was one of the few times she backed down.

Traveling and lecturing for weeks at a time took their toll. Stress and exhaustion brought about a return of the migraines Lucy had suffered in college. In early spring 1853, she admitted, "I am tired and nervous and half sick, too, and just this minute can't help wishing that my body was safely at rest. . . . I am tired of the hard labor, of stirring this state to do something." The work was draining; too many people ignored her message; and opponents were often vocal, rude, even frightening. But she always seemed to rally, often remarking the next week that she would "go at it again."[56] On occasion, fatigue prevented Lucy from speaking effectively. After lecturing at New York's Tabernacle, she deemed herself a "failure," for "I could not command my mind."[57] Still, she worked relentlessly in the fall and into the first several weeks of the winter of 1853–1854, though exhaustion and back pain finally forced her to rest. Totally worn down by weeks of lecturing and endless travel, she cancelled at least one scheduled speech before heading to West Brookfield, her refuge.[58]

Media coverage, though generally positive, was not universally complimentary. Some newspapers, especially those whose editors opposed abolition and women's rights, had a field day denouncing Lucy. Papers tended to be more critical of her campaign for women's rights than for antislavery, regarding the upending of gender roles as a far more dangerous idea than abolishing slavery. The *New York Times* and several other papers had little use for Lucy's women's rights lectures. "Miss Stone is an agreeable orator, with an agreeable manner, an agreeable person, and a disagreeable subject," the *Times* reported after her spring lectures in New York. While her audience seemed deeply moved by her message, "one sentiment seemed to pervade it: what a delightful woman was spoiled when Miss Stone abandoned good sense, society, and duty, and addicted herself to 'Woman's Rights.'" The writer admonished her for having "mistaken the normal theatre of woman's exertions." "All your grace and eloquence captivate us as they must, [but] cannot convince us. You are doubtless sincere. We are willing to believe that to turn away from the sanctities of domestic life and become a public haranguer, cost you many regrets and some mortification. You are a woman ... and you have erred." The patronizing tone must have upset Lucy, especially when being reminded that "you will nowhere feel more noble, dignified, and holy than the inner chambers of home."[59]

Yet Lucy drove herself relentlessly. While her voice was invariably described as "sweet," her antislavery rhetoric was unapologetic, typically evoking strong reactions from her audiences. Early on during a speech she delivered at the Unitarian Church in West Cambridge, Massachusetts, Lucy appealed to women in the audience by describing, as she often did, the plight of slave women. Then she boldly attacked the church, calling it one of the greatest obstacles to the principles of Christianity because denominations and their ministers failed to speak out against slavery. "The galling chains of slavery" had to be "removed from the limbs of the oppressed." Lucy also denounced the federal government—both Congress and the President—for making no effort to end slavery. And it was not just the government but everyone who supported slavery who was "guilty of the inhumanity and wickedness of slaveholding."[60]

Lucy was equally and relentlessly daring in addressing women's rights. At that 1852 National Women's Rights convention in Syracuse, she decried laws that gave husbands total control over their wives' earnings and property, no doubt thinking back to the Robinson wedding she had attended years earlier and to her father's tightfistedness. She challenged one heckler who accused her of ignoring God's role in the Creation. Lucy turned his words against him, saying he lacked faith in God since he failed to see that God had made women, just as he had made men. Women deserved all the rights that men enjoyed.[61] Lucy did more than just criticize men. She often censured women, hoping they would stand up for what they believed, just as she did. "Learn self-help—to mind not ridicule, or sneers, or flatteries," she insisted. She had little use for a "womanhood of blushing cheek, languishing eyes, and garments that draggle in the dirt."[62] Lucy encouraged the founding of more co-educational institutions, for she "abhorred" all-female schools, feeling they delivered a clear message that women were less worthy of the quality education that men received.[63] As Lucy later explained, on any topic, she sought to make women uneasy about the laws and traditions that kept them in a subordinate role and to instill in them a desire to change them.

Lucy, as we have seen, became skilled at spontaneous remarks, particularly in reacting to comments from the floor. When a heckler interrupted the proceedings at the 1855 Cincinnati Woman's Rights Convention by calling female speakers a "few disappointed women," Lucy seized the moment, using the point to her advantage. In what became some of her most celebrated remarks, she agreed that she was, indeed, a "disappointed woman." "In education, in marriage, in religion, in everything, disappointment is the lot of woman. It shall be the business of my life to deepen this disappointment in every woman's heart until she bows down to it no longer." Commenting that nearly all lucrative jobs had been closed to her when she was seeking a livelihood, she continued, "The same society that drives forth the young man, keeps woman at home—a dependent" and ultimately creates "a horrible perversion of the marriage relation."[64] She was a disappointed woman, indeed.

A rare written speech, "The Province of Woman," reveals the range of Lucy's arguments in support of women's rights. She first examined the Bible, a book she and her audience knew well and the most effective way of going to the source of the prejudice. She challenged scripture that defined women as inferior. Many believed God had "commanded women to be subject to men." But, Lucy argued, God never articulated differences between the rights of man and woman. In His creating a "helpmate" for man, God did not intend that woman should serve man but that she should be his "intellectual companion" and equal partner. Lucy pointed out some of the many mistranslations in the Bible and noted that learning Hebrew had taught her their correct meaning. Many strong women in the Bible and throughout history had elevated themselves to be the equals of men, and they deserved celebrating. She addressed the need to educate women, though admitted from personal experience that in pursuing higher education, a woman had to "scale walls of prejudice high as heaven." Lucy also again criticized women who wore baubles and made themselves into "butterflies of fashion." They satisfied society's expectations of women, while those who filled their minds with learning never earned society's approbation. Those perceptions had to change.[65]

No one seemed above reproach. In an 1853 speech, she denounced the Democratic Party and President Franklin Pierce for supporting the Fugitive Slave Law. How could they live with themselves by supporting slavery? she asked of the Democrats. She went on in the speech to condemn most ministers for ignoring the slave question and the horrors that ensued from it. Clearly these men were more interested in expanding their congregations than in denouncing evil. To clergymen who called abolitionists "infidels," Lucy quoted abolitionist Sallie Holley who said of ministers, "Let them call us infidels if they please; but O, don't let them call themselves Christian." To great applause, Lucy closed by urging everyone to join the hand of God and the hand of the slave.[66]

Meanwhile the nation's growing divide over slavery intensified, and slavery's extension beyond the South became a distinct possibility. The Kansas territory now became the center of much of the debate. In early 1854, Illinois Senator Stephen Douglas fashioned a bill to deal with the future status of the Nebraska and Kansas territories, offering a compromise solution by using the concept of popular sovereignty. This held enormous implications for the nation, for the Missouri Compromise of 1820 had prohibited the expansion of slavery anywhere in the Louisiana Territory north of latitude 36 degrees 30 minutes. This new bill now portended the possible extension well beyond that imaginary line. Lucy and other abolitionists kept abreast of growing tensions as Congress struggled to determine whether the Kansas territory would be slave or free. Although women could not vote on the issue, of course, some spoke out against the westward and northward expansion of slavery. In March 1854, Susan B. Anthony announced that she was accompanying Ernestine Rose to Washington, DC, where Rose planned to publicly condemn "that abominable measure."[67] But their voices and those of other abolitionists had little impact in opposing the bill. Congress passed the Kansas–Nebraska Act, and President Franklin Pierce signed the bill into law on May 30, 1854.

A national divide was widening over the slave issue. A number of abolitionists, Lucy among them, had become as passionate about antislavery as
southern slaveholders were in defending their right to own slaves. Garrison's
most radical followers demanded disunion as the only way to resolve the
heightening tension. To Garrison, the solution was obvious: end slavery's
hold on the country by separating northern states from slaveholding states.
This, he believed, would allow the nation to become a stronger republic. By
the mid-1840s, abolitionists' speeches often included cries for disunion. As
early as January 1842, former president and now Congressman John Quincy
Adams, though opposed to such a radical solution, nevertheless introduced
into the House of Representatives a petition from forty-two residents of
Haverhill, Massachusetts, who prayed "for dissolution of the Union."[68]

In the *Liberator*, Garrison expressed growing outrage at northerners who
were complicit in perpetuating slavery by accepting it as an integral part of
the nation. In 1843, Wendell Phillips called for disunion, pointing out the
impossibility of slave and free states coexisting in the nation. The 1844 New
England Anti-Slavery Convention voted to adopt the idea by an overwhelming majority. This seemed the only way to sever ties with the growing power
of the southern "slaveocracy" and to support a free labor economy.[69] At
the New England Anti-Slavery Society's annual July 4, 1854 picnic, Garrison
in protest burned a copy of the Fugitive Slave Law and then the US
Constitution.

While at Oberlin, Lucy had become aware of and begun to embrace this
radical idea, writing home in 1847 that the family with whom she boarded
hated disunionism so she never brought up the subject.[70] By the early 1850s,
Lucy began to support the idea in her speeches, for it seemed impossible to
live in a nation that allowed slavery. In September 1853, speaking at Corinthian Hall in New York City, she argued that "if the union could only be
maintained by maintaining the institution of slavery, the Union must fall."
She suggested forming a northern republic that would sever all ties with the
slave South.[71] At the New England Anti-Slavery Convention on May 31,
1854, Lucy offered similar sentiments, declaring that a nation that allowed
slavery to exist was only helping to perpetuate a horrible wrong. "Slave
Power" had an insidious hold on the country. The North had to sever ties
with the South, she insisted. Lucy cited Samuel May who said he did not
want to live in shame as a citizen of a slaveholding nation. Lucy took a different stance: "I never so much wanted to live; I never so much saw that
every live man and woman, taking that life in his and her hand, ought to go

to Freedom's altar, and there make a new consecration of it to Justice and to Freedom." Great cheers interrupted her remarks when she demanded that everyone must have the strength to rid the nation of slavery. Referring to the clause in the Constitution that allowed southern states to count three-fifths of their slave populations for purposes of representation in Congress she asked, "Why do we let slaveholders claim representation in Congress based on slaves and use his power against those slaves?" Relating her story about the Missouri slave girl who had pleaded for her assistance—a story to which she returned frequently—Lucy concluded by crying out, "Let this Union be dissolved!" Only then could three million slaves find freedom. "I do not know what bloodshed may come by it. All I do know is, that we have no right to keep a Union with slave-holders." More cheers followed. "Slavery shall be abolished, or the Union shall be dissolved. We ought to make it anew our rallying cry. . . . No Union with slaveholders."[72] This was Lucy, as radical and passionate as any fellow abolitionist.

In late fall of 1853, Lucy embarked on a lecture tour across the Midwest and into the South. She spent several weeks in Ohio, Indiana, Illinois, Wisconsin, Missouri, and Kentucky. Lucy first spoke at an antislavery fair in Cincinnati and then in New Richmond, Ohio, where she delivered two speeches on women's rights and one on antislavery. She then made her first foray into the South. Her contact in Louisville welcomed her to the city, and in true southern style, insisted that her "fame for eloquence, earnestness . . . youth and beauty" would attract a crowd.[73] And he was right. Lucy's four nights in Louisville speaking on women's rights were unexpectedly triumphant. Beforehand, two prominent men came to interview her. When they asked her if she found inspiration in the Bible, Lucy responded "not altogether," though admitted she probably did as much as they did. The men were much "tickled" by her answer and realized she was not a "mud mill," as one man put it, but a person of earnestness. Every night it was standing room only in the hall. Effusive coverage in the local press also surprised her, for Lucy had assumed southerners had little use for women's rights.[74] Never having been exposed to southern manners, she was pleased by how well-behaved the crowds were wherever she spoke. Unlike some of the unruly mobs she had faced in New York and Massachusetts, southern audiences treated her with respect, even when she wore bloomers. She was also thrilled to have cleared $600.

Speaking in Indianapolis in early November, she had a "large and very attentive audience" and took in receipts of $317. That evening she lectured on marriage "to a full house and succeeded better than I had even hoped to do & was listened to with breathless interest."[75] In St. Louis, she attracted the largest crowds ever assembled in that city, with nearly 2,000 people filling an auditorium to hear her. Afterwards, she commented, "I had larger meetings than I ever had in my life, and they [her audience] are better for them."[76] Lucy remained in St. Louis nine nights and delivered eight lectures. The city's two leading newspapers had nothing but positive comments to make regarding her eloquence and style.[77] Her final stop on the tour was Chicago in early January 1854. There she met "some glorious workers" and a lawyer who told her: "Draw upon me for money for the Cause, whenever, in your judgment, it is needed."[78] Leaving the Midwest, she traveled to Pittsburgh, Philadelphia, Washington, DC, and New York City. Invitations poured in; everyone wanted to hear Lucy Stone.

4

"The Heart and Soul of This Crusade"

As Lucy's lecture career flourished and her fame grew, she also became a leader of and major presence in the nascent women's rights movement. The earliest women's rights conventions held at Seneca Falls and Rochester, New York, and Salem, Ohio, made an impact, but primarily on people living in those regions. Lucy and other women sensed the need for something grander in scale, a national meeting to draw the public's attention to their cause. At an antislavery convention in Boston in the spring of 1850, an announcement was made that anyone interested in organizing a women's rights convention should gather after the meeting. Lucy, Dr. Harriot K. Hunt, Paulina Wright Davis, Eliza J. Kenney, Abby Kelley Foster, and Dora and Eliza J. Taft responded and met in a small, dingy room where they came to an agreement to hold a national meeting.[1] They targeted the event for late October of that year and chose Worcester, Massachusetts, as a suitable location. The city had efficient train service, a growing manufacturing base, an engaged group of reformers, and a vibrant cultural life. Paulina Wright Davis, who had been lecturing on female physiology and had the time and financial resources to take charge, led the effort, with Lucy and several other women doing much to assist her.

Lucy then visited Garrison to seek his advice since this group of women had no money, little support, and no knowledge of how to organize a national meeting. He told her that the antislavery movement had once been in the same situation, but because the cause was "rich in truth," it had succeeded so far. "Yours is just as true, and it will succeed," Garrison reassured her.[2] Buoyed by his support, the eight women proceeded to send out a call for their convention. Funds to rent the hall and to reimburse speakers for travel expenses came from contributions, including from convention organizers.

The women contacted friends and reformers by letter and telegram, inviting them to attend what promised to be an exciting event. Lucy wrote Nette, asking her to "make a speech or two" and promising to cover her travel expenses. She also invited Sarah Grimké, Angelina Grimké Weld, and Lucretia Mott among others, noting "we need all the women who are accustomed to speaking in public—every stick of timber that is sound."[3]

Despite Lucy's involvement in what was to become the first national women's rights convention, she barely made it to Worcester in October and could not give Davis all the assistance she had promised. While lecturing in Illinois in mid-summer, she had traveled to Hutsonville to visit her brother Luther and his wife Phebe, who was several months pregnant. Luther contracted cholera, a frightening disease that had already killed tens of thousands of Americans. Luther endured "dreadful suffering" and died on July 18, only twenty-eight hours after becoming sick.[4] Because of her condition, Phebe was unable to nurse him, so Lucy was the only family member at her brother's bedside.

While staying on to settle Luther's finances and personal concerns, Lucy managed to lecture to local residents, many of them poor whites who had migrated to the area from the South. This exposure made her well aware of the need for speech-making in the West where many people hated the idea of slaves but not of slavery itself. She found locals "ignorant almost beyond conception," with scant interest in women's rights or abolition. Fifty years would have to pass, Lucy claimed, before anyone there would "recognize a moral principle."[5]

Because the region was so sickly, Lucy and Phebe started home for Massachusetts on August 20 despite Phebe's condition.[6] Three days into their travels, Phebe gave birth to a premature, stillborn son whom they buried in Indiana. While nursing Phebe back to health, Lucy contracted a serious case of typhoid fever, likely due to bad drinking water, and was bedridden in a "lowly," noisy hotel. Dangerously ill, she was in and out of consciousness for eighteen days, unable to sit up, with no one to care for her at night. Eventually she began to recover, and the two women gradually made their way home. Looking ahead to the Worcester Convention and thinking she could not attend, Lucy felt "grievous disappointment."[7]

The first National Woman's Rights Convention met on October 24 and 25, 1850, on a "fine autumn day."[8] While a few hundred people were present the first morning, by evening the crowd overflowed Brinley Hall. Eminent reformers were present, including Mott, Harriot K. Hunt, Abby Kelley Foster,

Pillsbury, Douglass, and former New York slave and abolitionist Sojourner Truth. Paulina Wright Davis, a woman of tall stature, with fashionable auburn ringlets and fair complexion, welcomed the crowd, and in her opening speech, insisted that women were endowed with the same "inherent and inalienable rights as men." As one newspaper noted, "being a pretty woman, of course [she] made a very pretty speech," but apparently it was so philosophical, reported one Boston newspaper, that "common minds" could not understand it.[9]

Over the next two days, speakers addressed various topics. Ernestine Rose, who emigrated from Poland to the United States with her husband in 1836 and became a dedicated campaigner for women's rights, gave a speech, which the *Boston Mail* called the most "eloquent" of the day. She insisted that women have access to the same educational opportunities as men had and that marriage be between equals so women would not become slaves to tyrannical husbands.[10] Unitarian minister and writer William Henry Channing denounced prostitution as contaminating all of humanity. He also urged the creation of a senate of women to meet annually to discuss pertinent issues. Phillips emphasized women's right to vote and to claim all the natural and political rights that men had, including access to public office and to jury service. Laws needed to change, he affirmed, and should apply to women at all levels of society. When Phillips suggested that women were partially accountable for their oppression, however, Lucretia Mott—described by one paper as an elderly Quaker lady, "all bone, gristle, and resolution" who rarely avoided a challenge—stepped up to the stage and insisted that "where there is oppression, there is an oppressor."[11]

Abby Kelley Foster, with her usual boldness, suggested that for women to gain the rights they deserved, blood might need to be shed; throats might need to be cut. The audience gasped rather than applauded, and she exited the stage in silence. Reflecting her Quaker beliefs, Mott then countered Foster, arguing for moral suasion rather than violence to achieve their goals.[12] Speaking extemporaneously, Antoinette Brown decried society's reluctance to ordain her as a minister because she was a woman. Sojourner Truth, with her "dark skin and uncomely exterior," "gratified the audience highly" by stating that women had set the world wrong by eating the forbidden fruit, and she urged them to set it right. Douglass also spoke, advocating that women be more aggressive and demand their rights and not wait for men to grant them. Garrison claimed it an honor to identify as a women's rights man and was thrilled that so many people were present. Too much had been lost to the world by depriving women of their rights, he added.[13]

At the last minute, Lucy determined she felt well enough to travel from her home to the convention in Worcester, imagining she would only be a "looker on." To stand on the sidelines was not Lucy's nature, however, and by the second evening she decided to speak briefly. She did so "with great simplicity and earnestness." Lucy confessed her initial misgivings about the convention and whether it would attract much interest but stated that she was thrilled with the hundreds of people seated before her. Lucy insisted that women demand all the rights they deserved, especially the right to vote and the right of married women to retain their own property. She urged everyone to engage in a massive petition drive to pressure state legislatures to give them these rights. At one point—perhaps her first public expression of a lifelong belief—Lucy stated that she never wanted her gravestone to identify her as merely "the relict" of a husband, a remark that met with thunderous applause.[14]

Press responses to the Worcester convention varied widely, reflecting, as always, Americans' ambivalence over demands to upend traditional gender roles. James Gordon Bennett's *New York Herald* had no use for women's rights or the convention, which the paper claimed struck "terror into the heart of the stoutest man." His paper's headlines called the convention an "awful combination of socialism, abolitionism, and infidelity" and described participants as "gloomy and warlike."[15] The paper mocked speakers, claiming that women wanted to dispense with Christianity and the Bible, abolish current political and social systems, and put all races and both sexes on an equal plane. Another *Herald* article suggested the absurd idea that women might pursue the next step and feel qualified to run for Congress or even for the White House. This "motley" gathering of "fantastical mongrels, of old grannies, male and female," it asserted, spent two days discussing "the most horrible trash" and "most monstrous and disgusting principles." Not an insane asylum in the country, claimed the *Herald*, would countenance discussions of such "lunacy, blasphemy, and horrible sentiments."[16]

At the other end of the spectrum were newspapers that were less sneering, including, unsurprisingly, Garrison's *Liberator*. It called the convention "the noblest series of meetings that we have ever attended" and described Brinley Hall as "crowded with as intelligent, orderly, and interested a class of people as we ever saw assembled."[17] Similarly, Horace Greeley's *New York Tribune*, chief rival to the *Herald*, was upbeat in its exhaustive coverage. Greeley was thrilled with the convention and claimed that it mattered not whether women actually went to the polls if they were allowed to vote. The nation should allow them to do so in order to live up to its democratic ideals. Nor did he believe that expanding women's liberties and rights meant they would neglect the home. Greeley insisted that women needed a larger sphere of action, with more job opportunities and higher wages paid to them.[18]

Individual responses to the convention varied as well. Davis later wrote her own account of the meeting, which she published in 1871. She air-brushed out any hint of internal conflicts and contrary views in relating the events at Worcester, for there was some disagreement, such as that between Lucretia Mott and Abby Kelley Foster.[19] In contrast, Dr. Elizabeth Blackwell, who was not present, was troubled when reading the convention proceedings. While she found the speeches full of energy and feeling, she felt they lacked clarity. Blackwell could not sympathize with what seemed to be an "anti-man movement" since, in her own strivings to become a doctor, she had benefited from men's kindness. Blackwell felt rights for women needed to be pursued in another manner, not by speech-making at conventions.[20] A *Tribune* reader, meanwhile, feared that if women gained the rights that men enjoyed, family dinners would go uncooked, children's faces unwashed, and homes ignored. He saw no reason for women to complain about their current status. A wife or mother should never regard herself as a slave but as someone consigned to an exalted position, "spiritually far above political intrigue and vulgarity of rowdies." To this reader, it seemed the women at Worcester had forgotten about the immense power that women exerted in the home, for no one wielded greater influence than did mothers and wives. They were "missionary angels," on earth to remind men "of their high calling and high duties."[21]

Raising an issue that would have greater implications for the women's movement later on, Jane Swisshelm, editor of Pittsburgh's *Sunday Visiter*, objected to a resolution suggested at the convention linking women's rights with abolition. "The convention was not called to discuss the rights of color," and having to consider antislavery there was "altogether irrelevant and unwise," Swisshelm asserted. The two issues were most effective if campaigned for separately. Parker Pillsbury, for one, was troubled after reading Swisshelm's comments. Writing in Douglass's *The North Star*, Pillsbury pointed out how African Americans were excluded from nearly all areas of public life and segregated into separate spaces or institutions. In fact, at Worcester, blacks were few in number, and none were appointed to the several committees set up to study women's condition. Considering rights for women should be inclusive, welcoming "women of sable as well as sallow complexion," Pillsbury insisted.[22]

Finally, from England came Harriet Taylor Mill's essay, "The Enfranchise-ment of Women," which caused great excitement. This essay first appeared in the *Westminster Review* and then in the *New York Tribune* in July 1851. Mill, married to the philosopher John Stuart Mill, celebrated American women for holding the first national women's rights convention, demanding that women be able to participate in government and to be treated as men's intel-lectual equals. Mill's essay was widely circulated. The convention organizers were delighted that their meeting had attracted global attention.[23]

On the whole, women's rights reformers felt inspired by the success of their first national convention. Over the next decade, with the exception of 1857, they held annual meetings to address women's rights that convened in different cities in order to reach people living in various regions of the country—in 1851 it met again in Worcester, and then in Syracuse, Cleveland, Philadelphia, Cincinnati, and the last four in New York City. Lectures and discussions formed the heart of each convention, covering such topics as women's wage labor and equal pay, temperance, prostitution, marital prop-erty rights, suffrage, educational and professional training for women, access to lucrative jobs, and, on occasion, even controversial subjects such as birth control and easier divorce laws.

Ye MAY SESSION OF Ye WOMAN'S RIGHTS CONVENTION—Ye ORATOR OF Ye DAY DENOUNCING Ye LORDS OF CREATION.

Figure 17. Women's Rights Convention, 1850s (From *Harper's Weekly*, v. 3, no. 128 (1859 June 11). LC-USZ62–135,681, Library of Congress, Washington, DC)

The second national convention, held October 15 and 16, 1851, was one of the most successful of those in which Lucy was involved. Attendance was higher than the previous year, with some 3,000 people crowded into Worcester's City Hall and characterized by eloquent speakers and favorable press coverage. Davis again presided. Committees appointed the previous year reported on their findings on paid labor, education, and political and social equality. Letters came from British writer Harriet Martineau and two French women, Jeanne Deroine and Pauline Roland, who were imprisoned in Paris for promoting socialism and demanding the right for women to vote and to hold public office. They reassured American women, "Your socialist sisters of France are with you."[24] This was heartening, for again such comments indicated that American women's efforts were continuing to inspire women abroad.

At the third national meeting, in Syracuse, New York, Susan B. Anthony made her debut as a speaker, beginning her lifelong campaign for women's rights. Though she was on the whole well-received, she chided many of the women present for being timid and afraid to speak out. In response, Samuel May reminded her that women needed to be encouraged, not scolded. Lucy later comforted Anthony, who was upset because she valued May's opinion.[25] This was the first time the two women met, and they soon struck up a close friendship, bonded by a shared commitment to fight for women's rights.

Anthony was born in 1820 in Rochester, New York. Her father was a Quaker and raised his children to believe in human equality. She received a solid education and, like Lucy, became a schoolteacher but was soon troubled by gender inequality when she learned her salary was far below what less experienced male teachers earned. Lucy's comment at the 1850 Worcester Convention that she never wanted her tombstone to list her as a husband's "relict" caught Anthony's eye when she read about the meeting and was a compelling reason that drew her into the movement. She had been lecturing on temperance previously but now turned to embrace women's rights. Her energy and dedication were boundless, such that in a few years, her nickname became "Little Napoleon." Anthony also developed a strong relationship or partnership with Elizabeth Cady Stanton that endured for decades. While Stanton stayed home to raise her seven children, Anthony traveled and lectured, inspired by Stanton's bold thoughts and dazzling rhetoric. Being single, Anthony never had to alter her lifestyle to care for husband or children. At times, in fact, she exhibited impatience with those who married and bore children, fearing they might lose that sense of mission she felt so deeply.[26]

The October 1853 National Women's Rights Convention in Cleveland was a tremendous success, lacking the internal squabbling and disruptions that had marred two previous meetings. The hall was filled to overflowing. As Lucy commented, "We are having a most beautiful grand time!" There was no jealousy, no in-fighting, "but one deep united purpose to serve the Cause." Press coverage was respectful. "All is so very different from our New York meeting!" she exclaimed. "There was no rowdyism; here deep, earnest interest."[27]

By the fifth National Woman's Rights Convention in Philadelphia in 1854, Lucy had become the acknowledged leader of the movement. She was thrilled with this meeting, affirming that there had been "no discord or disorder," the press was respectful, the speeches were moving, and they collected $700. "The good seed is being sown," she asserted.[28] Much of this success was directly due to her. Not only was Lucy a principal organizer, she possessed the star power that drew people to women's rights conventions. As the *New York Tribune* summed it up, "the public mind instinctively fastens upon this little person as being, what she really is, the heart and soul of this crusade."[29]

Much had been debated between Seneca Falls and this meeting in Philadelphia. Women had considered but then ultimately rejected the idea of adopting the 1848 Seneca Falls "Declaration of Rights and Sentiments," for many sensed that it placed too much blame on men and offered more grievances than goals. With all conventions, money remained an issue. Holding conventions was expensive, and at this point, women leading the movement still struggled to rent a hall, pay speakers and entertainers, reimburse travel expenses, and publish tracts and convention proceedings. While they charged admission or passed the hat for donations, the money collected at the meetings rarely covered expenses. Men of means like Phillips contributed to the cause, as did Mott, Lucy, and other women who donated money from their lecture fees. But the movement still operated on a shoestring.

Another frequent topic of debate was whether or not to create a formal structure to coordinate the women's movement and to plan all future conventions. Opposition arose almost immediately. Phillips believed everyone would get along better with the informal approach they had been using. Presciently, Nette believed a national society would be "a narrow minded partial affair of some stamp that will shame the cause and retard its progress," inevitably followed by another organization formed in "self defense."[30] She opposed the idea, also feeling that women were not yet ready for it. Ultimately they left things as they were, at least for the time being. Volunteers, including Lucy, served on a Business Committee to plan each convention, select the location, raise money, invite speakers and special guests, appoint people to study key issues, and publicize each meeting.[31]

However careful the planning, every convention had an air of uncertainty about it. Since meetings were open to everyone (unlike a number of men's conventions), protestors, naysayers, and unruly mobs could—and frequently did—show up. In advance of the third national convention in Syracuse, the call for the meeting stated that approach: "Our platform will, as ever, be free to all who are capable of discussing the subject with seriousness, candor, and truth." This open invitation sought to appeal to all men and women. But some men came not to listen or to learn but to drown out speakers or pelt them with rotten fruits and vegetables to express their displeasure. Syracuse was the first women's convention at which "coarse and ribald speech" interrupted the proceedings. At an 1853 spring women's rights meeting in New York, rowdies also appeared and tried to drown out speakers. Lucretia Mott presided, but even this resolute woman had trouble silencing the crowd and dealing with one protestor who defended the concept of women's separate sphere and a minister who questioned loudly and frequently whether women recognized the authority of the Bible.[32]

But women began to bring about a demand for change. In the winter of 1853, Lucy took on another project—trying to convince her home state of Massachusetts to support women's suffrage. In February, working on her own, she began circulating a petition for submission at a meeting scheduled for the following May when politicians planned to amend the state constitution. This petition, written by Phillips, demanded that the word "male" be struck from the state constitution so that women could vote and hold public office.[33] While circulating the petition, Lucy lectured statewide for nearly four months. In mid-March, exhaustion forced her to retire to the Boston home of longtime reformer and abolitionist Francis Jackson, where she recuperated and waited for an invitation to address the Massachusetts legislature. She recovered in time to speak to the annual national meeting of the American Anti-Slavery Society on May 11 and to attend the New England Anti-Slavery Convention later that month.[34]

Finally, on May 27, 1853, Lucy and Phillips were granted a hearing to address the Massachusetts Senate Committee on Qualifications of Voters. They presented reasons why women deserved the same political rights and privileges that men enjoyed and why women should have a voice in electing those who governed them. Women possessed the mental capacities of men, and, in fact, were as well or even better educated than many men who voted.[35] Despite "respectful and intellectual" crowds in the galleries, though, the speeches gained little media attention, and after all of Lucy's hard work, the outcome proved discouraging. The legislature debated their arguments. A few men joked about these two advocates of women's suffrage, calling them "Mr. Lucy Stone and Miss Wendell Phillips" and expressing worry that women might demand not only the right to vote but to hold office and even—imagine the thought—to become president of Harvard College.[36] Ultimately, the legislators concluded that since women could express their political feelings through petition drives, they had no need to vote. More importantly, since only 2,000 people in the entire state had signed Lucy's petition, it was obvious few women desired suffrage. In the eyes of these men, most women seemed content to maintain the status quo. Lucy's upset over the outcome turned into a determination to fight even harder, telling Stanton that women would "renew our forces, to such an extent that they will not again dare so insult us."[37]

As one might expect, with Lucy's reputation growing and her radical views becoming better known, she came under greater public scrutiny. West Brookfield's Congregational Church officials became increasingly uneasy about their outspoken member. In June 1851, Lucy received a letter from L. Sampson, Clerk of the Church, who informed her that she had been removed as a member because she had withdrawn from regular communion and, more importantly, because she was "engaged in a course of life inconsistent with her covenant engagement to this church." Within days, Lucy responded, claiming she knew of no church member who was dissatisfied with her work. Though she rarely entered the church's doors, this situation offered her another opportunity to protest an injustice. She requested the opportunity to explain what she was doing and how it reflected the basic tenets of the church and of Christianity. There is no record this meeting ever took place.[38] Lucy's ties with her childhood church, however, officially ended.[39]

This, though, was a small matter compared to two others that became public. The first was Lucy's rush to judgment when she publicly accused one of her former Oberlin professors, James Harris Fairchild, of engaging in the slave trade and of using profits from it to purchase his Oberlin home. In June 1852, Fairchild responded to Lucy's charge, accusing her of slander and explaining the true story. He admitted that his father-in-law was a slave owner. When he died, Fairchild and his wife bought a young slave girl from the estate and brought her to their home in Oberlin to raise her as a free person. He had purchased his home using his professor's salary. Fairchild scolded Lucy for not speaking to him before she accused him in public. Lucy admitted her error and apologized, explaining that her information came from an Oberlin theology student whom she had trusted. She sent Fairchild's letter and her apology to the *Liberator* and asked Garrison to publish both so the truth could be known. She signed her apology, "Yours, for truth and justice."[40]

The second event took place in Philadelphia where Lucy lectured in February 1854 at the city's Musical Fund Hall, whose manager at the last minute informed Lucy that he would not allow African Americans to attend her talk. Lucy had been misinformed and thought the Hall welcomed everyone. She and James Mott, who had helped her schedule the lecture, hoped blacks would know the rules and not show up, though Lucy had already distributed free tickets to them. Several did come and were turned away at the door. Because she could not find another location at the last minute, Lucy went ahead and spoke to an all-white audience. At the end of her speech, however, she explained the situation and told everyone present that she would never again speak in a hall that excluded blacks. The next day Lucy published a brief account of what had happened.[41]

Frederick Douglass, for one, was not satisfied with Lucy's explanation, however, and lashed out at her in his newspaper, the *Frederick Douglass Paper*, insisting that as soon as she understood the hall's policy, she should have refused to speak there. His accusation cut deep, and Lucy shared his comments with the Motts. James felt somewhat responsible and defended Lucy, believing she had done the right thing by first lecturing and then denouncing the hall's exclusion of blacks. After all, Mott pointed out, white people, including many abolitionists, did not shun Philadelphia's omnibuses because they refused black riders or boycott events that did the same.[42]

Douglass's reaction surprised others as well. His response reflected, in part, his irritation with Lucy because she had recently lectured in Kentucky and Missouri, where slaveholders welcomed her. Also upsetting Douglass was his four-month-long feud with Garrison over the direction of the American Anti-Slavery Society and their differing views on the use of violence to end slavery and on the meaning of slavery in the US Constitution. Abolitionists in turn were troubled by Douglass's relationship with a white British woman, Julia Griffiths, who had met Douglass when he was on tour in England from

Figure 18. Frederick Douglass (Image 485,472, New York Public Library)

1845 to 1847. She had settled in Rochester where Douglass resided with his family. Still others saw Douglass's reaction to the Philadelphia situation as a reflection of his character. "Poor Frederick," James Mott commented, "he seems very much disposed to quarrel or find fault with those who have been, & would be now, if he would let them, his best friends."[43]

Adding to Lucy's grief over this matter was a letter from abolitionist Lydia Mott, a friend and distant relative of James Mott's, who rebuked Lucy for the "very great error" she had committed. "I don't believe that one reformer can ever be advanced at the expense of another," Mott insisted. She believed that when Lucy rented the hall, she knew it would not admit black people. If she had been there, Mott would have refused to attend. She hoped Lucy would publicly admit her error. Lucy, wanting to defend her action, responded in a lengthy letter, setting forth details of the misunderstanding and claiming she felt she had made the wisest choice rather than cancel the talk altogether. Fortunately the issue died, and three years later when Lucy was again scheduled to speak at the still-segregated Musical Fund Hall, she refused to do so and insisted on speaking at another location that welcomed African Americans.[44]

It was not merely their presence and passionate words that fueled public censure of women speaking in public. In the late 1840s and early 1850s, female reformers, including Lucy, turned to fashion as another way to challenge the boundaries imposed on women's lives. They began to don "bloomers" in order to move about with greater freedom and comfort. In the mid-nineteenth century, middle- and upper-class women typically wore voluminous, physically restricting dresses, with skirts comprised of yards of material that reached nearly to the ground and could weigh as much as twelve pounds. To accentuate the ideal feminine figure, undergarments contorted women's bodies with corsets, tight lacing, whalebones, bustles, and hoop skirts, giving them a stylish hour-glass shape.[45]

Some sensible Americans, including a few physicians, medical advisors, and popular authors such as Catharine Beecher, began to advocate dress reform, proposing that women shed the corsets and "tight lacing," that constricted their bodies and crushed internal organs. In *Letters on the Equality of the Sexes*, Sarah Grimké complained that women too often adopted the latest fashion trend, donning "geegaws and trinkets" in order to "gratify the eye of man." Men, by contrast, did not bedeck themselves in extravagant, uncomfortable clothing that curtailed their freedom. Grimké regretted that even wage-earning women spent their hard-earned money on clothes in order to please their male employers. To Grimké—and as we have seen, to Lucy—simplicity of dress was the answer.

Amelia Bloomer, editor of a women's newspaper, the *Lily*, waged a campaign for simpler dress. Because the *Lily* did so much to promote the outfit, including printing patterns for women to copy, the dress took on the name of the paper's editor. Using dramatic, even frightening language, Bloomer pointed out the potential health hazards of the clothing women were expected to wear, warning them of the dangers they faced. The "excessive heat induced by an inordinate amount of clothing" would lead to "spinal afflictions," and extreme pressure would cause "torpidity of the liver and portal circulation, accompanied by constipation," she warned. One way to free women from these physical constraints to give them greater freedom of movement and improve their health was to don different clothing.[46]

That is exactly what Lucy did. In the summer of 1849, she made her first bloomer outfit to wear at home. In a year or two, she and a number of women adopted the new fashion statement by wearing bloomers in public. The costume included baggy pants that stopped above the ankles, a simple, knee-length dress, and no corsets. British actress and abolitionist Fannie

Kemble may have been the first to don this outfit in public in the United States when she wore the "Turkish dress" in the late 1840s. By the summer of 1851, the outfit had caught on with a number of reform-minded women. Female residents of Brook Farm, a short-lived utopian community outside Boston founded in 1841 by Unitarian George Ripley, wore a type of pantaloons under their dresses, and magazines promoting health reform and medical issues endorsed the costume. Elizabeth Cady Stanton in the early 1850s adopted the dress, as did several young factory workers at the textile mills in Lowell, Massachusetts. Women who tried bloomers found them comfortable and practical. No longer did they struggle to breathe. The new style required far fewer yards of material, and long skirts no longer dragged through mud and snow. Lucy, who had always dressed simply, was thrilled with the new outfit. Apparently on someone as petite as she was, the pants and short skirt were quite becoming.[47] Reading about the 1852 Syracuse convention, Stanton expressed great pleasure that someone wearing bloomers was "a pet of the Convention." That "pet" was Lucy.[48]

THE AMERICAN LADIES' NEW COSTUME.—(SEE NEXT PAGE.)

Figure 19. The American Ladies' New Costume (Image 817,698, New York Public Library)

Most Americans were far less thrilled with bloomers than were Lucy, Bloomer, and Stanton. In fact, most people were appalled. Women were now exposing their ankles, which apparently disturbed people far more than the sight of female performers on stage who exposed bare arms and a good deal of cleavage. Anthony, whose correspondence reveals her love of fine fashion, hesitated to adopt the outfit, claiming that women put pants on only to "better display their legs." She also worried that bloomers would not be warm in winter.[49] Many Americans found the outfit unattractive, and reactions were unrestrained and shrill. Women wearing bloomers appeared masculine, exposed, and tasteless. Members of the New England Anti-Slavery Society were aghast when Lucy showed up to lecture wearing pants. When Lucy stayed with Lucretia and James Mott, the Mott daughters were embarrassed because Lucy's bloomer outfit attracted so many unwelcome stares and rude comments from people on the street.[50] On another occasion, Lucy was wearing bloomers while walking in New York with Nette. Soon boys and men surrounded them, jeering and taunting her. The men blocked their movement. Fortunately an acquaintance walked by, saw the commotion, and summoned a policeman who broke up the crowd.[51]

The press deprecated the new costume, especially *Harper's* magazine. Its January 1852 issue contained pictures of strange looking men modeling a form of bloomers, clearly to spoof the fashion statement. To emphasize the contrast with proper feminine fashion, the magazine also included radiant-looking women bedecked in traditional attire with hoopskirts, ruffles, and many petticoats. Interestingly, Nette observed that more women expressed prejudice against bloomers than did men.[52]

In any case, the fad was short-lived. By early 1854, women developed second thoughts about wearing the bloomer costume. Stanton gave up the experiment that February. "Her petticoats have assumed their former length," Anthony reported, "and her wardrobe cleared of every short skirt."[53] The two women advised Lucy to do the same. "We put it on for greater freedom; but what is physical freedom compared with mental bondage?" they questioned. "If Lucy Stone, with all her reputation, her powers of eloquence, her loveliness of character, that wins all who once hear the sound of her voice, cannot bear the martyrdom of the dress, who, I ask, can?"[54] Apparently no one.

Reluctantly, Lucy gave up the bloomers. As she explained to Anthony, she believed no one should be judged by the clothing she wore. Suffragist Mary Livermore recalled years later that Lucy "would have gone on wearing it, had it not been for the daily crucifixion she had to endure in the streets from rude tongues."[55] Lucy believed that wherever she lectured, people listened to her and accepted her message, whether she was wearing bloomers or a long dress. But criticism continued. She was annoyed that so many people paid attention to her attire rather than to the truths she spoke. At this point, Lucy decided to travel with both long and short dresses when she lectured and to wear what seemed to fit the occasion, though she continued to shun corsets and wore dresses that were a bit shorter than was fashionable. As she later admitted with the acquired wisdom of age, she had been naïve in thinking she could alter entrenched ideas about female fashion. "I knew so little of the world," Lucy sighed, "that I thought the example of a dress so suited to the needs of life would be at once adopted."[56]

Another reform issue that briefly attracted Lucy's interest was temperance, though she never demonstrated as strong a commitment to that cause as did Anthony, Nette, and many other reformers. Alcohol consumption was a concern to many women, especially those who had fathers, brothers, or husbands who drank too much and were affected by the impact of men's excessive drinking. Certainly Lucy had good reason to support temperance since her father's drinking that fostered his abusive behavior had negatively affected the Stone family. An event that did attract Lucy's attention to the issue was the World's Temperance Convention held at the Broadway Tabernacle in New York on May 12, 1853. Men at the convention decried the presence of women who showed up to attend the meeting and refused to seat Anthony on their Business Committee after she had been nominated. They insisted that women return to their "proper sphere." In protest, some fifty men and women staged a walkout. They then held their own event the following September, the Whole World's Temperance Convention, that attracted some two thousand people. They renamed the earlier men's meeting the Half World's Temperance Convention since it had excluded women.[57]

At the Whole World Temperance Convention, Lucy spoke to some 3,000 people on "Women and Temperance." That first night she followed on the heels of a humorous speech by Phineas Barnum, who delighted the audience with mocking comments about drunkards. By contrast, Lucy spoke in dead seriousness in describing the dark side of alcohol. "Drink the intoxicating cup and you poison your whole being," she intoned. Then she offered a radical proposal and an unusual one for her to air in public: the right of a husband or wife to divorce a spouse who drank excessively. Lucy believed that laws, public shaming, and social pressure were insufficient to deliver the message to drunkards on the evils of alcohol. The threat of a drunkard losing a spouse and his or her children, she felt, would both shock and shame that person into sobriety. Lucy insisted that society had to make it impossible for anyone who was a drunkard "ever to sustain any marriage or parental relation." The threat of divorce, Lucy truly believed, could curb such behavior.[58] This alternative temperance convention and the radical speeches, including Lucy's, generated some negative media coverage. The *New York Times* wasted no words in damning the convention, claiming that women "have made every subject they have touched odious and contemptible in the public mind."[59]

As Lucy traveled and lectured on her own and organized women's rights conventions, her circle of friends and supporters expanded to include some of the most eminent reformers and intellectuals of the time—both male and female. An issue basic to her belief in human equality was welcoming men as equal participants in the women's rights movement. While the goals of the movement addressed women's grievances and most of those involved were women, a surprising number of men played pivotal roles, a situation that Lucy encouraged. She believed that men's presence added greater legitimacy and prestige—to say nothing of financial support—to women's efforts. She befriended several men who supported women's rights, and she found inspiration from them—men, as we have seen, like Garrison, Phillips, May, and Higginson. In the 1830s, it was Garrison who had convinced the Grimké sisters and Abby Kelley to get involved in the antislavery movement and encouraged Lucy and other women to hold conventions. May hired Lucy as a lecturer, scheduled many of her initial talks, and proved a lifelong friend. Phillips, as we've seen, was a stalwart supporter—both financially and emotionally—a man of wealth, social standing, and a law degree who found his life's calling in antislavery and women's rights. His wife Ann, who was plagued by a mysterious and debilitating illness throughout much of their married life, encouraged his commitment to the cause.[60]

Higginson and Lucy developed a particularly close relationship. Lucy identified him as one of three men who best understood what women needed, in addition to Phillips and William Ellery Channing, another Unitarian minister. Lucy and Higginson first met in Newburyport, Massachusetts, and their friendship flourished when Higginson and his wife moved to Worcester. He became an ardent admirer of Lucy's, commenting that she had "a little, sweet-looking Quakerish body with the sweetest modest manners, and yet is unshrinking and self-possessed as loaded cannon." He escorted her to the 1853 Whole World Temperance Convention, and their paths often

Figure 20. Wendell Phillips (LC-USZ62–129,165, Mathew Brady photograph, Library of Congress, Washington, DC)

crossed as they worked and lectured for abolition and women's rights.[61] He also wrote on women's issues, and one of his most famous essays, "Ought Women to Learn the Alphabet," argued for higher education for women. Like Lucy, he believed in co-educational institutions, seeing single-sex schools primarily as a transitional step to lift women to the same educational level as men.[62]

In the early 1850s, the famous abolitionist, Transcendentalist, and Unitarian minister Theodore Parker joined the women's movement. One evening after Phillips returned from a women's rights convention, Parker learned where his friend had been and cautioned, "Wendell, don't make a fool of yourself." To that remark, Phillips responded, "Theodore, this is the gravest question of the age. You ought to understand it." Struck by his friend's reply, Parker began to study the issues, and by the end of the year, dedicated himself to the movement as well. In 1853, Parker preached four sermons on the subject in a prominent Boston church, including "The Domestic Function of Woman" and "The Public Function of Woman." Lucy was thrilled to have

Figure 21. Thomas Wentworth Higginson (Image 1,254,942, New York Public Library)

this renowned minister's support, and she had the latter sermon published in pamphlet form.[63] As their support grew, even men's organizations began to pay some attention to the movement. When the Young Men's Mercantile Library Association of Pittsburgh invited Lucy to lecture on women's rights, she exclaimed, "Does not the world move!"[64]

But as can happen in all reform movements and within all organizations, carping, jealousy, and hurt feelings surfaced among female activists. At the 1852 Syracuse women's rights convention, tensions heightened among Paulina Wright Davis, Lucy, and other women, which did not abate until Davis left the movement. Davis, who had a healthy ego, wanted the convention to endorse the *Una*, the newspaper she had started and in whose pages she sought to elevate women and to provide a voice to "discuss the rights, sphere, duty and destiny of woman, fully and fearlessly."[65] Convention attendees turned her down, for money was tight. Davis also was critical of conventions, feeling they were not the best way for women to achieve their goals. She felt that too many women tried to grab the spotlight, an interesting comment from a woman who loved being the center of attention. Davis also wanted her friend Elizabeth Oakes Smith, a poet, lecturer, and women's rights activist, to serve as president of the Syracuse meeting; instead, a committee chose Lucretia Mott. Committee members may have been put off by Davis's efforts to try to control the meeting, or they may have been turned off by Smith's glamorous attire and her "thoroughly self-intoxicated" demeanor, as educator and activist Elizabeth Peabody put it.[66]

Davis would not let the situation die and decided to go public with her grievances. She wrote the *Liberator*, complaining that the women's movement was becoming politicized. She claimed that she disliked the tactic of women refusing to pay taxes because they could not vote, and she did not approve of Lucy's efforts to encourage open discussion at conventions. Davis also defended the elegant gowns she and Smith had worn, claiming they did so as an antidote to the unattractive bloomers worn by so many others. Lucy was dismayed by Davis's airing of these issues, and Nette, who heard about Davis's letter, was upset at such pettiness in exposing "these womanish jealousies."[67] Three years later, Lucy again disagreed with Davis when Davis wanted the next convention to subjects of marriage, divorce, and marital property rights. Lucy felt women were not yet ready to tackle those huge questions, with no two women thinking alike on them. The real question in Lucy's mind was whether or not a "woman, as wife, [has] a right to. . . . keep my body and its uses" to herself. Few wives could do that, she believed, for they were in "bondage" to their husbands. She hoped Davis "with her vanity and her jealousy" would not attend the next convention.[68]

Davis was not the only one who became disheartened by the movement. At times, even Lucy became discouraged. She complained to Anthony that the 1855 convention in Philadelphia was "the poorest" national meeting they had ever held. She felt speakers "showed little enthusiasm," and receipts were lower than anticipated. Afterwards, speakers complained that they were inadequately reimbursed for their travel expenses, with no one more upset than Ernestine Rose. Lucy felt Rose and others had little understanding of the time, energy, and expense that went into holding a convention. Lucy was so discouraged by the squabbling that she suggested they cancel the next year's convention.[69] She also expressed her distress to Anthony when she learned that Mary Nichols, a health reformer and women's rights activist, had complained to several people that "Lucy and her clique" had refused to let Nichols speak the year before in Cincinnati. Lucy called her an "artful creature" who presented herself as a victim in order to gain sympathy.[70]

Fortunately, these squabbles were infrequent, and friendships flourished and did much to sustain and to support Lucy and others during these early, challenging years of the women's movement. Lucy wrote scores of letters every year and received as many, if not more, in return. She often communicated with Samuel May who offered her solace and advice. Lucy's family also became a mainstay, for her parents had reconciled themselves to their daughter's unique career and fame. In fact, when West Brookfield neighbors criticized Lucy's activism as "crazy" and her behavior as "unwomanly," Hannah defended her daughter and in doing so, apparently "converted herself." Francis also had accepted Lucy's career choice and eventually told her, "I was wrong and you was [sic] right." In fact, the first time Lucy lectured in West Brookfield, her father came to listen. From the podium, Lucy occasionally glanced at him, "and I saw he was feeling satisfied."[71] Lucy remained close to Sarah and her family, evidenced by the many times she visited Gardner, Massachusetts, where the Lawrences now lived.

Of all the friendships, however, at this juncture her relationship with Anthony was one of her most critical. They corresponded for years, finding in one another a soul mate dedicated to seeking justice for women. Both lectured widely and played major roles in women's rights conventions. Each admired the work the other was doing for a cause they embraced as central to their very being. As single women, they shared much in common. In Anthony's eyes, Lucy was a model reformer and profound inspiration. Early on, Anthony wrote Lucy admiringly, "You are doing an amount of good rarely exceeded by any laborer in the reforms."[72] In return, Lucy wrote, "You are one of those who are sufficient to themselves. I thank God every day for you and me, who can work on and take care of oneself."[73]

The two became a formidable pair as they organized national women's rights conventions, frequently writing one another to discuss details and offer inspiration. By the early 1850s, as Anthony began to travel and to lecture, she could empathize with Lucy's demanding, exhausting life. The two were mutually solicitous, urging the other to pull back from a punishing schedule and to take time to rest and recover for future work. Lucy urged Anthony to "work <u>moderately</u>, but I am afraid you don't know what moderation is. . . . Suffrage is <u>sure</u> to come to women, God will wait for it, and so may you." Anthony invited Lucy to her Rochester home in the summer of 1853 so they could recuperate after lengthy travels and series of lectures,

Figure 22. Susan B. Anthony (LC–USZ62–111,871, Library of Congress. Used with the permission of the Nebraska State Historical Society)

promising her they could pick peaches and relax before setting out again.[74] After two of Lucy's lectures in New York City in September 1853, Anthony complimented Lucy on her success but urged her to rest. "Lucy, do live a long life. There is a vast deal of work for you to do; therefore, be prudent, that you may have the strength to accomplish it."[75] Anthony's letters suggest her deepening affection for her fellow worker, and by late September she was signing her letters, "Yours with love."[76]

Lucy never developed the intimate relationship with Stanton that she had with Anthony, although in the early years of the movement, she certainly admired her. Until 1860, their paths crossed infrequently, for Stanton was tied to home and to bearing and rearing her seven children. As Lucy recalled, the first time she met Stanton was at a convention in late 1852 or early 1853, shortly after Stanton gave birth to her first daughter, Margaret, on October 20, 1852.[77] Stanton was already the acknowledged intellectual force of the movement and one who never avoided controversy. Lucy appreciated that quality, expressing gratitude for Stanton's "brave, true words" in the essays and letters she sent to be read at women's rights conventions. "She is the bravest woman I know," Lucy wrote. "I love her dearly."[78] Lucy garnered Stanton's admiration in return when she addressed the 1853 temperance meeting and suggested that divorce be the solution for spouses married to alcoholics, for a woman's access to divorce was a vital issue to Stanton. Yet despite her admiration, Lucy always referred to her formally as "Mrs. Stanton," while she called Anthony, "Susan" or "Susan dear." Perhaps one reason for their distance was the differing views they held on the involvement of men in the movement. As was evident in the Seneca Falls "Declaration of Rights and Sentiments," Stanton had no problem blaming men as women's chief oppressor. Lucy, on the other hand, sought out men, welcoming their support.

Personality also may have been an issue, for Stanton was outgoing and charming, though she could be a bit intimidating. While Lucy was smart and quick to answer those who challenged her, she lacked Stanton's ebullience and sense of humor. Lucy did possess a sense of irony.[79] But she was self-effacing and humble and never demonstrated the bold confidence that Stanton exhibited. Class might also have prevented a close friendship from developing between Lucy and Stanton, for Stanton grew up in a privileged family, and she never had to farm or work for a living as Lucy did. No doubt Lucy and Stanton respected one another and their commitment to women's rights. But Stanton was always more ecumenical than Lucy in tackling women's causes, addressing any issue that struck her as relevant, any injustice that seemed odious. As the "Declaration of Rights and Sentiments" indicated, Stanton advocated a broad agenda for women's rights, even when the movement became focused on suffrage. For instance, in her speech delivered at the 1860 national women's rights convention, Stanton tackled divorce, open marriage, and birth control, startling many in the audience. And while Lucy was passionate about antislavery, that was a cause that garnered far less of Stanton's attention.[80]

Lucy continued to correspond with and visit Lucretia and James Mott. She admired the couple, seeing their relationship as an ideal example of a supportive, companionate union. James wrote Lucy long, thoughtful letters, dispensing advice and praising her accomplishments, often treating Lucy as he might have a daughter. Of the Motts, Lucy wrote, "Mrs. Mott was our ideal woman and one of the most persuasive advocates. James Mott was always with her, and the beautiful harmony of their lives answered the objection about discord in families."[81]

Aside from Anthony, Antoinette Brown remained the other mainstay in Lucy's life. After Oberlin's graduation, the two exchanged many letters, initially recalling their years at Oberlin and sharing their experiences as Nette pursued studies in theology at Oberlin while Lucy traveled and lectured. Their affection for one another ran deep and reflected typical homo-social feelings among women at this time. As Nette wrote Lucy in March 1848, "You will not believe I have at all forgotten you or loved you any less than I used to. . . . You do know that I did love you a great deal, for I remember your telling me I couldn't help it if I tried."[82] Despite their different views on religion, fashion, and other issues, "I loved you Lucy as I seldom loved any human being and as I much fear I shall never love another," Nette confessed. When Luther had died in 1850 and Lucy contracted typhoid fever, Nette expressed profound sympathy for all that Lucy had endured. She also worried about Lucy's health as she traveled and lectured, fearing her friend was driving herself too hard: "You will get worn out before your time and don't do that, Dear Lucy, for you will not do half the good in the end."[83]

The two women shared a deep level of trust and an open, honest friendship. Reacting to the creation of the 1853 Whole World Temperance Convention, Nette explained that she disliked forming a women's temperance organization that allowed men in as members but not as officers, a move she called "womanist" for its seeming retaliation against men for excluding women from their society. Women had to be above such pettiness. She believed the women's movement needed strong leadership, similar to Garrison's role in the antislavery movement. Nette's choice was Lucy, who unlike several other women, Nette believed, wanted no glory and had no "separate and higher interest" than seeking equality of rights for women and men.[84]

Beyond family, friends, and fellow reformers, Lucy found comfort in the written word, especially poetry. When seeking escape from the relentless challenges and solitary lifestyle, she read and then memorized William Cullen Bryant's poem, "Lines to a Waterfowl," especially the lines, "He who from zone to zone, Guides through the boundless sky thy certain flight, In the long way that I must tread alone, Will lead my steps aright." She also loved Anne Whitney's "Bertha" and found strength and the need for patience in its line, "If the aloe wait an hundred years," referring to a plant which only blossomed once a century.[85]

Despite friends and many personal and professional contacts, her growing fame as an orator, a comfortable income, and a frenetic but rewarding career, Lucy lacked a constant companion to comfort, listen to, and support her.

She admitted that while she was used to living and working alone, she did, at times, feel some doubt as to whether this was how she wanted to live out the rest of her life. But rather defensively she explained to the man who would eventually end that solo existence, "I have been all my life alone. I have planned and executed, without counsel, and without control & have shared thought, and feeling, and life, with myself alone. I have made a path for my feet, which I know is very useful, it brings me more intense and abundant happiness, by far, than comes to the life of the majority of men. And it seems to me, I cannot wish it by any change. And then I ask, 'Can I dare to change?' It rings an everlasting 'no.'" She added that the time when her love was not shared was "only as the drop to the ocean. The great whole of my life is richly blest; let it remain so."[86] Here was an independent woman who had created a rich and rewarding life on her own. But that situation was about to change.

5

"This Strange Union": Marriage and Motherhood

"I shall not be married ever," Lucy wrote Nette in August 1849. "I have not yet seen the person, whom I have the slightest wish to marry, and if I had, it will take longer than my lifetime for the obstacles to be removed."[1] Those "obstacles" included laws which declared a wife to be the possession of her husband—a *feme covert*—as the legal expression termed it—with virtually no rights to operate as an independent being. But a few years later, Lucy found that man—or, rather, he found her. With a relentless, well-crafted courtship over a two-year period, he wooed and finally won Lucy Stone. Yet their first meeting was hardly auspicious. Lucy, who was returning home after Luther's death and her bout with typhoid fever, stopped by a hardware store in Cincinnati to cash a check. The store's co-owner, after meeting her, told his brother that he had met a young woman whom he, his brother, might like. His brother was not interested, and perhaps at that moment Henry Browne Blackwell began to think about Lucy for himself.[2]

Blackwell, born in Bristol, England, was the second-youngest son of Samuel and Hannah Lane Blackwell and the fifth of their nine children.[3] Samuel was deeply religious but by all accounts, a tolerant, good-humored, and kind man. He was also well-read and an ardent reformer, with strong convictions about abolition, women's rights, and temperance, and he deeply instilled in his children progressive ideas about social reform. As a sugar refiner, Samuel had been able to provide his family with every comfort in England. But that situation changed when a fire destroyed his refinery in 1831. Facing financial ruin, he made the decision to move the family to New York in 1832, a year before Great Britain abolished slavery in its Caribbean islands. In America, Samuel could start over.[4] He quickly became involved in the antislavery movement and soon befriended a community of abolitionists, including Garrison, Samuel J. May, Gerrit Smith, and Theodore Dwight Weld. He established a sugar-beet refinery business, selling to those who, like himself, refused to purchase or to use sugar cane produced by slave labor. But that business faltered, in part due to the financial panic of 1837. The next year, the family left its Long Island home, briefly settled in Jersey City, and then moved to Cincinnati, hoping their financial situation would improve in the West. In August 1838, however, Samuel suffered a recurrence of malaria, and after being treated with calomel, he died, leaving his wife Hannah and the children on their own, with few financial resources.[5]

At that point, the Blackwell brothers, including 13-year-old Henry (born in 1825 and called "Harry" by his family), helped to support the family. He and Sam worked as clerks. Hannah and her three eldest daughters earned money by running a girls' school, the Cincinnati English and French Academy for Young Ladies, and taking in boarders. Somehow the family found the money to send Henry to Kemper College in St. Louis to study law. He left there after a year, claiming he lacked the ability to speak extemporaneously. Henry's departure also may have been for financial reasons or because he found it difficult to focus, not sleeping for days on end and suffering periodic mood swings, even bouts of depression. Harriet Beecher Stowe, who happened to be a neighbor of the Blackwell's, called Henry a "wild boy," and he may have been. Certainly he had a restless spirit, a trait he inherited from his father. His sister Marian despaired for him. "You seem to me ever like a comet that has not found its centre & goes wandering wildly through space," she wrote.[6] Henry worked as a clerk for six years and then invested in a flour mill business. In 1846, using borrowed funds, he went east and, following in the footsteps of his late father, invested in a sugar refinery in New York in order to learn the business.[7]

Again exhibiting his relentless "butterfly streak," Henry was soon drawn to a new adventure.[8] When the refinery burned down (evidently a danger with sugar refineries) in the late 1840s, Henry's dreams turned to the West. He announced his desire to join the tens of thousands of men who had migrated to California to try to make their fortune in gold. As daughter Alice later wrote of her father, all during his life he was drawn to anything that offered the hope of making money.[9] Probably influenced by family members who advised him—strenuously and on numerous occasions—to get serious about his future, Henry gave up on California. His sister Marian, in particular, urged him not to let the excitement of the gold rush entice him.[10] His mother Hannah was most "thankful" when he discarded the plan, concerned about the "horrid contingencies and desperadoes you would be in the midst of!" She warned that most men who migrated to California found a grave rather than gold. Instead, Hannah encouraged Henry to visit one of the nation's most celebrated ministers, the Rev. Henry Ward Beecher, hoping he might convert Henry and encourage him to become a minister.[11] Piety had never been a strong suit in Henry's character, however, and he ignored his mother's wishes. Instead, returning to Cincinnati, he and brother Sam each borrowed $5,000 from a cousin in England and invested in a wholesale hardware store—what became known as Coombs, Ryland & Blackwells. The two young men also became involved in Cincinnati's cultural and social life and organized a debating club.[12]

Although Henry's financial future seemed uncertain, he yearned to marry and seemed to fall in and out of love easily. He envisioned the type of woman he needed, for as he explained to his sister Emily, he wanted an "intelligent, go-ahead lady with a fortune to back her go-aheaditiveness." Lucy was hardly a woman of fortune, though when the two met in that hardware store,

Figure 23. Henry Browne Blackwell (LC-USZ62–76,998, Library of Congress, Washington, DC)

she was earning a substantial income from her lecturing, and, indeed, making far more than Henry. By this point, she also had become one of the most famous women in America.[13] Henry immediately saw that Lucy was smart, determined, serious, and independent, with a purposefulness that eluded him. It may have been the attraction of opposites. He, by nature, was fun-loving, charming, witty, dreamy, and romantic. Pleasant looking, though slightly short and stout, he had blue eyes and dark, wavy hair.[14] Henry was a man of sound habits, never drank alcohol, and shunned tobacco in all forms.[15]

After the check-cashing episode, the next time Henry saw Lucy was in the spring of 1853 when she and Phillips addressed the Massachusetts State legislature. He had gone east to try to find a publisher for some poems he had written and to attend an antislavery meeting. She then spoke at the New England Anti-Slavery convention, where Henry also spoke, apparently having overcome some of his fears about public speaking.[16] Lucy's lectures captivated him. "The beauty, charm, and eloquence of Miss Stone captured her hearers and greatly impressed me," he wrote Sam. He also was taken by her demeanor and her "strong moral character." He then met with Garrison to inquire about Lucy's status and learned she had no suitor, though Garrison also warned him that she had no desire ever to marry and had rejected other men. Henry reported to Sam that he would try to see more of Lucy, admitting he far preferred her above any other woman he had met.[17] Despite her being seven years his senior and dead-set against marriage, Henry initiated a campaign to woo and to wed Lucy Stone.

Henry began corresponding with Lucy, at first addressing her as "Miss Lucy" while she called him "Mr. Blackwell." Soon his greeting became "My dear friend." He sent her a translation of Plato and insisted she keep the book so that he could imagine her reading it as she sat "amongst the cool green granite hills of Massachusetts." He mentioned a visit he had paid to Sarah Grimké and Angelina Grimké Weld at their New Jersey home. He described his deep admiration for Lucy's profession and for the principled life she lived, in contrast to his own ill-defined pursuits. He admitted to being "naturally social in all my tastes and habits." And he knew himself well, for he confessed, "I love even too well the sympathy and approbation of my fellow creatures" to approach life in the same the way Lucy did, for she had learned to ignore the many taunts and insults she suffered and the opposition she encountered.[18] In a return letter, Lucy explained how lonely her life was because of her unique journey: earning a college degree, becoming a Garrisonian lecturer, and donning bloomers. But, she explained,

"It is better far, to be <u>alone, and be true</u>, than to procure companionship by being false."[19]

Henry's campaign to win Lucy's heart involved his composing lengthy, ardent, and quite beautifully crafted letters. As Lucy continued to travel and to lecture across the Northeast, Henry called her a "born locomotive."[20] At first, Lucy was not swayed by his verbal flourishes nor by his efforts to discuss ideas and topics she might find so appealing, including the martyrdom of Puritan dissident Anne Hutchinson; Ohio laws pertaining to marriage; the possibility of women becoming attorneys; and, of course, women's rights. In several letters he expounded on the evils of slavery while admitting he knew of no way to end it. He also believed in a truly "companionate" marriage, one in which husband and wife were equal partners in every respect. He would, he wrote, sacrifice anything to please her.

His letters were pages-long, many of them cross-hatch to save paper and postage, written in beautiful, tight penmanship. They combined pragmatic thoughts and romantic sentiments. Henry presented every possible reason why Lucy should marry him, though he was careful not to press too hard, at least at first. A month after they met, he wrote casually, "I believe some day you ought to & will marry somebody—perhaps not me—if not—a better person." He equated an unmarried state to the condition of a slave prohibited from legally marrying, by depriving her of enjoying close, personal relationships. To deflect the idea that marriage might be on his mind, Henry maintained that he needed three more years before he would be financially secure enough to wed. He then detailed his idea of a perfect marriage—"no sacrifice of individuality . . . no limitation of the career of one, or both, but its extension."[21]

He did not want his wife to be a "drudge," an image he had of Angelina Grimké Weld, who had married abolitionist Theodore Weld in 1838 and subsequently borne three children. He believed a wife should not remain at home taking care of babies as Angelina Grimké Weld was doing.[22] Comparing himself to other men, Henry insisted he would not want his wife confined to domesticity, adding that if either partner could not "study more, think more, feel more, talk more and work more than they could alone, I will remain an old bachelor & adopt a Newfoundland dog or a terrier as an object of affection." He would like his wife to pursue whatever interest or profession she desired.[23] Henry believed in this concept of companionate marriage, though he sensed that most women would likely be uncomfortable in that type of relationship because they preferred being dependent on their husbands. He hoped Lucy would welcome a marriage of equals. "Equality with me is a passion," he added.[24]

Somewhat surprisingly, Lucy defended the Welds' marriage and their current lifestyle. She admitted that they had chosen to withdraw from the antislavery movement, but in their own way were acting on their convictions by raising three "good, brave" children. She suggested that the couple was doing more to improve the world by raising and educating children than continuing to campaign for abolition. While Lucy saw this as the right choice for them, however, she did not feel it suited her. She saw no future for herself but fighting to undo "the horrid wrongs of society." She was willing to continue her lecturing even if that meant a less satisfying personal life. Her life was totally committed to abolition and to women's rights, but she hoped she and Henry could be friends.[25]

Lucy's ability to ignore public censure was a revelation to Henry. Even after seeing her attired in bloomers, Henry felt she had made all the right choices. He admitted that the very isolation that Lucy's life—and bloomer costume—created was "strangely attractive" and concluded that there was "something bracing in the air of solitude." Yet while Henry admired Lucy's dedication to reform, he chided her for being wedded to her profession and to her causes, having little time to develop close relationships. "A woman who united herself with a fellow worker with sufficient means & position to prevent the necessity of her drudgery—free to be at home when she pleases & to leave it when she thinks it best ... is this position necessarily less influential than your present one?" She responded stoically that she had learned to deal with "privations" and "isolation" and had found much happiness in her career.[26]

Of course, Henry's words must have affected Lucy, who knew from her own upbringing the joys of a large family. Still, even after months of being courted, she remained unconvinced that marriage suited her, again insisting they just be friends. Suggesting that they meet in Niagara Falls, New York, for a face-to-face conversation, Henry promised it would not "awaken unreasonable hopes of a speedy change of mind on your part."[27] Lucy agreed to the meeting, which took place in early October 1853. Henry, ever the romantic, later recalled sitting beside a whirlpool at Lucy's feet, "looking down into its dark waters with a passionate & unshared & unsatisfied yearning in my heart." Whether Lucy shared such dreamy sentiments is doubtful. When she wrote her mother to tell her she had visited Niagara, she mentioned the soothing, rushing water but gave no hint that anyone, much less a man, was with her.[28]

In October, Henry made a point of attending the fourth annual National Woman's Rights convention held in Cleveland. Obviously trying to impress Lucy, he delivered his first women's rights speech, lecturing for over an hour. A local newspaper felt his speech went on too long and commented, "He forgot it was a Woman's Convention."[29]

To prove how useful he might be to her, Henry arranged a fall and early winter lecture tour for Lucy throughout the Midwest, using his business contacts to set up engagements in several midwestern and a couple of southern cities. This service was impossible to refuse. Using the Blackwell home as her base, Lucy was drawn to Henry's "good and noble" family, especially to his mother. "I love them very much," she added.[30] She was grateful for the kindness shown her and the "home-like" feeling she enjoyed while staying there. Sam was taken with their visitor: "We have quite adopted her." Lucy described Henry's solicitude and how lovingly she felt toward him. While she was on the road, the two kept up their correspondence, though Lucy continued to insist that she was too much for any man to marry. "I value you and your happiness too much ever to consent to attach to you a life that all the affirmations of my reason conscience . . . for me to belong to you." Instead, they should remain friends, and she hoped she would be able "to add sunshine to your life."[31] As for the speaking tour, Lucy felt it had a profound effect on a number of new people whom she reached, and she gratefully acknowledged to Henry that its success was due to him.[32]

Meeting Lucy in Chicago where she ended her tour gave Henry hope, for in early January 1854, he wrote: "I am the most fortunate favored of all living men to have thus won the love of a woman so pure & true & noble." They could ignore marital laws and build a unique relationship. He vowed that when they married, he would publicly denounce all laws that made a wife subservient to her husband. He added, "I wish I could take the position of the wife under the law & give you that of a husband."[33] In their future life together, Henry at times seemed to do just that.

Yet when Henry suggested he come east to visit her, Lucy apparently had second thoughts and made it clear that, while she loved him, she did not want to marry him. She still could not envision living under the laws of marriage or sharing her life with anyone. Moreover, in Lucy's mind, Henry lacked the purposefulness that was by now second nature to her. She wished he could make more of his life and depend less on the approval of others. She realized how hard he struggled to lead a meaningful life and urged that he try to "cultivate steadiness of purpose and deliberations, and love of and trust in the Truth without regard to consequences."[34] Henry replied that he would do so but wait until she could give him "a fair chance of being loved by you."[35]

Whatever his shortcomings, Henry was tenacious in pursuing Lucy. Most men would have given up after a few months, but he did not. On the other hand, his relentless pursuit proved incredibly stressful to Lucy, for he challenged everything she had come to believe about marriage and about herself. Her punishing schedule, the constant lecturing, and her unassailable ambivalence toward marriage added to the tension. Exhausted by months of traveling, lecturing, and stress, Lucy returned to West Brookfield in early spring 1854, suffering migraines. But she was back in Cincinnati in early April for an antislavery convention, which Henry also attended. Days later, he wrote that while he worried that his long letters might tire her, he hoped they could see one another that summer. Revealing his profound neediness he added, "With you I live—without you I vegetate."[36]

Appealing to her desire for quiet moments amidst her hectic schedule, he proposed joining her and spending time with her at Sarah's home in Gardner, where no one could observe them, "all by ourselves, with God and the Angels. The blue sky over our heads, the green earth beneath us, and the bright summer air around us—I would ask no other heaven to invoke, no other mediator but you, dear Lucy." Lucy hesitated to invite him to visit and so left the decision to him. In early May, Henry admitted he had planned to remain "cool & philosophical" but finally wrote, "I love you!" He was determined his love would never limit her life or impede any activity.[37] Business prospects brought him to New York in early May where he lectured at an antislavery meeting. He visited Lucy in Boston several days later, and they traveled to Sarah's home, there to sort out their relationship.[38] Apparently the outcome was not favorable to Henry, for in July 1854 Lucy again explained that they did not belong together as husband and wife. "If we did, I should not so often feel my spirit protesting against it."[39]

But a turning point took place that September after Henry attended the Western Anti-Slavery convention in Salem, Ohio. His crowning achievement as an activist was his role in rescuing a slave girl from her master and mistress as they passed by train through Salem en route to Tennessee. Abolitionists had advance word about the family's travels, and hundreds of them assembled at the train depot. When the train arrived, Henry boarded first and asked the girl and her mistress if the girl was a slave, which they acknowledged she was.

He then asked the girl if she wished to be free, and she responded yes. Henry informed the master that the girl was legally free since they were traveling in a free state. According to eyewitnesses, he calmly picked up the girl and handed her to another man who pulled the slave girl off the train and fled with her. The deed received a good deal of publicity. Abolitionists celebrated this open defiance of the nation's Fugitive Slave Law. But many Americans in both the North and South—including members of Henry's family—were shocked. These men had broken a federal law. Some newspapers overdramatized the event, reporting that the girl's rescuers were abusive and that Henry had assaulted the woman and had thrown her baby, whom she had been holding, on the floor. A few people threatened the Blackwell brothers' hardware business. Southerners were outraged, calling this the "Salem Robbery" and offered a $1,000 reward for Henry's capture.[40]

Lucy, however, was thrilled, now seeing Henry in a new light. Here he displayed a willingness to act on his antislavery convictions, no doubt also motivated by what he knew Lucy most desired to see in him. Finally he stood up for a cause and risked public disapproval. "What an exciting scene it must have been! How much of intense thought, feeling, and action have crowded in that little space of time! What a change in one human destiny!," she wrote him excitedly. Initially, Henry took great pride in what he had done, at last proving to Lucy that he could act decisively to defend a cause and not be swayed by public approval. Later, however, uneasy over mounting criticism aimed at him, Henry worried that he might have carried his convictions too far. But this event did change Henry's life. After Lucy's death, he admitted, "I was told later that this act of mine was what gained me my wife. If that was so, I received the most heavenly reward that ever came to earthly man for any deed."[41]

Of course, Henry's lengthy courtship of Lucy made the rounds of the Blackwell family. At least three of Henry's unmarried sisters—Elizabeth, Anna, and Emily—were upset by it. They were a formidable group. Elizabeth, four years Henry's senior, was already famous as the first woman in the United States to graduate from medical school and become a doctor. After earning her medical degree at Geneva College in upstate New York and studying in Paris and England, she returned to New York City where she struggled to establish a practice, finally opening a one-room dispensary on the lower East Side.[42] Three years later, Emily joined her. Born in 1826, Emily pursued a medical degree at Rush Medical College of Chicago and then Western Reserve University in Cleveland. Following her graduation in

1854, she studied in England before joining Elizabeth in New York.[43] Anna lived abroad and made a life for herself as a writer, intellect, and women's rights activist.

These three Blackwell sisters felt much was at stake in their brother's deepening interest in Lucy. Anna wrote Henry as soon as she heard of a possible engagement, explaining that she had little feeling for "Yankee women" and sensed, with more than a trace of British snobbishness, that Lucy was far beneath the Blackwell family in both her intellect and accomplishments.[44] Nonetheless, Elizabeth wrote Lucy in June 1854, to welcome her into the Blackwell family, assuring her she would always have everyone's support and affection. "Therefore, dear Lucy, let me offer you most cordially and with special meaning the hand of sisterly affection and assure you that we shall all be proud to welcome you when you see fit to claim the recognition." She awaited confirmation of an engagement.[45]

In the same letter, however, Elizabeth could not refrain from commenting on Lucy's involvement in the women's rights movement. While she shared with her a commitment to create a more just world, Elizabeth disapproved of women's rights conventions. Their usefulness had long ago been exhausted. She considered their continuance "a waste of time to those whose time is of value, and an injury rather than a benefit to the Cause." Elizabeth felt meetings to discuss abstract principles and rights "become mere displays of vain oratory or the theatre of vanity and petty ambitions." The women's movement, Elizabeth argued, could not even support a newspaper, unlike other major reform movements that published one. Ever since the national convention at Worcester in 1850, women's rights conventions had "degenerated in moral force," she added, and should end because they lacked "true vitality." She did hope Lucy and Ernestine Rose would continue lecturing since they had a "God-given power" to influence others.[46]

Lucy answered Elizabeth, noting that a union with Henry was only "possible" rather than "probable." She admitted that Henry was becoming more dear to her, "but we both felt that a relation upon which so much is depending requires that the parties should have the fullest knowledge of each other." Lucy questioned whether they were suited. She then defended women's rights conventions. She was well satisfied with their results, she opined, for meetings paved the way for individual work as well as for expanding the public's interest in women's issues. Sending out calls for annual meetings and listing famous supporters such as Ralph Waldo Emerson, Ohio congressman and abolitionist Joshua Giddings, and newspaper editor Horace Greeley gave these conventions

weight in the public mind. Lucy confessed that she possessed "a natural isolation in my character, which renders it difficult for me to assimilate with others,
yet I work heartily with conventions because I think them vastly useful."[47] If
she did not sense the meetings were doing any good, she would not be involved
in them. Whether Lucy's comments had any impact on an opinionated
Elizabeth is unknown.

Throughout the lengthy two-year courtship, Henry struggled to find a
fulfilling occupation. Like a number of Americans of this era who articulated
numerous thoughts in their quest for self-improvement, he sought a meaningful career that would help him lead a more perfect life. Although he
would struggle his entire life to find that ideal career, he was conscious of his
shortcomings. As he admitted to Theodore Parker in 1853, his life up to this
point had been a series of "blunders & weaknesses" and "neglected opportunities." His business ventures were "paltry," and all he could claim as a
"memorial" to his struggles were the few poems he had written. Henry
hoped he might, at some future date, "cooperate with you in some humble
form in the great work of human progress."[48] Ultimately, it would be Lucy,
rather than Parker, who aided Henry in working for "human progress."

Searching for lucrative business opportunities, Sam and Henry, along with
many others in the mid-nineteenth century, became caught up in speculative land fever in the Old Northwest. By the 1830s, the federal government
had forcibly removed Indian tribes, including the Black Hawks, from the
region and had begun to encourage the purchase and settlement of land
"ceded" to the government by various tribes.[49] A group of Cincinnati investors hired Sam and Henry to serve as agents to buy land in Wisconsin and
Illinois. In January 1854 Henry traveled to Wisconsin, intending to purchase
seventy-five sections of 640 acres each. He planned to retain eight to ten
parcels for himself and anticipated making a $1,500 commission on the bal-
ance. By June, he had bought 10,000 acres, holding on to 6,000 of them and
hoping to sell the rest. Writing to Lucy, he elaborated on the glories of
Wisconsin, describing the beautiful prairie, farm land, and healthful climate.
What he found especially appealing was that it took little capital to acquire
a name for oneself. Even Elizabeth bought land, and she and Henry dreamed
of a future "Blackwell Exodus" to the "finest tract of Wisconsin land" where
the entire family and close friends could unite in some sort of communal
colony.[50] Four weeks later, Henry was in Illinois, buying more property and
exulting in rising land prices. He urged Lucy to invest in western land as
well, which eventually she did.[51]

Something significant seemed to have transpired in the relationship in October and early November 1854. Attending the fifth National Woman's Rights convention in Philadelphia that fall, Lucy found she could not concentrate. "While the minutes are being read, my thoughts run away to you, and to our future," she confessed to Henry. She described the convention as a great success, but images of him kept distracting her. Lucy still believed another type of woman would best suit Henry, but now she expressed a desire for his love and support and hoped she could aid him in every way possible. While "a false step" could imperil their relationship, she yearned to see him.[52] A couple of weeks later, she wrote Henry, "To-day I have been out two hours and more, walking. With my long dress . . . and that glorious indifference, that 'don't care where,' I strolled everywhere, unseen and unknown. And I returned as rosy and fresh as though I had been twenty years younger." Lucy Stone was in love. After being alone for so long, she now realized that she wanted what most nineteenth-century women yearned for—a husband, a family, and a home. At last she accepted Henry's proposal.[53] Nette reported, "Very happy she seems, too."[54]

In late December, well in advance of their wedding, Henry encouraged Lucy to settle her personal property and earnings in her own name. After they were wed, he pledged to let her live as an independent woman, to support all her causes, and to consider her his equal. He now announced to his family and friends that he and Lucy would wed and encouraged her to do the same. He again suggested she invest some of her savings in railroad land in Illinois, reassuring her that his judgment on such matters was sound.[55] In addition to purchasing property in the West, Lucy began buying items for their future home. Now sensing the advantages of their unique relationship, she wrote Henry on Christmas Day, "We will be forever better for our wedded love." Garrison visited her in Boston and gave his blessing to the union, reassuring Lucy that Henry was dedicated to his beliefs and would never try to "shackle" her convictions. Such comments from a man she revered no doubt further convinced Lucy that she had made the right decision to marry.[56]

Emily and Elizabeth Blackwell, however, were less than thrilled with their brother's engagement. They continued to exhibit a degree of social snobbery and were as surprised as their sister Anna had been that Henry had fallen for a Massachusetts farm girl rather than a woman whom they felt matched their own intellects. While studying in Edinburg, Emily wrote Elizabeth, reporting she had heard that Lucy had accepted Henry's proposal, which she greatly regretted. The two worried about their brother's welfare, since all the Blackwell men, unlike the women in the family, struggled to find rewarding careers. "I hope L. Stone has given H a second refusal—her influence over him hitherto has been so unfavourable that though I respect her personally I sincerely hope she will not have H," Emily commented and reiterated her disapproval of Henry's plan to wed Lucy. She continued, "Harry's engagement does not of course surprise us—it was not very welcome—but few marriages are ever all we could desire." Finding it in herself to compliment Lucy, she added, "I believe the foundation of her character is really noble."[57] Elizabeth hoped that once Lucy became part of the Blackwell family, she would "lay aside some of the ultra peculiarities that are so disagreeable to us. Certainly we will not allow it to break the strong feeling that has always existed among us if possible."[58] Henry's sisters felt that Lucy's marriage to their brother might do much to elevate her character.

But to Henry, Elizabeth sent congratulations when she learned the engagement was definite. She admitted that she did not know Lucy very well. Her impressions had come through "the eccentricities and accidents of the American phase of this nineteenth century in bloomerism, abolitionism, woman's rightisms."[59] It would take time as well for Elizabeth and Emily to embrace Lucy as part of the Blackwell family.

Some of their concern is understandable. Lucy was the first outsider to breach that close family circle. Henry was the first Blackwell sibling to wed. All the Blackwells shared a great deal with one another—especially advice. Letters written to one family member typically circulated among all siblings and Hannah. Emily worried that Henry's marriage would inhibit that closeness. Perceptively she added, though she had not yet met Lucy, "If we can influence Lucy we can Harry—she will be always the stronger one." When Emily learned the couple contemplated a visit to England, the thought of Lucy lecturing in their homeland horrified her and hoped she would cancel any plans to do so. "You cannot conceive the strong prejudice here against that particular manifestation of woman's independence—the people are so different that it would create a violent prejudice." But Emily had begun to accept Henry's decision and hoped the marriage would be a happy one, realizing that her brother's feelings for Lucy, unlike his several past romances, were "no passing fancy on his part."[60] Sam and Hannah, on the other hand, had been elated from the start.

In March 1855, two months before the wedding, an ecstatic Henry wrote Emily to share his happiness. He mentioned that Lucy had saved $6,000 (nearly $164,000 in today's currency), noting that she planned to put it in the hands of trustees to "escape the present iniquitous law, which would make it mine if not prevented." He estimated that Lucy would draw an income of $600 a year "& so I feel no hesitancy in marrying." In an understatement, Henry admitted that his "pecuniary affairs" were not in an altogether satisfactory condition and would not be for several years. Anticipating that his western lands would increase in value, Henry hoped to clear $5,000 when they sold.[61]

Lucy had other thoughts on her mind other than money, and she mostly confided in Sarah about the impact of marriage laws, her sexual inhibitions, and concerns about bearing healthy babies in her late thirties. She gave Henry a copy of Henry C. Wright's 1854 book, *Marriage and Parentage*, in which Wright insisted that a man "has no more right to compel her [a wife] to yield to his passion" or to force on her "the conditions of maternity." Wright suggested that the woman should determine the couple's sexual activity and advocated that intercourse occur only for purposes of reproduction.[62] Henry promised Lucy she could "choose when, where & how often you shall become a mother." Yet despite her concerns but reflecting widely shared nineteenth-century values, Lucy wanted not only the comfort of a husband's love but also the opportunity to have children. Already she was thinking about a family. To Nette, Lucy explained that she wanted to have a baby "right away." Ultimately, she hoped that she and Henry could have four children. Wanting to complete the matter expeditiously, she told Nette that she preferred two pregnancies, to "dispatch matters so as to gain twins."[63] Henry tried to reassure Lucy about their having children and suggested they wait until after the wedding to discuss the issue. He hoped she would become "a cheerful & happy Mother by me" just as she would become a "loved & cherished & happy wife."[64]

Finally, on May 1, 1855, after some delays due to Lucy's hectic lecture schedule and serious migraines, the Stone-Blackwell wedding took place in the Stone family home. Henry had suggested they have the ceremony at her home in order to make the event appear as normal as possible. The peaceful, simple ceremony caused Lucy's months of worrying to evaporate. No other Blackwells were present, though Elizabeth and sister Marian, who were living in New York, had been invited. Bo and his three children, as well as a family friend, Charles Burleigh, attended.[65] Lucy's parents had never met Henry before this but no doubt were relieved and happy that their independent daughter finally found a husband. Conducting the 7:00 a.m. ceremony was Thomas Wentworth Higginson. The minister and his wife Mary had traveled from Worcester the previous afternoon, armed with bouquets of greenhouse flowers. Lucy's friend Anna Parsons sent orange blossoms to decorate the farmhouse. Nor had Higginson met Henry, but he wrote afterwards that he "liked [him] more and more; he is thoroughly true and manly, earnest, sensible, and discriminating; not inspired, but valuable. They seem perfectly happy together." Lucy looked lovely in an ashes of roses-colored silk dress; Henry was dapper in a proper white waistcoat. They had written their own wedding vows, removing the word "obey," and declared their relationship would be a partnership of equals. Lucy cried at the end. Higginson concluded "it was the most beautiful bridal I ever attended."[66]

A week later, Henry wrote Emily:

> I am flourishing in all the happiness of married life. Lucy & I were betrothed on the 1st of May at her father's house on a wild, rocky mountain farm where she was born & reared.... The ceremony was short & simple. After I had read the protest, Lucy & I standing side by side & Mr. Higginson before us, he made a few very kind & earnest remarks upon the occasion & then asked the same question necessarily of each whether we took each other to love, honor, & cherish in joy & sorrow, in sickness & health so long as we both should live & then joined our hands, pronounced us husband & wife, made a short prayer & all was over. Our friend Charles Burleigh, however, made a short speech ending by laying his hands upon our heads & bestowing a very fervent benediction, which gave the children of the house occasion to say afterwards that Mr. Higginson joined our hands, but that Mr. Burleigh joined our heads.

Henry characterized the Stone family as "excellent, kind, honest, intelligent, simple people all of them." As to his bride, he reassured Emily that she would come to like Lucy after she came to know her. "She is one of the most frank, kind, warmhearted & considerate persons in the world—full of spirit, cheerfulness & energy." Immediately following the wedding breakfast, the newlyweds caught a train for New York to visit Marian. Lucy could not participate in festivities that evening but took to bed with a headache. The newlyweds remained there until May 3 when they set out for Cincinnati by train, reaching the Blackwell home two days later. Henry predicted they would live with his mother for a while but eventually move east since Lucy preferred that region of the country, and his own feelings were "not very strong in the opposite direction."[67]

Although the ceremony had been quiet, the Stone-Blackwell wedding attracted national attention. Few people could have imagined that the famous Lucy Stone, with her strong convictions and fearless independence, would ever marry. Calling additional attention to the event was the couple's marriage "Protest" that Henry had suggested months earlier and which the two of them composed. Elizabeth Blackwell and Wendell Phillips received advance copies to edit.[68] The "Protest" addressed the very issues that caused Lucy to question marriage. This was not the first time newlyweds had protested marital laws. For instance, Theodore Weld, upon his marriage to Angelina Grimké in 1838, denounced laws that gave a husband control over his wife's property. But the Stone-Blackwell statement attracted far more attention. Released to the press after the ceremony, the "Protest" censured laws that turned wives into chattel and caused them to lose their rights and independence. "This action on our part implies no sanction of, nor promise of voluntary obedience to such of the present laws that refuse to recognize a wife as an independent, rational being, while they confer upon the husband an injurious and unnatural superiority," the "Protest" read. It went on to state Henry's and Lucy's objections to a woman's legal existence being "suspended during marriage," and they condemned laws that gave a husband automatic claim to a wife's property and earnings and that upheld a father's right as sole guardian of any children in rare cases of divorce.[69]

Following the ceremony, Higginson sent the "Protest" to a few newspapers and added a forward. "I never perform the marriage ceremony without a renewed sense of the inequity of our present system of laws, in respect to marriage—a system by which 'man and wife are one, and that one is the husband.'" He added his "hearty concurrence" to sentiments in the "Protest" and hoped it would receive wide coverage.[70] It did.

Many Americans were surprised that any man would marry a woman like Lucy Stone. Others could not understand how a couple could wed yet at the same time publicly object to marriage in its current legal state. But female reformers, even those who were surprised by Lucy's decision to marry, were thrilled with the "Protest." Abolitionist and suffragist Frances Jocelyn Gage defended Lucy when newspapers began to "sneer and insinuate and talk about Lucy's repudiating her principles." Gage argued that Lucy had never rejected marriage outright but simply opposed the odious laws that subjugated married women. Gage hoped the "Protest" would foster larger discussion about women's subordinate status in marriage.[71]

The press, of course, did sneer. Most newspapers carried at least brief notices of the event. The *New York Times* noted condescendingly that "Miss Lucy Stone has succumbed at last. In spite of all her diatribes against the tyranny of marriage, and her assertion of woman's rights, she has come under the yoke, and is now the lawfully wedded wife of Mr. Henry B. Blackwell. There is a great deal of human nature in Miss Lucy, after all." The paper mistakenly assumed it was Lucy who had conceived the idea of the "Protest" and that "her husband, like a docile, affectionate partner, as we no doubt he is, joined the protest." The *Times* hoped, however, that marriage would not mean Lucy would abandon lecturing. News coverage of reformers would "lack their usual spice if she abandons the rostrum."[72]

In addition to the *New York Times*, several papers published the entire text of the "Protest," including the *Liberator*, the *Philadelphia Inquirer*, the *New Albany (Indiana) Daily Ledger*, South Carolina's *Charleston Courier*, and the *Jackson Citizen* of Jackson, Minnesota. The *Boston Daily Atlas* had no use for the document and noted sarcastically that it was a "singular and important omission, that there is no provision that Mr. Blackwell shall make his share of the baby clothes." The *New Albany Daily Ledger* denounced the protest and asked, "Who are Lucy Stone and Henry B. Blackwell that they can't be married in the simple, confiding, honest way of our fathers and others! . . . It is superb nonsense all around."[73] The paper hoped this would not give other couples similar ideas. As was common at the time, several papers borrowed word-for-word from one another, copying the same brief comments alluding to Henry's earlier involvement in the slave girl incident: "Retributive Justice—Blackwell, who choked the lady in the cars and robbed her of a servant girl, has been married to Miss Lucy Stone. Justice is sometimes slow, but always sure."[74] Predicting that marriage would impede Lucy's lecturing, the *Springfield Republican* warned: "the name of Miss Lucy Stone, the sweetest orator of reform conventions, who could roar you the hardest epithets as gently as a sucking dove—has been suddenly and unexpectedly extinguished by her becoming Mrs. Henry Blackwell."[75]

Naturally Henry's sisters continued to worry about their brother's situation. In September, Elizabeth wrote to Emily that the two of them were the "only sane ones in the family," and thus only they knew what was best for their brother. They worried that "Garrisonians, and reformer issues, and westernisms, and approbationess will really ruin the life of an excellent fellow." More to the point was Elizabeth's admission, "I have lost much of my former influence over him." She worried that Henry might head to Kansas where violence over the slavery issue was escalating. "The fellow is so carried away by the influence of those he is with," she added, suggesting that Lucy's commitment to abolition and women's rights could pull Henry into the fray. The sisters now hoped the two would move to England where Henry could find a suitable business and "not let him toil all his days for nothing. . . . He might become a healthier and more useful man than I fear he will ever be here," Elizabeth mused.[76]

Taking another step to remain an independent woman, Lucy decided to keep her maiden name. Although it generated little publicity at the time, this was an even bolder move than the wording of the "Protest." For the first year of married life, she went by "Blackwell," but in the spring of 1856, decided to revert to "Stone." Recalling the question she had asked her Oberlin professor, since no man ever took his wife's name, she thought, why should a woman automatically take the last name of her husband? This was another way in which a wife became subsumed under her husband. Henry had no objection to her doing so. A number of women reformers had compromised on this issue by using their full names, such as Elizabeth Cady Stanton, Angelina Grimké Weld, and Abby Kelley Foster, rather than being identified solely by their husband's surname. Lucy's decision was far more radical and not a step she took lightly. She consulted several eminent lawyers, including Salmon Chase of Ohio (later Lincoln's Secretary of the Treasury and then Chief Justice of the Supreme Court) and Samuel E. Sewall of Massachusetts, and found there was nothing illegal about keeping her maiden name.[77]

From that point forward, she was known as Lucy Stone, although for clarity and on legal documents and hotel ledgers she occasionally added "wife of Henry Blackwell" after her name. She first announced this at an antislavery meeting in the spring of 1856. While most women's rights reformers opposed her decision, Stanton, Anthony, and Higginson wrote to support her. Stanton reasoned that a woman's sense of self-respect demanded that she retain her name from birth to death.[78] Lucy took the decision so seriously that she became visibly upset when someone referred to her by "Blackwell." She never hesitated to correct those who called her "Mrs. Blackwell" either in public or in private. One time, when riding on a train, a neighbor spotted her and greeted her with, "How do you do, Mrs. Blackwell." "Lucy Stone if you please," was her chilly response.[79] When invited to lecture, she often reminded her host not to add Blackwell to her name on any publicity.[80]

Lucy's sensitivity about her name was especially evident in September 1856 when the *New York Tribune* listed her as Lucy Stone Blackwell on the call for that year's National Woman's Rights convention. "I feel grieved and hurt. It was so unjust, so cruel!" she wrote in despair to Anthony. Lucy's reaction was driven, in part, because she assumed that Anthony and Higginson, who had put out the convention call, were responsible for the mistake. To Anthony, Lucy wrote, "At New York last spring I had announced that I kept my own name. The public understood it. Newspaper criticism was nearly over, and the battle more than half fought." She seemed to have no mind of her own, and now had to fight this battle all over again. Lucy believed it would take years to correct the situation. "I have lost something which has darkened all my heavens," she wrote melodramatically.[81] The whole episode seemed almost more than she could bear. A letter from Anthony, however, cleared up the matter. She explained that Higginson had simply made an honest mistake. He apologized and said that he had been out of the country and apparently did not realize Lucy had changed her name. Still, tradition died hard, for some newspapers referred to her as Lucy Stone Blackwell in her obituaries decades later.

Despite all her worries during the lengthy courtship, Lucy found that marriage suited her well. Her relationship with Henry was far different than what Lucy had witnessed of her own father's relationship with her mother. Their early letters to one another when they were apart reveal a very affectionate Henry confessing, "I love you with my whole soul" and Lucy glowingly replying, "you are the best husband in the world" and that she was "more grateful than ever, that God has given me you to love, you and no one else."[82] Lucy found that as a married woman, she indeed could operate as an independent being. Only weeks after the wedding, she learned about a women's rights convention being held in Saratoga, New York. She asked Henry if she could attend. He responded that he did not need to give her permission; the person she should ask was Lucy. An astonished Lucy shared the incident with Anthony: "I can't get him to govern me at all!"[83]

While she did not let marriage interfere with her lecturing, Lucy was learning the joys and intimacy of a cozy home and loving spouse. After returning from a speaking tour, she admitted that life was far pleasanter at home than on the road. To her mother, she described Henry as "always kind and good and never gets in any way mad." In their early weeks together, she was learning to love and trust him. Besides their mutual interest in abolition and women's rights, the two shared a love of literature, and they often read to one another in the evenings or sat side by side, each engrossed in a book. "I grow more grateful of Harry's love. . . . I try to be a good wife—and I know he loves me very much," she confessed.[84] Months later Lucy wrote her father, describing Henry as one of the kindest men in all the world and from whom she had not yet heard any unpleasant words. To Anthony she commented on all that Henry was doing to support her: "God bless him! I can't tell you how infinitely dear he is to me."[85]

Yet Lucy's commitment to antislavery and to the women's rights movement remained undiminished, as was evident in February 1856 when she learned about an enslaved woman, Margaret Garner, who was being held in an Ohio jail while awaiting trial. Garner was a 23-year-old fugitive slave from Kentucky who had fled to southern Ohio with her husband, his parents, and the couple's four young children. The family members had scarcely made their way to Cincinnati when authorities found them. "When she saw that escape was impossible, [she] seized the little daughter, a child of great beauty, nearly three years old, and nearly severed her head from her body," Lucy explained. Before Garner could take the lives of her other children, authorities stopped her. "It was no wild desperation that had impelled her," reported Lucy, "but a calm determination that if she could not find freedom here, she would get it with the angels."[86]

Lucy met with Garner in prison and then delivered a speech to presiding Commissioner John L. Pendery and others at the hearing. She had asked Garner if she had possessed a knife to kill herself, would she choose to go to God or go back to slavery? Lucy told Pendery that Garner preferred "liberty with God to oppression with man." But her efforts did little good, and Lucy was distraught after the trial when Garner was returned to bondage and suffered a fate feared by all slaves: being shipped to the Deep South. Lucy used this tale in future speeches, claiming that if she ever found herself in a similar situation, "with the law against me, and society against me, and the church against me, and with no death-dealing weapon at hand," she announced, "I would with my own teeth tear open my veins and send my soul back to God who gave it."[87] A Virginia newspaper reflected what must have been a common southern reaction to the episode, denouncing Lucy's involvement in the trial and describing her as a "modern" female reformer who was "continually interfering with other people's business."[88]

Living in the Blackwell home during these first months of marriage, Lucy was as busy as ever, traveling and lecturing in towns and cities across the Midwest. In the fall of 1856, she spoke in Racine, Milwaukee, Madison, and Janesville, Wisconsin, spending two or three nights in each city. Compared to crowds in the East, though, attendance was sparse. Lucy blamed this on the many foreigners living there who evidenced little interest in reform.[89] A speech she delivered in Dayton, Ohio, she termed "pretty successful," but she was "<u>completely discouraged</u>" after speaking in Milwaukee. The city had a population of 35,000, but only 200 people came out to hear her. She found not a single soul in the state to circulate petitions on women's suffrage, so she did the work herself.[90] After submitting them to the Wisconsin state legislature, she found two "progressive" assemblymen who gave her momentary hope, for they promised to send the petitions on to a select committee. Lucy admitted she had never felt better "or capable of more work." Ever the realist, however, she cautioned, "We must learn to wait, as well as to labor." Apparently the petitions fostered a "rousing" discussion in the legislature, but ultimately only three politicians supported the radical idea. Predictably, Wisconsin legislators tabled the petitions.[91] Greater effort was needed to convince men there and everywhere to share political power with women.

Lucy's travels across the rural Midwest reminded her of how hardscrabble the lives of frontier women were. She shared her observations with Sarah, concluding that these women worked much harder than did the men. They were up and about only four days after giving birth. Some situations appalled her. For instance, one husband forced his wife, who had borne a daughter, to sleep in their outhouse all winter long while he enjoyed their warm cabin. His explanation was that "If she will have girls, cold is good enough for her." Lucy wryly concluded, "He is a very good specimen of the whole."[92]

For the first several years of married life, Lucy and Henry led a peripatetic existence as Henry sought work and managed land holdings in the Midwest. In May 1856, the couple temporarily settled in Viroqua, Wisconsin, a town comprised of some thirty shanties, located in an area where Henry held 6,000 acres of land. Traveling across 250 miles of frontier to get there was a challenge; living there proved even more of one. They found themselves removed from any cultural stimulation and far from people with whom they shared anything in common. To her father, Lucy described the beauty of the land and the abundant wildlife yet also wrote that she was miserable because settlers were so indifferent to abolition and to women's rights. After a few weeks, the couple gave serious thought to moving East. Henry admitted that they had grown "weary of this slipshod, scrambling, dissipated Western life." As soon as some of Henry's land sold, they planned to purchase a home in the East. These were difficult months, and Lucy acknowledged, "This wandering life is a wretchedly unnatural one."[93] She yearned for a home where they could engage in "self-improvement, with noble aims, and good resolutions coined into deeds."[94]

In late fall they packed up and moved east, with Lucy temporarily residing in West Brookfield with her parents and then with Sarah's family in Gardner and Henry staying in New York with Elizabeth while he looked for work and a home. The New York area was especially appealing because several Blackwell family members now lived there. Elizabeth and Emily both practiced medicine in New York, and Hannah and Marian had left Cincinnati and followed family members east. Surprising and pleasing nearly everyone was the marriage of Nette and Sam, which had taken place on January 24, 1856. Lucy was thrilled for both, writing that she hoped the marriage would "ripen to the richest fullness and prove for you what my love has to me, constantly more beatific, more soulful, more necessary."[95] Together, the two brothers studied business opportunities and real estate in and around New York, hoping to purchase homes in exchange for cash and some Wisconsin land. Ever the optimist, Henry wrote that while it was difficult to find work in such a crowded city, he believed business possibilities were limitless, New York "being the center of the whole Continent."[96]

In the midst of this upheaval, Lucy and Henry kept abreast of national events, especially the ongoing debates over the westward extension of slavery. Few Americans had anticipated that the 1854 Kansas-Nebraska Act would foster such outbursts of violence as proslavery and antislavery proponents settled in the territory. Adopting popular sovereignty to resolve the future of slavery there, the Act intensified the divided reactions in Congress and among the public over the possibility of southerners bringing their slaves into western territories. The 1820 Missouri Compromise now seemed mute. Men both in the North and in the South sensed much was at stake and urged settlers to populate Kansas in order to influence a future vote on the slave question there. The New England Immigrant Aid Company, organized in the summer of 1854, raised money to assist northerners moving to the territory, while slave owners, especially those living in Missouri, crossed the border into Kansas to stake out a home.[97] Each side established a territorial capital and government—northerners at Topeka and southerners at Lecompton—and each claimed the right to govern the region. Both sides tried to elect a delegate to Congress in a series of rowdy, fraudulent elections.

And then violence in Kansas and elsewhere grabbed the nation's attention. A group of southern ruffians attacked the abolitionist stronghold of Lawrence, Kansas, destroyed a newspaper office, and burned down buildings. In reaction, on May 23-24, 1856, the ardent (some say crazed) John Brown and his followers massacred five proslavery settlers at Pottawatomie. Many Americans were horrified by such brutality. A day later on the Senate floor, Congressman Preston Brooks of South Carolina, using his metal-tipped

cane, beat Massachusetts Senator Charles Sumner into a state of uncon-
sciousness because Brooks felt that Sumner's two-day antislavery speech,
"Crime Against Kansas," had insulted the South and the honor of Brook's
elderly cousin, South Carolina Senator Andrew Butler. Sumner survived the
attack but bore the scars for the rest of his life. Several weeks later, Lucy
wrote Anthony that "The Cause of Kansans and of the Country are still <u>our</u>
<u>Cause</u> even tho, we <u>are</u> disenfranchised & we shall suffer all its wrong." She
saw it in women's interest to help secure justice there.[98] Lucy and other
women reformers weighed the possible impact of the situation in Kansas on
their next convention. Higginson turned down an invitation to speak at
their fall meeting, for at that moment he saw antislavery as far more important than women's rights. Lucretia Mott and others concluded that the Kansas situation was so enormous it "will have no space for us."[99] Debates over
the extension of slavery were consuming the nation—and women.

"Bleeding Kansas" did become a theme at the 1856 national women's
rights convention in New York. Wendell Phillips used the opportunity to
deliver a spirited address, detailing how violence was harming not only men
but also affecting women living in the territory. Lucy composed a lecture
called "Border Ruffians at Home" in which she compared those in Kansas
who were trying to suppress free elections to men everywhere who tried to
prevent women from gaining the right to vote. In her eyes, all those who
opposed women's rights deserved to be labeled "border ruffians."[100]

Offering American women reformers a counterbalance to the situation in
Kansas was the growing interest among their sisters overseas who shared
their concerns. Women had been thrilled with Harriet Taylor Mill's 1851
essay and Jeanne Deroine's and Pauline Roland's support of American wom-
en's efforts. At the 1856 National Woman's Rights convention, Lucy listed
the many advances women had made since they held their 1850 national
meeting. Remarkable in her eyes was the global interest in "human equality."
She noted the petition that "noble" British women had submitted to Parliament, citing the work of Harriet Martineau, Elizabeth Barrett Browning,
and her sister-in-law, Anna Blackwell. Lucy concluded that the battle for
equality in Great Britain was even harder than theirs because of that country's entrenched class system. No petition by English women gained attention from men in Parliament unless it included the signatures and support of
upper-class women.[101]

Alongside Kansas and a greater global interest in women's rights, Henry
and Lucy had family issues to consider: buying a home, Henry's job, and,

finally, Lucy's pregnancy. That spring, Henry and Lucy purchased and moved into what was described as a "fine" gothic farm house in Orange, New Jersey, a two-story cottage with nine rooms on an acre of land. Emily visited them and was pleased, describing the "open fresh country and fine hills" and their house situated close to the "well built neat village" of Orange.[102] The purchase price was $5,000, nearly half of it paid for with Lucy's savings and the balance with a few hundred acres of Wisconsin land. They moved in April 1. Lucy was delighted. She was now living close to Blackwell family members and friends, a vibrant metropolitan area, and access to reliable transportation across the Northeast. She reported to her mother that she was "using her 'farm lessons'" to plant their large garden of potatoes, corn, peas, and pole beans and making her own bread dough, baked by a local baker for a penny a loaf.[103] Lucy and Henry spent many happy hours improving their new home.[104]

By the spring of 1856, however, Henry was becoming increasingly worried about land investments, especially uneasy about property he had purchased with Lucy's money. Feeling pressure to earn a living, in December Henry negotiated what seemed to be both a solid business investment and a new job, buying partial interest in the publisher C. M. Saxton & Company of New York and working as an agent selling agricultural books. His annual salary was $1,500, with a third of his wages going to pay interest on the $5,000 he had borrowed to invest in the business. The remaining $1,000 he earned covered annual household expenses, debts, and interest and taxes on western lands.[105] While Sam initially declared Henry's partnership a "safe" situation, within months another business partner left the firm, and Henry was unwilling or unable to buy out Saxton. By July 1857, the business, like thousands of others affected by the nation's sudden economic downturn that year, failed. Henry blamed himself for this bad investment. "I came into the firm without having an account of stock taken & was deceived in the results of the business," he explained. Henry was also startled to discover the company had made bad investments and was heavily in debt. He lost land worth $2,200 as well as some of Lucy's savings.[106] These financial worries seemed to be nothing new, for as Lucy admitted, "we have been and still are very 'hard up'—a chronic complaint with us."[107] To pay off interest and taxes on their land, Lucy borrowed $500 from an elderly female friend. Several of Lucy's letters to Henry's youngest brother George explained their dire situation as they struggled to repay the several hundred dollars they owed him.[108] Lucy helped ease their precarious financial situation by lecturing well into her pregnancy. Two months earlier, Henry had explained, "Poor Lucy proposes going away for three weeks" to lecture. "This she would not do but for our exceeding scarcity of money—and the urgent need for a well & cistern."[109]

Without a job and few prospects in the East, Henry's thoughts again turned westward, and in July 1857, he wrote George that if he could just spend three to five years out West, he could return a wealthy man. In typical male fashion, he asserted that Lucy would follow him anywhere, even to Wisconsin, if he asked her to do so. But Lucy was now seven months pregnant. "With a young infant with perhaps no help & in a log cabin," Henry explained, "a woman is not in an enviable position in a new country with the thermometer at 40 degrees below zero and the snow three feet deep." Instead of moving west, Henry searched for a position in New York or in New England that paid a decent salary.

Excitement over the birth of a child, however, tempered their worries. It had taken Lucy a while to conceive. Ten months into their marriage, Nette commented that Lucy was still without "any maternal prospects," much to "the regret of several people!" Nette knew Lucy and Henry loved one another, and, in veiled language typical of the time, she hoped "that this one tie to their union may yet be completed."[110] Lucy was eager to have children, had read about motherhood, and given serious thought to make that happen. Months after Lucy and Henry wed, when Anthony urged her to accept more invitations to lecture, Lucy responded, "I do not intend to lose my opportunity of securing the blessings of Motherhood. I shall only be absent when I know it is not possible, while I wait for results."[111] When Nettie conceived only months after her wedding, Lucy congratulated her but obviously regretted that she was not so fortunate. "For myself I almost despair," she admitted and then teased Nette, asking her, "Will you give me one of your seven"?[112] Months passed before conception occurred. Now Lucy's due date was September 1857.

Late into her pregnancy, Lucy remained active in antislavery and women's rights by working from home, but this was a challenge. In the spring of 1857, Anthony again turned to Lucy for her indispensable role in organizing the next national women's rights convention, selecting speakers, and determining where the meeting should be held. No doubt Anthony had become frustrated with her friend. Lucy delayed responding, most likely because of her pregnancy. Becoming excited about a convention was hard when carrying a baby and anticipating the possible dangers ahead. Knowing all too well the inherent risks of childbirth in mid-nineteenth-century America and recalling that Luther's wife Phebe had suffered a miscarriage and Lucy's sister Eliza had died in childbirth, both Lucy and Henry were anxious "until the crisis passes safely." In early August, Anthony wrote that while she rejoiced at Lucy becoming a Mother, "how I shall miss you." Anthony anticipated that motherhood would make the same demands on Lucy that it had made on Stanton and was now making on Nette, who had given birth to a daughter a few months earlier. Anthony could not imagine the movement without Lucy and Nette but closed her letter in a generous spirit, hoping Lucy would be "blessed with a second Lucy" and pass through "the ordeal of maternity & be saved to work on for humanity."[113] With Lucy unable to organize the next women's rights convention and with Lucretia Mott's sense that conventions had become repetitive and cost more than they brought in, the 1857 convention never took place.[114]

In early September, Henry was able to report that Lucy was "hoping for a happy release from the annoyances & discomforts of her present position in a few weeks." Less than two weeks later, on September 14 at 12:50 a.m., Henry exclaimed, "Lucy ushered into the world a brave, vigorous little girl." Emily came out from New York to attend the birth. Henry described the healthy baby as having dark blue eyes and black hair who immediately made herself known to the world by adopting "as her own Mr. Garrison's celebrated motto which hangs underneath his portrait at the side of our bed, vis 'I will not equivocate; I will not conceal; I will not recede a single inch & I will be heard!!!!'" He reported that mother and daughter were doing well.[115] The baby initially remained nameless, and for more than a year was called "Sarah" in honor of Lucy's sister. Finally, however, Henry and Lucy settled on "Alice" as her name—Alice Stone Blackwell.

If marriage had altered Lucy's life to some degree, the birth of a baby transformed it. Like all new mothers, Lucy found the responsibilities of nursing and caring for an infant exhausting and unremitting. Breastfeeding and infant care kept her homebound.[116] During her first two years, Alice suffered numerous illnesses that were all too common among infants and young children in nineteenth-century America. In late November, however, in a fairly typical remark, Henry wrote that the baby had a cold but was "fat and flourishing," while Lucy was weary "with the never ending labor of nursing."[117]

Two months after giving birth, Lucy decided to do something significant while tied to home. Like writer and Transcendentalist Henry David Thoreau had done in 1846 when refusing to pay his taxes, Lucy engaged in a similar act of civil disobedience—an especially bold gesture for a woman. She carried through on an earlier threat she had made not to pay her city taxes since she could not vote. Dr. Harriot Hunt of Boston had been doing this for several years, questioning why women property owners had to pay taxes when they had no voice in their government. Lucy wrote the tax collector of Orange, New Jersey, in January 1858, hoping he would understand the injustice of the law. The current policy was unjust to one half of the adult population and contradicted the nation's concept of government, Lucy argued. The city tax collector did not see it that way. When Lucy refused to pay the money she owed, the town constable seized several household goods—two tables, four chairs, and engraved portraits of Garrison and Salmon P. Chase—and sold all of them at public auction to pay the taxes. As had been planned in advance, a sympathetic neighbor purchased the items, and Lucy bought them back. Lucy declared that she would do the same thing next year and every year thereafter until the law changed.[118] That, however, did not happen.

Lucy's action generated a good deal of publicity, though ultimately had no impact on the law. The *New York Times* criticized her for making such a scene. The entire gesture seemed like a "sham" since friends were waiting in the wings to purchase her furniture. One reader took this opportunity also to criticize Lucy for refusing to take her husband's last name, questioning if she even had the right to claim she was married. A couple of weeks later, another *Times* article expressed disapproval that Lucy and Harriot Hunt were using non-payment of taxes to demand women's right to vote, though the writer ignored or forgot that New England's patriots had made this same case against the British in the 1770s. He added that society might feel less admiration for women "if all women [were] like them."[119]

Such notoriety notwithstanding, motherhood imposed new demands on Lucy, and her situation became even more difficult when Alice was less than six months old. Henry left for Chicago in early March to work as a book agent, selling books for A. O. Moore & Co., run by his friend Augustus Moore. Living in Chicago also would allow Henry to keep better track of their western lands. His departure left Lucy alone to care for Alice over the next five months. What discussion took place in advance of Henry's lengthy absence is unknown, but earlier promises to one another to allow independence of action meant that Lucy must have seen this as Henry's right, whatever hardships it imposed on her. An important factor, of course, was that they needed money. While Lucy devoted herself to caring for sickly Alice, Henry became consumed by his new job.[120]

Lucy had anticipated a return to lecturing after Alice's birth but found that she had little time or energy to prepare speeches or to travel. Also, she was reluctant to leave Alice. Finding a capable baby nurse who met Lucy's high standards was a challenge, though Hannah Blackwell sometimes came to assist her.[121] On April 22, 1858, Lucy did join three of the country's most renowned male lecturers—lawyer James Topham Brady, author George William Curtis, and clergyman Edwin Hubbell Chapin—to speak on "The Future of Woman in America" in New York as part of a series to benefit the Shirt-Sewers' and Seamstresses' Union.[122] Lucy regarded this as a most worthwhile cause since thousands of women were working in deplorable conditions in sweatshops, earning barely enough to stay alive. Anthony, who often exhibited little patience with fellow reformers marrying and bearing children, wrote Nette when she heard the news, fussing that Lucy was ill-prepared to present this lecture, being "tired and worn" by baby care and having no time to engage in "careful, close continued intellectual effort." Lucy, however, did just fine. The *New York Times* was quite complimentary, claiming that Lucy was the only speaker to be "sincere and hearty."[123]

Figure 24. Lucy Stone with Alice Stone Blackwell, 1858 (LC-USZ62–13,524, Library of Congress, Washington, DC)

But such speech-making was rare. And when Anthony wrote and complained about the demands she was experiencing on the lecture circuit, Lucy found it difficult to be empathic while she cared for an infant. "You are tired with four months work," she countered. "If you had measles and whooping cough added to all you have done, it would not be half as hard as the taking care of a child day and night is. I know. I shall not take any responsibility about another convention till I have had my ten daughters."[124] During the summer months, while Henry was gone, she and Alice spent several weeks in West Brookfield and Gardner visiting her parents and sister. No doubt Lucy appreciated the help she received in caring for Alice.

Despite Henry's steady income, money worries continued to haunt the couple. In the spring of 1858, Augustus Moore advanced Henry six months' salary to ease him through financial demands that included interest payments and taxes owed on western lands. Henry also cashed in Lucy's remaining bank stock. He felt guilty about using her savings, admitting to George that he did so only "because my honor is implicated & I feel not at liberty to refuse."[125] He hoped to be able to repay her in full. Lucy was far less troubled by this than was Henry, and she reassured him, "If you knew how freely I part with it, I am sure you would accept it cheerfully."[126] Befitting their ideals of a true companionate marriage meant sharing assets. And a generous spirit to Lucy was a far cry from the behavior of her tight-fisted father. Ever hopeful, Henry imagined some of their land would soon sell since immigrants were pouring into the region.

This prolonged, five-month separation was hard on both of them, but especially on Lucy. She often commented on her exhausting days and sleepless nights but also regretted that Henry was missing the magical moments of Alice's physical growth and development. Henry's musings revealed how much he missed Lucy and the baby, and he repeatedly vowed never again to be away from the family for such a long time. "Dear Lucy, if you only could know and realize all I feel for you—you would know that we are <u>married</u> in soul and forever." Dreams of rejoining his family came over him "as sweet as the breath of flowers," though he felt his contribution to Moore's firm was "indispensable." At the same time, he admitted that he hated the separation and cursed the "library business, my own folly and western lands, the root of all evil."[127] Henry engaged in some soul-searching and admitted that he had kept Lucy in an "<u>unsatisfied</u>" situation by moving constantly, allowing her "no rest or permanent home" and being "a drag instead of a helpmate to you." Ever seeking his dream to become a more perfect individual, he thought long and hard about his character. Inspired by reading Washington Irving's biography of George Washington, Henry explained how much he admired the nation's first president, who had learned to control "all his wanderings and irregular impulses and to move onwards in a steady, constant, noble life," traits that eluded Henry. "Lucy dear, I have it in me—you shall help me to bring it out."[128]

Lucy missed Henry and did a good deal of soul-searching of her own during his absence, fretting she had not been the best of wives. She hoped he knew how hard she had been trying to be a good wife and mother, "but I have tried before and my miserable failures hitherto make me silent now. But if I have conquered myself or gained anything in all these weary weeks you will find it in my actions." She yearned for them to become a model family.[129] Ever optimistic, Henry fully expected Moore's book firm to turn a profit, anticipating he would then receive a third of the profits, and their money worries would end.[130] But working so hard also caused him to admit that he was tired of the struggle.[131] By late June, not until Henry's job had almost ended, did Lucy feel comfortable in confessing, "in no other absence have I ever felt your loss so much, never so longed for you, never needed you, as I have these four weary months." In response to Henry's suggestion that she rest, a testy-sounding Lucy retorted, "No one who takes care of a baby can rest."[132]

By late June, Henry boasted that his presence had saved Moore's business from failing, and he was bringing his duties to a "wonderfully and unexpectedly successful" end. In assessing his contributions to the company, Henry reconceived his original motive for taking the job, now representing it as a selfless, rather than a money-making, gesture. He claimed to have accepted the job because Moore needed him.[133] He could have stayed on, but that would have meant moving the family to Chicago or longer absences from home. As he left Chicago, Henry wrote Lucy that he felt satisfaction with the "very great and almost inestimable service" he had performed. But he longed to be home and hoped he and Lucy could climb New Hampshire's Mount Monadnock together.[134]

Despite Henry's success as a book agent, his and Lucy's financial situation remained in jeopardy. They were land-rich and cash-poor, for their western properties were not selling as anticipated, especially following the recession of 1857. Besides the property taxes and interest on loans that Henry owed, some of the purchased land had not been properly surveyed and filed, and legal challenges to land claims poured in, which demanded time and money to sort out.

In order to save money, in August 1858 Lucy and Henry exchanged the Orange, New Jersey, home for twenty acres of land and what Sam described as "a dilapidated" farm house in West Bloomfield (later Montclair), New Jersey, lowering their annual mortgage by $600. As Sam observed, the unimproved land was beautiful but the house practically uninhabitable.[135] Writing to her father, Lucy made an effort to be cheerful about the move, describing the land as having good fruit trees and three building sites. Being a mile from town pleased Lucy. They planned to rent out one house on the land for $50 a year and their pasture land to local farmers for $4 a week.[136] A month after they moved, Henry developed a painful boil on his nose, and Lucy became more worn down with nursing him and one-year-old Alice while living in a ramshackle house.[137]

In early December 1858, their living situation changed again. In order to be closer to the property they owned and for Henry again to work temporarily as a book agent for Augustus Moore, the three moved to Chicago and rented out their West Bloomfield home. There they lived in a boarding house. The upheaval had to be hard on everyone. In February 1859, Henry reported that while business was slow and times were hard, he had placed 125 book orders. And Lucy was pregnant again.

During this pregnancy, Lucy faced a crisis as her confidence in her speaking ability waned. In February 1859 from Chicago, Lucy admitted to Nette that she wished she felt "the old impulse and power to lecture" as she had in the past, both to promote the principles she embraced and to aid the family financially. But she also knew "I dare not trust Lucy Stone." After hearing a speech one evening, she considered the possibility of returning to the lecture circuit. "But when I came home and looked in Alice's sleeping face and thought of the possible evil that might befall her if my guardian eye was turned away, I shrank like a snail into its shell." Likely exhaustion, hormonal changes, and mood swings during the first trimester of her pregnancy exacerbated such reactions. She realized that "for these years, I can only be a mother—no trivial thing either."[138] She was torn. Her commitment to motherhood and her desire to lecture and sway minds as she had done in years past affected her deeply. Lucy did what she could to help organize the 1859 National Woman's Rights convention in New York, though she acknowledged that she could not attend or take full responsibility for the meeting.

The family planned to spend an enjoyable summer, and they settled north of Chicago in the town of Evanston. But tragedy interrupted this pleasant summer when in July, Lucy gave birth to a premature seven-month-old baby boy who did not survive. This was a devastating loss to Lucy and Henry, since both had wanted another child. Lucy wrote little about this tragedy and shared the news of the infant's death with few others. She had no one to console her—no mother, sister, or close female friend—except Henry, who was also dealing with the loss. Finding strength in her faith, Lucy rationalized the baby's death, writing, "He is garnered from all harm. The circle widens on the other side, that will welcome us when we go."[139] Nette, who had also lost her second baby, a four-month-old daughter, to what was called cholera infantum, empathized with Lucy and urged her to share her loss with others. She reasoned that Lucy's friends would better understand why she had temporarily shut herself off from the world. "I think every body who is so anxious to have Lucy speak again would feel better if they knew how impossible that has been and still must be for the present," Nette commented. She closed, "I know how it has made your heart ache to lose so many new hopes."[140] Henry, Lucy, and Alice moved back to New Jersey late that summer and for a time, Henry sold real estate.[141] For the next three years, Lucy devoted herself to caring for Alice. No doubt the loss of their baby boy made her more determined than ever to be an attentive parent to their only child. She proved to be just that, for as Nette later observed, Lucy was "an almost too careful and self-sacrificing a mother."[142]

Lucy did recover and briefly returned to the stage on February 2, 1860, sharing the podium with one of the nation's most famous ministers, Henry Ward Beecher, and delivering a speech at the Cooper Institute in New York on "Woman's Rights and Woman's Wrongs." The timing was perfect, for the New York legislature was currently debating a more liberal married women's property rights bill. On that very same stage less than four weeks later, Abraham Lincoln delivered a powerful speech that defined his stance on slavery and did much to enhance his national standing.[143]

In her talk, Lucy sought to clarify the women's movement, for too many people misunderstood what it sought to achieve and too few women understood the laws that kept them oppressed. She tied women's duties to the antislavery movement, calling women "educators of the race" who had to act on their "God given responsibilities" to abolish slavery. Since men and women stood equal before the eyes of God, should they not stand "equal before human laws"? she asked. One newspaper reporter covering the event recounted that it was difficult to connect this Lucy Stone to the Lucy Stone of the past. "The bright cheeks were there, the girlish figure, the musical voice; but the old assurance, the perfect self-poise, the rapid, confident, slightly saucy utterance, were all wanting." It was not what Lucy said but how she said it that surprised him. The writer concluded, "The mother's heart has dissolved the woman's voice, and what was once pertness is now pathos; what it has lost in vigor it has gained in tenderness." He felt that Antoinette Brown Blackwell had experienced a similar change in her speaking ability, and both women, now mothers, were "more subdued and womanly." He observed that Lucy stood on the stage "blushing and trembling" as she had never done in years past.[144]

Another tragedy in Lucy's life was the death of her mother on September 14, 1860, Alice's third birthday. During that summer, Lucy and Alice had spent weeks in West Brookfield caring for Hannah as she was "sinking away." Lucy described her mother's passing as painless and peaceful. For Lucy, who had loved her mother so deeply, the loss caused her profound sorrow. She wrote Henry, who had remained in New York, wishing he were with her to tend her "bruised" heart. She shared the love she always felt for her mother, appreciating her generous spirit and her "wealth of truths." The Stone siblings held a funeral for Hannah. Lucy and Alice then stayed on for several more days to comfort her father, whom Lucy described as "old, alone."[145] For the rest of her life, Lucy thought fondly of her mother. She sensed that when she was born, her mother was sorry to have another girl "to share and bear the hard life of a woman," but concluded, "I am wholly glad that I came, and she is too, if she sees."[146]

Days after Hannah's funeral, Lucy attended a meeting in Worcester on September 19, convened by Stephen Foster, to consider the idea of forming a new political party that would focus on abolition. A number of passionate abolitionists were dissatisfied with the four candidates running for president in the 1860 election. The Democratic Party had split into three factions with three candidates, suggesting a possible victory for Republicans. Yet the Republican candidate, Abraham Lincoln, was not committed to end slavery. He supported his party's platform, wanting to prevent slavery from spreading westward but leaving it intact in southern states. Foster's meeting proved a disappointment, with only one invited speaker supporting Foster's idea. Lucy spoke and urged everyone to avoid all political engagements.[147]

But good news occurred toward the end of the decade when the women's movement received major contributions from two generous donors. Women reformers had eked by for almost a decade, paying for conventions and publishing tracts as best they could. Now that situation changed. The first of

Figure 25. Hannah Matthews Stone (Schlesinger Library, Radcliffe Institute, Harvard University)

these contributions was an anonymous gift of $5,000 (later disclosed to be from Francis Jackson, a strong supporter of abolition and women's rights) to publish tracts, pay lecturers, and "obtain equal civil and social position for woman." From his considerable fortune, Jackson also left Lucy, Abby Kelley Foster, and several other abolitionists $100 each "as a token of esteem for their fidelity to moral principle, and their devotion to the cause of human freedom."[148] Wendell Phillips was appointed trustee of the funds.[149] The next year, Charles F. Hovey, a reformer and successful department store owner in Boston, set up a $50,000 trust fund to aid the antislavery movement, free religion, and women's suffrage. The Jackson and Hovey gifts gave women a sound financial basis to carry on their work. Lucy hoped some of the money could be used to challenge state laws that taxed women property owners but refused to let them vote.[150] Other women suggested they use the money to publish and distribute more tracts, while some felt the money should generously compensate lecturers at their conventions. Over the years, the money supported a variety of projects.

While these bequests were welcome news, Lucy and other activists were discouraged when confronting women who remained indifferent or hostile to suffrage and to women's rights in general. Too many regarded politics as nasty business and evidenced no desire to vote. Some believed that an expansion of their rights would undermine women's privileged place in the home and their dependence on men. Typical was Anna Raymond of Mystic, Connecticut, who wrote her local paper about Lucy's supposedly "brilliant" speech on "Woman's Rights and Woman's Wrongs." Who would take care of the children or cook supper on Election Day if women were out voting? she wondered. While some women might want to vote, many would not, "if it is half as rowdy on election days as the men report." Instead, Raymond heralded the latest female fashions, especially huge new bonnets and a welcome return to hoop skirts.[151] As Lucretia Mott aptly summarized statements such as Raymond's: "So circumscribed have been her limits that she does not realize the misery of her condition." Elizabeth Cady Stanton was more disheartened by this situation. "It is most humiliating to know that many educated women so stultify their consciences as to declare they have all the rights they want," she observed. They seemed to have no idea about the many "barbarous laws" that constricted their lives, and they had lost all sense of self-respect.[152] This made Lucy ever more determined that when she lectured, she would make women feel such discomfort with their inferior status that they would demand that laws and traditions be changed.

The 1850s had proved a transformative decade in Lucy's life. She had achieved national renown as an orator for antislavery and for women's rights and had become one of the most famous women in America. She was a pivotal figure in organizing national women's rights conventions. She married a man who loved her and who treated her as his equal. She had become a mother and temporarily withdrawn from an active role in the two major reform issues that had been the focus of her life. Being a mother to Alice was her most important responsibility right now. But events in the country at large would eventually draw Lucy back fully into the fray.

6

War and Division, 1861–1869

While the Civil War was perhaps the most transformative event in American history, it had little impact on the women's movement. A number of activists had hoped the war would offer women the possibility of achieving suffrage and full citizenship. That did not happen. Instead, for four years reformers shifted their attention from demanding women's rights to working for Union victory and the abolition of slavery. When President Abraham Lincoln called for 75,000 Union troops after the bombardment of Fort Sumter in Charleston Harbor on April 12, 1861, northern women cancelled their national convention, which had been planned for May. Susan B. Anthony confessed to being "sick at heart" as women put their campaign on hold.[1] In fact, throughout the war, no national women's rights convention was held. Instead, as we shall see, it was Reconstruction that drew women into major debates as Congress passed three constitutional amendments to give black men citizenship and suffrage rights. Passage of these landmark amendments and their implications profoundly altered—and ultimately divided—the women's movement.

Initially, it was the nation that was divided. The growing acrimony between North and South over the possible westward extension of slavery and Lincoln's election in November 1860 precipitated the exit of seven southern states from the Union. In February 1861 they formed the Confederate States of America; within weeks, four other southern states joined them. In the months between Lincoln's election and his inauguration, few efforts were made to deal with the secession crisis. The situation in the North became increasingly volatile, at times even dangerous. A number of people faulted abolitionists, with their strident voices and radical agenda, for worsening the crisis. Mobs challenged Anthony and Stanton as they lectured in upstate New York. Henry Stanton urged his wife to cease public speaking, worried that she was risking her life by addressing "mobocrats" who "would as soon kill you as not."[2]

But the threat of danger did not stop Lucy. In early January 1861, she left three-year-old Alice in the care of Henry's sisters and traveled to the Midwest to lecture. She and Henry needed money, and Lucy needed what public speaking could give her—self-esteem and a focus for her life. In Fort Wayne, Indiana, she delivered her first major speech since Alice was a baby. From Dayton, Ohio, she happily reported that all three of her lectures were a success. "I am so glad to find again the old inspiration and it came to me more and more," she commented. Press coverage was positive, and Lucy cleared $130 after expenses. Being far from home made her feel lonely. "Every night when I lie down," she wrote Henry, "I do miss the sheltering love of your arms." She brought along the Christmas present Henry had given her—a volume of William Cullen Bryant's poems, which she suggested the two of them read together when she returned home in late February.[3]

The war did prompt women to take action to support the Union. Within days after the war began, Elizabeth Blackwell announced plans to organize volunteer relief efforts to aid Union soldiers and to create a capable nursing corps. The war, in her mind, could open new opportunities for women. On April 26, 1861, she and a number of others convened a meeting in Cooper Union in New York to discuss ideas. Addressing the 4,000 people who turned out, Elizabeth Blackwell announced the formation of the Woman's Central Association for Relief (WCAR). Twenty-four men and women were appointed to serve on its board of managers and coordinate soldiers' aid societies and women's volunteer efforts.[4]

Two months later, the United States Sanitary Commission (USSC) formed under the leadership of landscape architect and journalist Frederick Law Olmsted and Unitarian minister Henry Whitney Bellows. They were anything but enlightened about women's potential and what the WCAR could accomplish. Olmsted wrote Bellows that caring for the sick and wounded was "not a feminine business. It must have a masculine discipline" or it was doomed to fail.[5] Nonetheless, the USSC sought to encourage and coordinate volunteer efforts, including those involving women, to support the war. Over time, the USSC hired hundreds of agents to oversee some seven thousand local associations. As historian Nina Silber writes, the two volunteer organizations—the WCAR and the USSC—"coexisted in an at times uneasy working alliance" throughout the war.[6]

Despite Olmsted's views, women on the home front proved vital to the Union war effort. Thousands of volunteers performed charitable work, rolling bandages, sewing, knitting, and collecting food and medical supplies to

Figure 26. Elizabeth Blackwell (LC-USZ62–57,850, Library of Congress, Washington, DC)

send to hospitals and to soldiers on the battle front. In many communities, women organized and held what were called "sanitary fairs" where they sold food and homemade goods in order to raise money and to heighten people's patriotism and commitment to the cause. Some of the larger fairs, including those held in major cities such as Chicago, New York, and Philadelphia, were amazingly successful, raising hundreds of thousands of dollars.[7] Philadelphia's 1864 Great Central Fair held in Logan Square was six months in the planning, and during the three weeks it was open, raised over a million dollars.[8] Women also held dramatic and musical productions and tableaux vivants to raise money. For instance, members of the Soldiers Aid Society in Cleveland, Ohio, put on two evenings of "charming musical performances" and tableaux that were described as "superb."[9] With so many men serving in the military, women also moved into paid jobs formerly held by men, laboring as nurses, teachers, government clerks, and factory workers.[10] A few hundred women even dressed in drag and joined the Army; others such as former slave Harriet Tubman, who escorted some 300 slaves to freedom, and actress Pauline Cushman, were willing to serve as Union spies.[11] Hundreds of thousands of women in the Union and Confederacy became full-time farmers, planting and harvesting crops to feed their families and to supply surplus food to the military.

There is no indication, however, that Lucy showed real interest in any of these activities, in part because the war did not directly affect her family, although she did keep abreast of wartime events. Henry, his brothers, and Lucy's two brothers never served in the military. Also, it was all too clear to Lucy that both Democrats and Republicans had no interest in supporting women's suffrage, so she had no interest in politics. Her correspondence declined during these four years, for without women's rights conventions to organize and with only limited lecturing opportunities, there were few reasons to write letters. The war did affect Lucy and Henry's relationship, however, for they lived apart for long stretches of time. Henry had to earn a living, and Lucy had to care for Alice and various family members.

Lucy's main wartime contribution was her involvement in a new organization that demanded an end to slavery. In the spring of 1863, while Lucy, Henry, and Alice boarded in a house near Gramercy Park in New York, she, Stanton, and Anthony presided over the creation of the Woman's Loyal National League (WLNL).[12] Following Lincoln's Emancipation Proclamation on January 1, 1863, northern women realized they needed to push the government to emancipate slaves and to support the Union war effort. Even among some Republicans, interest in the war was flagging as it dragged on and the body count rose. Their idea was to organize associations of women throughout the Union, organizations that would work for these goals in a nonpartisan manner, meaning without direct association with any politician or party. In part because most of the war was fought on southern soil and a larger percentage of southern men were fighting, Confederate women, they argued, were demonstrating greater dedication to the cause than were northern women. As Stanton pointed out, "they see and feel the horrors of the war; the foe is at their firesides; while we, in peace and plenty, live and move as heretofore."[13] Northern women had to rally. She called for the first meeting of the WLNL.[14]

That meeting took place in Cooper Union on May 14, 1863, a two-day event which one newspaper characterized as "thinly attended."[15] This was the first convention Lucy had been to in several years, but she was chosen president and took charge as best she could. Along with Ernestine Rose, Angelina Grimké Weld, Anthony, Nette, and others, she addressed the crowd, urging women to view themselves as "educators of the race" and to act on their "God given responsibilities" to abolish slavery.[16] But those who were present held conflicting ideas on what the WLNL should try to accomplish. Some felt that supporting the war effort should be its only goal, for that would attract the broadest support. Others urged the organization to demand an end to slavery and to fight for the rights of slaves and former slaves. The most contentious issue was whether or not to add women's suffrage to the agenda. Some saw this as a distraction. Others like Lucy and Ernestine Rose defended the idea. Lucy harkened back to the country's origins and to the mistake the founding fathers had made when they condoned slavery by protecting it in the Constitution and letting "the wretched monster live." In the same way, she argued, the WLNL could not be truly loyal if it ignored women. "Leave them out and we take the same backward step that our fathers took when they left out slavery."[17] Ultimately, the convention resolved to stand behind Lincoln's 1863 Emancipation Proclamation, despite its limitations, and to promote political and civil equality of "all citizens of African descent and all women."[18] Despite these lofty pronouncements, not everyone felt the meeting had been a success. Garrison grumbled that it was almost impossible to hear any of the women speakers, and he called the meeting "almost a dead failure" by becoming a women's rights convention.[19]

Undaunted, the WLNL leadership set up headquarters in Cooper Union and composed a pledge for women to sign. Members promised to support the war so long as the government made it a war to end slavery. An artist designed a membership badge that depicted a slave breaking his chains. The organizers planned to hire twelve lecturers in groups of four—with at least one black man, one white man, and one woman in each corps of four speakers—to spread their message across the Northeast and Midwest. Lucy had done little public speaking since the late 1850s, but she was still at the top of the list. "I know the old fires are in her—or, if not the <u>old ones</u>—still brighter and grander ones," Anthony commented in a letter to Stanton. The Committee would write her and "may the powers of all the good & true & earnest help her to say <u>yes</u>."[20]

Almost immediately, the WLNL undertook a petition drive to collect a million signatures and to submit the petition to Congress demanding an immediate end to slavery. Anthony took charge of this colossal effort, appointing some 2,000 volunteers to obtain signatures from different regions across the North.[21] The organization submitted its first 100,000 signatures by February 1864, with Massachusetts Senator Charles Sumner celebrating what women had accomplished thus far. And the work continued.[22] By the war's end, women had gathered some 400,000 signatures, an impressive number though well below their ambitious goal. Canvassers discovered that many in the North did not support abolition, fearing the impact freed slaves might have on the welfare of the nation. What would these people do? Where would they go? Others felt the petition merely replicated the Emancipation Proclamation. And still others rejected the petition outright, believing that women engaged in an activity of this kind had moved out of their proper domestic sphere. Nevertheless, these efforts had a significant impact on Congress. Sumner presented the petitions to his colleagues, pointing out to them that never had so many signatures been secured proving Americans in the North detested slavery. The campaign revealed that the Union was willing to wage a war to free slaves, giving politicians and Lincoln greater support to push for emancipation. Eric Foner asserts that the Thirteenth Amendment to end slavery forever, eventually passed by Congress in January 1865, "originated not with Lincoln but with a petition campaign" undertaken by the WLNL.[23]

Lucy only engaged in limited public speaking during the war and only some of it on behalf of the WLNL. In December 1863, she addressed the American Anti-Slavery Society's convention in Philadelphia's Concert Hall, part of a celebration of the organization's third decade. A local paper dismissed the meeting as the most "strangely constituted" it had ever witnessed, being comprised of "semi-feminine men and strong-minded women." It went on to describe what it called the weird attire and odd hair styles of black and white "big gun" lecturers as well as of those in the audience. The paper added that the hall was only half full. Garrison's *Liberator* was far more charitable in its assessment. Reporting on Lucy's speech, the paper noted excitedly that "after her long silence, [she] spoke as naturally as if she had never lost a day's practice."[24]

Out of necessity, Henry and Lucy lived apart for significant portions of the war. Henry continued to seek paid work. He had hoped to find a job with the Lincoln administration but, unsuccessful, had to take what he could get. He dabbled in real estate and then worked as a clerk and salesman for Dennis Harris's Congress Steam Sugar Refinery in New York. He moved into the city while Lucy and Alice stayed in West Bloomfield. Lucy oversaw the landscaping and planting of fruit trees, a cherry orchard, and a vegetable garden. She also nursed Marian and Hannah when they became ill.[25] Henry spent some time at home in the spring and summer of 1862, and he and Lucy entertained a number of guests, including Ainsworth Spofford and his wife and Elizabeth and Theodore Tilton who visited in early June. In August, nearly every member of the Blackwell family in the New York area paid them a visit.[26] Following in his father's footsteps, Henry convinced his boss to try to produce sugar out of beets. In mid-summer, he traveled to Ohio to investigate the possibility of sugar beet production in that state and to locate farmers who might grow them. He planned to remain there until early February, claiming the work was "absorbing" and took "every minute of my available time."[27]

Despite what seemed to be a stable family life and Henry now employed, the Blackwell sisters continued to worry about their brother. When Henry was home in August 1862, Elizabeth despaired—yet again—over his "imperfect character, his imprudence, his speculativeness, his restless unsatisfied aspirations." She had never approved of Lucy and now concluded that the marriage had "linked two excellent but unsuitable natures together." Nonetheless, the two were fairly happily married, and she concluded rather spitefully that Henry "must take life as it comes to him, or as he has made it."[28] The sisters also worried about their brother's physical and mental health. Emily fretted over Henry's job, feeling that Dennis Harris was taking advantage of him and using him "for all the public peddling & puffing of his business in a way which is very undesirable." She predicted that the business association would end within a year. Emily understood that Henry's optimism carried him through trying times, for invariably he felt the next opportunity would provide him the income and satisfaction he craved. When a job possibility opened in Washington, DC, Emily opposed this change of locale, knowing it would not subdue his restless nature. His "property entanglements" also meant he could not leave, and she knew Lucy would not go, presumably because she refused to live any place where slavery had recently been legal.[29]

During the war, West Brookfield and Gardner, Massachusetts, proved welcome escapes for Lucy, and she went as often as she could, prompted by family needs, her desire for quiet, and for welcome visits with Sarah. In the summer of 1861, Lucy and Alice spent several weeks in West Brookfield. There, Lucy suffered from boils that broke out all over her body. To Henry she described the large boils that had erupted on her body. "You won't find me very attractive. I am red and corpulent and covered with sores, Will you want a divorce?" she teased.[30] In May 1862 Lucy and Alice visited again, and this time Lucy's migraines returned. Henry joined them in mid-summer. Lucy and Alice returned to West Brookfield during the summer of 1863

while work was being done on their New Jersey home. A lonely Henry
confessed to Lucy that their home "is no longer home without you." He
oversaw renovations while staying with his mother in New York.[31] In writing Lucy, he described the satisfying time he was spending with his mother,
gossiping and sharing tales of the past, though he wished she had been there.
He also worried about the bad weather affecting New England that summer
when Lucy and Alice visited Cape Cod. His letter closed, "With truest love
and good wishes dearest wifekin."[32]

In 1864, Lucy and Alice settled in West Brookfield and Gardner for six
months. This proved an especially trying time for Lucy. Her father was seriously ill and nearly blind. Reading, which had been one of his favorite pas-
times, was now impossible, and Lucy realized he had little to live for.[33]
Spending days in the Stone farmhouse was hard on her, for she felt like a
stranger even in the room where she was born.[34] Her father's condition
worsened, and she and her siblings took turns nursing him.

In early fall, Lucy rented a home in Gardner and enrolled Alice in a common school there. She again felt a profound loss of confidence in her ability

Figure 27. Francis Stone (Schlesinger Library, Radcliffe Institute, Harvard
University)

to lecture. Having delivered only a few speeches over the past several years, she again wondered if she could ever be the inspiring speaker she had been in the past. Compounding her self-doubt was her struggle with menopause, which had a significant effect on her emotional state. Lucy seemed to suffer severely from this life change, experiencing depression and mood swings which likely heightened her loss of confidence. During a time before doctors could do much to alleviate or lighten the symptoms of menopause, Lucy had to suffer through these hormonal changes.[35]

The peaceful, rural surroundings, however, proved an antidote to these miseries. In mid-summer she wrote Anthony that her headaches were nearly gone, as was "the mental confusion that has so tormented before. The quiet of the farm—the old associations, —the total change, are worth a world to me and if I can only survive the inevitable change of constitution and be right side up, at the end of it, I shall pray again for the return of the great impulse that drove me into the world, with words that <u>must</u> be spoken." She planned to lecture but only when her self-confidence returned and "my feet are firm under me."[36] This was a far different Lucy from the woman who had lectured with such passion and self-assurance and stirred audiences a decade earlier.

Amidst the tranquility of rural Massachusetts, there was much to keep her busy. Lucy's days were filled with cooking, washing, ironing, cleaning, and instructing Alice an hour each day. She also found time to write Henry frequently. Their absence seemed to make her heart grow fonder. In July 1864 she expressed how much she missed him and was sad that he had not written recently. She imagined he was enjoying himself as he vacationed with friends on New Jersey's Lake Hopatcong. "I have felt very near to you all day, darling, dear, and have wandered around . . . glad that in all the world, no one is so dear to me as you—and thankful, for this strange union, which draws me by pleasant, tender ties to you." She urged them both to correct their faults and "let us be made perfect, not through suffering, but through love." She could imagine no better husband than he was and knew she would rather live with him than with anyone else. "But we will abide our lot, this year— save what we can—and gain strength, & courage, and patience, and hope, and all graces & virtues, for future use."[37] Yet one can't help but wonder if Lucy felt a bit envious that Henry was happily vacationing with friends as she cared for her dying father and confronted her waning confidence.

Lucy sensed that her troubled state of mind had been hard on their marriage but also felt that their current separation and peaceful surroundings were proving restorative. To Henry she explained, "Here, with fewer cares, & almost nothing to vex me, I hope to get back, somewhere near to the state of soul & spirit, in which I was, when you first found me." She ultimately hoped they could "come nearer our ideal of what a wedded home life, ought to be." Time spent with Alice and Lucy's immediate family was the best remedy for now. Being in the quiet of her former home, far from crowds and constant scrutiny allowed her "to find that better self of me." She needed to remain there until "the Angels of healing make me whole again."[38] Lucy reiterated her distaste for urban living, which they had experienced for several months when the family had lived in New York during the winter of 1863–64.

For all Lucy's emotional turmoil, the letters she and Henry wrote one another suggest a solid marriage, one in which neither partner lost sight of the affection, concern, and interests they shared. Lucy described her reactions to a sermon she had read by Henry Ward Beecher and lectures on education by Ralph Waldo Emerson. When on July 18, 1864, President Lincoln put out a call for an additional 500,000 soldiers and the possibility of a draft to fill military deficiencies, she insisted, "Harry dear if you should be drafted, you must buy a substitute at any price—Draw on my credit if necessary!!! I wish this infernal war were over."[39] She knew he would have no trouble paying a substitute to serve in his stead. In early September, Henry sent Lucy's family a huge barrel containing a large ham, tea, smoked tongue, salmon, and sugar, all food items hard to come by during the war. Lucy was most grateful for his kindness. She hoped he would visit soon.[40] In September, with the 1864 presidential campaign looming and knowing Henry's love of politics, Lucy encouraged him to quit his job and to campaign for Lincoln's re-election, hoping this would invigorate him and make good use of his talents. Such work was sure to make him fresher, fairer, stronger, and looking ten years younger than now. She included advice on public speaking, urging him to use facts, not generalities, not to overstate his points, and to avoid mentioning personalities. Solicitously she reminded her "little boy" to buy warm stockings and to travel with his blanket shawl while he campaigned.[41] That fall Henry spent five weeks stumping and lecturing for Lincoln in New Jersey. Anticipating the end of the war, Lucy hoped they could rent their West Bloomfield house and vacation together on Nantucket, Martha's Vineyard, or Labrador. "We will fish, learn to boat, & swim, read, study, think, and grow together."[42]

More than one historian has characterized the Stone-Blackwell marriage as reaching a crisis stage during the war years.[43] Lucy's and Henry's letters do not support that assessment. Theirs was hardly a unique situation; couples often live apart at some point in their marriages, and certainly many did during the Civil War. Lucy was well aware of her fragile mental state and the impact of menopause, believing that the quiet of her childhood home and Sarah's presence were what she most needed. Henry enjoyed city life; Lucy did not. Henry had to earn a living and to try to sell western lands, so for much of the war he was tied to New York and to the Midwest. Lucy's concern for Henry was poignant and natural. In June 1864 she urged him to go west to sell land. Once the war ended, she hoped he would consider becoming a "missionary at large." Lucy felt there would be an outpouring of vice and immorality, and Henry was just the person to thwart them.[44]

Amidst their personal reflections, Lucy and Henry's letters did comment on larger events, especially issues related to abolition. In July 1862, Henry was upset with Congress for adjourning without taking a stance on emancipation. After the Union's surprising defeat at the First Battle of Manassas that same month, Henry realized, as did many Americans, that the war would not be a short one. After reading about Union troops fleeing back to Washington, DC, he held out little hope for a victorious Union. He was also disheartened by President Lincoln, for he was anything but "progressive" on the issue of slavery.[45] Lucy also expressed initial disappointment in Lincoln, feeling he was doing too little and moving too slowly on slavery. But with Lincoln's issuing the preliminary Emancipation Proclamation in September 1862, Lucy looked forward to a final "proclamation of freedom to the slaves," though she worried Lincoln might not carry through as promised because so many Union officers and soldiers were pro-slavery.[46]

But by the 1864 presidential campaign, Lucy expressed support for Lincoln over Democrat challenger George McClellan: "As bad as Lincoln is, a union with him and his supporters, seems to me, less bad than a union with peace Democrats." She felt the Democratic Party was doing everything possible to undermine Lincoln's presidency. "Its love of country is less than its hate of Lincoln," she commented insightfully. Lucy was also upset that Garrison was now fully vocal in his support of Lincoln, despite the president's cautious approach to abolition. Lucy wished Garrison would shun all politics as he had in the past. "O, if he would only cry out as in the earlier days!" Seeming to reject his earlier radicalism, Garrison now believed that a political solution was the most expedient way to end slavery. In July 1864, with the war dragging on, Lucy questioned the nation's identity as a true democracy, since it excluded so many people from full citizenship. She felt discouraged by the war and by her country. "All that I see of the New Nation, too, I dislike. Its spirit is bad."[47] She did, however, celebrate General William Tecumseh Sherman and his soldiers after they captured Atlanta in September 1864, and she rejoiced when reading about their occupation of Savannah in December which brought hope of a swift Union victory.

For Lucy, the war years when her speaking career was less demanding gave her more opportunities to spend time with Alice. Lucy's approach to mothering combined deep affection with high expectations. In her letters during periods when they were apart, Lucy often called Alice "my dear little cub" or "cubbe," nicknames both she and Henry used. She signed her letters "Mamma." She hoped she and Alice could "have a grand cuddle" but in the same letter added, "You know my dear I expect a great deal of you," a comment that must have resonated with an impressionable 12-year-old.[48]

Lucy also developed close relationships with her nieces and nephews, especially with Emma, Sarah's eldest daughter, to whom she felt like—and in some cases, acted like—a second mother. "You must learn by your mistakes as well as your successes. You must try to distinguish between the good and bad, the geese and the swans and be sure that you are always true to yourself," she advised. Lucy urged Emma, then 16, to study French as well as music and drawing, to visit art galleries and the nearby insane asylum, to window shop, and to use the public library. "Cultivate your taste for history," she advised, pressing her to read newspapers in order to keep abreast of national events. Lucy reminded Emma that people would judge her by her words and actions, that she should respect herself and always do her best, never tease others, keep up with her mending, and care for her teeth and nails. Also important was keeping a list of dirty clothes she sent to the washer woman.[49]

Francis Stone died on September 30, 1864, just shy of his eighty-fifth birthday. Frank and Bo were at his side. "He seemed to be just waiting, and was glad when he knew that his last hour drew near," Lucy explained to Hannah Blackwell. She described to her how they had prepared their father's body, placing autumn leaves around his pale face, which she described as sweeter and calmer than she had ever seen it in his life. He was buried beside Hannah. Lucy admitted that his last years were his best, no doubt recalling his abusive approach to childrearing after drinking too much. But she was sad: "I cannot tell you, the sense of loneliness & loss, we all felt when we returned from the grave to the house, which had been the home of the family, for 50 years. The house, and the beautiful hills, remain, but the home is gone."[50] Lucy's final thoughts of her father were lovingly sentimental, but his death also meant an end to her close ties to the family home at Coy's Hill.

Lucy and Alice remained in Gardner through December. Lucy was beginning to feel happier and more confident, and she hoped the family could move to Boston that winter. There, she imagined she would find like-minded people and a sympathetic audience. "It will be like a perpetual benediction to be in the society of those with whose labors and sympathies, I have so long shared," she explained to Henry.[51] Two weeks later, after receiving a letter from him in which he described the travails of his travels, she wrote one of her most effusive letters, no doubt partly inspired by her acute sense of loss. "How I longed to put my arms all around you, to warm and comfort you! O! Harry darling, I love you dearly, I can almost measure how much, by the sense of pain, and loss, which tho not hearing from you made me suffer."[52]

Although 1864 proved a difficult year for Lucy—poor health, loss of her father, a sense of drifting from her professional career, and, of course, the seemingly endless war—one event was worth celebrating. By August, Henry had sold several of his and Lucy's western and New Jersey properties, taking advantage of war-time inflation to make a substantial profit. He was able to clear himself of all debts and emerge with cash in hand. To Lucy, enormously relieved, this meant Henry no longer had to be tied to the "treadmill of business" and could feel "free."[53] Lucy shared the welcome news with Hannah, noting that they had much to celebrate with Henry's freedom from wage work and several thousand dollars in his pocket. Since some of Lucy's land had also sold, she pressed her need for financial independence. Lucy insisted they keep their money and investments separate, noting "It is more important to me than you have ever known, that I should have the income of my property." She asked Henry to purchase bonds with the money from her land sales and to put them in her name so she could draw interest.[54] Lucy hoped Henry could find some enjoyable pursuit in public service without worrying about earning a living and could spend the winter in a warm climate. She worried because he was all "skin and bone" from his years of hard work, mentioning nothing about her own years of equally hard labor.[55] The profits from their property sales led to a major change in the family's financial status. By the early 1870s, Lucy and Henry had an estimated personal worth of $50,000, close to a million dollars in today's money.[56]

The final months of the war brought welcome news on all fronts. In December 1864, as Henry headed to Chicago, Lucy urged him to read Lincoln's

message asking the House of Representatives to pass the Thirteenth Amendment and end slavery in this nation forever.[57] The Senate had passed the
Amendment in April. On January 31, 1865, the House finally passed the measure as well, which then went out to the states for ratification.[58] Abolitionists
and ministers, including Henry Ward Beecher, delivered sermons celebrating
what they viewed as the nation's movement toward becoming a true democracy. Lucy's reactions were more complicated. While she, of course, embraced
the end of slavery, Beecher's words made her "sick and faint," for men failed
to understand that a true democracy did not exist as long as women still were
without rights. Such speechmakers, she explained, "forget that every man's
wife, mother, and daughter has [sic] no political existence." "You and I," she
announced to Henry, "will work together (Moses, and Mrs. Moses) to make
this country a democracy without sham or humbug."[59]

Having rented out their home in West Bloomfield, in January 1865, Lucy,
Henry, and Alice visited Boston, seeing some of Lucy's friends and looking
for a house to purchase. They found the city to be as expensive as New York.
Boarding soon proved too costly, and they returned home. Instead of the
Boston residence of which Lucy dreamed, that winter she purchased a house
in Roseville, New Jersey. They also adopted an orphan named Annie, as a
companion for 12-year-old Alice. The two girls, however, did not get along,
and ultimately they placed Annie with another family.[60]

The war finally ended with Robert E. Lee's surrender to Ulysses S. Grant
at Appomattox on April 9, 1865. Five days later, John Wilkes Booth assassi-
nated President Abraham Lincoln, shocking the nation, which mourned his
death. Andrew Johnson of Tennessee became President. As part of Reconstruction, an immediate task at hand was to deal with four million enslaved
individuals. In addition to Congress's passing the Thirteenth Amendment to
end slavery forever, in March 1865 Congress established the Bureau of Refugees, Freedmen, and Abandoned Lands, better known as the Freedmen's
Bureau. This government agency sought to help newly freed slaves find jobs,
acquire an education, gain access to health care, and search for family members who had been sold during slavery. The Republican-dominated Congress now turned its attention to the status and rights of former male slaves,
showing no interest in the status and rights of women. Reformers who had
put the women's movement on hold during the war hoped that with the
war's conclusion, Congress would reward women by giving them the right
to vote. Lucy planned a fall lecture tour in New York and New England to
remind Americans of the need for women's suffrage.

As the Thirteenth Amendment went out to the states for ratification, Congress began debating a Fourteenth Amendment to give black men full citizenship and suffrage and limit states' congressional representation if they prevented black men from voting. In May 1865 at the American Anti-Slavery Society's annual meeting, Wendell Phillips expressed support for this amendment, regarding the rights of former male slaves as essential for their own and for the nation's future well-being. Demanding women's suffrage at this time, Phillips felt, would dilute the most vital issues of the day—black male citizenship and their right to vote. "One question at a time," he intoned at the meeting. "This hour belongs to the negro." His words astonished Lucy and other women. Here was the man who had steadfastly lectured and for years sustained and supported the women's movement and now seemed to be deserting them. He was hardly alone. Elected officials and many supporters—at least at this time—avoided the issue of women's rights, now regarding former male slaves as more deserving. After all, they had endured slavery for hundreds of years. Lucy was dejected and tried to explain why men seemed to be shrinking from "the van[guard] of our movement." "I think God rarely gives to one man or one set of men, more than one great moral victory to win," she reasoned.[61] Lucy's comment was an intriguing one since she, herself, was committed to two great causes for justice. Perhaps she sensed that most politicians could not see beyond a single goal—in this case the abolition of slavery. And not only was it evident that the hour seemed to belong to the "negro"; it also belonged to men.

Nonetheless, the new amendments galvanized organizers. For years, women had worked at the state level, lecturing, petitioning, and pleading with state legislatures to change laws that oppressed women. What they now realized was that Congress might do for women what it was trying to do for freed slaves, thus opening a second option for women campaigning to gain the right to vote. A constitutional amendment would trump any state laws preventing women from voting. Most women also sensed the need to concentrate their energy on suffrage rather than address other issues such as marital property rights and divorce laws. If they could vote, women would gain the power needed to enact other reforms to end their oppression. At this point women reformers like Lucy began to call themselves suffragists.

To that end, in December 1865, as Congress debated the Fourteenth Amendment, Lucy, Stanton, and Anthony submitted a petition to Congress asking it to pass another Constitutional amendment to prohibit states from disenfranchising citizens on account of sex. They demanded universal suffrage, which meant giving women and former slaves the right to vote.[62] Stanton fired off an essay to the *National Anti-Slavery Standard*, insisting this was the perfect time for the nation to demonstrate its true democratic character by enfranchising everyone. She found the notion that black men might win suffrage before white women a step backwards. Expanding the number of male voters would create even greater barriers to women's enfranchisement. Adding insult to injury, for the first time in the US Constitution, the Fourteenth Amendment inserted the word "male" three times. "Male" does not have the same generic properties as "men," as in "all men are created equal," and its gender-specific meaning was all too clear.

The eleventh National Woman's Rights Convention met on May 10, 1866, at the Church of the Puritans in New York, the first national meeting held in six years. Lucy, who was visiting family in Massachusetts, was absent, likely because she feared the outbreak of cholera that hit New York at the beginning of the month and had caused her brother Luther's death years earlier.[63] At this meeting, suffragists and abolitionists formed the American Equal Rights Association (AERA) to work for universal suffrage. Their goal was to create a united front by demanding the vote both for women and for newly freed slaves. Lucretia Mott was named president of that new organization; Stanton became vice president, Henry, secretary, and Lucy, a member of the executive committee. That spring, Lucy and Henry traveled to Washington, DC, to try to persuade Senator Charles Sumner, principal author of the Fourteenth Amendment, to remove the word "male" from it. Sumner was polite but refused to change the wording, claiming he had already edited the amendment fourteen times.[64]

Women soon discovered that only a handful of men in either political party had any interest in extending suffrage to women. Rising racial violence in the South—pillaging, burning, lynching, and raping—showed that freedmen were the ones in need of political power and federal protection. While treating former slaves with compassion was certainly paramount in the minds of some Republicans, there is no doubt politics sharpened their interest in giving black men the vote. Republicans who now dominated Congress knew former male slaves would vote for the party that freed them, and their votes would give the Republican Party many new members and additional power. Women offered no such assurance to either political party since their votes would be as divided between Republicans and Democrats as were those of white men. As Nina Silber argues, men also emerged from the war with a heightened sense of masculinity, a sense that they had paid the full price of war, providing another rationale to oppose women's suffrage. Congressmen now tied the right of suffrage to the war, claiming that only those who could fight deserved the right to vote.[65] (Women pointed out that many men never served in the Civil War or were ineligible to serve, but this seemed to be a moot point.) In these debates, congressional Republicans also paid more attention to freed slaves in the South than to free blacks in the North, where several states had enacted anti-miscegenation laws, and some, like Indiana, insisted on segregated schools.[66] Giving former male slaves citizenship and suffrage dominated the Republican political agenda.

All of this was profoundly disillusioning to Lucy. The first months after the war ended were unsettling ones for her and Henry, though both were happy to have the family together again. In 1866, they had moved back into their West Bloomfield, New Jersey, home, which Emily reported still needed "lots of work," though she incorrectly assumed they did not have the money to improve it. Hannah and Marian were living in nearby Roseville.[67] In May, Henry headed west but soon returned home. "You & Alice make my home & where you are not, home no longer exists for me," he wrote Lucy. He hoped the three of them could spend the summer in the mountains or at the beach. Ever eager to make money, Henry considered purchasing more western lands.[68]

Lucy experienced another period of self-doubt, and Henry tried to boost her confidence and encourage her return to lecturing. His plan was that they do it together, presenting a series of speeches on women's rights. Traveling by horse and carriage, they could lecture in twenty-five Massachusetts towns. "You shall speak <u>first</u>," he insisted gallantly, and he would follow, "picking up" and "weaving in" what she had omitted. "If you choose, you can close." Henry hoped they could carry on this great cause together and was certain that if she were willing, "good will come of it." Whether they fully carried out Henry's plan is unclear, although they did lecture together on women's suffrage. Their 1866 flyer announced: "Woman Suffrage! Constitutional Amendment. Lucy Stone and Henry Browne Blackwell of Boston will speak at the _____ at 7:30 p.m. Admission Free. Come one! Come all!"[69]

Meanwhile Congress continued the debates over rights. Most Republicans and some abolitionists, including Abby Kelley Foster and Thomas Higginson, agreed with Wendell Phillips that Congress should first end the wrongs of slavery by giving black men the right to vote before it addressed women's rights. Lucy wrote Foster in January 1867 after attending an AERA meeting at which most men found no reason to support women's suffrage.

Even several "colored men" spoke up and reasoned that women were already well represented at the polls by their husbands and thus had no need to vote. Lucy felt otherwise. "The broad principle of universal justice put into the foundation of our Temple of Liberty, is the only thing that can save it," she insisted to Foster. She detected a "strange blindness" in those who demanded a "poor half-loaf of justice for the negro, poisoned by its lack of justice for every woman in the land." Advancing only black male suffrage contradicted the nation's democratic principles. "O Abby, it is a terrible mistake you are all making. . . . There is no other name given by which this country <u>can</u> be saved, but that of <u>woman</u>." Lucy also mourned for the many women living overseas "whose longing eyes are turned from all shores to our own." They admired the United States as a democratic public that "derives its just powers from the consent of the government. They alas will be disappointed, as shall we." Adding even more drama to her letter, she concluded: "The tears are in my eyes and a nail goes through my heart."[70] For Lucy, only universal justice, including all voices engaged in the political process, could save the nation.

At the same time Lucy was expounding on universal justice, Henry wrote and had published a startling four-page letter addressed to southern legislatures, "What the South Can Do: How the Southern States Can Make Themselves Masters of the Situation." In it, he explained in brief the current tension between North and South over black male suffrage and offered "common ground for reconciliation." In order to get southern states to support women's suffrage, he urged them to give white women the vote since the number of white women voters would counterbalance the power of black voters and "thus the political supremacy of your white race will remain unchanged." Whether Henry discussed this first with Lucy is unknown, and if he did, how she reacted to his idea, though it is hard to believe she was not aware of what he had written.[71] For years, at least in the back of his mind, Henry tied women's suffrage in the South to white supremacy, narrowing his idea in 1885 by suggesting the vote only be given to educated white women.[72]

Lucy was becoming determined to do her part. On March 6, 1867, she turned to her home state and addressed a committee of the New Jersey legislature on "Woman Suffrage in New Jersey." Despite the lecture's title highlighting women, she asked elected officials to remove both "white" and "male" from the state constitution, reflecting her belief in universal rights. Both women and African Americans had demonstrated their loyalty during the Civil War. Nearly 200,000 black men had fought for the Union, she pointed out, and millions of women worked and sacrificed on the home front. Lucy summarized current laws that oppressed married women and sustained their dependency and secondary status. In the United States, she noted, the idea that "governments derive their just powers from the consent of the governed" had never been fulfilled. Giving both blacks and women the vote would ensure them access to a decent education, good jobs, and equitable wages. It would also fulfill the nation's destiny.

As Lucy had often done in earlier speeches, she answered each argument that people articulated to keep women and African Americans from voting: they were not well-educated enough to vote; a wife's casting a ballot could foster discord if she supported a different candidate from her husband; voting would undermine women's purity when they encountered "rowdies" at the polls; women and blacks might take the next step and demand the right to hold public office; children and the home would be neglected while mothers voted; and finally, a sense that most women did not want to vote anyway. Lucy pointed out that between 1776 and 1807, New Jersey had been the only state to allow women and blacks the right to vote. During those years, none of the dire warnings many had articulated held true. Now was the opportune time to make the nation truly democratic. States owed "to the country and to God" the establishment of institutions based on the "immutable principles of the Declaration of Independence."[73] New Jersey could lead the way. Committee members discussed Lucy's arguments and found no logical reason why women should not vote. They recommended that the state hold a constitutional convention to consider women's suffrage. When the proposal was submitted to the entire New Jersey legislature, however, members voted to postpone a convention. It never took place.

Enjoying financial security for the first time in their marriage and even in their lives, Henry and Lucy discovered the joys of a vacation retreat. At the time, Martha's Vineyard was a sparsely inhabited island, hardly the upscale resort it is today. Their first visit to the island was in the summer of 1866 when they accompanied their friend Ainsworth Spofford, whose father was a minister in the town of Chilmark. Since the Vineyard had no hotels and few services, the next summer Lucy and Henry rented a furnished home, paying $30 for six months, a "fabulously cheap" deal according to Sam. The cottage was situated outside of West Tisbury, high on a hill overlooking the sea. Lucy was absolutely taken with the beauty of the island, its pounding surf and splendid beaches, the sheep grazing in meadows, the rolling hills, and cool summer temperatures—all of it relaxing and uplifting.[74] Henry gloried in the fine hills for walking, the lovely beaches, the fresh air, and "the excitement of a new locality." He invited all his family to join them.[75] Emily Blackwell visited and waxed positive on the trout streams, the yellow, sandy beaches, and excellent boating. The character of the people charmed her: "It is so very anti-New York. There is no poverty, no Irish," she wrote, managing to ignore the presence of their Irish maid Mary. "It is a quite primitive well to do country population with all New England domestic neatness, cleanliness, and thrift," Emily added. Seeking to hire additional household help during their visit, together she and Lucy explored the southwestern end of the island and visited Gay Head, a community whose population comprised one-quarter Indians, one-quarter whites, and one-half blacks.[76] For years, Martha's Vineyard served as the favorite vacation spot for Henry and Alice—and for Lucy when she was able to get away. Eventually they and several others in the Blackwell family purchased property near Nashquitsa Pond on the western end of the island.[77]

In the fall of 1866 Lucy gave serious thought to starting a women's newspaper, noting in a letter that she and Henry were trying to raise money for "our paper." She wrote suffragists and friends, including reformer and abolitionist Elizabeth Buffum Chace of Rhode Island, asking for financial support to assist the venture. Anthony heard about the idea and deemed this project a pivotal one for the movement, writing that Lucy and Henry were willing to undertake the paper.[78] Fundraising efforts continued into early 1867, but by March, Lucy had second thoughts, unsure if she could ever raise enough money. More importantly, her attention now turned to the new state of Kansas which had scheduled a fall 1867 referendum to bring two issues before its male voters: whether to give blacks and women universal suffrage. Kansas suffragists were urging women in the East to help them campaign for both measures. Lucy again wrote Chace and others, asking that instead of donating to a newspaper, they support the Kansas campaign.[79] In thanking Chace for her donation, Lucy expressed optimism about the work ahead, seeing the Kansas referendum as a first step in giving all women the vote. Lucy saw this vote as vital, for it was the nation's first statewide referendum on universal suffrage.

In April 1867, Lucy and Henry headed to Kansas under the auspices of the AERA to convince voters to remove the words "white" and "male" from voting requirements in the state constitution. They left Alice in the care of her Blackwell aunts. At this point, Henry had no other obligations and doubtless welcomed the opportunity to speak and to campaign for a worthwhile cause. Lucy was most grateful for Henry's assistance and before they set out, commented: "Henry has done much more than I and works for women, as man with a good mother, wife, child & 5 sisters should."[80] In Kansas, Colonel Sam N. Wood, a state senator and a champion of women's suffrage, heralded Lucy's arrival, proclaiming, "With the help of God and Lucy Stone, we shall carry Kansas!"[81] He organized and scheduled the couple's many engagements. Lucy and Henry brought thousands of suffrage tracts to distribute wherever they spoke.

Kansas proved to be a grueling campaign. Lucy and Henry traveled by train, carriage, and wagon, often covering twenty-five to forty miles each day. Overnight accommodations were frequently crude. Writing to Alice, Henry, in typical fashion, made light of their adventure: "We climb hills and dash down ravines, ford creeks, and ferry over rivers, rattle across limestone ledges, struggle through muddy bottoms, fight the high winds on the high rolling upland prairies, and address the most astonishing (and astonished) audiences in the most extraordinary places." They lectured in log school-houses, stone churches, stores, and even a court house without a roof.[82] Lucy was more realistic about the hardships they endured but relieved that her speaking ability had returned. She shared the good news with Anthony: "I speak as well as ever, thank God! The audiences move to tears or laughter, just as in old time. Harry makes capital speeches, and gets a louder cheer always than I do, though I believe I move a deeper feeling."[83] She was elated to meet the "grand" women in Kansas who were committed to universal suffrage. Back east, AERA members were effusive about Lucy's and Henry's campaign, claiming in their proceeding minutes that "their hearts [were] all aglow with enthusiasm, greeted everywhere by crowded audiences, brave men and women" so that "Kansas, the young and beautiful hero of the West, may be the first State in the Union to realize a genuine Republic." No doubt the eastern organization's need for additional support in part prompted such glowing comments.[84]

The three-month campaign was, nonetheless, an uphill battle. One man told Lucy that if his late wife had ever expressed a desire to vote, "he would have pounded her to death!" Lucy reported that the state Republican Party was trying to drop women's suffrage from the ballot and that "the Negroes are all against us." She feared that if black men could vote before women, there would be an even greater struggle ahead for women. Opponents argued that women should not meddle in politics and believed that most of them did not want the right to vote anyway. Others spread rumors that Henry and Lucy were advocating free love, a claim Lucy found absolutely preposterous.[85] As the two prepared to leave Kansas, Stanton summarized their situation: "Lucy is almost heartbroken at the turn of affairs in Kansas and probable failure of the suffrage question." Now it was her turn.

Anthony, Stanton, and Unitarian Universalist minister Olympia Brown followed Lucy and Henry to Kansas and optimistically embarked on their own campaign. They soon encountered problems, however, including a shortage of funds and the state Republican Party's support of black male suffrage but not women's suffrage. Anti-suffrage forces were becoming better organized and more vocal in fighting both state constitutional changes. In a desperate attempt to bolster their campaign, the three women aligned themselves with the Democratic Party and with a wealthy supporter, an unstable, racist dandy named George Francis Train. He offered to bankroll their efforts and to lecture with them across the state. Whereas Lucy and Henry worked for both propositions, Anthony, Stanton, and Train spoke on behalf of women's suffrage. They attracted enthusiastic crowds. People apparently loved the outrageous Train, who dressed in flashy outfits, joked, and uttered racist comments.[86] Topeka's *The Leader* reacted sarcastically: "For personal vanity unadulterated and sublimated.... For vapid incoherence and crazy rhetoric ... commend us to George Francis Train."[87]

News of their Kansas work filtered back to New York, and AERA members, including Lucy and Henry, were horrified by the turn of events, especially by Train's involvement. They could not fathom why Anthony and Stanton would damage their reputations and that of the organization by associating with this man. Garrison called Train a "ranting egoist" and a "crack-brained, harlequin, and semi-lunatic." He was an insult to everything the AERA was trying to achieve. Lucy was stunned that the three women had not consulted anyone and in dramatic fashion claimed, "I felt the hurt of this action of theirs, as though it had been a blow to my own child." Several members questioned Anthony and Stanton's judgment and their work on behalf of the organization.[88] Reacting to the mounting criticism, the two women defended Train and his support for their cause, calling him a "pure minded noble man" and touting his "moral probity of character and great executive ability."[89] After leaving Kansas, Stanton and Anthony traveled with Train to several cities to lecture, seemingly indifferent to or unaware of the stunned reactions they fostered among AERA members. Lucretia Mott, like many, was becoming increasingly disenchanted over the turn of events, and she longed for earlier days when women merely lectured and held conventions.

Unfortunate, too, were Stanton's racist comments, which intensified as she campaigned in Kansas and elsewhere and which became a regular feature of her rhetoric over the next few years. Giving black men, who only recently had emerged from slavery, the right to vote before giving it to educated white women disgusted her. Her list of undeserving male voters also included immigrants, Mexicans, and working-class laborers. Stanton was appalled that "all the lower stratas of manhood are to legislate in their interests" and ignore women.[90] She denounced the expansion of male suffrage to "ignorant foreigners" who would now be able to vote "the minute they reach our shores."[91] Stanton's biographer Lori Ginzberg writes that Stanton "was drawing upon a powerful sense of her own class and cultural superiority" and "deaf" to the impact of her words. Her comments had a profoundly negative effect on the women's movement and turned off a number of people. The "harm was deep and harmful," writes Ginzberg, adding that this was not "Stanton and Anthony's finest moment."[92]

Lucy and Henry were disheartened by the situation in Kansas and saw little hope for a positive outcome. Henry returned there in mid-October but soon concluded, "We are beat." And beat they were. The vote to remove the word "male" from the Kansas constitution was defeated by a vote of 19,857 to 9,070. Black suffrage had a slightly closer outcome but also lost. As the first statewide referendum on women's suffrage, the vote was a significant blow. Henry concluded that male voters were not yet ready to address such momentous issues in a single campaign.[93]

Ultimately, the Kansas vote on black suffrage had little meaning as Congress debated and then passed the Fifteenth Amendment, which prevented suffrage being denied to anyone (at this point, meaning any man) on the basis of race. Congressional Republicans realized the Fourteenth Amendment lacked the teeth to ensure black men the right to vote. Without political power, freed people would continue to suffer at the hands of whites. Stanton was furious with yet another effort to advance black men over women. She argued that the "daughters of Jefferson, Hancock, and Adams" should have the right to vote before black men. She feared for women's future, having written rather spitefully in an 1868 essay, "Manhood Suffrage," "what may she not be called to ensure when all the lower orders, natives and foreigners ... legislate for her and her daughters?" Stanton also pointed out that black men who had been voting in Washington, DC, for two years had yet to support women's suffrage in the nation's capital.[94]

But Lucy continued the fight and refrained from any of the racist rhetoric uttered by Stanton. Lucy lectured at the Brooklyn Academy of Music in late

December 1867 on "Woman Suffrage." Employing many of the same arguments she had used in Kansas, she insisted that women were as capable as
were men in making rational choices. Many women were better educated
and more qualified than were many of the men who voted. Women should
also be able to run for public office, adding that a woman would make a far
better president than Andrew Johnson, who was universally acknowledged
to be a disastrous leader. In closing her lengthy speech, Lucy said women
voters would purify the legislature and do much to enhance the "general
prosperity of the Union."[95]

Perhaps inevitably, it was at this point that Lucy's friendship with Anthony
began to unravel. Lucy was deeply troubled by Stanton's and Anthony's behavior in Kansas and their relationship with Train. Adding to the tension was
the suggestion that Anthony had squandered funds that should have gone to
pay suffrage workers in Kansas. In response, Anthony questioned where
Henry and Lucy had found money for their Kansas campaign. Henry defended their expenses, claiming they paid for some of the Kansas trip with
their own money and the remainder from the Charles F. Hovey bequest. A
day later, Lucy reported that she had received "two characteristic" letters
from Anthony, obviously upset by their accusatory tone.[96]

In January 1868, Stanton and Anthony initiated a huge new project:
founding and publishing a newspaper, the *Revolution*, initially funded by
George Train and David Melliss, a financial writer for the *New York World*.
The two undertook the paper on their own, with no affiliation to the AERA,
and set up an office in New York. For Stanton, this fulfilled a lifelong dream,
providing space where she could freely express her frank opinions on a wide
range of subjects. Anthony had long felt the need for a voice to represent the
women's movement, one that could give full coverage to all the work being
done to advance women's causes. Below the *Revolution's* masthead, it read:
"Principle, not policy; justice, not favor—men, their rights and nothing
more; women, their rights and nothing less." As a *feme sole* with the legal
standing to sign contracts, Anthony served as proprietor and office manager
and signed all documents while Stanton and Parker Pillsbury served as co-
editors. Stanton wrote much of the copy.[97]

The paper covered news on the status of women in various states as well
as abroad. By its second year, in order to attract more readers, the *Revolution*
broadened its appeal by carrying poetry and serialized fiction.

Despite Stanton's and Anthony's enthusiasm, it was soon all too apparent
that the paper faced significant problems. Advertising revenues never covered

expenses, and thousands of anticipated subscribers never materialized. The paper's radical tone turned off many readers. Train's funds dried up when he set sail for England and was then arrested and jailed in Ireland for transporting Fenian—anti-British—literature.[98] In May 1870, the paper was sold to a joint stock company, with Laura Curtis Bullard, a novelist, correspondent, and women's rights advocate, taking over as editor-in-chief. The paper folded that December. Anthony was left as the responsible party and spent a few years earning money by lecturing to pay off the paper's $10,000 debt.[99]

In April 1868, a number of women in the Boston area, including Caroline Severance and wealthy Boston matron and author Julia Ward Howe, helped to found the New England Woman Suffrage Association (NEWSA). They sensed the need for their own organization, regarding the AERA primarily as a New York association. Also, the actions of Anthony and Stanton in Kansas had deeply troubled them. Although still a resident of New Jersey, Lucy felt a strong affinity for this organization and its members, and she traveled to Boston for its first meeting. As always, she took full advantage of her visit to lecture in the Boston area. After her Kansas experience on the lecture circuit, Lucy felt renewed confidence and was able to tell Henry, "My blues are gone, I wish they may never return to trouble me or you."[100] In November she and Henry returned to Boston for the opening convention of the NEWSA. Julia Ward Howe was elected president and served until 1877; Lucy was appointed to the executive committee.

It was Lucy who had drawn Howe into the women's movement. Born in 1819 in New York City into a well-connected family, she married Samuel Gridley Howe, a well-known, highly esteemed reformer who headed the Perkins Institution for the Blind in Boston. He was eighteen years her senior. In addition to bearing and raising their five children, Julia Ward Howe wrote poetry, essays, and plays. Composing "The Battle Hymn of the Republic" in 1862 brought her fame, for this poem, when set to music, became the Union anthem. Well before the founding of the NEWSA but sometime after the Civil War ended, Higginson convinced Howe to allow her name to be included among those calling for a women's rights meeting. He urged her to attend that meeting in Boston's Horticultural Hall where Lucy was to be principal speaker. Howe hesitated, for she envisioned women's rights leaders to be unfeminine, shrill, and difficult. On the other hand, Howe could readily identify with women's oppression. Her husband was a domineering man in private who resented her independent income and her fame as a writer, criticized her ability as a mother, undermined her self-esteem, and tried to prevent her from engaging in reform activities. Twice Julia Ward Howe had considered divorcing him.[101]

Howe hoped to remain inconspicuous at the meeting, but she was invited to sit on the stage with Garrison, Higginson, Phillips, and others. She also had not been looking forward to hearing Lucy speak, for Stone "had long been the object of one of my dislikes," Howe admitted years later. What a surprise when she saw a "sweet, womanly face" and heard Lucy deliver a powerful message that resonated with her. Howe was transfixed. "Here stood the true woman, pure, noble, great-hearted, with the light of good life shining in every feature of her face." Lucy's arguments were "simple, strong, and convincing," in demanding for women all the rights that black men recently had been given. Asked to respond to Lucy's speech, Howe could only utter, "I am with you." And she was. As Howe later recounted, she went to the meeting "with a very rebellious heart. I came out very meek and have so continued ever since."[102] From that point forward, Howe was hardly meek. She ignored her husband's dictates and became fully engaged in the women's movement. Not only did this cause reflect her needs, she admired

JULIA WARD HOWE

Figure 28. Julia Ward Howe (LC-USZ62–8221, Library of Congress, Washington, DC)

the women who worked with such conviction, steadfastness of purpose, and self-sacrifice. Where Howe had once felt isolated because of her understanding of women's oppression, she now worked alongside women who shared her convictions. Howe's fame and social standing added enormous legitimacy to the movement.[103] She became one of Lucy's lifelong friends and most stalwart supporters and proved to be an effective, powerful voice for women's suffrage.

But while gaining a new friend, over the months Lucy's relationship with Stanton and Anthony continued to deteriorate. At the May 1868 AERA annual convention in New York, a debate resurfaced over women's suffrage versus black male suffrage. Lucy and others felt especially troubled by Train's relationship with Stanton and Anthony. At this meeting, Henry, Lucy, and Stephen Foster again accused Anthony of misusing funds in Kansas. Anthony defended herself, claiming she had had to raise money for the campaign, spend some of her own money, and left the state in debt.[104] Anthony's defense proved effective; Henry and Lucy garnered little support. At the same meeting, Lucy took Frederick Douglass to task, with "every spark of latent fire" when he asserted that unlike black men, women had never been persecuted when demanding their rights. Lucy angrily retorted that she had faced persecution on many occasions. In this instance, too, she stood alone. Afterwards, Anthony wrote Higginson, wishing he had been present "to see & hear Lucy Stone out do her old self even." She characterized this as a "most delightful" moment and explained somewhat snidely that at the meeting, she had somehow taken the high ground and was able to overlook "every word and insinuation" Lucy hurled against her.[105]

Personal issues aside, Lucy again turned her attention to her home state. In November 1868, she and Hannah Blackwell made a futile attempt to vote. As expected, they were turned away.[106] Then she and Nette organized the State Woman's Suffrage Association of New Jersey. Their call for the organization's first meeting urged all to attend who were "opposed to the existing aristocracy of sexes and who desire to establish a republican form of government." The call, with class, racist, and ethnic overtones, asked, "Shall women, alone, be omitted in the reconstruction? Shall our mothers, wives and sisters be ranked politically below the most ignorant and degraded men?" In December 1868, Lucy presided over the organization's first meeting and was chosen president; Nette became a vice president. The first task of the New Jersey organization was to conduct a petition drive demanding women's suffrage to submit to the state legislature and to Congress. One journalist who reported

on the meeting noted the absence of Stanton and Anthony, which he attributed to "coolness" between the two women and Lucy.[107]

Lucy traveled to Ohio in the winter of 1869. She visited the Blackwell's
former home outside Cincinnati, as well as Oberlin College, the "dear old
place," as she described it. The college had expanded significantly since she
graduated, and she told Nette that she "wandered round and round, with
my heart in my throat, trying in vain to find our Oberlin." She ran into
former pupils as well as Professor John Morgan and President James Harris
Fairchild.[108]

Returning to New England in the spring of 1869, Lucy lectured in various communities in Massachusetts, Maine, and Rhode Island. In March, she
and Phillips addressed the Joint Special Committee of the Massachusetts
state legislature, urging officials to "squelch" the word "male" from the state
constitution.[109] Massachusetts women had conducted a major petition drive
demanding suffrage, hoping the state would be the first in the nation and
perhaps in the world to get "the ball rolling." Female spectators packed the
Committee room to observe the joint hearing. Phillips was again women's
stalwart supporter since black male suffrage now seemed secure. In his opening remarks, he said that he had attended at least two-thirds of all women's
rights conventions over the years and never heard from men's lips anything
that began to compare to the eloquence of women. Lucy followed him, delivering a strong rationale for women's right to suffrage. The New York Times
reported her as being "eloquent and sometimes caustic," and the largely female audience applauded and wildly stamped its feet. In an unexpected but
happy outcome, the chair of the Committee was so impressed with their
arguments that he said he would recommend a bill in support of women's
suffrage. Lucy truly believed that "with a little help," Massachusetts could
become the first state to remove the word "male" from its constitution.[110]

Two months later the Massachusetts Joint Special Committee on Woman
Suffrage issued its report. Leading up to that report, the Committee had held
two public hearings, one on March 30, the second on April 14. It noted that
it had received 8,000 signatures on petitions demanding women's suffrage
but also received an anti-women's suffrage petition from 194 Lancaster, Massachusetts, women who argued that gaining the vote would "diminish the
purity, the dignity, and the moral influence of woman, and bring into the
family circle a danger element of discord." The Committee's final report
articulated all the reasons why women should have the right to vote: the
many women who were property owners and paid taxes; the many women

who demonstrated a keen interest in politics; and Massachusetts women who had loyally supported the war effort. Female voices would add much to the government by purifying it. The nation had been founded on the ideals in the Declaration of Independence. Since the country had recently ended slavery, its next responsibility was to enfranchise women. While the Committee also presented counter arguments against women's suffrage, it found far more compelling reasons in favor of the issue. "Why should not Massachusetts be the first to adopt this?" asked one man. "She has always led in all the great events which have marked our progress as a state or nation." The Committee then voted to support an amendment to the state constitution "to secure the elective franchise, and the right to hold office to women in this Commonwealth." Lucy was thrilled. But like the situation in New Jersey, when the Committee's recommendation was brought before the entire Massachusetts legislature, elected representatives rejected it.[111]

The third annual meeting of the AERA convened in New York's Steinway Hall on May 12, 1869, and proved a pivotal moment in the women's movement. More than a thousand people attended the convention. There was now a serious division in the ranks. In December 1868, the AERA executive committee had rebuked Anthony and Stanton and repudiated any responsibility for their Kansas campaign. Activist Caroline Severance questioned the two women's "strange, insane" association with Train and concluded, "They have been bewitched with him."[112]

Nonetheless, the major question before the assembly was whether or not to lend support to the Fifteenth Amendment, which the House of Representatives, after an affirmative Senate vote, had passed on January 31 and sent out to the states for ratification. Stanton, Anthony, and several others opposed the Fifteenth Amendment, since it only dealt with suffrage for black men. In response, Douglass described how angry mobs hunted down black men in the South like wild beasts, tore them from their homes, and hanged them from lamp posts. Women, he claimed, had never suffered such horrors. (Someone in the audience then asked him if such outrages were inflicted on black women. Douglass admitted they were but not because they were women but because they were black.) While he supported women's suffrage, he believed black male suffrage should come first. He objected to Stanton's referring to blacks as "Sambos" while elevating white women as "the daughters of Washington and Jefferson." In his thinking, the issue of black men voting was a "question of life and death."[113] Henry Ward Beecher and others reluctantly supported the Fifteenth Amendment, believing that after its ratification, Congress would consider women's suffrage in the form of a Sixteenth Amendment. Stanton and Anthony refused to accept any compromise, characterizing the debate over the Fifteenth Amendment as a "battle between the sexes."[114]

In recent months, Lucy's thinking about the Fifteenth Amendment had shifted, moving away from the opposition she had expressed to Abby Kelley Foster two years earlier. In addressing the AERA convention, she admitted that Stanton and Douglass had each presented convincing reasons for their conflicting views. Recounting the situation in the South, though, she reminded everyone of how whites were using terror and violence to uphold white supremacy. Lucy, in dramatic language, then denounced the North, which seemed little better than the South, for in the North, "the Ku Klux Klan in the shape of men" claimed legal custody of children in rare cases of divorce. However, she now declared her support of the Fifteenth Amendment, grateful that anyone "can get out of the terrible pit," referring to the nation's inequitable treatment of blacks and women. The Fifteenth Amendment was a positive move toward universal suffrage.[115] Lucy predicted that women in some parts of the country would be able to vote in the 1872 election. She closed by saying that success would come because women's demands "were founded on the principle of eternal justice."[116] Stanton was probably correct in later assessing Lucy's change of heart over the amendment by commenting, "Mrs. Stone felt the slaves' wrongs more deeply than her own—my philosophy was more egotistical."[117] She and Anthony continued to oppose its ratification.

The public sensed that many in the women's movement opposed the Fifteenth Amendment, an impression Lucy tried to counter. She insisted that at every convention "we have adopted resolutions heartily endorsing the 15th Amendment, and of necessity rejoice in every gain for the negro." Only Stanton, Anthony, Paulina Wright Davis, and Phoebe Cozzens openly opposed it, she claimed. But Lucy feared their strong voices and the impact that Stanton's comments in the Revolution could have, especially on people living in western states.[118] Having worked for abolition for so much of her adult life, Lucy had to support the Fifteenth Amendment and truly believed that women were next.

Other disagreements surfaced at the third annual AERA convention, and some became personal. Douglass characterized the meeting as a women's rights convention, not an equal rights meeting. Stephen Foster again accused Anthony of misusing funds in Kansas and asked that she and Stanton resign from their leadership roles in the organization since they opposed the Fifteenth Amendment. Anthony was already harboring resentment against "Lucy Stone & Co." for failing to pay her full salary from the Charles Hovey funds and to reimburse her for out-of-pocket expenses in Kansas, an amount she estimated to be $1,000.[119] She also blamed the "treachery of friends" for turning against them.[120] Two days later, no doubt frustrated, defensive, and feeling isolated from many in the AERA, Stanton and Anthony walked out of the meeting and hastily (some said secretly) formed a new organization, the National Woman Suffrage Association (NWSA). Invitations hurriedly went out to a select group of women to join them. Lucy and Henry were not included.[121]

In the midst of these squabbles, Lucy and Henry were able to enjoy some social diversions that took their minds off these problems. In the spring of 1869, Henry traveled to Florida with Abby and Ludlow Patton, a wealthy New York financier for whom Henry was doing some work and who lived nearby in Roseville, New Jersey. That July, Lucy and Henry visited friends in Pomfret, Connecticut, where they enjoyed a "luxurious world" of "pleasant rambles, pure fresh air, delightful shade, nice bathing, intelligent conversation, books & a croquet ground ... music & comfortable board."[122] Later that month they visited the Spoffords at their home in Kennebunkport, Maine.[123]

But another likely diversion proved far more disruptive. In the summer of 1869, Henry became involved with the beautiful and young Abby Patton.[124] She had been one of the celebrated Hutchinson Singers, a family of performers who often entertained at antislavery and women's rights conventions. The nature of this relationship remains unclear—it may have been a flirtation, a close friendship, or a full blown affair, perhaps begun that spring or summer—or during the trip to Florida. Lucy and members of the Blackwell family seemed aware of Henry's relationship with a "Mrs. P." As Emily wrote in September 1869, "I hope that Harry has made up his mind to break off his relations with Mrs. P, and I was glad to learn indirectly that she herself wished to do the same. . . . Things are more hopeful than they were, nor do we know what the result will be between Harry and Lucy."[125] In a revealing, anguished reaction, in April 1870, Lucy confided to Emily that Henry had received a letter from Ludlow Patton's office. "It is not good for him to go there to renew or take up the old snare," she warned. "I wish you would say to him in the friendly way which a sister may, in hope he does not make headquarters at Mr. Patton's for it is not good to do so. . . . I shall never even try to go through such another time as that of last summer. . . . I wish he could be kept away." At least in writing to Emily, Lucy seemed resigned to the situation, stoically closing her letter, "But what will be, will be."[126] Emily, for her part, was fed up with Henry and hoped he could find a job that would occupy his mind and redirect his interests instead of "running after Mrs. P. at Roseville."[127]

While Henry and "Mrs. P" likely had some sort of relationship, we do not know its intensity and then what words were exchanged in private between Henry and Lucy, nor what anger, recriminations, and accusations were expressed. Looking back, Lucy was relieved when the tumultuous year ended. It is all too easy to misjudge the relationships of others, taking clues from cryptic comments and reading into letters what may or may not have been the writer's intent. A number of Stone-Blackwell letters are missing. Lucy and Abby Patton rarely corresponded since they lived nearby. Some family letters were lost in a house fire in 1871. After her parents had died, Alice destroyed letters she felt did not reflect well on her parents. These missing letters might have revealed what happened and provide a better sense of the depth and character of the relationship. But perhaps not. Much of what happened likely was discussed in person rather than in letters, at least between Henry and Lucy. All we have are a few remarks by Henry's judgmental sisters, a notation by Abby Patton mentioning a passionate relationship she had with an unnamed male, and perhaps most telling of all, Lucy's distress. While Lucy seemed devastated, this must have been hard on Blackwell family members, especially Henry's sisters who, despite their occasional frustration with their brother, always sided with him rather than with Lucy. This situation, compounded by Anthony's and Stanton's break from the AERA and their founding the NWSA, was a painful development for Lucy and no doubt compounded her upset. For Lucy, who set such high standards for herself and others and had come to trust Henry implicitly, these months must have been heartbreaking.

If an affair did occur between Henry and Abby Patton—hardly a unique situation then or now—Lucy and Henry were able to rebuild their marriage beginning that fall, though not without relapses. In the winter of 1871, Henry's sister Marian observed of Henry and Lucy that "there is no home atmosphere about them, never the shadow of peace or domestic enjoyment." Forgiveness takes time, as was true for Lucy. Yet six months later when Marian visited them again, she seemed to find a more joyful home.[128] Whatever its nature, Henry's relationship with "Mrs. P" did end. As early as November 1869, he was writing affectionate, teasing letters to

"Dear Lucikin" and sharing observations on the women's movement as he headed to Wilmington, Delaware.[129] Over the years, Henry became more involved in women's suffrage, perhaps out of guilt, certainly out of a desire to support Lucy and work for such a worthy cause, and perhaps because he found nothing better to do with his time. In late 1869, he reluctantly agreed to move to Boston, perhaps to please Lucy and keep the family intact—or to remove himself from temptation.

The issue of black male versus female suffrage continued to reverberate and moved well beyond discussions in Congress and among AERA members. At the Western Woman Suffrage Association meeting held in Chicago in September 1869, participants discussed a resolution introduced by Henry which urged the extension of the voting franchise to every class of people and renounced anything that elevated one group above another. Lucy and Henry encouraged others to support the resolution in order to prove to a skeptical public that those demanding women's suffrage also stood behind universal suffrage. Lucy felt that when women opposed the Fifteenth Amendment, they hurt their own cause. Anthony, who was at the meeting, insisted that no convention on women's suffrage should ask members to endorse any other issue except women's right to vote. She then softened her statement and said she, too, supported black male suffrage. Sensing general support for the idea, Henry dropped his resolution.[130]

In the fall of 1869, in response to the founding of the NWSA, Lucy took a bold step and formed a rival organization, the American Woman Suffrage Association (AWSA). The group that served as the core of this new organization was the NEWSA established some eighteen months earlier in Boston. For months, Lucy engaged in careful planning, not wanting to have the new organization appear exclusive or planned in haste—in stark contrast to the NWSA. She sent out hundreds of invitations, wanting to attract both male and female members. In writing potential members, Lucy explained that the new organization would neither oppose the Fifteenth Amendment nor raise side issues. It promised to meet the needs of those "who cannot use the methods, and means, which Mrs. Stanton and Susan use," expressing her desire to create a very different organization and one, in Lucy's mind, that would be run correctly.[131] Lucy's work behind the scenes paid off, for the call for the first AWSA convention listed many luminaries and reformers including Garrison, Lydia Maria Child, Abby Kelley Foster, Amelia Bloomer, Higginson, Myra and James Bradwell, Samuel May Jr., Henry Ward Beecher, Charles Robinson, Gerrit Smith, and Lydia Mott.[132]

Lucy sought to make this an inclusive group by inviting both women and men. She even employed flattery and offered incentives to attract attendees. For instance, to the Rev. James Freeman Clarke, she wrote, "Our cause suffers today from the lack of the organizing talent of MEN, in its management." She promised to pay Clarke's travel expenses to attend the AWSA's first convention and apologized for not being able to do more. "If we can only organize wisely and well," she explained, "with half our officers men, of the right kind, there will be no end to the good that will come of it."[133] When she heard nothing from Clarke, a week before the convention was to open she wrote him again, claiming, "We need your organizing ability and large reputation, and we may need your power of speech in case we have a stormy time."[134] Whether Clarke appeared is unknown.

Lucy also wrote Stanton and enclosed a copy of the formal call for the AWSA's inaugural convention. She wished they could find a quiet time to discuss her organization. Lucy explained that the AWSA was not created to rival the NWSA, for she hoped both organizations, "each in harmony with itself" could do better, more effective work "than either could do alone." Each would attract different constituents, she explained, and thus strengthen the work by campaigning for suffrage using different methods. She reassured Stanton, "this soc[iety] shall never be an enemy or antagonist of yours in any way."[135]

It is hard to imagine that Stanton—or Lucy, for that matter—saw the AWSA as anything but a competitor of the NWSA. Stanton responded to its founding not by letter but in an article she wrote for the *Revolution*, calling the founders of the AWSA "a few dissatisfied minds" and "Boston malcontents" who had been "sedulously and malignantly working" to undermine certain NWSA officers. This division, caused by personality clashes, not grand goals, was to be "deplored."[136] Others were displeased with the founding of a second organization and let Lucy know it. Martha Wright, Lucretia Mott's sister and an organizer of the 1848 Seneca Falls Convention, wrote Lucy that unity rather than division would better serve the women's cause. Since Congress had already passed the Fifteenth Amendment, there seemed no reason to create two organizations, since the founders' initial disagreement had been over black male suffrage. Wright urged Lucy to move toward union and the passage of a Sixteenth Amendment and put behind her all former differences.[137]

Certainly Lucy saw the AWSA as an alternative, explaining to suffragist Esther Pugh that she founded it "to unite those who cannot use the methods, and means, which Mrs. Stanton and Susan use."[138] Those who did not oppose the Fifteenth Amendment and who wanted to focus their energy on suffrage rather than on side issues needed their own organization. Over time, however, some people concluded that what motivated Lucy to take action was her enmity toward Anthony. She often denied this accusation, explaining that her founding the AWSA was "not taken on account of personal feeling" but because of her "unspeakable regret and sorrow for the actions of the Nationals in 1869."[139]

Lucy's decision to create a competing organization to the NWSA deserves some pondering, though none of her writings reveal a clear-cut motivation. She received a fair amount of criticism in forming the AWSA, more so than did Anthony and Stanton for creating the NWSA, though those two women generated much of the criticism aimed at Lucy. By 1869, Lucy found it impossible to work with these women, questioning their judgment and disagreeing with their opposition to the Fifteenth Amendment and their unfortunate campaign in Kansas. One can also sense that with the upheaval in Lucy's personal life, she needed something to call her own, to absorb her energy and engage her mind, made up of followers loyal to her. Once the Fifteenth Amendment became a part of the Constitution and black male suffrage was no longer an issue, it was too late to bring the women together. Lucy had to continue her life's work, and she now believed she could only do so through an organization with members loyal to her, based on goals and actions she supported. But as a prescient Phillips had predicted to women back in 1852, establishing a formal women's organization would inevitably "develop divisions among yourselves."[140] That is exactly what happened. To many people, the existence of two organizations seemed counterproductive to a movement in which everyone allegedly was seeking the same goal. Many scholars then and since have offered mixed reactions on whether the two organizations ultimately helped or hindered the women's movement. Some have argued that the two energized one another as they campaigned and often competed for the most effective way to win women's suffrage. Others feel much time and energy were wasted and that more could have been accomplished had all women worked together as a united front rather than weighed down by jealousy and personal conflicts.[141] Whether they could have done so at this juncture is hard to say.

The AWSA's first convention met in Cleveland, Ohio, on November 24 and 25, 1869. The choice of this location made sense, being far from New York and NWSA headquarters. Lucy also recognized and took advantage of a vibrant reform spirit in parts of the Midwest, particularly in Ohio which had long evidenced a commitment to antislavery, women's rights, and other reform issues. Every seat in the hall was filled, with some attendees standing in the aisles and along the side galleries. Delegates representing twenty-one states were present, including Nette, Myra and Judge James Bradwell, Julia Ward Howe, Mary Livermore, and Stephen Foster. Reflecting Lucy's commitment to include men, Rev. Henry Ward Beecher was chosen president, even though he was not present, and Garrison spoke and expressed enthusiasm for the new organization.[142]

Anthony also attended the meeting, for Higginson, in a fit of "mistaken magnanimity" according to Lucy, invited both Stanton and Anthony to attend. Lucy was not pleased, fearing "it will be so dreadful an incubus to take them up again!" Anthony addressed the meeting, sharing her displeasure at the turn of events, claiming the AWSA sought to "nullify" the NWSA and undermine the *Revolution*. But she grudgingly accepted the reality of the situation and urged those in the audience to join either the AWSA or NWSA in order to try to persuade Congress to pass a Sixteenth Amendment. She hoped the two organizations could cooperate.[143] Ellen DuBois points out that this inaugural meeting did not address long-term goals and strategy and instead focused on organizational issues, suggesting that the AWSA's principal concern was to create a robust association, one that would start on a strong foothold.[144]

At least in her public remarks, Stanton, who served as the NWSA's first president, initially felt less charitable toward the AWSA than did Anthony. She "deplored" this division in the ranks, listing all that the NWSA had accomplished and concluded that those people drawn to the AWSA "have probably been betrayed into this indiscretion." Paulina Wright Davis, who had never harbored much affection for Lucy, insisted that the AWSA's purpose was "to destroy" Stanton and Anthony. Garrison, after reading Stanton's comments, called them "slanderous" for "attacking and misrepresenting" her rival.[145]

The two organizations were different, and both members and outsiders sensed rivalry between them. In its campaign, the NWSA made broader, more ecumenical demands, including expanded marital property rights and easier access to divorce, in addition to women's suffrage. It directed many of its efforts at the federal level, trying to convince Congress to pass a women's suffrage amendment similar to the Fifteenth Amendment. The AWSA saw itself as a "truly representative national organization," maintaining close ties to its auxiliary organizations established in various states.[146] It focused on winning suffrage through the states, which traditionally had determined voter eligibility, though in later years leaders also saw the wisdom of working for a federal amendment.[147] The AWSA, which had more members than the NWSA, had a more inclusive approach to membership, welcoming both men and women and allowing men to serve as officers. Initially the NWSA only welcomed female members and officers, although that policy changed within a few years.[148] The NWSA set up headquarters in New York; the AWSA found its home in Boston. The AWSA's convention structure was more formal than that of the NWSA. Each AWSA state chapter sent a certain number of delegates to annual meetings based on that state's congressional representation, and only delegates could vote on substantive issues. NWSA meetings were open to everyone.[149] Both organizations solicited new members, especially prominent individuals. Garrison and Henry Ward Beecher joined the AWSA. Lucretia Mott tried to remain neutral, although later her sympathies lay with the NWSA, probably because of her long-standing friendship with Stanton.[150]

Once the AWSA formed, individual efforts were underway almost immediately to try to unite the two organizations. Newspaper editor, poet, and suffragist Theodore Tilton attempted this in 1870. He was able to obtain Lucretia Mott's support in a letter he sent to each AWSA state association. At an arbitration meeting held in early April and which Lucy attended, Tilton proposed several ideas for unification, most of which subsumed the AWSA under the NWSA. Not surprisingly, "the Boston group" rejected them.[151] In 1874, Martha Wright contacted Lucy, wishing members of both organizations could meet to discuss a cause that all supported, although she feared this would not happen. Wright predicted the two organizations would impede, not advance, the women's movement. She believed Lucy's reasons for founding the AWSA made no sense and added that "petty or personal difference should have no place."[152] At this juncture, however, Lucy had no interest in unification, especially when all suggestions made the NWSA pre-eminent.

In late fall of 1869, Lucy reached two decisions she had been considering earlier: moving the family to Boston and starting a suffrage newspaper. Perhaps this was in response to Henry's alleged affair with Abby Patton, or to the exhausting life she had been leading, or to a desire to leave the New York area and distance herself from the NWSA. New York was home to the *Revolution*, and she did not want her newspaper competing for investors, subscribers, and advertisers. Her close friends in the Boston area—Garrison and his family, Phillips, May, Higginson, and Howe—gave her a sense of belonging. She and Henry enrolled 12-year-old Alice in Jane Andrew's progressive boarding school in Newburyport, just north of Boston. Lucy felt this was best because she was again traveling often, and Alice needed "regular habits" and "proper discipline." But she felt "crushed and torn and homeless" in having her daughter living away from home.[153] Doubtless it was Lucy's decision to move to Boston, for Henry initially evidenced little desire to settle in a city that he found "dull & provincial." Yet in late October 1869 Henry, whose work situation was still tentative, joined Lucy in Boston to help her raise money for a newspaper.[154]

Fundraising began immediately. To potential investors of what became known as the *Woman's Journal,* Lucy elucidated what she and Henry hoped to accomplish. She by no means saw the paper as a money-making venture. "We can live on our income and will cheerfully give our time and best efforts." Lucy hoped friends who sympathized with women's suffrage would provide funds to help support it. She wanted to attract the best writers and to have the paper become a powerful organ "against the evil it has to combat."[155] Lucy and Henry set up a joint stock company to raise $10,000, selling shares at $50 each. By year's end, Henry, who put up the first $1,000, had solicited several wealthy Boston businessmen and supporters of women's suffrage.[156] Lucy rented a two-room office at 3 Tremont Street, a block from the state capitol and adjacent to the Boston Common. That same building housed the New England Woman's Club and headquarters of the AWSA.[157] Lucy and Henry lived in an apartment above the *Journal* office while they looked for a house to buy.

The decade ended with heartening news from the far West, giving Lucy and others hope that women's struggles were finally reaping positive results. Although Massachusetts, Kansas, and New Jersey failed to act on women's suffrage, it was the Wyoming territory that became the first place in the nation to do so. In November 1869, the Wyoming territorial legislature considered a bill giving women the right to vote. After only a month's deliberation, elected representatives passed the bill. As one keen observer commented, "all great reforms take place, not where they are most needed, but in places where opposition is weakest."[158] Hostility to the issue had little time to develop, and Governor John A. Campbell quickly signed the bill into law. In September 1870, Wyoming women over 21 (of whom, admittedly, there were few) went to the polls and voted for the first time. That same year, the Wyoming territorial Supreme Court decreed that women could also sit on juries. Women in the East were thrilled and accorded Governor Campbell much credit for the victory. The *Woman's Journal* later heralded him as a "champion," claiming that "no man in America ever achieved, within a single month, so enviable a reputation" as he had.[159] Many western settlers hoped the right to vote would entice women to move to Wyoming, or as New York newspaper editor Horace Greeley expressed it, "the girls" would now yearn to come to this "higher plain of Human Rights."[160] Although women did not flock to the frontier territory in order to vote, Wyoming stood as an example to the rest of the nation.[161]

In February 1870, Utah's territorial legislature also voted to give women the right to vote. This was a more puzzling situation since Americans did not equate Mormons living in Utah with a liberal or enlightened view of women. Yet Mormons, who comprised a majority of the region's population, hoped this gesture would counter Americans' negative feelings toward their faith and their belief in polygamy. Adding women voters also became a way to ensure Mormons' power in future elections once more non-Mormons settled the Utah territory, since Utah, unlike most areas in the West, had nearly as many women living there as it did men. And unlike most Protestant sects that gave men total authority in church, Mormons allowed women limited decision-making on matters of faith. From the perspective of those in the East, a number of congressmen and senators welcomed Utah's women's suffrage bill as a positive measure. Allowing Utah women to vote "will be found a powerful aid in doing away with the horrible institution of polygamy," the Committee on the Judiciary concluded.[162] That, however, did not happen.

The 1860s were a transformative decade for the country, overwhelming and traumatic in the first half, and during its latter half, volatile for Lucy and for the women's movement. Slavery had been abolished at enormous cost. Now at the helm of the AWSA and soon of the *Woman's Journal*, Lucy continued her campaign for the other great cause and for universal justice.

7

Onward the Struggle,
1870–1888

By moving to Boston and starting a newspaper, Lucy had hoped to limit her lecturing and traveling. Perhaps thinking back to the recent upheaval in her personal life, she had told Nette that those activities were "not consistent with any home life, or any proper care of my family. I feel it more and more, and shall certainly not continue this mode of work. . . . I long for a snug home."[1] Lucy fondly wished that the *Woman's Journal* would keep her fully engaged in the women's movement but allow the family to spend more time together and provide her a quieter, less stressful life. Instead, for more than two decades, Lucy found herself working at full speed, each week producing what became the nation's most influential women's rights newspaper and continuing her leadership role in the fight for women's suffrage.

The first eight-page edition of the *Woman's Journal* appeared January 8, 1870. The paper promised to eliminate "a cargo of irrelevant opinions," to avoid partisan "warfare," and to push for suffrage, now the major goal of the movement. Lucy insisted that the paper adopt a moderate tone in order to attract the broadest readership and numerous advertisers. Other newspapers greeted the *Journal* warmly, highlighting its "excellent appearance" and "high-toned" articles, thankful that it avoided "sharpness," "demagoguerism or amazonianism or cant." Others cited the paper's "talented" writers and "high moral tone."[2] When an uncharitable review in the *New York Tribune* predicted the paper's early demise, Lucy retorted that the only way "to stop the *Woman's Journal* is to give women suffrage."[3]

While living above the *Journal* office, Lucy and Henry explored real estate around Boston. By the end of the year, they purchased a sprawling house in Dorchester, built around 1820, with a widow's walk and seven marble fireplaces. They paid $20,000 for it. According to Emily, the home was "the handsomest residence any member of the family has ever occupied."[4] It was located on Boutwell Street, high atop Pope's Hill, with views of Boston Harbor to the east and of the Blue Hills to the west. Dorchester had recently been annexed into the city proper. Before the 1850s, the area attracted few residents, but with an aqueduct now bringing fresh water to the neighborhood and with dependable transportation, Dorchester became a desirable place to live. Trains ran along Neponset Street and from Harrison Square below their property, providing regular service into the city. A number of wealthy merchants purchased or built large homes there. Lucy and Henry's ten acres of land and 160 stately trees held special appeal, giving Lucy a sense of rural living near downtown Boston. Their extensive acreage allowed them to plant vegetable and flower gardens and to have an orchard, stables, and a barn for their carriage, cows, and horses. When she had time, Lucy again employed the domestic skills she learned as a child—churning butter, making yeast and soap, canning fruit, and preparing dried beef. She liked to work in the garden and planted trees and bushes that thrived for years. In the fall of 1871, the entire family reunited when Alice left the private boarding school where she had been and moved home, attending nearby Harris Grammar School.[5]

Publishing the *Woman's Journal* proved to be a far greater challenge than Lucy had ever imagined. Being "saddled" with the paper did not please Henry, at least at this juncture, and he uncharacteristically grumbled to his brother George about working without being paid a salary "for no earthly reason but to try to make Lucy happy."[6] But he had no other steady job and had good reason to make her happy. Fortunately Lucy was able to hire Mary Livermore to edit the *Woman's Journal* after Livermore's Chicago suffrage newspaper, the *Agitator*, folded. Livermore, born in 1820, had been an ardent abolitionist and was a reformer and strong suffragist. During the Civil War, she played an active role in the US Sanitary Commission. In 1868, she served as the first president of the Illinois Woman Suffrage Association. With her new editorial position, Livermore and her family moved to Melrose, a small town north of Boston. From there, Livermore commuted into the city and oversaw the *Journal* for two years, using her considerable skill and knowledge to give the newspaper a solid footing.[7] After Livermore left in 1872 to pursue a lecturing career, Lucy took over as editor, with assistance from Henry, Higginson, Howe, and later Alice.[8] Henry eventually reconciled himself to this job, commenting that it provided an "occupation & social & political position" and was not "unpleasant work."[9]

Lucy had never published a newspaper or run a business, but she plunged in with her characteristic single-mindedness. In the spring of 1872, she reported proudly to Henry that the work was going well, and she was pleased she was up to the task. But the paper hardly gave her the "cozy" life she envisioned, for publishing an issue every week was unremitting and exhausting work. In the spring of 1871, even before she took over full-time editing, Lucy admitted she was "so over crowded and over worked that I have barely time to breathe."[10] And it was not only producing weekly copy. Lucy also had to raise money, sell subscriptions and advertising space, and find authors to write articles. Her traveling and lecturing continued but became less frequent, for the *Journal* tied her to Boston and demanded much of her time and energy.

Lucy devoted the rest of her life to publishing the *Woman's Journal*, which many came to see as the voice of the women's movement. Despite the constant toil, it must have been satisfying to Lucy to witness the fruits of her labor. She attracted some of the nation's most pre-eminent writers, including Howe, Higginson, Harriet Beecher Stowe, Henry Ward Beecher, John Greenleaf Whittier, Charlotte Perkins Gilman, Louisa May Alcott, and others. The paper covered a wide range of topics, basically anything touching upon women's issues and activities in this country and abroad. The paper's influence on the movement and on its readers was profound. Carrie Chapman Catt, who later served as president of the National American Woman Suffrage Association and played a key role in the 1920 passage of the Nineteenth Amendment that gave women the right to vote, called the *Woman's Journal* a "history-maker and history recorder for the suffrage cause" and claimed that the success of the movement was "not conceivable without the *Woman's Journal's* part in it."[11]

One of Lucy's greatest challenges in running the *Journal* was fundraising, an unrelenting task, for the paper more often than not operated in the red. This was especially true during its early years when, as Lucy quipped, the paper ran "on a very close margin." Never did subscriptions cover costs. In its first year that "very close margin" was a deficit of $7,000; $5,000 in its second year; and by year four, $1,500. Lucy constantly sought out new subscribers, more advertisers, and additional contributions. In 1874, having diverted a good deal of *Journal* money to support Michigan's unsuccessful women's suffrage campaign, Lucy literally went door to door begging for money.[12] The next year she reported that funds were "scarce" and a month later commented, "We are parched for money as we never were." Returning one evening after seeking more ads, Lucy confessed, "I wish I could rest. I am so tired today, body and soul, it seems as though I should never feel fresh again. I have been trying to get advertisements for the Woman's Journal to eke out its expenses." She had walked miles the previous day, climbed countless flights of stairs, and despite all her effort, returned empty-handed. When she arrived home that night, the house was cold, and fires were out in all the furnaces and fireplaces. In a rare moment of despairing candor, she admitted, "I do wish there was some way of carrying on the Woman's Journal without such a hard, constant tug."[13]

Most people had no idea that the *Journal* required ongoing financial support or that for years Lucy and Henry collected no salary from it. Few ever understood that it took a great deal of money and labor to produce the paper. As Lucy explained to potential donors, she and Henry had "a simple style of living and we do most willingly devote ourselves to this work." Their real estate holdings and western lands, which years before had seemed such futile and unreliable investments, were now producing cash, allowing the two of them to devote themselves to the paper and to suffrage. Lucy no longer had to lecture to earn money, nor did Henry have to hold a full-time job. In later years, Lucy tried to correct the public's misimpression of her as someone who was "rolling in wealth" due to a large bequest from the Eddy Fund. Eliza F. Eddy, daughter of Francis Jackson, died in 1882 and wanted to support a cause her father had embraced. She bequeathed $40,000 to be divided between Lucy and Susan B. Anthony to support the "Woman's Rights Cause." Several relatives contested the will, but finally in March 1885 a judge ruled the Eddy will was valid. While that was welcome news, Lucy's major portion of the estate was Francis Jackson's former Boston home. After she had spent a good deal of money enlarging and repairing the house—repapering walls, plastering, installing new plumbing, and buying a new furnace and kitchen range—she was able to rent out the home for $1,700 a year. What was left over after upkeep and taxes helped to support the *Journal* and some activities of the AWSA.[14]

Despite this source of income, the paper's financial problems never completely abated. Even after nearly two decades, Lucy noted the *Journal* was "in a tight place financially," and Henry had to pay its bills out of his own pocket. The year 1888 was especially hard. The woman who solicited advertisements was ill, and a number of subscribers were delinquent in paying what they owed. The NEWSA, which had been contributing to the paper, could no longer afford to do so. A few wealthy suffragists made occasional donations, and Lucy was never too proud to ask for what she deemed a worthy cause. At one point she brazenly but politely contacted a recent widow, Mrs. John L Whiting, reminding her of her late husband's financial commitment to the *Woman's Journal* and asked for the $100 contribution he had promised the paper.[15]

Lucy was constantly seeking new subscribers; their numbers waxed and waned over the years. To entice them, the *Journal* sometimes offered specials, such as two free months for an annual subscription or reduced rates for two or three months of the paper. On occasion, she hired women to sell subscriptions, though they had limited success. At its peak, the *Woman's Journal* claimed some 6,000 subscribers. Yet in the fall of 1878, Lucy despaired because the paper had 2,000 fewer subscribers than it had two years earlier. "I feel overpowered," she moaned.[16]

Reading the *Woman's Journal* today offers insights into women's myriad activities and accomplishments over the years. Suffrage was the paper's number one news item, of course, with detailed coverage of several state campaigns and various conventions and meetings, revealing the growing grassroots efforts nationwide. A regular feature, "Foreign Items," presented news from European countries as well as from such far flung places as New Zealand and the Sandwich Islands. Among the paper's regular columns was "What Women Are Doing," offering newsy tidbits, such as notice of a society of women who refused to kiss men who used tobacco; an Iowa woman who had become a notary public; and an announcement of sales of Louisa May Alcott's *Little Women* when it had surpassed 30,000 copies.[17] In the 1880s it provided detailed coverage of suffrage efforts abroad, especially in England, where the campaign was most active. Articles discussed Chinese prostitutes in San Francisco and a heated debate on enfranchising women held by male students at Harvard College.[18]

One delightful story that ran for months in the 1870s covered sisters Abby and Julia Smith of Glastonbury, Connecticut, who did what Lucy had done in the late 1850s: refused to pay their property taxes because they were not allowed to vote. Since both sisters were in their eighties, they elicited much sympathy, especially when the town seized their cows to pay the taxes they owed. The Smith sisters made great press, for as Lucy commented, they "seem to have hit the mark at the right time." The fact that they belonged to the AWSA and found inspiration for their defiance after attending a meeting no doubt heightened Lucy's sympathy. Lucy at one point likened the Smiths' victimization to those who suffered at the hands of the Ku Klux Klan, over-dramatizing their situation by claiming, rather brashly, that "nothing more dastardly can be found in all the records of southern violence."[19]

The paper included essays on wage-earning women, examining both their accomplishments and their plight. A column, "Progress among Colored Women," highlighted African American women who founded a school for black children in Philadelphia and a union of black washerwomen in Little Rock, Arkansas.[20] A long article addressing poor white women living in North Carolina questioned the positive image the New South was trying to create in the public mind. The truth was that many white women living there were in dire straits, having access to limited schooling, suffering domestic violence, and holding few paid jobs. The essay observed that northern philanthropic and missionary organizations, which reached out to assist African Americans, all but ignored the South's poor whites.[21]

The *Journal* brought readers' attention to Swarthmore College, a co-educational institution outside Philadelphia founded by Quakers in 1864, and the University of Michigan's decision in 1870 to admit women. An article, "Ennoble Domestic Work," detailed the positive aspects of domestic labor as an opportunity for the many unemployed women seeking paid jobs, dubbing it an "honorable" profession. The paper examined the situation of Myra Bradwell of Illinois, a law school graduate whose status as a married woman prevented her from practicing law.[22] Early on, the *Journal* ran a series, "People You Should Know," providing biographical essays on influential abolitionists and reformers including Angelina and Sarah Grimké, Gerrit Smith, and Jane Grey Swisshelm. Lucy must have been delighted to print the flurry of challenges to Dr. Edward Clarke's 1873 book, *Sex in Education, or a Fair Chance for the Girls*, in which he argued that young women's physiognomy made them ill-suited to pursue the same level of higher education as men enjoyed. Clarke believed young women could not handle a rigorous education while their reproductive organs were developing. Too much studying meant young women's limited "life force" was being diverted to their brains rather than to their uteruses. He feared for the nation's future. Harvard President Charles William Eliot agreed with Clarke, believing women could not "bear the mental stress that comes from too hard study."[23] Angry respondents, most of them women and many of them college graduates, went on the attack and presented countless examples of happy, healthy women who were attending college, including, after 1879, under Eliot's presidency, at Radcliffe.[24]

In addition to editing the *Journal*, Lucy kept up the fight for women's suffrage, traveling and lecturing, circulating petitions, corresponding with scores of suffragists across the nation, writing and speaking with politicians, organizing and attending AWSA conventions, and co-sponsoring bazaars and other fund-raising events. During her first years in Boston, her schedule seemed as busy as ever, despite her vow to cut back. For instance, during one week in February 1875, she spoke at a lyceum in Newton, Massachusetts, and hosted a suffrage club meeting in their Dorchester home the following night. The next evening she participated in a hearing at the State House in Boston. Lucy traveled to Belfast, Maine, to lecture on Thursday, and on Friday, set off for Augusta to give a speech. She managed to spend the weekend at home but two days later she spoke in Quincy, Massachusetts. As long as she remained healthy, Lucy rarely turned down an opportunity to campaign for the vote, now back in her element on stage.[25]

Amidst these frenetic activities, personal issues continued to affect Lucy's professional life. Tragedy struck in December 1871 while she and Henry were attending a convention in New York. A fire broke out in their Pope's Hill home, causing significant damage to several rooms, family heirlooms, and personal items, including books, papers, and most of the letters Henry had received since childhood. Alice and the family's Scottish maid, Annie McLeod, were inside, but both managed to escape. Fortunately, Lucy and Henry had insurance that covered most of the $10,000 in damages. When Emily Blackwell learned about the disaster, she wrote immediately, sympathizing that their "cheerful" house was ruined, knowing how hard Lucy had worked to create a "snug" home. Emily suggested they start over, sell the land for "13 or 14,000$," and find more suitable arrangements. Accustomed to urban living and concerned about the cost of rebuilding, Emily hoped they could find an apartment or decent boarding house in Boston.[26]

Lucy had no desire to give up Pope's Hill, and she and Henry rented a smaller house nearby while renovations and additions were made, a process that took nearly six months. While the family rarely enjoyed an indulged life, Lucy now refurnished the house in style. Alice for one felt the changes made it less homey, and she found some furniture "too splendid to use." Restoring their home proved to be a wise decision, however, for over the years, Pope's Hill served them well. Both Henry and Lucy were extremely hospitable. There was a constant stream of visitors through their home. Lucy enjoyed entertaining guests, especially young ones, although it was tiring. In April 1875, she reported that the house was full, and every meal for the past month had included one to five extra mouths to feed. A few years later she reported on a "houseful of company," which she predicted would be the situation all summer. "I seem to be over loaded always," she admitted. Often Lucy invited several people to join them for dinner or to spend the night. She welcomed students who were far from home to share holiday meals. Lucy was generous to extended family members, to suffragists and friends, and especially to her several nieces who often visited and stayed for months at a time.[27]

Without full-time help, Lucy could not possibly have published the *Journal*, lectured and traveled, overseen the household, and entertained so graciously. She hired a man to print the *Woman's Journal* and various women to typeset the paper, to run the office, and to take charge of bookkeeping. Alice often came to the office to help fold and mail copies of the paper. Finding competent, reliable domestic help was a greater challenge.[28] Lucy disliked the hiring and rehiring process, which she described as "the purgatory of changing girls."[29] Normally Lucy and Henry had at least a maid, a cook, a yardman, and a stable boy. Periodically a seamstress came and spent two weeks making clothes for the entire family. Lucy was never totally at ease in employing help, and at one point commented that if she had the time, she would perform her own housework, for she knew no one who could do it better.[30] Having always been a person of extreme orderliness, that comment rang true. But such free time was no longer hers.

Hints of an emerging sense of class and privilege began to appear in Lucy's correspondence, at least in regard to their hired help. The Irish most often upset her. "These Irish girls are rather too much, though I have a good cook, who is also a nice girl," she admitted. Reflecting values instilled since childhood, what really bothered Lucy was waste, and she longed for a "thrifty Yankee woman."[31] Maids seemed to come and go, either resigning for good cause or proving unsatisfactory. In September 1871 Lucy found a "slow, good Nova Scotia woman" whom she hired on trial to see if she would work out. Two years later Lucy happily reported she had employed a pleasant woman from Maine, a Mrs. Coe, who brought along her 6-year-old daughter Annie and a "strong Irish woman who gets drunk every week, but who is so much better than most of those who are sober." In 1875, Lucy found a "sensible and kind" woman who was "excellent" and willing to work hard, freeing Lucy from domestic worries so she could devote her time to the *Journal*.[32]

Despite Lucy's frustrations in finding competent help, she apparently was a kind and generous employer. Mary Flynn, who worked as a house maid, recalled that Lucy never treated her as a servant but rather "like a daughter." When Flynn became ill, Lucy nursed her. Lucy was typically good-natured, though she did try to impose some of her values on her servants. She warned Flynn not to wear corsets, for "you have only one gizzard and you must save that." Lucy encouraged her to attend night school, and when Flynn refused, Lucy tutored her. One Fourth of July, Lucy and Henry were going out of town. As they were leaving, Lucy told Flynn they might return in time for mid-day dinner. Lucy had purchased all the food needed to prepare a delicious meal and asked that it be ready by 1:00 p.m. Flynn was irritated because she had planned to join friends to celebrate the holiday, but she dutifully cooked the meal. Near dinner time, Flynn suddenly spied her brother, his wife, and their four children coming up the road. As a surprise, Lucy had invited them to spend the day—and mid-day dinner was ready. Flynn later resigned to be near her fiancé. Lucy put Flynn's final wages in an envelope with instructions not to open it until she got to Boston. When she did, Flynn found $50, far more than what she was owed. Flynn concluded that if Alice did not inherit much money from her parents, it would be because Lucy had given away most of it.[33]

For over two decades, in editing the *Journal* and leading the AWSA, Lucy's friendships with dedicated suffragists nationwide expanded. Her correspondence reveals the multiple relationships she developed, especially with suffragists working at the state level, and the many friends she depended on and nurtured. Nette and Julia Ward Howe were always there for her, and Mary Livermore remained a strong ally. Another loyal suffrage worker and close friend was Margaret Campbell of Maine, who attended the first AWSA convention. Campbell became an effective lecturer, contributor to the *Woman's Journal*, and dedicated suffragist. She and her husband sometimes stayed overnight at Pope's Hill. When she could afford it, Lucy paid Campbell a small salary for lecturing, working on state suffrage campaigns, and soliciting new subscribers for the *Journal*. After Campbell and her husband moved to Iowa in 1879, Campbell conducted an energetic suffrage campaign there and became an important contact for Lucy in the Midwest. Lucy felt a deep sense of comfort with Campbell, and she often confided in her, sharing her multiple health problems and frustrations with the NWSA and its officers, intimate thoughts she often kept from Henry and Alice.[34]

Besides editing the *Journal*, of course, Lucy's other responsibility was her leadership role in the AWSA, particularly working with its state affiliates and their members. While she only served as president of the organization in 1872, Lucy led its executive committee and played a pivotal role in organizing annual conventions, rallying members, raising money, and working on state suffrage campaigns. She attended every AWSA annual convention until poor health made travel too difficult for her. AWSA conventions met in various cities, often in the Midwest where support for the organization and for women's suffrage was strong: Minneapolis, Topeka, Detroit, Omaha, Louisville, Cleveland, Cincinnati, and elsewhere. None of the meetings, however, generated the kind of media attention that women's rights conventions had garnered in the 1850s when they were unique. Nor was every one a total success. At the AWSA's second annual meeting, again held in Cleveland, attendance was so low that one journalist bluntly characterized it as "pitiably small." According to a local newspaper, the previous year had shown evidence of a "good send-off" for the new organization but claimed that the 1870 convention was a "fizzle" and accomplished virtually nothing.[35]

A dramatic episode occurred at this 1870 meeting. Susan B. Anthony again attended, and in front of everyone, questioned why the AWSA did not campaign for other issues besides suffrage, such as easier divorce laws and women's marital property rights. Anthony contended that the *Woman's Journal* was in no position to ignore the need for women's greater freedom in marriage since one of its editors, Lucy Stone, "refused to submit to the legal form of marriage." She was referring to the "Protest" Lucy and Henry had written and issued following their 1855 wedding. Those in the auditorium were shocked. Higginson rose immediately and took Anthony to task for slandering Lucy. Since he had married the couple, he knew Lucy's marriage vows were "as pure and true" as "any woman on earth." Anthony apologized, claiming she did not mean to insult "my friend." But the damage was done.[36]

Every bit as disheartening as these moments of division were the growing number of women nationwide who were apathetic toward or opposed to women's suffrage and to gaining the rights that men enjoyed. At the 1878 AWSA meeting, Lucy despaired that even some members seemed indifferent to the cause. She hoped the AWSA could become more effective and that more women would petition and demand suffrage from their state legislators.[37] But this was nothing new; women's indifference had been evident since early in the women's movement. In 1855, Susan B. Anthony bluntly and all too accurately had assessed the situation: "Woman is the greatest enemy of her own sex."[38] Author Louisa May Alcott wrote Lucy (whom she addressed as "dear commander in chief") a letter in 1883 that was intended to be made public and reprinted in the *New York Times*. She believed that the movement's worst enemy was "the indifference or timidity of women." Many smart, well-connected women participated in church and charity work but seemed afraid to look beyond those activities and do the useful work that "so ennobles life." Alcott continued, "It is discouraging to see so many excellent women blessed with plenty of time, money and brains, content with trifles when so much good work is waiting to be done."[39]

Anthony's catty comment at the 1870 AWSA convention revealed the growing ill-will between the NWSA and the AWSA. In the years ahead, that relationship remained uneasy, and at times outright hostile, especially between Lucy and Anthony. Some of this can be explained by personalities and slights and comments, whether intended or not. Anthony, as we have seen, criticized Lucy for forming the AWSA and starting a newspaper, finding something almost sinister and counterproductive in their mere existence. She accused Lucy of splitting the movement, even though the NWSA was formed first and Anthony and Stanton had invited only a few select women to join it.

Outwardly, Lucy and Anthony tried to exhibit a semblance of mutual tolerance, but their correspondences are filled with snide comments about one another. Anthony believed that if she, Stanton, and Lucy had worked together, they might have led a united movement instead of one "distracted" by division. Early on, she denounced Lucy and the AWSA: "their Journal languishes—their society totters—I do not believe the friends east or west will sustain her in <u>undermining</u> efforts when they come to know their spirit & purpose."[40] Anthony must have been somewhat jealous of the success of the *Woman's Journal* since the *Revolution* had failed. Lucy now had the power of the pen, and the *Woman's Journal* sometimes gave negative coverage of NWSA events or ignored them altogether. For instance, after Stanton spoke on "Marriage and Divorce" at the Decade Celebration in October 1870, the *Woman's Journal* attacked her "loose notions of marriage and divorce," calling them "demoralizing." Stanton, whose own marriage had never been strong, seemed to be promoting free love. "Be not deceived—<u>free loves mean free lust</u>," warned the *Journal*. The *New York Tribune* picked up on the rivalry and depicted it as "War in the Woman Suffrage Camp."[41] A decade later, Anthony wrote a friend, saying that the AWSA was "too weak and too wicked for anything or anybody decent—They *do nothing*—give no *plan* of work to the people—but growl."[42]

This was not the movement's finest hour. Anthony accused Lucy of founding the AWSA on false premises, which Lucy sustained "by keeping a whole cabinet of lies." In 1875 Lucy summed up her reasons for not wanting to unite with the NWSA "after all the experiences we have had of [Anthony]."[43] Anthony responded that "Lucy, like the South, is incapable of understanding magnanimous overtures (thousands of which have been made to her)." The fact that they had once been such close friends likely made them more sensitive to each other's slights. A few women, including Lucretia Mott and Nette, tried to remain neutral (though Mott favored the NWSA, and Nette joined the AWSA). Nette likened the situation to a great "duel in the dark," even calling it a "civil war." Martha Wright, Mott's sister, yearned to see the division end and charitably concluded that it could be explained by the "large endowment of combativeness needed to make a reformer."[44]

Most comments no doubt reflected jealousy and hurt feelings. Neither Lucy nor Anthony seemed capable of forgiving the other and putting aside past misunderstandings. When officers of the NWSA and AWSA both campaigned for Ulysses S. Grant for president in 1868, they avoided appearing at the same event. For many years, Anthony felt resentful toward Lucy, and Lucy in turn was often curt and unpleasant. On one occasion, as Lucy was collecting donations after a lecture at which Anthony was present, she raised the hat as she walked past Anthony, declaring, "I don't want any of your money, Miss Anthony!" Anthony retorted that lecturers should never reject any donation. Lucy then lowered the hat, and Anthony dropped in a half dollar. Lucy snapped, "Well you can be sure you give it to a good cause."[45] Anthony for her part seemed to delight in any news that showed evidence of the AWSA's limited influence. Following the 1879 AWSA convention in Cincinnati, she chortled, "I have laughed in my sleeves" when learning that only twenty people attended the AWSA business meeting. On the election of Henry Blackwell and Higginson as AWSA officers, she commented "What a farce of a system" and called these choices Lucy's "two adorers— one on each side to shield and protect."[46]

Stanton made a few efforts to try to reconcile the two organizations. Henry wrote her in June 1872, emphasizing the need to adopt a new direction by seeking political alliances with the Republican Party and together support Grant as president for a second term.[47] Both organizations saw Grant and his party offering a chance to win suffrage for women. In the fall of 1872, Stanton (whom Alice described as a "pleasant, short, excessively fat little old lady with white curls"[48]) and daughter Harriot Blatch visited Lucy to see if they could get beyond their differences and campaign together for Grant. Nothing came of that. In December 1873, Stanton wrote Lucy and Nette, urging them to forget the past and to consider joining the NWSA. Nothing changed. A year later Stanton again wrote Lucy, asking why she refused to recognize the NWSA "merely because you have a personal feud with its president [Anthony]." She told Lucy she was harming herself by running a competing organization. "Too grand a work awaits the women of this generation to spend any thought or feeling on personalities," Stanton reasoned, and she asked Lucy to consider whether it was her "high principle" that caused her to treat Anthony so badly.[49] Whether she made similar gestures to Anthony is unknown.

This division only deepened with the appearance of a colorful, brassy woman named Victoria Woodhull, who briefly served as a poster child for the NWSA. She was everything Lucy was not, and Lucy was appalled by everything that Woodhull represented. Woodhull grew up in an impoverished, unstable family from the Midwest. She had little education and in her teens, married an older man, a quack and alcoholic. She gave birth to two children, though the marriage was never happy. Woodhull and her sister Tennessee (Tennie) then began earning money as spiritualists, fortune tellers, and psychic healers, traveling around the country plying their talents and selling elixirs. Woodhull divorced her first husband and married a radical anarchist and spiritualist, though she never took his name. The two sisters and the entire family made their way to New York. Settling there and working as clairvoyants, the two sisters caught the eye of Cornelius Vanderbilt, one of America's wealthiest men. They became his favored companions, and Tennie became one of his several mistresses. Vanderbilt set up the sisters in business, and in another unlikely chapter to their life story, they opened the nation's first female brokerage firm, Woodhull, Claflin, and Company, obtaining insider trading tips from Vanderbilt. In May 1870, the two began publishing a newspaper, *Woodhull and Claflin's Weekly*, also funded by Vanderbilt, which covered financial information as well as gossip, Wall Street fraud, scandals, and articles on free love.[50]

Having befriended Massachusetts Congressman Benjamin Butler, Victoria Woodhull won a unique privilege—the opportunity to address Congress. On January 11, 1871, she spoke before the House Judiciary Committee, arguing, in a speech largely written by Butler, for women's right to vote under the Fourteenth Amendment. Members of the NWSA, who were holding their annual meeting in Washington, DC, at the same time, packed the galleries and were thrilled in hearing Woodhull speak. NWSA officers immediately invited her to their convention. Members of the Judiciary Committee, however, ignored Woodhull's suffrage plea.[51]

Stanton and Anthony apparently were delighted with Woodhull—her fresh, exciting persona compared favorably to the tired, staid male politicians

Figure 29. Victoria C. Woodhull (Image TH-63,196, New York Public Library)

who continued to avoid women's demands. Even when she learned about Woodhull's checkered past and disreputable family, Stanton defended her, claiming in 1872 that everything about her indicated "the triumph of the moral, intellectual, spiritual over the sensuous in her nature." Women needed to support one another, not pry into their personal lives if they were to achieve their goals, she insisted. In another moment of hyperbole, Stanton trumpeted Woodhull as "one of the ablest speakers & writers of the century."[52]

But Woodhull's moment in the sun was brief. Vanderbilt remarried and showered less attention and fewer favors on the two sisters. Woodhull's radical views on free love and socialism, as well as her disgraceful family, turned off many people. In the spring of 1872, Henry reported to Lucy that Woodhull "and her set of odds and ends" were beginning to organize a quasi-political party, the People's Party. Woodhull declared herself its presidential candidate (though she was not old enough to serve) and named Frederick

Douglass as her running mate (though she had not asked him). Woodhull's brief campaign platform included a defense of free love, socialism, and women's suffrage.[53]

Lucy was horrified by Stanton's and the NWSA's embracing Woodhull as a worthy addition to the women's movement. Suffragists who were conducting campaigns in Iowa, Michigan, and elsewhere were equally aghast at this embarrassing woman; some blamed the failure of their state suffrage efforts on the negative publicity that Woodhull generated. When Margaret Campbell offered to lecture in Michigan to assist the suffrage cause there, women in the state recoiled, in part reflecting their jealousy toward eastern suffragists. Of greater importance, at least according to Lucy, were women's fears that "we are Woodhulls." Others agreed that Woodhull was harming the movement. A Chicago newspaper concluded that the Woodhull scandal "had killed woman suffrage." Eventually even Anthony became uneasy with Woodhull's antics and felt her presence was demoralizing to the NWSA and to the movement.[54] In 1874, Lucy commented, "The Woodhull & Claflin tribe are a real curse but they make only temporary nuisance. We are gaining all the time."[55] Lucy's competitive spirit was evident, for she seemed to regard Woodhull's negative impact on the NWSA as a boost for the AWSA.

Causing even greater upheaval was an October 1872 issue of *Woodhull and Claflin's Weekly*, which revealed one of the greatest scandals of the nineteenth century—the affair between Henry Ward Beecher and one of his parishioners, Elizabeth Tilton. Both were married. Theodore Tilton and Beecher, one of the country's most famous ministers, had been good friends. For a couple years, however, rumors had been circulating about a possible relationship between the two after Elizabeth Tilton confessed to her husband that she and Beecher had never engaged in "criminal intercourse" but in "a high religious love." As the story leaked, the *Woman's Journal* carried a letter Beecher had written to the *Brooklyn Eagle*, professing his innocence and denying all stories and gossip as "grossly untrue."[56] Elizabeth Tilton then retracted her statement about the innocence of their relationship. Word spread after Tilton told his mother-in-law, as well as Anthony and Stanton, about his wife's affair. Stanton revealed the scandal to Woodhull and to the public, and Woodhull announced the news to a group of spiritualists meeting in Boston. Six weeks later her newspaper exposed all the shocking details, with embellishments.[57] Lucy hoped both Elizabeth Tilton and Beecher would survive the shame but feared the harm Stanton's revelations would inflict on the women's movement. Stanton had put her "nasty" "foot too deep into it for our good," Lucy commented. Lucy wanted to have nothing to do with what she called "filthy" gossip.[58]

Ultimately, the scandal led to both a civil and a church trial. Theodore Tilton sued Beecher for damages, and the case went to civil court in January 1875. Leaders of the NWSA tended to support Beecher. Interestingly, despite Beecher's affiliation with the AWSA, Lucy and Henry stood behind Elizabeth Tilton, feeling she was a woman wronged. Believing Elizabeth Tilton was innocent (even though at one point she confessed to an affair), Lucy wanted to help her "so that she shall never get into the grip of Theodore. She has no money, nor resource of any kind . . . and her heart aching for her children may yield again to the power of her old tormenter."[59] An editorial in the *Woman's Journal* explained that Elizabeth Tilton was a long-time friend, and Lucy refused to imagine she was the type of woman who would commit adultery.[60] Lucy's support of Elizabeth Tilton also may have been influenced by her negative feelings toward Theodore Tilton and his earlier, unwelcome efforts to unite the NWSA and AWSA. Lucy was struck by his claiming rights to the couple's children yet at the same time questioning whether or not they were his. Weeks later, the civil trial ended in a hung jury, due in part to Elizabeth Tilton's ever-vacillating, often muddled testimony. Her reputation was ruined. In a subsequent church trial, Plymouth Church cleared Beecher of all wrong-doing and reinstated him as its minister, reflecting both the double standard but also the church's unwillingness to part with a man who attracted so many parishioners—and so much money. Beecher then took up lecturing at home and abroad in an effort to pay off his enormous legal bills. The Tiltons divorced; Theodore fled to Europe, and Elizabeth Tilton retreated to her mother's home to avoid public scrutiny.[61]

In the midst of this ongoing scandal, more uplifting events were taking place that harkened back to the nation's founding: Women's Tea Parties. The largest one was held in Boston on December 15, 1873, to commemorate the centennial celebration of the Boston Tea Party, this time to protest women's taxation without representation. Some three thousand supporters gathered in and around Boston's Faneuil Hall, which was festooned with banners denouncing a government that existed without the consent of the governed. Attendees, who paid a twenty-five cent admission fee to support the NEWSA, represented all walks of life and included suffragists Julia Ward Howe, Mary Livermore, Higginson, Douglass, Garrison, Lucy, and Henry. Wendell Phillips delivered the main address, and others spoke, read poems, and sang hymns. Lucy's "most stirring" speech drew parallels between the injustice that patriots confronted in 1773 and those that women now faced. The event was a tremendous success in rallying the converted, though it did nothing to change the minds of suffrage opponents.[62] On December 16, the New York Woman's Suffrage Society also held a centennial celebration of the Boston Tea Party. Anthony spoke, having recently been arrested, tried, and fined for illegally trying to cast a ballot with a group of women in Rochester, New York.[63]

Another issue that divided the two organizations was their choice of the convention that each claimed marked the beginning of the women's movement. The NWSA celebrated the 1848 Seneca Falls convention as its key event, given that Stanton had been an organizer and likely author of the "Declaration of Rights and Sentiments." Lucy and the AWSA harkened back to the first national women's rights convention held in Worcester in 1850, which Lucy had attended and helped organize. As Lucy later commented, Worcester "was the one really to stir the public thought," rather than Seneca Falls, which had only a regional attraction.[64] At the NWSA's thirtieth anniversary celebration of Seneca Falls in 1878, some 1,200 people were present for the grand affair in Rochester's Corinthian Hall where Stanton delivered an inspiring speech. The AWSA held a thirtieth anniversary celebration of Worcester two years later. Joining Lucy for the splendid event were some who had been present in 1850, including Nette, Abby Kelley Foster, Samuel May Jr., and William Howard Channing.

But in 1876, both women's organizations participated in the nation's centennial celebration in Philadelphia, an event four years in the planning. Initially, however, Lucy refused to take part. She saw little reason to revel in this moment, since women's suffrage seemed years away. It was "shameful," she felt, that on the nation's one hundredth anniversary, women were "politically and legally still in a bad place." Two years earlier at an AWSA convention, she had urged members to take no part in the centennial. Instead, she instructed them to shut their doors, pull down their window shades, dress in black, and stand on street corners protesting women's inequality.[65] Thus, it was hardly surprising that no suffragists served on the Women's Centennial Executive Committee, which was charged with planning a huge display of women's accomplishments in the main building. With growing demand by all participants for limited exhibit space, however, the Women's Committee decided to construct its own separate building. Appeals for donations went out to organizations and to individuals, and within four months, women raised $40,000 for the Woman's Pavilion. This building later was cited as one of the outstanding structures of the centennial.[66]

Eventually Lucy changed her mind about joining the celebration, seeing it as an opportunity to show off what women had accomplished. She was asked to submit an exhibit, and after receiving a permit, put together a display on tax protests by women, including those by Virginian Hannah Lee Corbin (sister of Richard Henry Lee), physician Harriot Hunt of Boston, Abby and Julia Smith, Abby Kelley Foster, Worcester suffragist Sarah E. Wall, and herself. She arranged the materials in a two-foot square black walnut box with glass cover and a large sign, "Protests of Women against Taxation without Representation," and sent it to Philadelphia. Visitors to the fair soon wrote to tell Lucy they could not find her display. When Lucy visited the fair, she discovered the walnut box placed high on a library shelf where no one could see it. The sign was gone. When she asked that the case be placed at eye-level, a Mrs. Gillespie, who had charge of the Woman's Pavilion, told Lucy the "Protest" was unsuitable to this "time and place."[67]

Lucy had hoped the display would inspire women to join "the peaceful methods" of the suffrage campaign. She saw an enormous irony in hiding an exhibit on women's protests at a centennial fair celebrating "the rights which, a century ago, cost years of bloodshed and strife to establish for men." To her, "the very people who call the world to honor the old defence of a principle see no fitness or need to show that there is now active defence for the application of the same principle to a much larger class, viz, all the women of the country." She sensed that Gillespie could not forgive suffragists for refusing to help plan the women's exhibit, for no one she knew had approved the Committee's decision to create a memorial to Queen Victoria. In retrospect, Lucy experienced "an ache in her heart" and regretted that women had participated at all. Their absence would have signaled women's anger toward a government that ruled without their consent. She also felt the entire women's exhibition presented only a fraction of what women actually were doing, ignoring their role in family, church, school, and community and failing to show the majority of women who toiled thanklessly in their homes.[68]

Lucy, Henry, and Alice did attend the Philadelphia exposition, though they complained of heat, exhaustion, and bad water. The AWSA held a meeting in the city's Horticultural Hall on July 3 to celebrate New Jersey women who, from 1776 to 1807, had been allowed to vote. The Hutchinson Singers entertained the crowd with the singing of "One Hundred Years Hence."[69] Lucy delivered a long speech on the history of New Jersey women voters. An Englishman named Raper also spoke, heralding the right to municipal suffrage that women in England now enjoyed, though he was well aware that far more work was needed to convince Parliament to give British women full voting rights.[70] Henry addressed the crowd and suggested that the nation celebrate July 2, not July 4, as its true Independence Day since on that day, decades ago, New Jersey gave women the right to vote. The NWSA also played an active role, with its leaders protesting what to them appeared to be a mockery of democracy. On July 4, in order to disrupt the Centennial's Independence Day celebration, Anthony and four other women marched into a hall, interrupted a reading of the Declaration of Independence, and presented their "Woman's Declaration of Independence," which denounced the subordination of women. They then exited and read the document to a crowd gathered outside. Even Lucy seemed pleased with this dramatic gesture, observing that the NWSA had "made a really good meeting" and that Anthony and her followers "seem to be on their best behavior."[71]

In the early 1870s, temperance re-emerged as a potent reform movement, making a significant impact—both positive and negative—on the campaign for women's suffrage. The founding of the Women's Christian Temperance Union (WCTU) in 1874 led to what became the nation's largest and most active women's organization in the last quarter of the nineteenth century. The WCTU became even more effective when Frances Willard assumed the presidency in 1879 and served in that capacity until her death in 1898. Willard, born in 1839, grew up on a Wisconsin farm and earned a bachelor's degree at North Western Female College. She taught, traveled in Europe, and for three years served as president of Evanston College for Ladies, a school associated with Northwestern University. It was in the WCTU, though, where Willard found her true calling, bringing her energy and organizational skills to move the association in an exciting new direction. She promoted a "do everything" campaign, meaning members could do whatever it took to curb or to eliminate the manufacture, sale, and consumption of alcohol.[72]

In 1879, Willard decided that supporting women's suffrage would be a positive step for the WCTU, for if women could vote, they would have the power to support laws to end the production and sale of alcohol. Not all members agreed with Willard, but the decision had been made. To Lucy, this alliance was a boost to the movement. She wrote that "Mrs. Willard is coming on grandly. I rejoice in her every day." But while having good reason from her childhood to oppose the consumption of alcohol, Lucy never fully engaged in the temperance cause, feeling that gaining suffrage was a far more important issue. The vote would elevate "all women to a plane when they can work for temperance and every other good thing."[73] If women could vote, they could use their political power to curb or end the consumption of alcohol. While this certainly broadened support for women's suffrage, as Lucy and Henry soon discovered, the decision also increased opposition; manufacturers and sellers of alcohol, saloon keepers, and the many men who enjoyed alcohol now had another reason to oppose women's enfranchisement.

Although the *Journal* tied her to Boston, Lucy and Henry traveled westward to support campaigns in territories as they sought admission to the Union and in states revising their constitutions to consider granting women the right to vote. In the fall of 1877, the two set out by train for Colorado, which had achieved statehood a year earlier. This was their first major statewide suffrage campaign since the disappointing defeat in Kansas. Beforehand, Lucy contacted several wealthy individuals to raise money for this campaign. This trip proved to be another exhausting undertaking, for travel conveyances were crude and distances long. Lucy had hoped they would be assigned to the western part of the state so she could visit the Rocky Mountains, but their initial assignment was in southeastern Colorado. They did get to see Pike's Peak covered with snow and had a "magnificent" meeting in Denver.[74]

Ultimately, however, their effort failed. The final vote on women's suffrage in Colorado was 6,612 for and 14,053 against. Henry likened this outcome to what had happened in Kansas, recognizing that without an endorsement by either political party, victory was impossible. He also accused Colorado politicians of using underhanded tactics, including vote tampering by manipulating the printing and distributing of voters' tickets that read "Woman Suffrage *not* approved." It was impossible to overcome the "fixed habit of masculine supremacy" and male voters' determination to resist anything new, he commented.[75] To Anthony, who also campaigned in Colorado, this defeat showed the wisdom of the NWSA's focus on Congress and on a Constitutional amendment. "It is worse than folly to expect to get suffrage by the state rights plan," she concluded. She was particularly upset by the "Whisky Ring" and, like Stanton, by the "ignorant, bigoted, priest-ridden and ruled masses. . . . native Mexicans, the negroes, and the Irish and German Catholics" who opposed women's suffrage.[76]

But a few years later Lucy and Henry tried again. This campaign in Nebraska would prove to be one of the hardest fought of the decade. The legislature agreed to submit a referendum on women's suffrage to all male voters in November 1882. Women in the state rallied, forming the Nebraska Woman

Suffrage Association and starting a monthly newspaper, the *Western Woman's Journal*. Nebraska suffragists sought support from both the AWSA and the NWSA. In the summer of 1882, while Henry and Alice vacationed on Martha's Vineyard, Lucy stayed home to edit the *Woman's Journal* and to organize the AWSA meeting planned for Omaha in early September. She felt some concern, since the city had not yet extended a welcome to the AWSA, and in an unprecedented move, the NWSA also planned to hold its annual convention there two weeks later. Lucy feared the two organizations might compete and reveal the "ill will" between them, especially after she learned Anthony might attend the AWSA convention. NWSA workers might do more harm than good, in her mind, for they tended to demand rather than to reason "and so create antagonism."[77]

In the late summer, Lucy and Henry journeyed to Nebraska, leaving Alice, now graduated from college and working for the *Journal*, in charge of the paper. They stayed there a month. The AWSA opened its convention in Omaha on September 12. Lucy had feared Anthony's appearance at the meeting, feeling she would cause a disturbance, but when she showed up, members warmly welcomed her. Apparently ignoring her earlier comment

Figure 30. Lucy Stone (LC-USZ62–77,002, Library of Congress, Washington, DC)

that state campaigns were fruitless, Anthony noted that Nebraska was the third state campaign she had shared with "her friend Lucy Stone."[78] Overall, Lucy felt the Omaha convention went well, especially when three-quarters of those at the meeting signed a petition demanding the right to vote. But in lecturing across the state to reach out to male voters, Lucy found travel as rough as it had been in Colorado. Trains ran infrequently, and after one event, Lucy spent twelve hours trying to reach her next destination. She hated the dust that poured in on them, turning their clothes black. By contrast, Henry described the dust as "fine as flour" and observed the "fleecy, gauzy clouds" and "rolling prairies with their beautifully curved outlines."[79] Lodgings were often dreadful. In Schuyler, their hotel room was "wretchedly uncomfortable," and in Wahoo, Lucy reported "primitive accommodations": a tiny room with one small towel, one small pitcher of water, no hooks, nails, or closets where they could hang their clothes, no chamber pot, and no table or shelves on which to put their things. "The bed had been slept in, and it is made up now for somebody else to sleep in, just as we left it." But, as Lucy reasoned, "without the shedding of blood there is no remission for sin."[80]

Lucy's normal optimism did, at times, elude her. It was disheartening to find that in Schuyler, no posters had been hung around town announcing their talks. As happened on every western trip, Henry suffered severe diarrhea. Lucy found Schuyler "very rough" compared to other communities they visited. While they found some dedicated supporters, they also encountered a state suffrage association that was disorganized, underfunded, and suffragists embroiled in disagreement. Lucy missed Alice and wrote her, "Poor little Cubbe! I wish I could hug you and I hope you feel strong." Several days later, she wrote again from Omaha, wondering if the flowers in the garden were blooming and commenting that she "should not mind if they all spoiled if we could carry Nebraska." But she knew they would not. Lucy and Henry sensed from the start that this was a lost cause—worse than Kansas fifteen years earlier—but they tried to hide their feelings in order to keep up the spirits of state workers.[81]

The hardy frontier women Lucy met in Nebraska once again exposed her to the hardscrabble lives of so many women in this country, and their tales affected her deeply. She met a 31-year-old woman who had borne nine children, five of whom had died. The family lived in a dugout, and the woman and her husband were overwhelmed by constant toil. The woman told Lucy that many Nebraska women chose to live in hotels with their children because they could not find the domestic help they needed.[82] To so many women like her, mere survival trumped any desire to fight for the vote.

Despite the commitment by both the AWSA and NWSA and statewide lecturing by Lucy, Henry, and Anthony, Nebraska's male voters decisively rejected the vote for women: 25,756 for and 50,693 against. As in Colorado, opponents engaged in vote tampering, deceptive wording on ballots, blank ballots automatically counting against suffrage, and inconsistent voting rules. The outcome was particularly disappointing to Lucy, Henry, and AWSA members. NWSA officers, by contrast, now seemed more determined than ever to put their energy into a national suffrage amendment to be passed by Congress. But all suffragists began to realize that a decision made by state legislators was a surer road to victory than leaving the issue up to all male voters, a number of whom were immigrants and in the eyes of many suffrage workers, evidenced little interest in women's rights.[83]

Disillusion and defeat thus fostered nativism and classism. Lucy and Henry were disheartened by the countless immigrants in Nebraska who rejected the measure. Creeping into their correspondence was obvious frustration with the number of immigrants pouring into the country and who were allowed to vote. No doubt an exaggeration, Lucy complained that 90 percent of Nebraska's population was foreign-born. The many Germans, Bohemians, Scandinavians, and Irish who had settled there had no interest in supporting women's suffrage. Similar to the words that Stanton had uttered in Kansas and using what can only be called prejudicial language, Henry asserted that the "filthy crowd of cheap fare passengers" he saw on trains made him all too aware that "the republican institutions and extended suffrage are on trial in this country." Only votes by women could improve the situation, for educated, native-born women could influence elections and counter the impact of the immigrant vote. Lucy agreed, noting that more women in Boston were native born rather than foreign born, and if they could vote, they would "save this dear old city from going to the bad!" She feared that "the power is going into the hands of the least valuable class."[84]

These nativist sentiments did not abate. Years later, Lucy was upset when reading about the behavior of young women who were acting like "furies" as they joined men in the 1893 strike against Andrew Carnegie's Homestead (Pennsylvania) steel works. As that labor protest escalated, Carnegie ordered some 300 Pinkerton agents in to quell the massive protest, and the entire Homestead community, including women, rose up in arms. Rather than admiring these women's spunk and bravery, Lucy concluded that all women should be at least 21 before they could vote, for "in that time they may [be] free from old world ideas" and learn "self control."[85] Lucy's moral rectitude and strict notions of proper behavior obviously outweighed concerns she might have felt for Carnegie's exploited workers and their families.

Amidst the state campaigns for women's suffrage, Henry engaged in yet another business venture that took him far from home, returning to his on-going interest in sugar beet production. His restless spirit sometimes made it hard for him to help Lucy, sitting in an office editing a newspaper. In 1870, he accompanied a group of men to Santo Domingo (now the Dominican Republic) as part of a commission appointed by President Grant to consider a plan to annex the island to the United States. That scheme went nowhere, but it rekindled an idea in Henry that harkened back to his late father's business—growing sugar beets on the island. In his thinking, not only might he reap financial rewards but do some good by undercutting the price of sugar cane still being produced in parts of the Caribbean by slave labor. He made a few more trips to Santo Domingo, including one in March 1872. Lucy, indicating that she now understood Henry's needs, reassured him he did not have to be tied down by her work. "I want you to feel that you are not burdened and limited by this place and by us. You <u>need</u> change, variety, sunshine and birds." She promised he could have all the freedom his nature demanded in order to pursue his dreams.[86]

Within a short while, the Santo Domingo venture failed, but in the late 1870s, Henry's interest in sugar beets turned to Maine. Henry, Sam, and several other men founded the Maine Sugar Beet Company and tried to introduce the crop to local farmers. As always, when undertaking any new project, Henry was ebullient, telegramming Lucy, "Sugar beet manufactur-ing a success. Slavery in Cuba is doomed." But that venture struggled. After four years trying to develop a process for turning beets and sorghum into sugar, the business proved unprofitable. One major hurdle was trying to convince Maine farmers to grow this labor-intensive crop, which to them promised little profit. Henry then tried to restart the company in Sche-nectady, New York, but that, too, failed. Throughout all this, Lucy and Nette displayed great patience, tolerating yet another of their husbands' dubious business ventures and the loss of substantial amounts of money. Likely they had no choice. So vested had Henry been in this venture that at one point, Lucy feared his reaction to another failed business could be the end of him.[87]

With the failure of the sugar beet business, Henry spent more time cam-paigning for women's suffrage and writing for and editing the *Journal*. Even in

Maine he had felt some guilt in leaving Lucy with the "load" of the *Journal*. He promised to return within a week with "unabated zeal and interest" in the paper. Two weeks later, he was still absent. Henry finally was home in the spring. Yet for Lucy, who seemed well used to Henry's broken promises, any assistance he provided was a help and a far cry from what most husbands at this time did for their wives. Over the years, Lucy expressed profound gratitude for his assistance, thanking him for his "constant efforts, the patient faith and courage with which you do single handed, year after year, try to secure political recognition for women." He, in turn, mused that in their old age, sitting "snug by the hearthstone," they would ponder "this very path you have taken in the interest of political justice for women."[88] But Henry's speculative tendencies and "butterfly" personality were hard to put to rest, and as late as 1889, he had undertaken a new project: spending thousands of dollars to purchase land to develop homes near Pope's Hill. "He is pleased and Mama disgusted," observed Alice.[89]

Figure 31. Henry Browne Blackwell (LC-USZ62–76,999, Library of Congress, Washington, DC)

Throughout the struggle for women's suffrage, Henry did offer Lucy much needed assistance, and despite his flighty personality, he often proved a supportive, loving husband. In late April 1878, from Portland, Maine, he wrote a revealing, heartfelt letter, concerned that his work meant they would be apart on their twenty-third wedding anniversary. "If I were only as sure that you had been the gainer as I, I should be still more happy," he wrote. "I know I have tried you in a thousand ways—but most of all by not being able to show you the sincere good will I have had. If it had been necessary I would have <u>died</u> for you at any time."[90] However conflicted and guilty Henry felt because of his restless spirit and his fling with "Mrs. P," there is no doubt he loved Lucy—and needed her. The two were apart on their next anniversary as well. In contrast to Henry's dreamy musings, the ever-pragmatic Lucy wrote him: "How long a time we have jogged on pulling together! Well, the last half has been much the best to me. May it get better and better for both of us till the end." A year later and weeks before their twenty-fifth anniversary, Henry addressed his "dearest little wife of mine" and insisted, "<u>Our silver wedding must not be spent apart</u>." He offered to travel wherever she might be so they could celebrate together. Lucy admitted she could not understand how Henry, with his dreamy, impulsive nature, could have married "so grim a person" as herself. That self-assessment contained more than a kernel of truth. In Lucy's hundreds of letters written over the decades, hints of humor were rare, and if present, usually self-directed. Outwardly gentle, kindly, and generous, underneath she exhibited a seriousness of purpose and "the firmness of a great rock."[91]

While Lucy's single-minded commitment to suffrage certainly shaped her life and her marriage, its most profound impact was on Alice. Life could not have been easy for the daughter of such a famous reformer, though Alice admitted, "I am uncommonly proud of being Lucy Stone's daughter." In 1874, Henry and Lucy enrolled Alice at Chauncey Hall against her wishes. This private, college-preparatory high school in downtown Boston had a student population of some 250 boys and fewer than 20 girls.[92] Alice was a sensitive young woman and a nervous student, but always determined to earn top grades and win academic prizes. When she graduated from Chauncey Hall, Alice won a gold medal for English composition. Her social life, however, was limited. Although smart, conscientious, and quick in conversation, she was tall and gangly, with a rather brooding expression. She had only a handful of girlfriends, and few young men were attracted to her. As Henry observed, Alice "lives the life of a grown person rather than of a child." At least through high school, her classmates rarely invited her to social events they hosted. One can imagine how her classmates' parents worried about their children associating with the daughter of such a radical family. Alice hated being left out, and that insecurity prompted her to play tricks on other girls and sometimes to act in a spiteful manner toward them. Mostly her social life involved visiting museums, attending the theater, and socializing with reformers and authors who spent time at their home or at the *Journal* office. She was a voracious reader and spent hours at the Boston Athenaeum, a private library near the *Journal* office, and the Boston Public Library. When Alice finished high school, Lucy encouraged her to attend Boston University, which had recently gone co-ed, thus fulfilling her mother's belief that co-educational schools were far preferable to single-sex institutions.[93] Alice graduated in June 1881 as president of her class and elected to Phi Beta Kappa.[94]

There is no doubt Lucy and Henry were extremely vigilant parents, constantly worried about their only child and anxious to protect her. They purposely hired young female servants to provide Alice with companions. Lucy was a devoted mother but also fussy and fretting, constantly reminding Alice to wear her coat and gloves in cold weather, helping her edit her school compositions, and insisting on accompanying her into Boston. Not surprisingly, Lucy and Henry did nothing to encourage suitors or introduce their shy young daughter to men her own age. When Alice was 16, Lucy had the "motherly" talk with her, relating "all kinds of queer things about boys" and warning Alice that "if you show them any attention they immediately think you want to marry them, and that they would like to marry you." When Alice was almost 22, Henry worried about the "apparent intimacy" between Alice and a young man she had met in school, whose character "we know so little." The solution was to keep them from being alone together.[95] This must have been crushing to a young woman who attracted so few men.

Two other examples of Lucy's attentive parenting—and heightened sense of morality—occurred when Alice was a grown woman. In 1878, when Alice was attending Boston University, Lucy wrote the school's president, Dr. William Warren, objecting to classics found in the school library which "will make a modest girl blush, or an impure boy giggle." She explained that Oberlin College "had expurgated editions of these classics so that they are fit to be read by students of both sexes in each others presence." She urged Warren to contact Oberlin President James Fairchild to determine how to obtain "cleaner editions."[96] In another situation, when Alice was in her early thirties and had gone camping in Canada with friends, Lucy and Henry learned that the conditions in the camp were extremely primitive. Worried about her, they urged Alice to come home by pretending that Lucy was ill and needed her. Alice loved her camp experience, but, dutifully, she returned home.

Alice respected and loved her mother. She understood the heavy load Lucy carried in running the *Journal*, campaigning for suffrage, overseeing the care of their large house and extensive garden, planning meals, and "keeping an absent minded daughter clothed and in running order. . . . I should think she would go cracked, but she pursues the even tenor of her way and shows no sign of breaking down."[97] But she adored her fun-loving, affectionate father, with whom Alice shared light-hearted, spontaneous moments. On summer nights Alice and Henry often sat in Pope's Hill's widow's walk and recited poetry. They read to one another, discussed books, and enjoyed taking carriage rides together, exploring unknown byways around Boston. Alice liked to write poetry, but being a very private person, she was mortified when Lucy published some of her poems in the *Journal* without asking permission. Alice hated drawing attention to herself and was sparing in nurturing close friendships. She did develop a close relationship with Lucy Anthony, Susan B. Anthony's niece. Another dear friend was Kitty Barry, her Aunt Elizabeth's adopted daughter.[98] The two corresponded for years while Kitty was living abroad, and Alice later took care of Kitty as she aged.

After graduating from Boston University, Alice took a few months off to relax and travel and then joined the *Journal* staff in the fall. Lucy always hoped Alice would follow in her footsteps. "She will make the world better and that is what I hope for her," Lucy commented to a friend.[99] In 1887, while working at the *Journal*, Alice started a new project, the "Woman's Column," which summarized suffrage news taken from the paper and was sent gratis to hundreds of newspapers nationwide. Writing for and editing the *Journal* were not tasks Alice undertook grudgingly. She was a superb writer and admitted that she enjoyed working on the *Journal*: "I can't think of any line of work open to me that I should like so well." Lucy was extremely grateful for Alice's commitment to the paper.[100]

Ever since she and Henry had married, Lucy had dreamed of a trip to Europe. That opportunity came in the summer of 1879 when Henry wanted to visit Blackwell family members living in England as well as examine and purchase sugar beet machinery in Germany. But as vacation plans progressed, Lucy decided she could not leave the *Journal* and her leadership role in the

AWSA, not even for a few weeks. Henry felt "grieved" to leave her with such a "heavy load of cares" and wished she could put the *Journal* in someone else's hands. Lucy could not be swayed. Henry and Alice enjoyed several weeks in Europe without her. Vicariously through their letters, Lucy enjoyed reading about their travels across the continent and Great Britain. But her disappointment was profound.[101]

That same year, Lucy at last had her first and only opportunity to vote. Following the lead of some other states, the Massachusetts legislature passed a partial-suffrage law in April that allowed adult women to vote for members of school district committees. The thinking was that mothers, who were responsible for their children's upbringing, should weigh in on school matters. Lucy paid the required $2 poll tax and appeared ready to exercise her hard-won right to cast her ballot as Lucy Stone. Boston's registrar, J. M. Wightman, told her the city solicitor had determined she could not vote "by any other name than that of her husband." Lucy explained that she had always been known as Stone, not Blackwell, and that no law required a woman to take her husband's last name. Wightman refused to let her vote unless she used her husband's surname. Lucy refused, and using this situation to make a point, issued a written protest. Wightman would not budge, insisting that Stone was not her last name. Lucy stood firm but to no avail. Her only opportunity to vote was lost.[102] To avoid similar situations in the future, that August the Massachusetts legislature passed a law requiring married women to use their husbands' names in order to vote.

In the early 1880s, another matter in her home state caught Lucy's attention. The issue was upsetting. In January 1882 she learned that two members of the NWSA, Harriet Jane Hanson Robinson and her daughter Harriet Lucy Robinson Shattuck, were trying to form a Massachusetts chapter of the NWSA, which in Lucy's mind would compete with the MWSA, the existing state association loyal to the AWSA. Higginson urged Lucy to ignore their efforts, but she could see no reason for two organizations to co-exist in the same state, especially on what she had assumed to be her turf. In the *Woman's Journal* she denounced what appeared to be an intrusion by a competitor to the MWSA. Using rather veiled language, Lucy commended the work of the MWSA, adding that suffrage efforts should not be wasted "in a multiplicity of societies" and thankful that "unfortunate affiliations with erratic and immoral movements" in other states had not "retarded" the work in Massachusetts. Robinson and Shattuck went ahead with their plans.[103]

Besides the ongoing conflict between the AWSA and NWSA, opposition to the women's movement intensified and began to cause Lucy and other suffragists a good deal of grief. Remonstrants, as women suffrage opponents were known, became more numerous, better organized, and more effective. On any issue that seemed to broaden women's voting privileges, they submitted petitions demonstrating solid opposition, and they wrote legislators to convince them to vote against bills on women's suffrage. The *Woman's Journal* had first mentioned remonstrants in 1871, listing Ellen Ewing Sherman, wife of General William Tecumseh Sherman, and Elmira Phelps, sister of educator Emma Willard, as among suffrage's strongest opponents. Like these two women, most remonstrants lived privileged lives, many of them married to politicians and professionals. They felt threatened by any rights that might upend their traditional role in the home. They embraced their dependence on men, warning in their petitions that suffrage would "imperil" women's peace and happiness.[104] As the *Woman's Journal* reported rather disparagingly, these women lived in beautiful homes, had healthy children, and lived comfortable lives. These women were too busy reading novels, attending balls and operas, and visiting one another to see the "toiling and suffering women" around them who would benefit by gaining the right to vote.[105]

And remonstrants were not only women; many men joined the organized opposition, including a number of ministers as well as President Eliot of Harvard.[106] William Lloyd Garrison Jr., who was as devoted to women's rights as his father had been, speculated that Eliot, though in many ways a progressive figure in American higher education, feared that granting suffrage to women might create turmoil in his "venerable" institution. Garrison reasoned that no worthy cause ever failed to encounter resistance, and remonstrants proved "that our movement has passed the epoch of contempt, and is deemed important enough to justify the opposition."[107]

Meanwhile, Lucy engaged in loftier actions by again encouraging Massachusetts to take the lead in granting women the right to vote. She and AWSA members tried to convince the state legislature to pass women's municipal suffrage. While the issue generated discussion in newspapers and among elected officials, this was a hopeless battle. Remonstrants came out in force, fighting the issue on all fronts. That same year, AWSA leaders tried to convince the chair of the state's Republican Party to include in its platform resolutions supporting suffrage and women's right to full citizenship. In part, perhaps because of Henry's lifelong interest in politics, Lucy was beginning to see the wisdom of convincing a political party to support their cause. She tried to shame the Republican Party's chairman by noting that Nebraska, Iowa, and Indiana had suffrage amendments pending, and Massachusetts should lead on this issue, not follow others. Her efforts came to naught.[108]

In reading about Lucy's life and her relentless fight for justice, it is hard to fathom how she sustained her spirit and dedication to a movement that lasted so long and stirred so much opposition. Yet her belief in the cause of women's suffrage never flagged. It was, to her, the bedrock of her existence, forming and informed by her character. It was little less than a form of religion, providing her with a way of reconciling herself to the world and making it better that gave her the strength to pursue endless campaigns for women's suffrage, despite crushing results and the many men and women who were indifferent or opposed to the cause. It was her strength and courage that often inspired others. Lucy advised a dispirited Margaret Campbell, who had been lecturing in New England, to ignore all vicious attacks. "It is because I have this quiet faith in the certain triumph of the right, that I am entirely undisturbed by anything which venom and ill nature can do," she explained.[109]

As has become clear, Lucy was a far more complicated individual than she appeared to the public and to the hundreds of suffragists who admired her courageous spirit and dedication to the cause. She straddled a place in two worlds: in private, someone bound by traditional ideas as a wife and mother versus her embodiment as a modern, very public woman campaigning to create a truly just nation. Lucy could not have been easy to live with—so determined, moralistic, and occasionally self-righteous. At times, she put the campaign for women's suffrage and the weekly publication of the *Woman's Journal* above her family—giving up on a lifelong dream of a trip to Europe and family vacations on Martha's Vineyard, and undertaking frequent and lengthy absences from home. Lucy believed the suffrage campaign needed her; the AWSA demanded her leadership; the *Journal* could not survive without her. Lucy drove herself relentlessly in pursuing her dream for this country, but often left little time for quiet, reflective moments alone and with her family.

Perhaps exacerbated by the constant battles she faced and the demanding work she undertook, serious health problems began to plague Lucy. They multiplied over the years and began to affect her ability to work and to travel. Rheumatism flared up frequently and caused increasing pain. In the spring of 1874, now 55 years old, she confessed to Margaret Campbell, "The rheumatism stiffens all my joints, and my active days are over." Finding it difficult to walk long distances, she now rode a carriage between the train station and the *Journal* office. At times her handwriting became almost illegible. In early March 1880, Lucy traveled to New York to consult with Emily about her health. A worried Henry, working in Maine at the time, wrote Lucy, "I love you with my whole soul and if anything happens to you[,] life will have very little worth to me afterwards."[110] Emily detected bronchitis and pneumonia in Lucy's right lung and brought in a specialist who confirmed the diagnosis.[111] "The attack was essentially the result of her over work and over worry," Emily told her brother. She felt Lucy's nervous system was strained and recommended absolute quiet, far from the *Journal* office.

Lucy heeded Emily's advice. In late March, Alice took time off from school to accompany her mother to Wilmington, Delaware, where for two months under a doctor's care, Lucy rested and recovered from her infected lung and irritated larynx. Alice tended her mother, taking "away every burden" and treating her "as tenderly as a baby." Emily again told Henry how anxious she was about Lucy's condition, worrying that another year of overwork could lead to another breakdown. Lucy ignored Emily's warning and returned home in July to get back to work. She suffered another case of bronchitis in 1883 and in late summer, confessed to Campbell that she had been experiencing heart trouble for two years, as well as pain in her throat and back and weight loss. Two months was all she could afford to take from the *Journal*, and she rallied and returned to the office "just as usual." Lucy's main worry was not her own health but Henry, Alice, and her work.[112]

Even though the family enjoyed financial comfort, Lucy continued to dress modestly, shunned corsets, and for lecturing, invariably wore a black silk dress, white cap, white lace collar, and a shawl of fine white lace. Pope's Hill's orchard and gardens produced abundant fruits and vegetables, some of which the family consumed, some of which Lucy gave away, some of which Henry and Alice made into jam, and some of which Lucy sold at a local market. To Lucy, even selling a single box of blackberries or strawberries helped the family, and she continually sought to find a "multitude of economies" in order to save money.[113]

Lucy was beginning to understand and accept her place in history. She responded positively to an invitation to speak at Oberlin's Jubilee, its fiftieth anniversary, held June 29 to July 4, 1883. Once there, she found she was one of only a few women on stage, a far cry from her college graduation when she had not been allowed to read her senior essay. In her address, Lucy

Figure 32. Group Portrait of Blackwell Family on lawn (l. to r. standing: Dr. Emily Blackwell, Ainsworth Spofford, Alice, Lucy, and Mrs. Spofford; seated: Henry and Florence Spofford) (LC-DIG-ds-03,394, Library of Congress, Washington, DC)

heralded Oberlin's achievement as the first college to accept women and blacks. In a very personal comment, she added that early on, Oberlin was the only place where women could get a college education, when "even their own fathers did not know it was wise and safe to educate a woman." All students had to work hard, but that was "small dust in the balance in comparison with the treasure of knowledge which has opened us here." She did not avoid criticizing the school, acknowledging that Oberlin had "held women to silence" and "shook its minatory finger at the daring girls" (like herself) who wanted to debate in public and read their own essays at commencement. But she was grateful that attitudes had changed. So, too, had women's access to higher education, for half the colleges in the country were now open to women. In closing, she chided a school that had helped to free slaves and given women and African Americans access to higher education, but had yet to support women's suffrage.[114]

The celebratory event proved that Lucy had become one of Oberlin's most famous graduates, and even something of a household name. She shared the oddness of this experience with Alice: "Young women have kissed me and some brought their children, telling them to remember they had shaken hands with me—all for the love of our Cause, which they knew I had served."

Lucy took advantage of her trip to the Midwest by lecturing in several towns in the region, holding suffrage meetings every night, and "stirring things up, and they do need much to be stirred." In Painesville, Ohio, she stayed in the most "magnificent house I was ever in," with gas heating and a gas stove, two modern conveniences that astonished her. Lucy was amazed that someone could cook without wood or coal merely by turning on a switch.[115] The world was changing.

Change was also happening to women across the nation and around the world, showing that the movement was, at long last, taking hold, as women's accomplishments multiplied and some barriers fell. The *Woman's Journal* reported on many of these achievements. The paper heralded the founding of Sorosis, a professional women's association, and made note of its anniversary each year. In 1884, an article covered Belva Lockwood's candidacy for president of the United States, running on the newly created National Equal Rights Party ticket. Her presidential platform included women's suffrage, equal rights for all, an end to the liquor trade, and uniform marriage and divorce laws. Interestingly, Lockwood's campaign received little support from either the AWSA or NWSA, for members tended to support a two-party system.[116] In November 1883, the *Journal* was thrilled to report the Washington Territory had struck out the word "male" on its voting requirements. (The paper displayed a more sober reaction five years later when the territorial Supreme Court declared the Washington act unconstitutional since Congress oversaw the territories, and a majority in Congress did not support women's suffrage. Washington had overstepped its authority, and women there lost the right to vote.) The *Journal* celebrated Barnard College's opening in New York as an "annex" to Columbia University and London University's decision to admit women. Still, Lucy added, she had no such hope for this country's premier college, commenting that "Harvard will hold out as long as it can." The paper also noted another first for women with the opening in 1888 of the first publicly funded, all-female college: the Industrial Institute and College of Mississippi located in Columbus.[117]

Ironically, by the early 1880s, as women gained new rights and greater visibility, Lucy's role in the nineteenth-century woman's movement seemed to vanish. She became nearly invisible, leading some historians of the women's movement to all but ignore Lucy and instead focus on other reformers and suffragists, especially Stanton and Anthony. This was due, in part, to the success of the *Journal*, which seemed greater than any individual and which subsumed Lucy. More importantly, Lucy's near obscurity also began with the writing, editing, and publishing of the first three volumes of *History of Woman Suffrage*, undertaken by Stanton, Anthony, and Joslyn Matilda Gage.

The three women first conceived the idea of compiling a history of the movement following the Philadelphia Centennial celebration, which made them more aware of women's role in the nation's past and the need to celebrate it. Four years passed before they began their work in earnest. In part, the outpouring of works on the Civil War, all of which highlighted men's military exploits, motivated them. Women felt their own history could and should become part of the nation's historical memory. Lucretia Mott had long been urging Stanton to produce a history of the movement, and before her death in 1880, she had encouraged Stanton to inaugurate the project. The volumes' publication and near-disappearance of Lucy are reminders of how we come to understand our past, what sources are used, who produces them, and what they include and exclude. It is also true that those who are most assertive in heralding their role often receive the most attention. In these volumes, one of the most pre-eminent figures in the nineteenth-century struggle for women's suffrage was all but absent.

Some of this was Lucy's own doing; she shunned the limelight. Unlike Stanton and Anthony who were skilled self-promoters and delighted in huge, fancy celebrations held in their honor, Lucy discouraged any fuss. Despite her protests, friends found ways to commemorate her birthdays, but always in a low-key manner. For her sixtieth birthday in 1878, the New England Woman's Club held a reception and presented her with a handsome gold watch and purse containing sixty dollars in gold. A few women composed and read birthday poems to honor her. Lucy's seventieth birthday was equally sedate, held in the *Woman's Journal* office where Mr. and Mrs. Samuel E. Sewall presented her with a handsome crescent-shaped broach of pearls and a star of diamonds.[118] She was totally self-effacing. A number of writers, journalists, and publishers throughout her adult life had approached her, wanting to write about "one of the most famous women of the world." She turned them all down.[119]

As early as 1868, Stanton began to record women's history by writing an encyclopedia article on the suffrage movement for *Eminent Women of the Age*. She contacted a number of women reformers, including Lucy, to collect biographical material. Lucy rejected her request. Had Nette not provided Stanton with background information on Lucy, she might have been left out altogether. Although this piece was brief, Stanton was generous in her praise, calling Lucy a "young, magnetic, eloquent" speaker who "was eulogized everywhere by the press."[120]

Eight years later, Anthony was invited to serve as editor of the "woman suffrage department" for *Johnson's Universal Cyclopaedia* and to produce an essay on the suffrage movement as well as brief biographies of its principal activists. Stanton also contributed entries to this publication, including one on Lucy. After writing the essay, Stanton sent Lucy page proofs for editing. Lucy did little other than to correct a few glaring errors, so Henry dutifully edited the copy. Lucy wrote Stanton, "In regard to the History of the Woman's Rights Movement, I do not think it can be written by any one who is alive to-day.... Your 'wing' surely are [*sic*] not competent to write the history of 'our wing,' nor should we be of yours." Lucy reasoned that "there will come a time when this greatest of all the world movements will have made history and <u>then</u> it can be written" but insisted that she did not want to be part of this one.[121] Nette interceded at this moment, informing Anthony that Lucy hated being written about and explaining that when she had tried to gather a few facts on Lucy's life, Lucy had hesitated to share anything, fearing Nette might "print 'em."[122]

Lucy again refused to participate when Stanton, Anthony, and Gage began their new, multi-volume project. She did not want these women to write about her, about other AWSA suffragists, or about AWSA activities. Stanton requested information but heard nothing from Lucy. Though offended, Stanton sent another request. Lucy responded, saying she had never kept records or a diary, did not want to be included and hoped Stanton would not make up anything about her past. After learning about Lucy's reaction, Anthony attributed her behavior to "narrow <u>pig-headedness</u>."[123] As historian Lori Ginzberg writes, accumulated enmity between the two organizations that had developed over the years had "hardened" Lucy against this project. As Lucy herself explained to NWSA member Harriet Robinson, "I must decline all, and any participation in the suffrage history which Mrs. Stanton and Susan Anthony are preparing.... I am more than content to be left entirely out of any history those ladies may publish of suffrage work." Stanton, obviously miffed, observed that Lucy "thinks it a desecration of her immaculate being to be even mentioned by such profane lips as ours."[124] There was some truth to this, though Lucy did believe more perspective was needed. It was, as she had told Stanton, too soon to write the history of a movement that was still in progress, since suffrage had not been won. Lucy also felt uneasy about one organization's members writing the account, for it would—and did—present a biased view of events, putting the NWSA and its supporters front and center, in a most favorable light, while slighting others.[125]

But it was more than high-minded principles, a sense of history, and her profound humility that caused Lucy to refuse to participate in the project. As her correspondence with AWSA members and friends reveals, she had difficulty forgiving or overlooking what she regarded as completely inappropriate past behavior by Stanton and Anthony, despite the passage of time. She remained deeply troubled by their earlier partnership with George Train in Kansas, their embracing Victoria Woodhull as a worthy representative of women, and, more recently, their welcoming Mormon women (or as Lucy referred to them, "the polygamous wives of Utah") into the NWSA. Lucy's high-mindedness and refusal to participate influenced some other AWSA members who also were contacted about contributing to the *History*. Lucy cautioned Margaret Campbell and Ohio Quaker Rebecca Smith Janney from sending in material, telling them, "I think I should do nothing about it if I were you," since the three editors "will do as they please, whatever you do." Stanton, Anthony, and Gage went ahead without a word from Lucy or some other AWSA members.[126]

Producing these enormous volumes was a huge undertaking. The three editors contacted scores of women involved in the suffrage movement, most of whom were alive and associated with the NWSA. They collected biographical material, photographs, posters, convention minutes, excerpts from the *Congressional Record*, essays, newspaper articles, court cases—all related to the struggle for women's rights. The first volume, covering up to 1860 and over 800 pages long, appeared in 1881, having taken six months to compile. Overall, it presented a fairly comprehensive view of the movement during a decade when women had worked together. Since she refused to contribute any information, Lucy's role in the women's movement appeared slight. Nevertheless, brief comments in the *Woman's Journal* review called the volume "large, interesting, and handsome."[127]

The second volume of *History of Woman Suffrage*, which covered the Civil War and the decade following it, upset Lucy and several AWSA members. The book left out any mention of George Train, Victoria Woodhull, the movement's split and the subsequent formation of two suffrage organizations, Stanton's racist comments, the Beecher-Tilton scandal and Stanton's role in revealing it, and any events that conveyed a negative view of Stanton and Anthony. The volume all but ignored the AWSA. This was history from the perspective of the NWSA and its leaders. After Gage left the project for personal reasons, including difficulty in working with two women with such healthy egos, Stanton's younger daughter Harriot Blatch arrived from England

Figure 33. Elizabeth Cady Stanton and Susan B. Anthony (LC-USZ61–791, Library of Congress, Washington, DC)

to assist with the work. She was startled to discover that the second volume had nothing about the work of the AWSA and its leaders; it was as if Lucy, her organization, and its members did not exist. The story focused on suffrage efforts by NWSA members at the federal level, simplifying the multifaceted struggles at the state and local levels, as well as in "club and temperance" ranks, according to historian Julie Des Jardin. Blatch convinced her mother that the volume would be highly suspect without covering the AWSA. She contacted Lucy and Julia Ward Howe, but again both refused to participate. Blatch then gathered what material she could find from the *Woman's Journal*, other newspapers, and convention reports to add a final 120-page chapter covering the activities of the AWSA.[128]

While the *Woman's Journal* had offered positive comments on volume one, it was far less charitable toward the second volume when it appeared in 1882. "No one reading this book would get an accurate or adequate idea of the real history of the woman suffrage movement in this country from autumn of 1867 to 1871 and '72, its most critical and trying time," the paper noted.[129] Lucy was upset that in the second volume, a number of "unworthy and discreditable incidents" were left out, giving the mistaken idea that presented "all the performers as saints." The *New York Nation* agreed, commenting,

"The facts are neither clearly nor ingeniously set forth in this history."[130] Yet no doubt Lucy was partly responsible for the situation since she and other women associated with the AWSA refused to contribute. Certainly her strong sense of right and wrong, her continuing anger with Stanton and Anthony, and her pride led her to refuse to cooperate. Stanton and Anthony had created a history, and they and the NWSA were now in the limelight. The publication heightened Lucy's pique and perhaps fostered in her some feelings of jealousy toward the two women, though she did feel that, someday, history would get the story right.

Lucy could not have foreseen that these two volumes and a subsequent one would become the most definitive work on the nineteenth-century women's suffrage movement and a major reference tool for scholars, even today. While the massive amount of material included in them is noteworthy, bias is pervasive. The heroines in the first two volumes met the approval of Anthony and Stanton. Alice, in an understatement, called the volumes "somewhat one-sided." During her remaining years, Lucy continued to be troubled by such skewed history. In 1886, she commented on the many suffragists and their work that were left out. "No one who reads it would ever dream of the hard and constant part we have had in it."[131] She failed, however, to admit any complicity in creating such skewed history.

In these volumes, one also learns little about the AWSA's statewide efforts such as those undertaken in Vermont, Maine, Ohio, and New Hampshire. Margaret Campbell found the Maine chapter "very faulty," for it was riddled with incorrect dates and failed to mention the five months she and her husband had campaigned there. Mary Livermore felt the Indiana chapter was filled with inaccuracies. The work of Elizabeth Jones in Ohio was all but ignored. Lucy noted that while the editors conveniently left out George Train and Victoria Woodhull, they did "blow a loud trumpet for all the work done by the authors and their immediate fellow workers." But she rationalized that the value of the volumes lay in presenting dates and events, even if some of those were wrong.[132] These volumes presented and perpetuated an inaccurate view of the early women's rights movement and its most significant players. Stanton and Anthony made themselves the movement's nineteenth-century heroines, a view that continues today.

But as women looked to their past, they also looked to the future and realized that the movement was changing. A new generation of women reformers was emerging. Many first-generation activists were in poor health or had died. Paulina Wright Davis died of consumption in the fall of 1876.[133] Lucy's hero in the fight against slavery, William Lloyd Garrison, died of kidney disease at his daughter's New York home on May 24, 1879. Lucretia Mott's death on November 11, 1880, was a blow to all who admired her wisdom, her effective and often biting oratory, and her ability to remain above the fray. The death of Wendell Phillips on February 2 1884, following a brief illness, was an especially sad moment for Lucy, who bemoaned the loss of her dear friend who had been so supportive and generous during the long struggle. She extolled Phillips as a "steadfast defender and advocate of the right to better laws, better wages, to better education and to equal civil and political rights as such." She hoped women would hold a special memorial service for him, since "for more than thirty years he shared the fortunes of Woman's cause and was one with it."[134] She mourned his death for another reason, for he was the last person who could credibly attest to the inaccuracies in the *History of Woman Suffrage*.

"We are all passing away," Lucy wrote Samuel May Jr. in 1884.[135] Another blow was the death of Abby Kelley Foster on January 14, 1887, who suffered a seizure, took to bed, and never got up.[136] At Foster's memorial service, Lucy once again linked the courage of Kelley and the Grimké sisters who took "their lives in their hands" and "secured the right of free speech for every woman." Three years later Lucy's brother Bo died, and Lucy and Henry attended his funeral in West Brookfield, along with many people who came from miles around to honor their esteemed neighbor and friend.[137]

Lucy also lost the close friendship she had long enjoyed with Thomas Higginson. In the 1884 presidential race, the *Woman's Journal* took a rare political stance and came out in support of Republican James Blaine against Democrat Grover Cleveland. Lucy could not stomach the idea of a man occupying the White House who had fathered a child out of wedlock. One of her editorials claimed that his election would be "an indignity" to women. Not only had Cleveland admitted his transgression, but as Lucy learned from a friend, Cleveland had seduced that friend's niece and ruined her reputation. "Think of it a male prostitute and no woman a voter!" she commented.[138] Higginson, however, was one of many Republicans, known as Mugwumps, who opposed Blaine because of revelations of corruption and close ties with railroad barons. Mugwumps like Higginson were able to look beyond Cleveland's transgression—as were many Americans. Higginson objected to the *Woman's Journal*'s support of Blaine and used the *Journal* to express his opinion on the election.[139] He then penned a brief note to sever his ties with the *Journal* and to end his service as a vice president of the

AWAS. Lucy was troubled by Higginson's reasoning, feeling she had always treated him fairly and paid him well, even when the *Journal* operated in the red. We "shall miss his good articles (and his bad ones too.)," she wrote. A number of subscribers also objected to the *Journal's* stance during this election, writing letters that were "bitter and personal." These Lucy promptly threw into the wastebasket, unread.[140] She buried her disappointment and wished Higginson well, stating their political differences had no impact on the respect she felt toward him.[141]

Despite the deaths of these stalwart supporters and her declining health, Lucy was hardly ready to give up the fight. In mid-October 1885, she and Henry traveled to Minneapolis for the AWSA's annual meeting. Here she found "excellent people" and "good single-hearted suffragists." Local papers interviewed several AWSA members and reported positively on the convention. Many people congratulated Lucy on the *Woman's Journal*, praise she passed on to Alice.[142] At the end of the month, Lucy traveled to Indiana where she met a number of women who had never attended a convention or heard a suffrage speech. One woman brought along her four-month-old baby to dedicate him to the suffrage cause. "And as she nursed him from her own breast, he will probably drink in all his mother's spirit," Lucy reported.[143] In November, Lucy attended a reception in Cambridge, Massachusetts, to honor the French author Mme. Alice Durand, better known by her penname, Henry Greville. Lucy was presented to Durand as the "great leader of the woman's movement." Durand was impressed. She told Lucy that Europeans would not welcome women's suffrage for at least another twenty years, but she sensed Americans were ready for it. Lucy told her it took no courage to advocate for women's rights today, as it had in the past.[144]

That same year she wrote a stinging letter to New Hampshire's chairman of the Committee on Statutes, urging him to introduce a bill demanding women's municipal suffrage. She dramatized the situation, noting how women were beaten down by "measureless humiliation and helplessness" and from birth had almost no control over their own interests. She urged New Hampshire, which had given women the right to vote in school board elections, to lead the way in supporting women's municipal suffrage.[145]

No, Lucy had not lost her fighting spirit, and she reacted strongly to issues that negatively affected women. For instance, in early March 1886 she wrote to a Dr. Gleason, protesting a bill that lightly punished men for raping young girls. Lucy was upset that the age of consent for girls was 10, and she reasoned: "She cannot dispose of her property till she is of age. She should not be permitted to dispose of her honor any earlier than she is permitted to dispose of her property."[146] Whether Gleason was moved by her words is unknown.

In 1887, Lucy delivered a spirited lecture to the New England Woman's Club. She insisted on the importance of educating women, citing the founding of Mt. Holyoke and Oberlin. In an effort to correct misinformation in the *History of Woman Suffrage*, which highlighted Seneca Falls as the start of the women's movement, Lucy discussed her career and those who preceded her. She noted that when women first began to speak in public, "an earthquake shock could hardly have startled the community more." The church was "moved to its very foundation in opposition." She continued, "I think with never-ending gratitude that the young women of today do not know, and can never know, at what price their right to free speech, and to speak at all in public has been earned." Lucy described how when she first began lecturing, mobs pelted her with eggs and rotten vegetables and jeered and mocked her. A woman speaking on stage challenged society's traditional view of her proper place. The idea that a woman's sphere was in the home "was like a band of steel on society; challenging that idea brought enormous resistance." In leading the fight for suffrage, "we endeavored to create that wholesome discontent in women which would compel them to reach for better things." Lucy urged women to pursue new occupations by citing notable women who had created successful careers, including sculptor Anne Whitney, a female shoe store owner in Lowell, Massachusetts, and a woman who ran a profitable import business. Appealing to her audience, she celebrated the many women's clubs that now existed nationwide, the opening of numerous women's colleges and co-educational institutions, and the many female professors teaching at them. None of those existed a half century ago. But the work was far from complete, for the greatest challenge remained: ending women's "political disability."[147]

Health issues continued to impede Lucy's commitment to the movement and began to affect her work and daily life. Comments on various ills and even a few thoughts on her possible demise began to appear in her correspondence. For instance, when mentioning the death of an acquaintance, Lucy added, "I thought I should go to her funeral. But I seem much more likely to be at my own."[148] To Campbell, she wryly commented: "I am likely to become real estate." At one point she feared she was going blind, but an oculist prescribed eyeglasses which instantly cured that problem. During the spring of 1886, Lucy's rheumatism worsened, she suffered a serious case of sciatica and experienced severe pain in her kidneys. But she managed to carry on. The pain she suffered increased each year, and she feared she would have to give up her work.[149] In the fall of 1888 she suffered another bout of bronchitis and had to use crutches because of her rheumatism and severe pain in her left leg. She was unsure she could attend the annual AWSA convention in Cincinnati but did not want to admit that possibility.[150] The *Journal* and women's suffrage impelled Lucy to keep going.

As Lucy's rheumatism and bronchitis grew worse, again Emily insisted that she leave the *Journal* and spend time in a warm climate. Lucy finally heeded her advice. Emma, Sarah's oldest daughter, had surprised everyone by marrying George Blackwell, Henry's youngest brother, in late 1875. George, who at the time they wed was almost twice Emma's age, was now a wealthy man, thanks to his many wise investments. Several years after they married, the couple and their young children moved to Thomasville, Georgia, for their son Howard's health. In March 1887 Lucy traveled south to spend time with a niece she adored and to bask in a warm climate. Alice took charge of the *Journal*.

Lucy found the Deep South fascinating, and she shared her insights in long letters home. She was astonished to see peach and pear trees in bloom, leaves budding on trees, and green grass everywhere. But it was a rude awakening to witness the situation of southern blacks. Her visit to a school for black children left her appalled. Lucy soon realized that southern whites did not want blacks to be well-educated, for "they like to have them inferior" so they "would not cause trouble." Attending a black church and hearing its minister preach were eye-opening. She was especially struck by the lengthy sermon, the many well-behaved children who sat still during the long service, and women wearing "all the cast off finery of Thomasville," in their brightly colored dresses, bustles, and fancy hats. Everyone appeared respectable though "utterly poor." Even from afar, though, Lucy still thought of home. She wrote, reminding their caretaker to plant the flower and vegetable gardens, fix the screens and doors, clean the windows, trim the hedges, and exercise their cow.[151]

In Georgia, Lucy found opportunities to meet with local women to discuss their rights and describe the work of the suffrage movement in the North. She was invited to a suffrage meeting where she found a packed hall and much sympathy for the cause. Lucy then conducted a series of intimate meetings on women's right to vote and explained the laws that sustained women's subordination. The Georgia women admitted they could not have demanded their rights forty years ago but felt they should have the right to vote, even though they feared the problems it might cause in the legislature and for their husbands. Lucy showed them a suffrage petition that had circulated in Minnesota, and they signed it. But racism crept in. As one woman signed the petition, she explained that she had been widowed during the Civil War and had supported herself ever since. She would "as soon ask an ourang outang [*sic*] as to ask a negro" to vote. Nevertheless, Lucy felt "very glad to have helped to set the ball in motion."[152] At the end of May when she returned home and in better health, she incorporated her observations and experiences from the South in a speech she delivered to the New England Woman Suffrage Festival, "Condition of Women in the South."[153]

During Lucy's sojourn in Georgia, Alice and Henry carried on with suffrage work. They traveled to Rhode Island to assist the campaign there. It proved to be another uphill battle. Liquor interests were in full force in opposing suffrage, which by this point was closely allied to calls for prohibition. The state's influential newspaper, the *Providence Journal*, took a strong stand against the issue, insisting that women voters would be too emotional and not "discriminating" enough to make sound choices in the voting booth. This so angered some women that they immediately embraced the cause. Since the newspaper would not provide positive or fair coverage of their campaign, Alice and Henry purchased space in it to write and run their own stories. The newspaper took their money but then placed all their articles in the "most obscure corner" of the paper.[154] From afar, Lucy worried about the rigorous campaign's toll on Alice's and Henry's health. "I do not want the sole daughter of my heart to be drawn to death in it, nor the man whose name I do not take hurried to death by it," she commented. Although Henry and Alice continued to campaign, Alice grew discouraged. At the end of March she wrote her mother that defeat was certain. She looked forward to the end and "to have papa able to spend his evenings quietly at home again." She added, "I love you so much it makes me ache."[155] Rhode Island became another state unwilling at this point to give women the vote.

While recuperating in Georgia, Lucy gave serious thought to the idea of uniting the AWSA and the NWSA. The time seemed right. Lucy worried about her declining health. Suffrage work had to continue, with or without her. Achieving suffrage was more important than her uneasy relationship with Stanton, Anthony, and the NWSA. And, in any case, there were a few moments when her relationship with the two women seemed to thaw slightly. In March 1884, Lucy congratulated Anthony on a successful NWSA convention in Washington, DC, and the next year, she offered the help of the

AWSA in pushing for a federal suffrage amendment, closing her letter, "yours for our common cause."[156] But misunderstandings also continued. Two years later, Stanton sent a letter to Sidney Doane Shattock, husband of Harriet Lucy Robinson Shattock, who had helped her mother organize the Massachusetts branch of the NWSA. To a group of women, he read aloud Stanton's letter in which she called Lucy "the biggest liar and hypocrite she had ever seen." In another situation, when Anthony traveled to Boston to claim her share of the Eddy Fund, she ignored Lucy's invitation to spend the day with her. "Instead, she sent me a hateful note," Lucy explained to Nette, "that made me feel the last plank between us had broken."[157] Lucy insisted she was too busy to try to repair relations with Anthony.

Yet both Lucy and Anthony did share the dream of seeing the nation live up to its democratic ideals by granting women the right to vote. If suffrage were to succeed, a new generation of women had to assume the mantle and carry on the work that had defined Lucy's life. A united front now made sense. Younger suffragists could not comprehend why two women's organizations existed, each one pursuing the same goal. When Lucy learned that Anthony was planning a week-long fortieth anniversary celebration to commemorate the Seneca Falls Convention, she suggested they consult their state affiliates to see if both organizations could jointly sponsor this Jubilee Anniversary. Henry was more cautious and feared the submerging of the AWSA. He sensed that Stanton's appearance at the event would be a "great blow" to the AWSA and promote the NWSA by making much of the 1848 Seneca Falls convention which "really was not a very special landmark" in the women's movement.[158] But the seed had been sewn, and the herculean task in merging the two women's organizations into one had begun.

8

"Make the World Better,"
1889–1893

By the late 1880s, Lucy saw unification of the AWSA and NWSA as essential. "This is the Cause not of one woman, but of all women and of the whole race," she explained to Alice and Nette. In words that did not ring quite true, she continued, "Its success and prosperity have always been more to me than any personal feeling. So I could always rejoice in good work no matter who did it." While in Georgia, Lucy had outlined ideas for creating a united women's rights association. She suggested it be an umbrella organization, the "United Suffrage Societies." Under her plan, the AWSA and NWSA would continue to operate as separate entities, allowing each to conduct the work it had been doing for years.[1] She hoped unity would end any lingering resentment and be a positive step forward for the women's movement.

Between October 30 and November 2, 1887, the AWSA held its annual meeting in Philadelphia, and members voted to consider joining forces with the NWSA. The timing seemed right since "the causes of the subsequent separation" of the two had largely been removed. The AWSA appointed Lucy a committee of one to represent the AWSA and to meet with Anthony. If they could agree on general principles, a committee from each organization could then work out details.[2]

An initial breakthrough took place at a meeting between Lucy and Anthony on December 21, 1887. Anthony and her assistant, Rachel Foster, took the train to Boston and met in the *Journal* office since Lucy was not in any condition to travel. Anthony asked that Alice be present as well as a stenographer to take notes.[3] The four women apparently had a fruitful conversation, discussing ideas for unification, a new name and constitution, the inclusion of men as members, officer and membership requirements, and the relationship of the new organization with existing state suffrage associations.

The issue that aroused the greatest concern in Anthony's mind was Lucy's suggestion that she, Anthony, and Stanton be ineligible to lead the new organization since some people held the three of them responsible for the 1869 split. Lucy also hoped a younger woman could serve as president.[4] Anthony opposed this idea, claiming it was not because she wanted to be president (though Lucy rightly suspected she did), but because they should honor Stanton by selecting her to serve in that position.

The process of bringing together the two organizations proved to be a complicated one, taking more than two years to achieve. Lucy's main concern was that the suffrage campaign would continue after she was gone. Although the first meeting with Anthony went reasonably well, within weeks Lucy felt uneasy because she disliked "so many of those who are in that [NWSA] society." It seemed impossible they could ever work together. Above all, Lucy distrusted Anthony, sensing her "old grasping spirit is just as fully alive as ever" in wanting to lead the new organization. In a moment of despair, she lamented that she would prefer that the AWSA "die altogether than to seem to condone Susan's past."[5] She felt the AWSA would be at a distinct disadvantage if Anthony became president, "without any apology or confession." If that happened, Lucy felt it would have been as if there had been "no cause for separation" in the past, validating Stanton's and Anthony's former behavior. Disheartened by the entire situation, Lucy confessed, "I wish we had never offered to unite. . . . it is like trying to make republicans and democrats work together."[6]

The NWSA's executive committee met in Washington, DC, on March 27, 1888, and it soon became apparent that, unlike the AWSA, many of its members opposed unification. Too much time had elapsed to imagine the two groups ever working amicably, posited one member. Clara Neymann, for one, felt that both organizations engaged in good work and that their different approaches were bringing positive results, albeit slowly. There seemed little reason to join forces. Isabella Beecher Hooker, sister of Henry Ward Beecher, argued that some members felt such deep loyalty to the NWSA that it would be impossible for them to sever those ties or transfer their allegiance. The idea of Stanton not serving as president appalled Eliza Anne Chambers, for one, because for forty years, she claimed, Stanton had led "without spot, without blemish, without prejudice and without selfishness."[7]

Anthony, on the other hand, stood solidly behind unification and eventually masterminded NWSA approval, though she grumbled to friends that "Lucy Stone & Co" wanted the NWSA to surrender its name and its leaders and to make the *Woman's Journal* the official organ of a new organization. That paper "has for the whole score of years—either ignored us & our work altogether—or reported so meagerly & crookedly as to give its readers no just idea of us or our work," she muttered. Anthony absolved herself and Stanton of all responsibility for the 1869 split and claimed they would never stand in the way of unification, for it was the AWSA that had them "ostracized—twenty years ago!!"[8] Anthony was effectively reframing the past, insisting that Lucy was responsible for the split and had been the first to create a suffrage organization. In a twisted sense of logic, Anthony suggested she submit Stanton's name as president, in part because she suspected Lucy would never stand for it. She knew Stanton might enjoy the honor but would also have no desire to lead any organization, since she had never shown much interest in participating in organized meetings and conventions and now wanted to spend more time in England. Anthony hoped Lucy would so oppose the mere thought of Stanton as president that she, Lucy, would ask the AWSA to continue on as a separate entity.[9] If that happened, Anthony concluded, everyone would know whom to blame.

Lucy indeed objected to several ideas the NWSA proposed because that organization retained much of the power and was "fresh proof that to unite means for us [AWSA] to be gobbled up." In January 1889, with another planning meeting ahead, she confessed to Campbell, "I dread to work or try to work with these women. The old spirit is in them," but added defensively, "They will find we are not too easy to be managed."[10] Alice tried to moderate her mother's reactions, though she, too, disliked Stanton and Anthony, describing the latter as "tall, sharp, dictatorial, conceited, pugnacious and selfish."[11] But she wanted her mother to support unification, knowing she could no longer continue at the pace she had been working. Lucy rightly sensed that Alice worried about her and supported a new organization "more to save me the burden of the American than with any hope of fair dealing." The second meeting with Anthony in late spring went nowhere.[12]

Alice now found it difficult to sleep, worried that her mother was not getting the recognition she deserved and upset with the NWSA's plan. "She takes all the care and anxiety that belongs to her parents," Lucy acknowledged.[13] Nevertheless, Alice realized that a new generation of younger suffragists desired a single society that would prove stronger than two working independently of one another. Ultimately she was determined to make unification succeed.[14]

Another issue that created tension, at least for Lucy and Nette, was Anthony's and Stanton's continuing insistence that the 1848 Seneca Falls Convention be celebrated as initiating the women's rights movement. To Nette, Lucy wrote, "I think we ought to puncture the bubble that the Seneca Falls meeting was the first public meeting to demand woman suffrage." Lucy had a well-informed view of history, one that went beyond seeing a single convention as the moment when women first began to demand their rights. When Nette informed Anthony that she and Lucy objected to her claim about Seneca Falls, Anthony modified her wording, describing Seneca Falls as the first "organized" convention to demand women's rights. Anthony and Stanton, who made much of the Seneca Falls meeting in their *History of Woman Suffrage*, continued to insist it was the first meeting that initiated the fight for suffrage. In preparing speeches for the 1888 convention, Nette commented that she and Lucy could not publicly state "what Mrs. Stantons [sic] convention was *not*" but she could and did mention the debating club she and Lucy formed at Oberlin as an early example of an organization promoting women's rights.[15]

Amid these squabbles over unification and the starting point of the movement, the fight for women's suffrage at the state level continued. Lucy's rheumatism and heart condition now made lengthy travel all but impossible, so Henry campaigned in her stead. In the summer and fall of 1889, he traveled to the Dakotas and then to the Far West, keeping Lucy informed of his every move. As he departed for the West, Lucy worried about his traveling alone but recognized his need to get away.

In June 1889, North Dakota was holding a convention to write a new constitution as it sought statehood. Women hoped the new constitution would contain a clause allowing them to vote. Once in North Dakota, Henry felt confident that women there would be voting within two or three years.[16] His optimism proved premature, for after meeting with a group of politicians, he realized suffrage was not popular despite support from the territory's top newspapers and from many "public spirited" women. Again, he blamed the many immigrants who were "totally unacquainted with our institutions and controlled by European prejudices to vote against the social and political rights of American women." Liquor interests, fearing the power of women demanding temperance if they could vote, were out in force to oppose the suffrage measure. Despite the hurdles, Henry left North Dakota in his typical over-confident fashion, boasting to Lucy, "If Dakota is saved it will be wholly due to my coming & I think I could surely save it by remaining two or three weeks longer."[17] Dakota was not saved, but women there wrote Lucy to commend Henry's efforts. To Lucy, the defeat was full of irony, since Dakota men "gave more votes for the enfranchisement of Indians who are now after their scalps than they did for women!"[18]

Henry's next stop was Montana, which was also seeking admission to the Union. No women's suffrage meeting had ever been held in the territory, and he feared that submitting women's suffrage to all male voters would be certain defeat. It would be Colorado and Kansas all over again. Like North Dakota, he felt Montana should put the vote on enfranchising women in the hands of the legislature rather than let male voters have a say. If elected officials could vote on the idea, Henry predicted Montana women would have the vote within five years. Yet he was again overly optimistic as to the benefits of legislative action, for he soon realized that politicians were "timid," and their only desire was to remain in office or ascend to a higher position. Supporting women's suffrage was political suicide. In their frenzy to achieve statehood, Montana politicians "are afraid of <u>anything</u> that may endanger the ratification of their new constitution by the voters," Henry concluded.[19] He observed that with the completion of the Northern Pacific Railroad, many "rough, ignorant and depraved" men had settled in Helena, where every other building seemed to be a saloon, gambling hall, or brothel. Despite support from twenty-two legislators and the territory's Republican newspapers, "saloon interests" seemed to control the state legislature and stood firm against giving women the right to vote. Both political parties there opposed prohibition and feared that if women voted, they would make the issue the law of the land.[20]

From Montana, Henry traveled west to Washington which had voted for women's suffrage in 1883, only to witness the territorial Supreme Court overturn it five years later. The issue had little chance of being included in a new constitution, since it jeopardized Washington's chances of achieving statehood. A petition was circulating whose signers promised to vote against the new state constitution if it did not include women's suffrage, a threat that did little good.[21] The constitutional convention, comprised primarily of lawyers and politicians, seemed "to be in a conspiracy to shut women out," Henry reported. The men who supported women's rights "are shunned and avoided."[22] He saw no future for the measure and returned home, now with little hope that any state, even in the West, would pass suffrage any time soon.

In the East, with unresolved issues over unification pending, the AWSA and NWSA moved ahead with their week-long joint celebration of the

Seneca Falls Convention. This event, better known as the International Council of Women, convened at Albaugh's Opera House in Washington, DC, from March 25 to April 1, 1888. Some eighty speakers came from across the globe, representing fifty-two different women's organizations and eight foreign countries. The air was festive, with banners draped across the huge hall. Above the stage hung a portrait of "that loved, venerated woman," Lucretia Mott. In advance and from behind the scenes, Anthony begged NWSA members to avoid any mention of Woodhull "scandals" or any other negative events from the past.[23] Each tightly scheduled day was chock full of activities, musical performances, and speeches on numerous topics, including suffrage, temperance, industrial labor, education, prostitution, religion, and the law. Women from India, Denmark, France, Italy, and elsewhere reported on the status of women in their countries.[24]

The convention scheduled a special session for Saturday, March 31, the "Conference of the Pioneers," to honor several first-generation activists, including Lucy, Anthony, Stanton, Nette, Henry, Douglass, and others. Anthony introduced Lucy, calling her "one of the oldest and most persistent of the pioneers," and then took her hand as they came forward together on stage, prompting loud cheering from the audience. In the twenty minutes she had been allotted to speak, Lucy shared her own awakening to the cause and her early struggles in campaigning for the rights of women.[25]

Because both Anthony and Douglass made much of the Seneca Falls convention as the starting point of the women's rights movement, Lucy intentionally harkened back to events that preceded it. "Long before our time, the idea of woman's rights was in the air," she intoned. Lucy mentioned occasions that predated Seneca Falls, including women involved in the abolition movement who realized their demand for equal rights applied to women as well as to slaves. She highlighted Oberlin College's opening its doors to women, and she paid tribute to Sarah Grimké, Angelina Grimké Weld, and Abby Kelley Foster, who in the late 1830s broke barriers by gaining women the right to speak in public. Lucy then shared personal moments that had drawn her into the fight for women's rights—being rejected as a voting member of her church because she was a woman, being inspired by Hiram Powers's statute of the Greek slave, and her early struggles as she began a career in public lecturing before Seneca Falls. Applause constantly interrupted Lucy's remarks.[26]

Despite the celebratory nature of the meeting and an impressive turnout, not everyone was pleased, least so Alice. While she described the convention as "fine," the attendance "large," and the papers "good," she grew disenchanted. She was upset with Anthony, who had failed to tell her mother she would be called upon to speak, and she found Anthony's hand-holding of her mother an example of "ostensible friendliness and real unfriendliness." While admitting the convention accomplished much good, Alice felt that in spite of their triumphant speeches, NWSA members did not want to unite.[27] NWSA officials had asked that both organizations convene their conference committees in Washington to share details for forming a new organization. The NWSA then communicated that it could not discuss anything until plans had been presented to its members, creating another delay in the process.

Also distressing to Alice was that Stanton's and Anthony's speeches avoided any mention of George Train, Victoria Woodhull, and other embarrassing topics. Alice felt especially defensive when she heard others criticizing her mother. "It is rather irritating to see unworthy women who hate your mother and have constantly maligned her, receiving a week's continuous ovation." She found Anthony's introduction of her mother insincere. "I hate the Nationals," she complained. Furthermore, Alice could not fathom how NWSA members could attend a session discussing social purity and then parade over to the White House to be feted by President Grover Cleveland, knowing full well that he had fathered a child out of wedlock. To Lucy this also proved that "the unclean side is still uppermost with them [NWSA]." Naturally Alice and Lucy did not attend the president's reception. Alice concluded that she had never spent "a more disagreeable week."[28] Unlike Alice, Lucy took it all "placidly" and felt Anthony had presided effectively.

Alice was nonetheless able to move beyond her disgruntlement, realizing that the greater good would come by uniting the two organizations. The two sides finally were able to come together and on February 8, 1889, issued an "Open Letter to the Women of America," signed by Lucy, Julia Ward Howe, Mary Livermore, and Mary Eastman for the AWSA and Stanton, Anthony, Belva Lockwood, Matilda Joslyn Gage, and Frances Willard for the NSWA. In their joint letter, the women declared they were ready "to work in harmony with all other Associations of like character—and as in union there is strength." Lucy and the AWSA offered to cover the expenses of a fortieth anniversary celebration of the 1850 Worcester convention two years hence to celebrate the unification of the two organizations. That November, announcements began to publicize this 1890 meeting, and unification efforts moved ahead.[29]

Both in public and private, however, the relationship among AWSA and NWSA officers and members remained rather tense. In a May 1890 article in the *Woman's Journal*, Henry challenged Stanton's reminiscences of the 1867 Kansas campaign and the involvement of George Train. Upset by his essay, Stanton wrote Anthony and Clara Colby, a Nebraska suffragist and editor of the *Woman's Tribune*, claiming that Henry was presenting "lies & insults" instead of facts. He had attacked her and seemed "determined if possible to kill me." Stanton insisted that she and Anthony were not responsible for Train's presence in Kansas, claiming he had mustered support from Democrats and come to the state on his own. She felt their friends and AERA members in the East had then deserted them and blamed them for the loss in Kansas.[30] From England, Stanton sent a letter to read at the fortieth anniversary of the Worcester Convention to air her distress, especially with Henry. He again had accused Stanton and Anthony of aligning themselves with Train. In a most revealing statement about herself, Stanton fussed, "I am afraid we shall always have trouble with Blackwell, & Lucy. You see they make a point of contradicting what I say." In looking back at the 1850 Worcester convention, which she had not attended, Stanton gave full credit to Paulina Wright Davis for doing all the work.[31] When learning of this, Lucy corrected Stanton, pointing out that several women, including herself, had helped organize the meeting. Weeks later, Stanton asserted that Lucy never planned to be at Worcester and only showed up "when she saw it was to be a success." This infuriated Henry, knowing how ill Lucy had been at the time, having barely recovered from her near-fatal bout with typhoid fever. He now regretted that they had ever agreed to unite with the NWSA. Stanton, who did not appreciate being challenged, now accused Henry of being "autocratic" in his dealings with her.[32]

Despite such acrimony, the two organizations carried out Lucy's suggestion and held their first joint annual convention in Washington, DC, which met from February 18 to 21, 1890, under a new name, the National American Woman Suffrage Association (NAWSA). On the first day of the meeting, the two organizations announced their formal merger. Stanton was present, along with her two daughters, though they did not stay long. As soon as Stanton was named president of the NAWSA, the three women left and sailed for England. Lucy's worst fears were realized: Anthony, as vice president, now took over the new organization in Stanton's absence. Lucy could do little to counter the direction of the new organization and the appointment of officers, for she was at home, ill with a wracking cough and unable to attend this important meeting.

Due to her age and declining health, Lucy never played a major role in the NAWSA, though officially she served as head of its executive committee. She did attend its 1892 convention in Washington, DC, where she and Stanton testified on behalf of women's suffrage before the House Committee on the Judiciary. There, Stanton delivered her most eloquent and inspiring speech, "Solitude of Self." In it, she urged all women to end their dependence on others by gaining a sound education and developing a strong sense of self. "No matter how much women prefer to lean, to be protected, and supported, nor how much men desire to have them do so, they must make the voyage of life alone. . . . able to guide our own craft," intoned Stanton.[33] Women had to develop strength and self-reliance to handle the challenges they would face in life. Lucy was so moved by this speech that she printed it in its entirety in the *Woman's Journal*. No doubt Stanton's words hit home, for Lucy could readily identify with Stanton's call for women's access to higher education and for developing self-mastery. She herself had served as a model for both.[34]

Although her lecturing days were mostly behind her, Lucy occasionally spoke to groups near home. In early March 1892, the Mothers' Club of Cambridge invited her to speak. This was an elite, conservative women's group, comprised primarily of professors' wives as well as Wellesley College President Alice Freeman Palmer. Daughter Alice learned that some members were upset when they heard that the radical Lucy Stone was to address their meeting; others were excited. For the event, Alice helped Lucy don her usual black silk dress and white cap, making her "the sweetest looking old lady you ever saw." A carriage picked her up and took her into Cambridge. Lucy spoke on "The Progress of Women in 50 Years," again moving beyond Seneca Falls to include earlier events and apparently captivating club members. The women applauded loudly, fawned over her, and asked so many questions that she missed her train home.[35]

Lucy also lectured at a Farmers' Institute meeting in West Brookfield, where she sought to convince the men to pass a resolution favoring women's suffrage. At the end of her speech, she received a rousing ovation, and the suffrage resolution carried with only a couple dissenting votes. Afterward, several older men came to talk to her. Some had had Lucy as a teacher years ago or had attended school with her. "She was petted and made much of. She felt great comfort among the farmers of West Brookfield," reported a contented Alice. Lucy felt perfectly at ease, for as she often said of herself, "there was a good farmer spoiled when I went into reform." When she returned home that night, she was "rosy, beaming, and perfectly happy."[36]

For over a year, several women had begged Lucy to sit for her bust, which could then be exhibited at the 1893 World's Columbian Exposition to be held in Chicago. Lucy insisted, however, "It was not my wish" and hoped the women would use any money they raised "to help the Cause of Women" rather than spend it on a sculpture. Members of the New England Woman's Club ignored her wish and moved ahead. When Lucy was absent from one meeting, members announced their plans and collected $150 on the spot. A committee was appointed to raise the rest of the money. Two women finally wore down Lucy, convincing her that the money was given to honor her and would not have gone to support suffrage work. The Club then secured the noted sculptor Anne Whitney to carve the bust, a choice that must have pleased Lucy. In 1892, the bust of Lucy was finished. Alice saw the carved image of her mother and felt it conveyed her "fine noble face" with "an expression of confidence" and sense of "motherliness toward the whole human race."[37]

Now feeling proud of the sculpture, Lucy invited her brother Frank and his wife Harriet to see it before it was sent to Chicago. She urged the two to visit for a week. "[W]e are now so old that we cannot put off our visits if we expect to see each other here any more," she wrote. She also invited Sarah, hoping the three Stone siblings could spend time together. She offered to pay their train fares and sent along $5 in spending money. Lucy promised to show Frank all the sights of Boston and hoped he could come. "We may never have another chance to visit." She admitted she was increasingly lame and finding it harder to travel and, at times, even to move.[38] Frank and Harriet, though not Sarah, came in March, and the Stone siblings reminisced about their childhood. Lucy told her brother she wished she had given their mother "an easier time" when she was young. One of Hannah's major worries had always been Lucy's lecturing on Sundays rather than devoting that day to the Lord. Nevertheless, the two siblings concluded that Hannah must have been happy to see her children become such respected figures.[39]

The final trip Lucy undertook was in May 1893 when she and Alice traveled by train to Chicago to attend the World's Columbian Exposition, or as it is also known, the Chicago World's Fair. This was an extravagant undertaking, a virtual city covering nearly 650 acres built on Chicago's South Side. Unlike women's efforts to create their own Woman's Pavilion for Philadelphia's 1876 centennial celebration, this time they did not have to raise money for a special building to display their activities and achievements. The US government funded this structure, which was regarded as an integral part of the Exposition from day one. The building's purpose was to showcase women's accomplishments from around the world.[40]

Although Lucy was frail and often in pain, she could not pass up this opportunity to attend the Exposition. She was one of 330 women chosen to speak during the week-long speaker's forum held in late May, the Congress of Representative Women. When Lucy was presented at one session to discuss dress reform, the woman introducing her was "drowned in a wave of applause."[41] When she and other American suffragists were scheduled to speak, hoards of women rushed into the hall and were "nearly unmanageable."[42] On May 24 at another event held in the Art Palace, the new home of the Art Institute of Chicago, Lucy delivered her final public address: "The Progress of Fifty Years." She made a "sweet picture" dressed again in her black silk gown and lace cap and collar. Speaking in her "inimitable style, half humorous, half pathetic," according to one newspaper, Lucy explained women's accomplishments over the past decades, touching on education, employment, and suffrage. She described the difficulty colonial girls encountered in trying to acquire an education, limited in some places to attending school in the early morning before boys appeared for their school day. In stark contrast, she celebrated the present by citing the University of Chicago, which now admitted women and even had female professors and female regents. She urged women in the audience to pressure their husbands to support suffrage for women and to end the injustice of grouping women with "criminals, idiots, felons, and lunatics"—those in this country who were not allowed to vote.[43]

Lucy and Alice also met with a number of suffragists, including Carrie Chapman Catt who had visited Lucy a couple of years earlier when she traveled to Boston. In Chicago the two discussed the possibility of a victory for women's suffrage in Colorado, though Lucy deemed the case "hopeless."[44] Henry, who remained at home, urged Lucy and Alice to travel home by way of Mammoth Caves in Kentucky, whatever the cost, so they could see that amazing natural wonder. He also hoped the warm, dry air there might do Lucy a world of good. Henry constantly worried about Lucy's health and insisted that if she sensed she was coming down with pneumonia again, she should take two doses of calomel, still a popular mercury chloride remedy.[45] He sent Lucy updates on the suffrage campaign in Colorado, details of stories from the *Woman's Journal*, and news on labor union unrest.[46]

In these final few months of her life, Lucy had more time to reflect on her role in the women's suffrage movement. A few years earlier, she had commented, "I am glad to have been born when it was needed. Very early in life

I knew this was my work. . . . Very thankful am I for the noble women and men, my fellow workers. . . . Perhaps we shall see its fulfillment[,] perhaps not."[47] She also took time to settle her finances, insisting to Henry that all her collected rents and interest now be deposited in her own bank account. Still determined to operate as an independent women, she explained that she had never liked having her money in his account and only had gone along with it because "you did so much for women that I felt I had allowed it."[48]

Upon her return home from Chicago, Lucy's health spiraled downward, and her appetite and ability to digest failed her. She could not eat solid food and continued to lose weight and strength every week, though she felt no pain. In August, Lucy journeyed to Gardner, Massachusetts, to be with Sarah and to enjoy the tranquility and fresh air of rural Massachusetts, hoping her condition might improve. But she knew she was dying. Emily and several specialists diagnosed stomach cancer. At this time, there was nothing anyone could do to effectively fight cancer, other than to make a patient as comfortable as possible. While doctors could identify it and sometimes amputated an external tumor, they were not able to perform surgery successfully on internal organs. Infection and bleeding were too great a risk and usually speeded death rather than slowed it.[49] Emily prescribed a variety of possible cures, including pepsin, dandelion, Valentine's beet juice, milk, and quinine pills—all to no effect. From Gardner, Lucy wrote Henry, describing her condition: vomiting "dark matter" and bowel movements that were "as black as ink." Even milk upset her stomach. Lucy spent her days in Gardner sitting or lying down, interspersed by short walks in the garden. She tried to console Henry about her condition: "I hope to be better but think my working days are over." Realizing he and Alice would soon be without her, Lucy urged him to take care of his health, "for Alice's sake. She will need you."[50] On receiving this letter, Henry, who had been overseeing the *Woman's Journal*, immediately dashed off a note to her and then boarded a train for Gardner. "I shall stay by you till I get you restored to your usual health, which I think will not be long. <u>Don't feel discouraged</u>," he wrote with his typical optimism.[51] His visit apparently restored Lucy's spirits but did nothing to improve her condition.

Henry and Alice reluctantly accepted the fact that Lucy was dying. Alice had returned from her annual summer camping trip in Canada and now dropped everything to tend her mother. Doctors pumped Lucy's stomach since she could not digest food, but that provided no relief. In desperation, Henry consulted other physicians, including a homeopath. Henry told Julia

Ward Howe that doctors saw little chance of Lucy's ever recovering. He urged Howe to contact Lucy, for "you have been more to her than a sister for twenty years, and she has relied on you in her work as on hardly any other human being." He asked her not to call Lucy's case hopeless, for they had not yet related the physicians' prognosis to Lucy. Henry closed, "Dear Mrs. Howe, what shall I do without her?"

As instructed, Howe wrote Lucy with a false sense of optimism, urging her to get well, for "No one can fill your place." She suggested a change of scenery and drinking milk and promised to visit soon.[52]

As word spread about Lucy's condition, friends, acquaintances, as well as strangers began to visit Pope's Hill to pay their respects; others wrote heartfelt notes and letters. Ada Bowles of Gloucester told Lucy how much she and other women owed her for her relentless pursuit of women's rights, such that "another generation will rise up and call you 'blessed.'" Bowles said that Lucy had made friends around the world, "won by your lifelong fidelity to one of the world's greatest needs—equal justice."[53] Nette wrote Lucy a tender letter, wanting to visit so they could "talk over the many things in which we were both so much interested and for which we have both given the best of our lives." Higginson wrote and signed his letter "your old friend."[54] Samuel May Jr., who had launched Lucy's lecture career and remained a close friend, wrote after receiving a note from her, distressed in learning of her condition. He celebrated the cause they had shared together, to "which you have been so true to, which you have seen so wonderfully advanced and prospered in your life-time; growing from nothing, so to speak, until it is now a mighty power . . . and on the eve of becoming a triumphant one." While she would not live to see women's suffrage triumph, Alice would, due "to your faithful perseverance."[55]

News of Lucy's illness also appeared in the *Woman's Journal*, and scores of notes and letters of concern followed, as did many more visitors who came to pay their respects and bring flowers and gifts. Mr. and Mrs. Bowditch visited. He had known Lucy since she first began lecturing. So moved was he when seeing her now that he cried and kissed Lucy's hand repeatedly. Adeline Howland and Sarah Henshaw paid their respects and expressed hope that Lucy would live to see women gain the right to vote. "Oh I shall know it. I think I shall know it in the next world," Lucy responded, a remark she repeated to several visitors. A neighbor, Mrs. Pratt, urged Lucy to have courage, to which Lucy replied that she did not lack courage, nor had she ever. "I like to go to the other side; I have not the least fear of it." Hattie

Turner wished Lucy would live to see suffrage become a reality, and again Lucy answered that she might know about it. If she did not, "I shall be doing something better. I haven't a fear, nor a doubt, nor a dread." Frank Garrison visited, and Lucy expressed her gratitude for the work of his father and all of Frank's siblings.[56]

Knowing she could not be cured, Lucy told Henry and Alice, "the kindest thing you can do is to let me pass on. It costs too much to be cured—in suffering to myself."[57] She thanked Henry for his recent participation in the New England Agricultural Fair by going in her stead and added, "Dear Mr. Blackwell! How he has helped!" Everyone commented on how Lucy was as brave facing death as she had been courageous throughout her entire life. At peace with herself and with a faith still present from her mother's early ministrations, Lucy regarded death as a part of the natural progression of human life. For the past few years, she had often expressed that same attitude when seeing various parts of her body fail her, commenting calmly that whatever part of her body was giving out had served her well.[58]

Lucy continued to weaken, but every so often she rallied and became her former take-charge self, giving directions on housekeeping matters, expressing worries about Henry and Alice when she was gone, establishing who would inherit her money, which libraries should receive the many tracts and records she had saved over the decades, and discussing details of her funeral service and burial.[59] Lucy's will, which was to be executed by Henry and his brother George, stipulated that all her property was to go to Henry and Alice, but with unexpended funds to benefit the women's suffrage movement.[60] What Lucy most regretted about dying was leaving Henry and Alice. "I have not the smallest apprehension. I know the Eternal Order, and I believe in it." She told Alice, "I fully expect that the next world will be just as good as this—very likely better." Her daily worry was how much work she was creating for everyone. "I am afraid I have strength enough left to last two or three weeks, and then you will all be worn out." But to one of the Garrison sons she admitted, "I am glad I was born, and that at a time when the world needed the service I could give."[61]

According to everyone who visited Lucy, she was "perfectly placid and fearless" and faced the end with sweetness and calm in her final weeks of life. When she finally forced her doctor to admit that she would never recover, he urged her to approach the end as serenely as possible. Lucy responded, "There is nothing to be unserene about." Although she had not been a regular churchgoer as an adult, her profound belief in an afterlife surprised even

Henry. When a visitor mentioned her coming back to communicate to those who were still here, she responded, "I expect to be too busy to come back." And to another friend, she commented, "I look forward to the other side as the brighter side."[62]

Having returned to Pope's Hill, Lucy spent time in bed looking out the window at the flowers and trees, the sunlight, and the natural world that had always provided her such solace and strength. Lucy thought about Coy's Hill and the several babbling brooks on the Stone farm. She thought back to her childhood, to her distress when she learned from the Bible that God had supposedly made women inferior, to her studying and being tutored, and to her teaching school for a dollar a week. To Frank, she wrote her final farewell to inform him she was very ill. "But you have always been a dearly beloved brother, and I have always had profound respect for your integrity, your honesty, your love of truth. . . . I have no fear or dread of the life beyond, and sometime, somewhere, I hope to meet you there."[63] Both Emma Blackwell and Sarah visited her.

Even as she was dying, Lucy could not let go of women's suffrage. In mid-September, she wrote Mrs. John Hanna of Denver, expressing support for the suffrage campaign in Colorado and urging her to meet Carrie Chapman Catt.[64] And Lucy continued to ponder women's proper role. In a fascinating revelation that underscored this very modern, emancipated woman's deeply ingrained, traditional ideas about women, Lucy told Alice that a woman's "truest place is in a home, with a husband and with children, and with large freedom, pecuniary freedom, personal freedom, and the right to vote." She was not convinced that a woman should necessarily share equally in "bread-winning," since she had to bear and rear children "and her hands are full." But if the need to earn a living fell to her, as it had for Lucy, she "must be equal to it."[65] Whether Lucy spoke these words out of concern for Alice's future, hoping she would marry and bear children, or she had come to value home and family above all else is difficult to say. For almost forty years, Lucy had tried to balance family needs with her lecturing career and profound commitment to women's rights, at times with less success than at others. Here, on her deathbed, she expressed the importance of family, the proper role of women, and her love for Alice.

Lucy spent her final few days lying in bed, weak, vomiting, often unable to open her eyes or to speak. Among her last words, she expressed hope that "woman Suffrage and all other good things will come."[66] She admitted, "I feel as if there were ten years more of work in me, but if I am to go now, doubtless other work awaits me elsewhere." Lucy revived momentarily when she learned the exciting news that New Zealand had passed a law giving women there the right to vote, becoming the first nation to do so and giving Lucy's "loved cause" new strength.[67]

On October 18, 1893, at 10:45 p.m., Lucy Stone passed away. As Alice leaned over her dying mother, Lucy's whispered her final words to her daughter: "Make the world better."

Lucy's funeral service was held three days later in Dorchester's Church of the Disciples. Over 1,100 people attended, lining up well before noon for the 2:00 p.m. service. Many could not find seats and had to stand throughout the service. Bunches and garlands of yellow roses and nasturtiums and white flowers, the colors of the women's movement, presented by a number of women's suffrage organizations, festooned the church's interior. At the side of the pulpit was a plaster cast of the bust Anne Whitney had sculpted of Lucy and beside it, a life-size portrait of Wendell Phillips. The casket was open. The Rev. Charles G. Ames conducted the service. Six men and six women served as pall bearers. A number of friends spoke as Lucy had requested, including Mary Livermore, suffragist and Unitarian minister Anna Garlin Spencer, and Thomas Higginson.[68]

William Lloyd Garrison Jr. spoke and celebrated Lucy for having devoted most of her life to working to make this nation a true democracy. "She takes her place among the founders of the true republic."[69] Garrison said that it did not fit the spirit of Lucy's life to "indulge in sorrow and regret"; instead everyone should rejoice at the life she had led and the impact she had on the world. "The influence of that sweet, benignant face, of that sympathetic voice which never failed to inspire affectionate respect, of that character so simple and genuine and steadfast" encouraged many to take up the cause.[70] A letter read at the service from British reformer Laura Ormiston Chant said that Lucy represented the voices of thousands from England whose "hearts will be very sore at the thought of the loss we have sustained."[71]

Several days later, the minister of Boston's Church of the Unity, Minot J. Savage, delivered a eulogy, or what he called a "lecture," in Lucy's honor. He provided a brief background of Lucy's life, including vignettes that demonstrated her character, her determination to acquire a college education, and her dedication to improve the lives of all people. He highlighted the positive changes that had occurred to women because of her: marital property rights and women's freedom to travel, to attend college, and to work in most professions that men had long dominated. He extolled her "womanliness," her "gentleness" and "sweetness." Her persistence was admirable, for despite "defeat after defeat," she pushed for the cause of human equality and women's rights.[72]

Tributes came from far and wide. The press was most admiring. The *Washington Post*'s obituary called her the "first woman suffragist," since the cause had been her life's quest. It quoted Elizabeth Cady Stanton who, in a rare moment of crediting Lucy with her pivotal role in the fight for women's rights, acknowledged that "Lucy Stone first really stirred the Nation's heart on the subject of woman's wrongs."[73] Three days later, the *Post* carried another article on Lucy, "Make the World Better." "Were all men and all women to do as well their part as Mrs. Blackwell did hers the world would, indeed, be better." No one should forget her legacy, the paper continued, for "it is a legacy rich in suggestion, noble in inspiration. May we not hope that the world will be better for it; that the sum of good works will be multiplied thereby; that the influences to higher endeavor will find broader expansion and more complete fruition because of Lucy Stone's example?"[74] Not surprisingly, the October 28, 1893, issue of the *Woman's Journal* was devoted to Lucy, including a complete transcription of the funeral service as well as a brief biography by Alice, comments by Henry, and newspaper tributes. Friends and acquaintances could not find enough words to praise her. Mrs. Ednah D. Cheney wrote, "We hold in our hearts the memory of a loving and gracious presence, a voice like the music of brooks in the ear of a thirsty traveler, a smile that brightened the day, a hand ever ready to help; a young Joan of Arc, who listened to the voices in her youth, and whose fidelity to their demands kept her ever young and beautiful."[75]

Breaking another barrier, as she had been doing all her life, Lucy had insisted on being cremated, claiming she did not want her body to occupy much space on earth. Henry was not excited about cremating Lucy's body, but he acceded to her wishes. The idea of cremation was hardly a new approach to burial practices, having been performed by ancient civilizations including the Greeks, Romans, and Hindus. The method regained attention in Europe in the second third of the nineteenth century and began to attract proponents in the United States by the 1870s. Supporters argued that this was a more hygienic approach to burial than putting a body in a casket underground. No cemetery in New England yet had built a crematorium since the process had only recently become an acceptable burial option in this country. At Forest Hills Cemetery in Roxbury outside Boston, Lucy's body remained in a receiving tomb while a crematorium was being constructed by the Massachusetts Crematorium Society. Lucy's cremation was carried out in secret.[76]

On December 30, Henry and Alice, accompanied by Frank Garrison, rode a carriage to the Forest Hills Cemetery. They met the undertaker who then removed Lucy's coffin where she had been placed and waited for over an hour for the brick chamber to reach the proper temperature, at one point aided by a spray of kerosene and petroleum to hasten the proceeding. Then the iron doors opened, the lid of the coffin was removed, and Henry wrote, "I saw for the last time the dear form & face, lying in the same peaceful attitude as when the coffin was closed" ten weeks earlier. "The hands were folded upon her breast; the lace around her throat was undisturbed but its features were almost unchanged." Henry and Alice rode home by sleigh through a snowstorm with plans to return the following day to receive the ashes.[77]

Returning the next day, Henry described the inside of the furnace with "a few white bones still retaining their shape but crumbling almost at a touch" and two quarts of white and gray ashes all that remained of Lucy's body. On top of one of the two urns, Henry wrote "Lucy Stone, Dec. 31, 1893." The urns were placed in a vault to await their disposition. "Everything was quiet, decorous, and cleanly. Nothing could have been more reverent and in better taste," Henry observed. He had come to realize that cremation was only expediting a natural process and felt reconciled to Lucy's burial choice, especially knowing this is what she wanted. "It seemed appropriate that our Lucy, the pioneer in woman's rights, should have thus become a pioneer in Boston as cremation thus, in death as in life, seeing to make the world better."[78] Lucy's ashes were placed in the crematorium at Forest Hills Cemetery in Boston. Lucy became the first New England woman to be cremated in that region. Forty years earlier, Lucy interestingly had predicted that "the objects I seek to accomplish will not be attained until long after my body has gone to ashes."[79] Her body was now ashes, and that goal of women's suffrage took another twenty-seven years to achieve.

A few days after Lucy died, Emily Blackwell wrote Henry, conveying what their brother Sam had told her as they traveled home following Lucy's funeral: "Well there is one thing Harry can think of his 40 years of married life without any shade of self-reproach, for certainly he has been a most exceptionally good husband." Emily agreed, noting that few men would have modified their lives to fit their wives' needs as Henry had. "If there were imperfections on your side, there were also on the other. No one is perfect, and in any close association, there must be forbearance, and the acceptance of imperfections on both sides." Emily hoped his "morbid" feelings had dissipated.[80] Yet it took more than a year for Henry fully to recover from Lucy's death. He mourned for months, sitting in his room alone at night, hoping her spirit would return, missing the companion he had needed so much and who had given such meaning to his life.[81] Emily feared her brother was inconsolable and unable to rid himself of thoughts of his own shortcomings and failings, ignoring the fact that Lucy could be "difficult and trying." Emily felt Henry had reset the course of his life in order to adapt to Lucy's.[82] Many agreed with her and saw Henry as the best possible husband for Lucy Stone. No doubt, too, Lucy was the best possible wife for Henry.

The NAWSA's second annual convention, which met in Washington, DC, in February 1894, set aside time to pay tribute to Lucy. Despite his disagreement with Lucy in years past, Douglass praised her pivotal role in the antislavery and women's movements. "We cannot soon forget the voice, the face and form of the remarkable personage to whom we so long looked, and never in vain, for wise counsel and noble inspiration in our work for the advancement of woman's cause." Her name has been "a tower of strength to the woman's movement" for decades. Lucy left behind thousands of converts. Her first work was in the antislavery movement, and she came at the right moment when it needed help as the South's commitment to slavery strengthened. No one who came into the movement captured as much attention as did Lucy Stone. "To listen to her at that time was like listening to delightful music," Douglass added.[83]

Henry and Alice had to move on. Alice apparently had an easier time doing so than did Henry. The two continued to live at Pope's Hill and to publish the *Woman's Journal*, which remained the official organ of the women's movement. Alice served as editor-in-chief and wrote much of the copy. In 1917 the *Woman's Journal* merged with two other suffrage papers and became the *Woman Citizen*. When the Nineteenth Amendment giving American women the right to vote finally was ratified in 1920, the newspaper ceased publishing, just as Lucy had predicted long ago. After her mother's death, Alice became more of her own person. As Emily observed, "Alice is wonderfully developing her individuality in her independent position. . . . she shows a sort of self-will and positive determination in everyday life which is quite new."[84] In 1893 Alice had fallen in love with an Armenian theology student, Johannes Chatschumian, whom she met at the camp in

Canada. The two worked together to translate a number of Armenian poets. He returned to Europe to continue his studies but died tragically in 1896. Alice never married.

Henry did move on. Despite the constant shortage of funds for the *Woman's Journal*, Henry was determined to keep the paper afloat, and he managed to do so. He still harbored doubts about his success in life, having failed to become a millionaire or as financially secure as brothers Sam and George. He continued to campaign for women's suffrage. In 1895, he delivered an address before the NAWSA Convention in Atlanta, the organization's first meeting held in the South. There, reiterating a message he had expressed earlier, he insisted on the importance of educated white women voting since they could outnumber potential immigrant and black women voters who were illiterate, words that no doubt resonated with his audience.[85] Henry also engaged in other social and political issues, denounced imperialism, protested the Armenian massacre of 1895, and opposed the deportation of refugees. He enjoyed another trip to Europe, traveled to the Caribbean with George and Emma, and participated in Portland, Oregon's 1905 NAWSA convention, the first held on the West Coast. There he climbed a glacier, pleased that he could do so at the age of 80. Four years later, he and Alice attended the NAWSA annual convention in Seattle. Later that summer, he caught a bad cold and on September 7, 1909, died, peacefully at home. He was cremated and his ashes added to Lucy's in the urns at Forest Hills Cemetery.[86]

Alice developed a deep interest in humanitarian issues, especially in the dispossessed. With help from several foreign friends, she translated volumes of poetry into English from Russian, Yiddish, Spanish, Hungarian, and French. Her views tended toward the radical and socialistic, and she became involved with the Woman's Trade Union League, the WCTU, and the National Association for the Advancement of Colored People. Alice helped to found the League of Women Voters in Massachusetts. She became interested in convicted anarchists Nicola Sacco and Bartomoleo Vanzetti and defended Vanzetti until the two men were executed in Massachusetts in 1927. Alice retained a lifelong devotion to Armenian causes and to the refugee Armenian community in this country. She edited *The Little Grandmother of the Russian Revolution; Reminiscences and Letters of Catherine Breshkovsky* in 1914. Alice witnessed the passage of the Nineteenth Amendment, as her mother had hoped, and was able to cast her vote in the 1920 presidential election.

Alice continued to live at Pope's Hill but eventually moved to a smaller residence in Dorchester until relocating to Cambridge in 1936. When in

Figure 34. Alice Stone Blackwell (LC-USZ62-93,550, Library of Congress, Washington, DC)

good health, she vacationed on Martha's Vineyard. Her later years were increasingly difficult and spent in reduced circumstances after an "unscrupulous agent" lost most of her savings. Fortunately, several women, including Carrie Chapman Catt and Eleanor Roosevelt, contributed money to her upkeep, recognizing the important role she had played in the women's suffrage movement. By her early eighties, Alice was blind. One biographer described her as "a nervous recluse, living off the charity of family and friends," with a hired reader to visit her. She died March 15, 1950 and was also cremated at Forest Hills Cemetery and her ashes deposited there with her parents.[87]

Age did little to stop Elizabeth Cady Stanton from taking on controversial issues. She resigned from her leadership role in the NAWSA to spend more time in Europe with two of her children and to work on other projects. Her most radical idea was to tackle the Bible, having long blamed the Bible and ministers for sustaining women's subordination. Working virtually alone, she gathered every biblical reference on women and compiled these into two volumes, *A Woman's Bible*, published in 1895 and 1898. Many suffragists thought Stanton had gone too far in tampering with this sacred text, and at an NAWSA convention in 1896, they voted to censure the publication. On the other hand, the *New York Times* later heralded this as her "crowning achievement." Stanton completed her memoir in 1898, emphasizing her central role in the women's movement. She spent her final years struggling with her weight and failing eyesight. She died in her West Side apartment in New York on October 26, 1903. Her daughter Harriot Blatch carried on the family torch for women's rights. Blatch returned from England and played a pivotal role in winning women's suffrage for New York State in 1917, the first state east of the Mississippi River to give women the right to vote.

Susan B. Anthony maintained her tight leadership over the NAWSA until 1900 and continued to travel and lecture on behalf of women's suffrage. She then named her successor, Carrie Chapman Catt, to take over the organization. In the eyes of many younger suffragists, however, Anthony was the beloved leader of the movement. Anthony caught a cold while traveling to the 1906 NAWSA convention in Baltimore. Making only a brief appearance there, she returned to her home in Rochester, New York, where she died on March 13, 1906.

The cause for which Lucy devoted so much of her life finally happened, but it took another twenty-seven years after she died for the United States to add the Nineteenth Amendment to the Constitution. Catt, then Anna Howard Shaw, and Catt again assumed leadership of the NAWSA during its fight for women's suffrage.[88] Both that organization and a new, more radical group, the Congressional Union, founded in 1913 by Alice Paul and Lucy Burns, pressured Congress and President Woodrow Wilson to support women's right to vote. In the interim, fifteen states, almost all in the West, passed legislation giving women universal suffrage.[89] A new generation of suffragists expanded their activities by holding parades, participating in automobile tours, and using mass marketing to publicize their cause. Congressional Union members mimicked tactics of British suffragists and picketed the White House, held huge rallies in the nation's capital, and interrupted political meetings. When jailed, they went on hunger strikes. President Wilson finally and rather reluctantly acknowledged women's role in the nation's effort during World War I and gave his support to enfranchising women. First the House of Representatives and then the Senate finally passed the Nineteenth Amendment, which then went out to the states for ratification.

On August 26, 1920, thanks to a vote in the Tennessee legislature by a young representative, Harry Burn, whose mother urged him to do the right thing for women, the Nineteenth Amendment became part of the US Constitution. Only one woman who had attended the Seneca Falls Convention was still alive and voted. Among the suffragists who stood beside Lucy, Nette was still alive and could have voted, though she was 95 years old and in poor health. For Alice, it must have thrilling to see her mother's campaign finally succeed.

A year following the passage of the Nineteenth Amendment, another legacy of Lucy's took place: the founding of the Lucy Stone League in 1921. Its members, like Lucy, decided to keep their maiden name upon marriage, an act symbolizing women's independence that continues today.[90]

In later years, some suffragists began to try to revise the skewed image of the women's movement presented in the *History of Woman Suffrage* by writing about the movement as well as their roles in it. In the 1890s and early 1900s, Mary Livermore, Julia Ward Howe, Caroline Severance, a suffragist and active AWSA member, and Frances Willard among others wrote their stories and tried to correct the distortion of events. To counter these accounts, Anthony asked Ida B. Harper to write an authorized biography. Before its publication, Anthony approved every word of this work that eventually expanded to three volumes, the first one appearing in 1898.[91]

Lucy had never made an effort to correct the story. She did not write about her life before she died. Bothered by all the attention paid to Stanton and Anthony as the proclaimed leaders of the nineteenth-century women's movement and especially by Harper's glowing biography, Alice was determined to immortalize her mother. After years of work, she produced *Lucy Stone: Pioneer of Woman's Rights* in 1930. In the book, she challenged the unified vision of the movement, especially the one perpetuated by Stanton and Anthony. Besides emphasizing the central role her mother played in the women's movement, Alice showed that the movement, as seen through Lucy's thoughts and actions, involved far more than the fight for abolition and for women's suffrage. Her mother lived the very life she professed. Alice emphasized other events that spoke to Lucy's search for independence and selfhood, including her mother's determination to earn a college degree, her encouraging other women to become well educated, her tireless lecturing, and her creating an influential women's newspaper. Alice also portrayed her mother as a woman living multiple roles—orator, wife, mother, editor, and activist—in essence, the embodiment of women who had to learn to balance both their private and professional lives.[92] Feminist and writer Charlotte Perkins Gilman called Alice's biography "a noble and beautiful book." The *Philadelphia Public Ledger* praised the book as an "enriching memorial to a mother." More pointedly, the *Unity* of Chicago commented that the book "contributes to our hitherto much too scanty knowledge of the private life and character of Lucy Stone."[93]

Little physical evidence and few artifacts remain of Lucy's life. The Stone family farmhouse atop Coy's Hill in West Brookfield burned to the ground in 1950, with only a small part of the original stone foundation still remaining. Much of the Stone's original acreage became part of the "Coy's Hill Project." A trust in Massachusetts purchased 367 acres in 2001 and then re-sold 306 acres back to the state, which today includes the old home site.[94] The family home in Orange, New Jersey, where Lucy refused to pay her property taxes, was torn down in 1956 to make way for a church parking lot.[95] When Alice moved out of Pope's Hill, she willed the house to the Morgan Memorial which used it as a center for poor and immigrant children and youth, offering group activities, daily outings, and free lunches.[96] It was sold seven years later and torn down in 1971, today replaced by contemporary homes on smaller lots.[97]

In 1853, Lucy had written Henry to explain her passionate commitment to antislavery and to women's rights: "While so few can, or are willing, to give themselves wholly to the work the world so imperatively needs, all the more necessary is it, that those who can do so, should not falter."[98] Lucy not only believed in those words but lived them. She was one of those rare individuals who, throughout her life, could and did give herself "wholly" and unapologetically to two causes and never faltered. She expressed satisfaction for what she had been able to do: "How glad I am to have had so long a life to devote [to] it." Always she held out hope that universal justice would be attained, for "we know it is only waiting to bless the world."[99] For her part and in her own way, Lucy made our world better.

Notes

INTRODUCTION

1. Each state is allowed to have two statues in the rotunda representing famous individuals in its past. Today, there are ninety-one men and ten women. Each state selects two individuals who best represent its history. The women include Helen Keller, Sakakawea, Sarah Winnemucca, Florence Sabin, Frances Willard, Maria Sanford, Jeanette Rankin, Mother Joseph, Esther Morris—and Rosa Parks, who was added last year. The women's monument is in addition to the 100 individual statues. "Portrait Monument to Lucretia Mott, Elizabeth Cady Stanton, and Susan B. Anthony," http://www.aoc.gov/capitol-hill/other/statues/portrait-monument; and Susan Brandell, "Out of the Broom Closet and into the Rotunda," http://www.feminist.com/resources/artspeech/wword/ww3.htm. This statue of the three suffragists was sculpted by Adelaide Johnson (1859-1955) from an eight-ton slab of Italian marble, copied from statues created for the 1893 Columbian exhibition held in Chicago. The National Woman's Party, wanting to commemorate women's victory in finally winning the right to vote, presented the statue as a gift to the nation. Congress and its Joint Committee on the Library accepted it on February 10, 1921, with an unveiling ceremony five days later. Over seventy women's groups attended the event. But rather than remain in the rotunda where visitors could see it, the monument was then stored in a broom closet and in 1963, moved to a crypt below the rotunda. There it remained until September 1996 when Congress, responding to pressure from various women's groups, passed a resolution to have it returned to the Capitol. Private funds totaling some $89,000 were raised to have it moved. The statue returned to its rightful place on Mother's Day, May 10, 1997. It since attracted attention in an editorial, "A Women's History Museum, at Last?" *New York Times*, March 21, 2014, in reference to the possibility of a National Women's History Museum in Washington, DC. See also "About the National Statuary Hall Collection," http://www.aoc.gov/capitol-hill/national-statuary-hall-collection/about-national-statuary-hall-collection.

2. Reflective of Lucy Stone's omission is Karlyn Kohrs Campbell's edited collection, *Women Public Speakers in the United States, 1800-1925: A Bio-Critical Sourcebook* (Westport, CT: Greenwood Press, 1993), which does not include an essay on Stone among the thirty-seven women in the book. Campbell does explain

that she could find no one to write an essay on Stone, though it is surprising that this most famous of orators was not included.

3. Alice Stone Blackwell, *Lucy Stone: Pioneer of Woman's Rights* (Charlottesville and London: University Press of Virginia, [1930] 2001); Elinor Rice Hays, *Morning Star: A Biography of Lucy Stone, 1818–1893* (New York: Harcourt, Brace & World, 1961); Andrea Moore Kerr, *Lucy Stone: Speaking Out for Equality* (New Brunswick, NJ: Rutgers University Press, 1992); and Joelle Million, *Woman's Voice, Woman's Place: Lucy Stone and the Birth of the Woman's Rights Movement* (Westport, CT and London: Praeger, 2003).

CHAPTER I

1. Alice Stone Blackwell, *Lucy Stone: Pioneer of Woman's Rights* ([Boston: Little Brown, 1930] Charlottesville and London: University Press of Virginia, 2001), 3; and M. J. Savage, "Lucy Stone," November 3, 1893, Boston Unity Pulpit, in *Sermons of M. J. Savage*, vol. 15, no. 5 (Boston: George Ellis, 1893). According to a tale Lucy Stone often told, her mother milked eight cows the night before Lucy was born.

2. Two children died in infancy, and only two daughters, Lucy and Sarah, and two sons, Francis and Bowman, survived beyond early adulthood.

3. Fire destroyed the Stone family home on September 9, 1950. Author's visit to Quaboag Historical Society, West Brookfield, MA. All that remains of the home today are its stone foundation and a sign telling an occasional visitor that Lucy Stone lived there.

4. Henry Blackwell to George Blackwell, West Brookfield, MA, July 4, 1870, Blackwell Family Papers, Schlesinger Library, Radcliffe Institute for Advanced Study, Harvard University, Cambridge, MA, hereinafter cited as BFPS.

5. Lucy Stone to Antoinette Brown, August 1849, West Brookfield, MA, in Carol Lasser and Marlene Deahl Merrill, eds., *Friends and Sisters: Letters between Lucy Stone and Antoinette Brown Blackwell, 1846–1893* (Urbana and Chicago: University of Illinois Press, 1987), 57.

6. Brookfield initially included what today are Brookfield, West Brookfield, and North Brookfield, which were incorporated as independent communities in the nineteenth century. See Josiah H. Temple, *History of North Brookfield, Massachusetts* (Boston: Rand Avery, printer, 1887). Other insights come from the author's visit to West Brookfield in June 2011.

7. Massachusetts Historical Commission, *Reconnaissance Survey Town Report, West Brookfield,* 1984. http://www.sec.state.ma.us/mhc; Massachusetts Historical Commission State Survey Team, *Historical and Archeological Resources of Central Massachusetts: A Framework for Preservation Decision* (February 1985), 59–64.

8. The current First Congregational Church of West Brookfield was built in 1942. See also "Manual of the Congregational Church of West Brookfield, Massachusetts" (West Brookfield: Steam Press of O. S. Coke and Company, 1853) at

the Massachusetts Historical Society, Boston. See also *Vital Records of Brookfield, Massachusetts, to the End of the Year 1849* (Worcester: Franklin P. Price, 1909).

9. Massachusetts Historic Commission, *Reconnaissance Survey*; Jack Larkin, "The Merriams of Brookfield: Printing in the Economy and Culture of Rural Massachusetts in the Early Nineteenth Century," *Proceedings of the American Antiquarian Society*, 39–41. http://www.americanantiquarian.org/proceedings/44539371; George Merriam, "Genealogy in West Brookfield, Massachusetts," http://www.geneologyinwestbrookfield.blogspot.com. George Merriam apprenticed under the famous Revolutionary newspaper editor Isaiah Thomas who published his radical newspaper, *The Massachusetts Spy*, in Worcester, MA.

10. Henry Blackwell to Lucy Stone, West Brookfield, MA, October 28, 1868, Blackwell Family Papers, microfilm in Library of Congress, hereinafter cited as BFP. Henry and Bowman Stone visited Hannah Stone's childhood home in New Braintree and Francis's tannery.

11. Blackwell, *Lucy Stone*, 19–20.

12. Ibid., 9.

13. Lucy Stone to Alice Stone Blackwell, Reminiscences, BFP.

14. Ibid., October 7, 1893, BFP; "Interesting Facts Concerning Lucy Stone Home," folder of Blackwell family clippings, BFPS. Lucy's sampler is on display in the Quaboag Historical Society, West Brookfield, MA.

15. Massachusetts Historic Commission, *Reconnaissance Survey*, 6.

16. Blackwell, *Lucy Stone*, 11 and Lucy Stone to Alice Stone Blackwell, Reminiscences, January 2, 1892, BFP. For background on manufacturing in New England, see Thomas Dublin, *Transforming Women's Work: New England Lives in the Industrial Revolution* (Ithaca, NY: Cornell University Press, 1994).

17. Blackwell, *Lucy Stone*, 12.

18. Lucy Stone to Alice Stone Blackwell, Reminiscences, January 2, 1892, BFP.

19. Ibid.

20. Lucy Stone to Frances Stone Jr., Oberlin, Ohio, May 20, 1844, BFP.

21. Lucy Stone to Francis Stone Jr., Oberlin, OH, July 4, 1845, BFP.

22. Lucy Stone to Francis Stone Jr., West Brookfield, MA, 1836, BFP.

23. Lucy Stone to Charles Franklin Twing, Dorchester, MA, February 3, 1893, BFP.

24. Lucy Stone to Alice Stone Blackwell, Reminiscences, October 8, 1892, BFP.

25. Emily T. Pierce to Lucy Stone, West Brookfield, MA, January 2, 1847, BFP.

26. Blackwell, *Lucy Stone*, 11.

27. Alice Stone Blackwell, *Growing Up in Boston's Gilded Age: The Journal of Alice Stone Blackwell, 1872–1874*, ed. Marlene Deahl Merrill (New Haven and London: Yale University Press, 1990), 104.

28. Lucy Stone to Alice Stone Blackwell, Reminiscences, October 7, 1893, BFP.

29. Alice Stone Blackwell, "Early Years," October 9, 1893, BFP; and Blackwell, *Lucy Stone*, 9.

30. Lucy Stone to Alice Stone Blackwell, Reminiscences, BFP; and Blackwell, *Lucy Stone*, 17, 18.

31. Lucy Stone to Alice Stone Blackwell, Dorchester, MA, May 8, 1891, BFP.

32. Lucy Stone to Alice Stone Blackwell, Reminiscences, September 30, 1893, BEP.

33. Sarah Stone Lawrence to Alice Stone Blackwell, Gardner, MA, January 13, 1894, BFP; and Sarah Stone Lawrence, "Reminiscences of Lucy Stone," Gardner, August 11, 1898, BFP.

34. Lucy Stone to Alice Stone Blackwell, Reminiscences, December 13, 1891, BFP.

35. Alice Stone Blackwell, "Early Years," December 31, 1891, BFP.

36. Lucy Stone to Alice Stone Blackwell, Reminiscences, October 8, 1892, BFP.

37. Lucy Stone to Alice Stone Blackwell, Reminiscences, December 31, 1891, BFP.

38. Lucy Stone to Hannah Stone, Cincinnati, OH, May 1855, BFP.

39. Lucy Stone to Mr. O'Reilly, Boston, MA, December 8, 1878, BFP.

40. Lucy Stone to Alice Stone Blackwell, Reminiscences 1891, BFP and Alice Stone Blackwell, "Early Years."

41. Lucy Stone to Alice Stone Blackwell, Reminiscences January 6, 1892, BFP.

42. Lucy Stone to Francis Stone Jr., West Brookfield, MA, 1836, BFP.

43. Lucy Stone to Francis Stone Jr., West Brookfield, MA, June 14, 1840, BFP; and Blackwell, *Lucy Stone.*

44. Alice Stone Blackwell, "Early Years," 1881, BFP; and Sarah Stone Lawrence to Alice Stone Blackwell, n.p., August 16, 1898, BFP.

45. *Catalogue of the Members of the Congregational Church in West Brookfield from 1758 to 1861* (West Brookfield: Thomas Morey, 1861), Massachusetts Historical Society, Boston, MA.

46. Sarah Lawrence to Alice Stone Blackwell, n.p., August 16, 1898 and Lucy Stone to William Bowman Stone, Wilbraham Academy, MA, June 18, 1840, BFP.

47. Lucy Stone to Francis Stone, Jr., Paxton, MA, November 29, 1838, BFP.

48. See Linda K. Kerber, *Women of the Republic: Intellect and Ideology in Revolutionary America* (Chapel Hill: University of North Carolina Press, 1980); Kathryn Kish Sklar, *Catharine Beecher: A Study in American Domesticity* (New York: W. W. Norton, 1976); and Mary Kelley, *Learning to Stand and Speak: Women, Education, and Public Life in America's Republic* (Chapel Hill: University of North Carolina Press, 2006).

49. Maria Barlow, "Reminiscence" in BFP, and Blackwell, *Lucy Stone*, 29.

50. Isaiah Thomas started his newspaper in Boston but moved to Worcester in the early nineteenth century. Amassing considerable wealth, he used that money to found a library in 1812—the American Antiquarian Society in Worcester, MA.

51. Lucy Stone to Francis Stone Jr., West Brookfield, MA, February 25, 1836, BFP. Daughter Alice described her mother as a voracious reader. See Blackwell, *Lucy Stone*, 15.

52. Blackwell, *Lucy Stone*, 18 and Sarah Stone Lawrence to Alice Stone Blackwell, Gardner, MA, August 16, 1898, BFP. Those novels were Regina Maria Roche, *The Children of the Abbey: A Tale*, 4 vols. (1796) and Mrs. Sherwood (Mary Martha Butt), *The Lady of the Manor* (1836).

53. See "Who Was Mary Lyon?" https://www.mholyoke.edu/marylyon/founder.

54. Blackwell, *Lucy Stone*, 20; Handwritten article for the *Woman's Journal*, February 6, 1892 in BFP. Lucy mentioned the training of Mt. Holyoke women to become missionary wives in "Speech to the New England Woman's Club," 1887, BFP.

55. For information on Mary Lyon and Mt. Holyoke, see Elizabeth Arden Green, *Mary Lyon and Mt. Holyoke: Opening the Gates* (Hanover, NH: University Press of New England, 1979); Kathryn Kish Sklar, "The Founding of Mt. Holyoke Female College," in Carol Berkin and Mary Beth Norton, eds., *Women of America: A History* (Boston: Houghton Mifflin, 1979) and Lyon, Mary, s.v., *American National Biography*.

56. William Bowman Stone to Francis Stone Jr., West Brookfield, MA, August 31, 1838, BFP. Bo and a male friend also were tutored.

57. Lucy Stone, "Address," *Proceedings of the Woman's Rights Convention Held at Worcester, October 15, 16, 1851,* American Memory, Library of Congress, http://memory.loc.gov/cgi-bin/query/r?ammen/saw.:@field, hereinafter cited as American Memory.

58. Lucy Stone to Alice Stone Blackwell, Reminiscences, October 8, 1893, BFP; Blackwell, *Lucy Stone*, 40; and Lucy Stone, "Address," *Proceedings of the Woman's Rights Convention Held at Worcester, October 15, 16, 1851.*

59. Lucy's married sister Eliza had died in childbirth the year before on March 17, 1838, at the age of 29. This experience at Mt. Holyoke likely affected Lucy's preference for co-educational institutions. See Blackwell, *Lucy Stone*, 40.

60. Emma Blackwell to Alice Stone Blackwell, Gardner, MA, March 19, 1901, BFP and David Sherman, *History of the Wesleyan Academy at Wilbraham, Mass., 1817–90* (Boston: The McDonald & Gill Company, 1893), 230-31. Lucy was mentioned as a student in this publication: "the well-known advocate of anti-slavery and woman's rights." Wilbraham and Monson Academies later merged to become Wilbraham and Monson Academy. The school is still in operation, educating grades 6 through 12.

61. "Principles of the Quaboag Seminary" flyer found at http://www.knowwarren.org. Quaboag Seminary was sold to the town of Warren in 1856, and it became a public school.

62. Maria Barlow, "Reminiscence of Lucy Stone," n.d., BFP.

63. Lucy Stone to Alice Stone Blackwell, Reminiscences, March 31, 1893 and August 16, 1893, BFP; and Blackwell, *Lucy Stone*, 21. Bartlett later married a fashionable young woman, was drawn into New York society, and apparently led a rather dissipated life—a far cry from his early dreams of becoming a pious missionary.

64. For background on women's education, see Kelley, *Learning to Stand & Speak*.

65. Rhoda taught in nearby Warren; Luther mentioned teaching seventy pupils in his school. Bo also taught school.

66. Lucy Stone to Francis Stone Jr., West Brookfield, MA, 1836, BEP; and Henry Blackwell, Notes, n.d., BFP.

67. Lucy Stone to Alice Stone Blackwell, Reminiscences May 8, 1891, BFP.

68. Ronald G. Walters, *American Reformers, 1815–1860* (New York: Hill and Wang, 1978), 3; and Daniel Walker Howe, *What Hath God Wrought: The Transformation of America, 1815–1848* (New York and Oxford: Oxford University Press, 2007), 164–202.

69. Rev. Minot J. Savage, "Lucy Stone, November 3, 1893," *Sermons of M.J. Savage* (Boston: George H. Ellis, 1893).

70. Lucy Stone to Alice Stone Blackwell, Reminiscences, October 1, 1893, BFP; Blackwell, *Lucy Stone*, 7–8.

71. Blackwell, *Lucy Stone*, 7–8.

72. William Lloyd Garrison, "To the Public," the *Liberator*, January 1, 1831.

73. Sally G. McMillen, *Seneca Falls and the Origins of the Women's Rights Movement* (New York and London: Oxford University Press, 2008), 58; Garrison, William Lloyd, s.v., *American National Biography*.

74. For background on Garrison, see George M. Frederickson, *William Lloyd Garrison* (Englewood Cliffs, NJ: Prentice Hall, 1968); and Henry Mayer, *All on Fire: William Lloyd Garrison and the Abolition of Slavery* (New York: St. Martin's Press, 1996).

75. Rhoda was the only Stone family member who supported colonization, which promoted a plan to send slaves and free blacks to Liberia in Africa or to some other country. The American Colonization Society, formed in 1816, attracted a number of prominent members including James Madison and Henry Clay. Abraham Lincoln supported colonization well into his presidency.

76. Lucy Stone to Francis Stone Jr., West Brookfield, MA, December 1, 1837, BFPS.

77. Ibid. See also Eric Foner, *The Fiery Trial: Abraham Lincoln and American Slavery* (New York: W. W. Norton, 2010), 23–24.

78. Lucy Stone to Francis Stone Jr., West Brookfield, MA, December 1, 1837 and Lucy Stone to Francis Stone Jr., Oberlin, OH, May 20, 1844, BFPS. It is unclear if the reference was to Sarah or Angelina Grimké, since both wrote on abolition.

79. Blackwell, *Lucy Stone*, 16.

80. Martha Fullam Blair, Account in Frank Warren Blair autograph collection, Massachusetts Historical Society. Sarah Robinson died three years later giving birth to twins. Charles Robinson went to California and later became the first governor of Kansas.

81. Lucy Stone to Alice Stone Blackwell, Reminiscences, October 8, 1892, BFP. Coins at the time were worth 6½ and 12½ cents. Also, in the incident concerning the cheese and her father, Lucy told Alice never to include it in any biography because she did not want her father to look bad. Lucy explained that her father embraced the Puritan idea that women were to be governed and that "he had the right to hold the purse and to rule his own house."

82. Lucy Stone to Alice Stone Blackwell, Reminiscences, October 8, 1892, BFP.

83. Howe, *What Hath God Wrought*, 167.

84. Wright's lecture topics were radical for the time. One of her most popular speeches was "Moral and Political Questions of the Day, including Woman's Rights." She also set up a utopian community for slaves, Nashoba, north of Memphis, which failed. See Harriet H. Robinson, *Massachusetts in the Woman Suffrage Movement, A General, Political, Legal and Legislative History from 1774 to 1881* (Boston: Roberts Brothers, 1881).

85. For background on the Grimké sisters, see Gerda Lerner, *The Grimké Sisters of South Carolina* (Boston: Houghton Mifflin, 1967) and "Grimké, Sarah Moore" and "Grimké, Angelina Emily," s.v., *American National Biography*.

86. Lucy Stone, "Speech to the New England Woman's Club," 1887, BFP; and Million, *Woman's Voice, Woman's Place*, 29-31.

87. "Pastoral Letter of the General Association of Massachusetts," in Elizabeth Cady Stanton, Susan B. Anthony, and Joselyn Gage, eds., *History of Woman Suffrage*, vol. 1, *1848–1861* (Rochester, NY: Charles Mann, 1881), 81.

88. Lucy Stone to Francis Stone Jr., West Brookfield, MA, December 3, 1836, BFP; Blackwell, *Lucy Stone*, 24–25; and McMillen, *Seneca Falls*, 63-64.

89. John Greenleaf Whittier, "The Pastoral Letter," in Stanton, Anthony, and Gage, eds., *History of Woman Suffrage*, 1:84-86; and McMillen, *Seneca Falls*, 64.

90. Sarah M. Grimké, letter 8, "On the Condition of Women in the United States," in Sarah Grimké and Angelina Grimké, *The Public Years of Sarah and Angelina Grimké: Selected Writings, 1835–1839*, ed. Larry Ceplair (New York: Columbia University Press, 1989), 225.

91. Sarah Grimké, *Letters on the Equality of the Sexes and the Condition of Women* (Boston: Isaac Knapp, 1838).

92. Lucy Stone to William Bowman Stone, West Brookfield, MA, 1838, in Blackwell, *Lucy Stone*, 37.

93. Lerner, *The Grimké Sisters from South Carolina*, 1-5.

94. "Foster, Abby Kelley," s.v., *American National Biography*; Keith Melder, "Abby Kelley and the Process of Liberation," in *The Abolitionist Sisterhood: Women's Political Culture in Antebellum America*, ed. Jean Fagan Yellin and John C. Van Horne (Ithaca and London: Cornell University Press, 1994), 231–48; and Dorothy Sterling, *Ahead of Her Time: Abby Kelley and the Politics of Antislavery* (New York and London: W. W. Norton and Company, 1991), 13–59.

95. Lucy Stone to William Bowman Stone, West Brookfield, MA, June 18, 1840, BFP.

96. Blackwell, *Lucy Stone*, 36. After the 1850 Worcester Women's Rights Convention, the manager of the meeting hall expressed concern when he learned Kelley would be present, declaring "She is so odious."

97. Lucy Stone to Alice Stone Blackwell, Reminiscences, January 1, 1892, BFP.

98. Ibid.

99. *Woman's Journal*, January 22, 1887 and Sterling, *Ahead of Her Time*, 146-47.

100. Lucy Stone, "Workers for the Cause" speech, n.d., BFP.

101. Congregational Church (West Brookfield, MA), "A Statement of Facts in the Trial of Dea. Josiah Henshaw, and a Review of the Result of Council" (n.p., 1843); Lucy Stone to Alice Stone Blackwell, Reminiscences, September 30, 1893, BFP; Blackwell, *Lucy Stone*, 22–23; Alice Stone Blackwell, "Pioneers of the Woman's Movement," *Zion's Herald*, August 14, 1918, in "Lucy Stone, Biographical Material," Sophia Smith Collection, College Archives, Smith College, Northampton, MA.

102. Lucy Stone to Alice Stone Blackwell, Reminiscences, March 31, 1893, BFP.

103. Lucy had also taught Walker's son. See Antoinette Brown Blackwell, "Reminiscences of Lucy Stone," April 26, 1914, BFPS.

104. Antoinette Brown Blackwell, "Notes," April 26, 1914, BFPS; Angelina Grimké, "Proceedings," Anti-Slavery Convention of American Women, May 9–12, 1837, *Philadelphia National Enquirer*, July 8, 1837; "Oberlin Collegiate Institute," the *Liberator*, November 15, 1839. The three women who earned a degree were Elizabeth Prall, Mary Hosford, and Caroline Rudd. See article in *Oberlin Today* 21, no. 1 (1963) in Lucy Stone File, Oberlin.

105. Maria S. Porter, "Lucy Stone," *National Magazine* 3 (1895): 45.

CHAPTER 2

1. Lucy Stone to "Dear Friends," Oberlin, OH, August 30, 1843, BFP.

2. Robert Samuel Fletcher, "Oberlin, 1833–1866," typeset copy in Oberlin College Archives, Mudd Library, Oberlin College, n.d., 12–25, hereinafter cited as Oberlin; and Fletcher, *History of Oberlin College from Its Foundation through the Civil War* (Oberlin, OH: Oberlin College, 1943). Shipherd envisioned a series of colleges like Oberlin, and he left the area in 1843 to found Olivet College in Michigan. Unfortunately, he died from malaria in September 1844 before the new campus became a reality.

3. Nathan O. Hatch, *The Democratization of American Christianity* (New Haven: Yale University Press, 1989), 196.

4. "John J. Shipherd," http://www.oberlin.edu/arcive/holdings/finding.

5. Fletcher, *History of Oberlin College*, 34–50, quote, 50.

6. Fletcher, "Oberlin, 1833–1866."

7. Geoffrey Blodgett, *Oberlin History: Essays and Impressions* (Kent, OH: Kent State University Press, 2007), 10.

8. "Oberlin Collegiate Institute," *Emancipator and Weekly Chronicle*, Boston, MA, September 10, 1845 and Fletcher, "Oberlin, 1833–1866," Oberlin.

9. "The First Annual Report," November 1834, Oberlin Collegiate Institute, Oberlin.

10. Fletcher, *History of Oberlin College*, 91–94; and Fletcher, "Oberlin, 1833–1866," 59.

11. J. J. Shipherd to Fayette Shipherd, August 13, 1832, in Fletcher, *History of Oberlin College*, 88, 92.

12. "Report on Educating the Sexes Together," Oberlin Collegiate Institute, August 1945, Oberlin.

13. Lasser and Merrill, *Friends and Sisters*, 8; and "Oberlin Collegiate Institute," March 1834, circular, in Robert S. Fletcher Papers, Oberlin. Lori Ginzberg places Oberlin's co-educational approach within the context of its time. See Ginzberg, "The 'Joint Education of the Sexes': Oberlin's Original Vision," in Carol Lasser, ed., *Educating Men and Women Together: Coeducation in a Changing World* (Urbana and Chicago: University of Illinois Press, 1987), 67–80. By the 1850s, a handful of institutions experimented with co-education, including Antioch College, Genesee Wesleyan Seminary, and New York Central College.

14. *Catalogue of the Officers and Students in Oberlin Collegiate Institute, 1846–7* (Oberlin, OH: J. M. Fitch, 1846), 36.

15. Fletcher, "Oberlin, 1833–66," 102.

16. Young ladies to John Keep and William Dawes, July 10, 1839, Oberlin.

17. *Catalogue of Oberlin College, 1843– 44*, Oberlin. Required manual labor was scrapped entirely a few years after Lucy graduated.

18. Blodgett, *Oberlin History*, 33. Plymouth Church's minister as of 1847 was the charismatic Henry Ward Beecher.

19. *Catalogue, 1843–44* and "By Laws of the College," Oberlin. For background on Oberlin's religious climate, see Timothy L. Smith, *Revivalism and Social Reform: American Protestantism on the Eve of the Civil War* (Baltimore and London: Johns Hopkins University Press, 1980), 103–8.

20. Charlotte Hickox to Helen Remington, November 12, 1843, Oberlin, OH, "Student File," Oberlin; and Lucy Stone to Hannah and Francis Stone, Oberlin, OH, spring, 1845, BFP.

21. *Catalogue of Oberlin, 1843–44*; Charles Livingstone to his parents, May 1840, Oberlin, OH, Oberlin; and Antoinette Brown Blackwell, "Reminiscences," BFP.

22. Lucy Stone to her parents, August 30, 1843, Oberlin, OH, BFP; Thomas D. Matiasic, "Abolition vs. Colonization: The Battle for Ohio," *Queen City Heritage* (Spring 1987): 27–40; Fletcher, *History of Oberlin College*, 168–71; and Lasser and Merrill, *Friends and Sisters*, 9. Mahan was a difficult man, known to be overbearing, thin-skinned, and egotistical. He was forced to resign in 1850 after annoying faculty and trustees. See Fletcher, "Oberlin," 55. For background on the controversy at Lane Seminary, see Robert H. Abzug, *Passionate Liberator: Theodore Dwight Weld and the Dilemma of Reform* (New York and Oxford: Oxford University Press, 1980), 74–122.

23. John J. Shipherd to Charles Grandison Finney, March 14, 1831, Elyria, OH, in Appendix, Robert S. Fletcher Papers, Oberlin. Arthur Tappan and his brother Lewis initially made their money in a silk-importing business. After the financial crisis of 1837, that business failed, but they then founded a lucrative credit-rating service in New York.

24. Lucy Stone to Hannah and Francis Stone, Oberlin, OH, August 30, 1843; "1840 Laws and Regulations of the Oberlin Collegiate Institute," both in Oberlin.

25. Lucy Stone to Hannah and Francis Stone, Oberlin, OH, spring 1845, BFP.

26. Fletcher, *History of Oberlin*, 171; Woodbury quoted in Blodgett, *Oberlin History*, 16–17.

27. John Shipherd to Oberlin Trustees, New York, NY, January 19, 1835, Oberlin.

28. "Minutes of the Faculty Meeting," February 9–10, 1835, Oberlin.

29. By 1860, 250 black students had enrolled at Oberlin, many of them in the Preparatory Department. In 1862, Mary Jane Patterson became the first black woman to earn a bachelor's degree from Oberlin. Blodgett, *Oberlin History*, 62.

30. Cally L. Waite, "The Segregation of Black Students at Oberlin College after Reconstruction," *History of Education Society* 41, no. 3 (Autumn 2001): 347.

31. *Catalogue of the Officers and Students, 1843–44*; and "By Laws of the College," Oberlin.

32. Lucy Stone to Alice Stone Blackwell, Reminiscences, May 13, 1893, BFP.

33. Blackwell, *Lucy Stone*, 44–45; "Francis E. Spinner," *New York Times*, October 30, 1875. Spinner was the first cabinet member to hire female clerks—a pragmatic move due to the shortage of men to serve in such jobs during the Civil War. But one would like to think that perhaps this meeting with Lucy had an impact on his ideas about what jobs women could perform.

34. Lucy Stone to "Dear Friends," Oberlin, OH, August 30, 1843, BFP; and Lucy Stone to Alice Stone Blackwell, June 30, 1888, BFP. Because dirt roads became muddy after a rain, logs were often laid down side by side to create a solid—although very bumpy—surface. Hence the name corduroy road.

35. Lucy Stone to her family, Oberlin, OH, August 30, 1843, Oberlin; and "The Barrier Seemed Impassable," *Oberlin Today* 21, no. 1 (1963): 9.

36. Blackwell, *Lucy Stone*, 49.

37. "Taught by a Woman," Lucy Stone File, Oberlin; and William Cheek and Aimee Lee Cheek, *John Mercer Langston and the Fight for Black Freedom* (Urbana and Chicago: University of Illinois Press, 1989), 110.

38. Lucy Stone to Sarah Stone Lawrence, Oberlin, OH, September 14, 1845, BFP.

39. Lucy Stone to Sarah Stone Lawrence, Oberlin, OH, March 13, 1846, BFP.

40. Lucy Stone to Hannah and Francis Stone, Oberlin, OH, May 12, 1845, Oberlin.

41. Hannah and Francis Stone to Lucy Stone, West Brookfield, MA, January 11, 1845, BFP.

42. Lucy Stone to Hannah and Francis Stone, Oberlin, OH, spring 1845, BFP.

43. Antoinette Brown Blackwell, "Aunt Nettie's Reminiscences," August 16, 1896, BFP.

44. Lucy Stone to Hannah and Francis Stone, Oberlin, OH, spring 1845, BFP.

45. Lucy Stone to Francis Stone, Jr., Oberlin, OH, May 12, 1845, BFP. See also "Postal Act of 1845," http://www.jcampbell.com/Reference/us/184503_law.pdf.

46. Lucy Stone to Francis and Hannah Stone, Oberlin, OH, August 16, 1846, Robert S. Fletcher File, Oberlin.

47. Lucy Stone to Hannah and Francis Stone, Oberlin, OH, August 16, 1846, Robert S. Fletcher File, Oberlin; and Francis Stone, Jr., Oberlin, OH, May 12, 1845, BFP.

48. Lucy Stone to Hannah and Frank Stone, Oberlin, OH, spring 1845, BFP.

49. Lucy Stone to Stone Family, Oberlin, OH, August 30 and September 11, 1843, BFP.

50. Blackwell, *Lucy Stone*, 56.

51. *Loraine County News*, August 4, 11, 1870, and September 21, 1871, in Cheek and Cheek, *John Mercer Langston*, 11, 295; and Oberlin College Archives. http://www.oberlin.edu/external/EOG/OYTT-images/JMLangston.html. I thank Carol Lasser for informing me of this relationship.

52. The only extant newspaper essay, noted as vol. 1, no. 2, is "Let Every Man Speak Truth with his Neighbor," Oberlin, June 9, 1845, BFP. The essay has Lucy's professor's corrections on it, including comments such as "bad logic" and "two misspelt words."

53. Lucy Stone to Frank Stone Jr., Oberlin, OH, May 12, 1846, BFP.

54. Lucy Stone to Sarah Stone Lawrence, Oberlin, OH, September 14, 1845, in Million, 63.

55. Lucy Stone to Hannah and Francis Stone, Oberlin, OH, August 16, 1846, BFP.

56. Lucy Stone to Hannah and Francis Stone, Oberlin, OH, August 16, 1846 (typeset), in Robert S. Fletcher Collection, Lucy Stone Folder, Oberlin.

57. *Catalogue of the Officers and Students in Oberlin Collegiate Institute, 1846–47* (Oberlin, OH: J. M. Fitch, 1846), 13; and Brown, "Aunt Nettie's Reminiscences, August 16, 1896," BFP.

58. Lucy Stone to Hannah and Francis Stone, Oberlin, OH, August 16, 1846, Oberlin.

59. James P. McKinney, "Lucy Stone at Oberlin College," *Woman's Journal*, June 1902.

60. "Clay, Cassius Marcellus," s.v., *American National Biography*. Henry Clay was a distant cousin of his.

61. Lucy Stone to Francis Stone Jr., Oberlin, OH, April 12, 1846, BFP.

62. Based on mathematical calculations of scripture by Baptist minister William Miller and publicized by a savvy promoter, Millerites believed the second coming would occur in the spring of 1844. When Christ failed to appear, Miller revisited his calculations and came up with a new fall date. That, too, disappointed followers, and the movement disintegrated.

63. Lucy Stone to Francis Stone Jr., Oberlin, OH, July 4, 1845, BFP; Lucy Stone to Francis and Harriet Stone, Oberlin, OH, February 15, 1846, BFP. Among the leaders of this Party were Birney, Salmon P. Chase, who later became Chief Justice of the United States, and Gerrit Smith, an avowed abolitionist who was part of the Secret Six supporting John Brown's raid at Harper's Ferry in 1859.

The Liberty Party collapsed in 1848, many of its members gravitating to the Free Soil Party, which opposed the expansion of slavery in western territories. Smith was the uncle of Elizabeth Cady Stanton.

64. Lasser and Merrill, *Friends and Sisters*, 9; and Lucy Stone to the Stone Family, Oberlin, OH, September 11, 1843, BFP.

65. Lucy Stone in Fletcher, *History of Oberlin College*, 1:290.

66. Lucy Stone to her family, Oberlin, OH, March 14, 1847, BFP. Stephen Foster was an even more ardent abolitionist than his wife.

67. Lucy Stone to Francis Stone Jr., Oberlin, OH, May 12, 1845, BFP. Ohio abolitionists, including Asa Mahan and Charles Finney, founded the Ohio Anti-Slavery Society in April 1835.

68. Fletcher, *A History of Oberlin College*, 291.

69. Lucy Stone to Abby Kelley Foster, in Dorothy Sterling, *Ahead of her Time: Abby Kelley and the Politics of Antislavery* (New York and London: W.W. Norton, 1991), 231; and Lucy Stone to Sarah Stone Lawrence, March 13, 1846, Oberlin, OH, BFP.

70. Fletcher, *A History of Oberlin College*, 1:266–68.

71. James H. Fairchild, "Woman's Rights and Duties," *The Oberlin Quarterly Review* (July 1849): 251, 249.

72. William Bowman Stone to Lucy Stone, Gardner, MA, June 8, 1846, BFP.

73. Lucy Stone to Alice Stone Blackwell, Boston, MA, June 30, 1888, BFP; and Fletcher, *A History of Oberlin College*, 1:303.

74. Alice listed several of Lucy's female friends, including Nette, Sarah Pellet, Lettice Smith, Emmeline French (who was expelled), Eliza Fairchild, and Helen Cook. All were not at Oberlin when Lucy attended. See Alice Stone Blackwell, Reminiscences, August 17, 1903, BFP. For the poem, see Edward Henry, "A Parting Gem for Lucy Stone," August 27, 1847, BFP. For background on Nette, see Lasser and Merrill, *Friends and Sisters*, 7 and "Blackwell, Antoinette Louisa Brown," s.v., *American National Biography*.

75. Antoinette Blackwell, "Aunt Nettie's Reminiscences" and Lasser and Merrill, *Friends and Sisters*, 5.

76. Antoinette Blackwell, "Memoir of Lucy Stone," Memorial Meeting for Lucy Stone, New Jersey State Suffrage Association, February 10, 1894, BFP; Antoinette Brown to Lucy Stone, Oberlin, OH, undated, BFPS; and "The Barrier Seemed Impassible," 9.

77. Antoinette Brown Blackwell, "Reminiscences," BFP. Quakers were an exception, for they allowed women to serve as preachers, Lucretia Mott being the best example. On the other hand, Quaker services did not include sermons.

78. Lucy Stone to Antoinette Brown, West Brookfield, MA, c. August 1849, BFP.

79. Antoinette Blackwell, "Lucy Stone at Oberlin College," BFP; and Antoinette Brown to Lucy Stone, Oberlin, OH, February, 1850, BFP.

80. Ibid. See also Lasser and Merrill, *Friends and Sisters*, 8.

81. *Woman's Journal*, April 14, 1888, 117, in Lasser and Merrill, *Friends and Sisters*, 8.

82. Antoinette Brown to Lucy Stone, Oberlin, OH, September 22, 1847, BFPS; Edward D. Mansfield (1801–1888), *The Legal Rights, Liabilities and Duties of Women* (Salem: John P. Jewett & Co, 1845). Mansfield was a lawyer and professor of history at Cincinnati College. He aimed his 369-page book at women in order to give them a history and understanding of the law, pointing out differences in the law among various states. Interestingly, Mansfield dedicated his book to his mother. See http://www.lawbookexchange/pages/books/40702.

83. Antoinette Brown to Lucy Stone, Oberlin, OH, September 22, 1847, and Lucy Stone to Antoinette Brown, West Brookfield, MA, August 1849, both in Lasser and Merrill, *Friends and Sisters*, 31, 56.

84. Lucy Stone to Sarah Stone, Oberlin, OH, March 31, 1845, BFP.

85. Lucy Stone to Sarah Stone Lawrence, Oberlin, OH, September 14, 1845, BFP.

86. "Earning an Education," Lucy Stone file, Oberlin.

87. Hannah Stone to Lucy Stone, West Brookfield, MA, September 28, 1845, BFP; Lucy Stone to Francis Stone Jr., Oberlin, OH, May 12, 1845, BFP.

88. Lucy Stone to Sarah Stone Lawrence, Oberlin, OH, September 14, 1845, BFP.

89. Lucy Stone to Frank Stone Jr., May 20, 1844, Oberlin, OH, BFPS and Mark 41:9-23. The essay was by Mr. Hill and Mr. Beecher, the latter most likely Henry Ward Beecher, though there were several Beecher brothers.

90. Lucy Stone to Sarah Stone Lawrence, March 13, 1846, Oberlin, OH, BFP.

91. Lucy Stone to Alice Stone Blackwell, Reminiscences, 1885; and Lucy Stone to Francis Stone Jr., Oberlin, OH, May 12, 1846, both in BFP.

92. James Harris Fairchild, *Woman's Rights and Duties* (Oberlin, OH: n.p., 1849), 18, 290. Fairchild later became president of Oberlin.

93. Fletcher, *A History of Oberlin College*, 1:187.

94. Blodgett, *Oberlin History*, 26.

95. *Catalogue of the Officers and Students of the Oberlin Collegiate Institute 1843–44* (Oberlin, OH: The Evangelist Office, 1843).

96. "Report on Educating the Sexes Together," August 1845, Oberlin.

97. *Catalogue of the Officers and Students in Oberlin Collegiate Institute*, 1846–47.

98. Lucy Stone to Hannah and Francis Stone, Oberlin, OH, August 16, 1846; and "Lucy Stone at College," Lucy Stone File, Oberlin.

99. Alice Stone Blackwell, "Reminiscences," 1885, BFP.

100. Antoinette Blackwell, "Lucy Stone at Oberlin College"; and Blackwell, *Lucy Stone*, 62.

101. Account in Marianne Finch, *An Englishwoman's Experience in America* (London: Richard Bentley, 1853), 358. Finch visited Oberlin in 1851, and students were still heralding Lucy for achieving equitable pay. Of course, women students paid lower tuition than did male students, an issue that Lucy ignored here.

102. Quote in Fletcher, *History of Oberlin College*, 1:291; and Blackwell, *Lucy Stone*, 71.

103. Hugh Blair, *Lectures on Rhetoric and Belles Lettres*, 3 vols. (London and Edinburgh, 1787). Lillian O'Connor examined Oberlin's library records and discovered that Lucy had checked out this work. See Lillian O'Connor, *Pioneer*

Women Orators: Rhetoric in the Ante-Bellum Reforms Movement (New York: Columbia University Press, 1954), 69.

104. Antoinette Blackwell, "Lucy Stone at Oberlin College," February 10, 1894, BFP; and Frances J. Hosford, "The Pioneer Women of Oberlin College: Antoinette Brown Blackwell," *The Oberlin Alumni Magazine* 23, no. 4 (January 1927): 7–10.

105. "The First Girls' Debating Club," *Woman's Journal*, October 28, 1893; Manuscript book, "Minutes of the Young Ladies Association of Oberlin Collegiate Institute for the Promotion of Literature and Religion," in Cazden, *Antoinette Brown Blackwell*, 29; and Antoinette Blackwell, "Lucy Stone at Oberlin College."

106. Lucy Stone to Hannah and Francis Stone, Oberlin, OH, August 16, 1846, BFP.

107. Alice Stone Blackwell, "Memoirs: Stories Related by her Mother," April 5, 1885, BFP; and "Lucy Stone's Early Eloquence," Lucy Stone File, Oberlin.

108. Lucy Stone to Hannah and Francis Stone, Oberlin, OH, August 16, 1846, BFP. According to Fletcher, women in some respects brought this on themselves by upholding tradition. The first female students at Oberlin chose not to read their essay, for they deemed it inappropriate. See Fletcher, *History of Oberlin College*, 1:292.

109. Antoinette Brown Blackwell, "Reminiscences," BFP. She commented on this because several graduates that year supported equal rights for women.

110. Lucy Stone to Sarah Stone Lawrence, Oberlin, OH, March 14, 1847, BFP; Antoinette Brown Blackwell, "Memoir," BFP; and Blackwell, *Lucy Stone*, 68. Apparently only President Mahan supported her reading her own essay since his daughter Anna was to graduate the next year, and he hoped she would enjoy the privilege as well.

111. Sarah Stone Lawrence to Lucy Stone, West Brookfield, MA, June 18, 1847, BFP.

112. William Lloyd Garrison to Helen Garrison, August 28, 1847, in William Lloyd Garrison, *The Letters of William Lloyd Garrison*, vol. 3: *No Union with the Slaveholders*, ed. Walter M. Merrill (Cambridge, MA: Harvard University Press, 1974), 212–13; Antoinette Brown Blackwell, "Reminiscences," 74, BFP; and Blackwell, *Lucy Stone*, 74.

CHAPTER 3

1. Francis Stone Jr. to Lucy Stone, West Brookfield, MA, January 10, 1847, BFP.

2. Lucy Stone to Hannah Stone, Oberlin, OH, March 14, 1847, BFP.

3. Sarah Stone Lawrence to Lucy Stone, n.p., November 28, 1846, BFP.

4. Sarah Stone Lawrence to Lucy Stone, n.p., March 28, 1847, BFP.

5. Samuel J. May, "The Rights and Condition of Women: A Sermon" (Syracuse: Lathrop's Print, 1846); Sarah Stone Lawrence to Lucy Stone, March 28, 1847, BFP. In this letter, Sarah mentioned she had not yet received May's sermon that Lucy had sent.

6. William Bowman Stone to Lucy Stone, Gardner, MA, June 13, 1847, and July 15, 1847, BFP.

7. "Lucy Stone's Early Eloquence," Lucy Stone File, Oberlin College; William Bowman Stone to Lucy Stone, Gardner, MA, June 18, 1847, BFP; and Leslie Wheeler, *Loving Warriors: Selected Letters of Lucy Stone and Henry B. Blackwell, 1853 to 1893* (New York: The Dial Press, 1981), 18.

8. For background on women and antislavery, see Deborah Bingham Van Broekhoven, "'Let Your Names Be Enrolled': Method and Ideology in Women's Antislavery Petitioning," in Yellin and Van Horne, eds., *The Abolitionist Sisterhood*, 179–200; and Julie Roy Jeffrey, *The Great Silent Army of Abolitionism: Ordinary Women in the Antislavery Movement* (Chapel Hill and London: University of North Carolina Press, 1998).

9. Jeffrey, *The Great Silent Army of Abolitionism*, 88–93.

10. Yellin and Van Horne, "Introduction," *The Abolitionist Sisterhood*, 10–14; McMillen, *Seneca Falls*, 67–68. Such mob violence was all too common in the 1830s. Eric Foner writes, "literally hundreds of riots of one kind or another took place in the United States in the 1830s." See Foner, *Fiery Trial: Abraham Lincoln and American Slavery* (New York and London: W. W. Norton, 2010), 27.

11. Stanton's husband, Henry, was a delegate to the London convention. Mott had a different story. She reminded Stanton that they had made the decision to hold a convention when they met in Boston a year later. See McMillen, *Seneca Falls*, 81–82.

12. Two agents that listed Lucy as a speaker were the People's Literary Institute, promising in 1856 a "Brilliant Course of Lectures" and the International Lecture Bureau of Young Men's Christian Associations. In the latter, it noted that Lucy Stone charged $100 per lecture while Frederick Douglass's fee was $75 to $100. "Speech Announcements," BFP. A few lecturers earned even more. See J. Matthew Gallman, *America's Joan of Arc: The Life of Anna Elizabeth Dickinson* (New York and London: Oxford University Press, 2006), 66.

13. See Lisa Tetrault, "The Incorporation of American Feminism: Suffragists and the Postbellum Lyceum," *Journal of American History* 96, no. 4 (March 2010): 1033–35. For the huge crowds who heard Parker Pillsbury, see Stacey M. Robertson, *Parker Pillsbury: Radical Abolitionist, Male Feminist* (Ithaca and London: Cornell University Press, 2000), 80.

14. Elizabeth Jones to Lucy Stone, Salem, OH, July 1, 1847, BFP.

15. Henry Blackwell, "Early Years," in a notebook, n.d., BFP; and Million, *Woman's Voice*, 117. This Samuel May Jr. is different from the Rev. Samuel Joseph May of New York, though they were cousins and both ardent abolitionists and women's rights advocates. For a study of the MASS in the 1830s when it worked actively to broaden its support, see Richard Newman, *The Transformation of American Abolitionism* (Chapel Hill: University of North Carolina Press, 2002).

16. "Lucy Stone's Early Hardships," Lucy Stone File, Oberlin College.

17. Massachusetts Anti-Slavery Society, "Seventeenth Annual Report," January 24, 1849 (Boston: Andrews & Prentiss, 1849), 57.
18. Lucy Stone to Samuel May Jr., West Brookfield, MA, October 13, 1850, BFP.
19. Lucy Stone to Ednah Cheney, Boston, MA, June 13, 1883, New England Hospital Records, Sophia Smith Collection, Smith College Libraries, Smith College, Northampton, MA.
20. See http://www1assumption.edu/WHW/IconsFemale/TheGreekSlave. html. Apparently many Americans were most startled that the sculpture was nude.
21. This was a story Lucy often told. See Lucy Stone, "The International Council," extemporaneous speech, Woman's Journal, April 14, 1888; Blackwell, Lucy Stone, 89–90.
22. "Mrs. Livermore on Lucy Stone," Oberlin College. Ann Terry Greene Phillips was an invalid during much of her married life but totally committed to women's rights. At the 1840 World Anti-Slavery Convention in London, she, as one of the eight female delegates, had urged her husband Wendell to take a lead in giving women the right to participate.
23. Lucy Stone, "Workers for the Cause," speech, n.d. and Alice Stone Blackwell, "How Mamma Began to Take Money for her Woman's Rights Lectures," January 17, 1882, BFP.
24. Alice Stone Blackwell letter, recipient unknown, n.p., January 17, 1882, BFP; and "Lucy Stone's Early Hardships," Lucy Stone Folder, Oberlin College.
25. Isenberg, Sex and Citizenship, 16; and McMillen, Seneca Falls, 71–103.
26. Elizabeth Cady Stanton to Amy Kirby Post, Seneca Falls, NY, September 24, 1848, and Phoebe Hathaway to Elizabeth Cady Stanton, Farmington, NY, November 11, 1848, in Elizabeth Cady Stanton and Susan B. Anthony, The Selected Papers of Elizabeth Cady Stanton and Susan B. Anthony, vol. 1: In the School of Anti-Slavery, 1840 to 1866, ed. Ann D. Gordon (New Brunswick, NJ: Rutgers University Press, 1997), 123, 132. For background on Stanton, see Lori D. Ginzberg, Elizabeth Cady Stanton: An American Life (New York: Hill and Wang, 2009); and Elisabeth Griffith, In Her Own Right: The Life of Elizabeth Cady Stanton (New York: Oxford University Press, 1984).
27. Carol Faulkner, Lucretia Mott's Heresy: Abolition and Women's Rights in Nineteenth-Century America (Philadelphia: University of Pennsylvania Press, 2011); "Mott, Lucretia Coffin," s.v., American National Biography, and McMillen, Seneca Falls, 36–37. After the Civil War, the Motts helped found Swarthmore College, which they insisted be co-educational.
28. Philadelphia Female Anti-Slavery Society, "Sixteenth Annual Report" (Philadelphia: Merrihew and Thompson, 1850), 7, 15. Its records show that Lucy was paid $42.72 and brought in $14.38.
29. Frederick Douglass, "Eulogy to Lucy Stone" and Elizabeth Cady Stanton, "Tribute to Lucy Stone," in Proceedings of the 26th Annual Convention of the National American Woman's Suffrage Association, February 15–20, 1894,

Washington, DC, ed. Harriet Taylor Upton (Warren, OH: Chronicle Print, 1894), 73, 83.

30. Thomas Wentworth Higginson from Bangor, ME, 1855, in *Letters and Journals of Thomas Wentworth Higginson, 1846–1906*, ed. Mary Thatcher Higginson (Boston and New York: Houghton Mifflin Company, 1921), 59. Recipient is unknown. See also "The Power of Sweetness," *Springfield Republican*, n.d., in Lucy Stone File, Oberlin.

31. Maria S. Porter, "Lucy Stone," *National Magazine* 3 (1895): 42–54, quotes 43, 50.

32. "Pioneer Experiences," Lucy Stone File, Oberlin College; and Lucy Stone "Reminiscences" to Alice Stone Blackwell, October 5, 1891, BFP.

33. Ednah D. Cheney in "Lucy Stone, 1818–1893," n.p., in Florence Hazzard Papers, Sophia Smith Collection, Smith College Library, Northampton, MA.

34. "Lucy Stone's Seventieth Birthday," *Springfield Republican*, August 19, 1888.

35. "Mrs. Livermore on Lucy Stone," Lucy Stone File, Oberlin College.

36. Juliet Ward Howe, "Eulogy to Lucy Stone," in Upton, *Proceedings*, 58, 62.

37. Lucy Stone, "Speech," *Proceedings of the Woman's Rights Convention at Broadway Tabernacle*, September 6, 7, 1853, American Memory.

38. Lucy Stone, "Speech of Miss Lucy Stone," the *Liberator*, May 27, 1853.

39. "Woman's Rights Convention," *New York Times*, September 7, 1853; and "The Women Pests," *New York Times*, September 8, 1853. Brown was ordained by the church September 1853, right before Lucy's speech.

40. "Speech of Lucy Stone," New England Anti-Slavery Convention, the *Liberator*, June 16, 1854, BFP.

41. Million, *Woman's Voice*, 170.

42. Horatio Alger to Lucy Stone, Marlborough, MA, September 22, 1856, BFP.

43. Lasser and Merrill, *Friends and Sisters*, 87. On her western tour in the winter of 1853–54, Lucy allegedly grossed over $5,000.

44. "Speech at New York Anti-Slavery Convention," *National Anti-Slavery Standard*, September 10, 1853.

45. "The National Woman's Rights Convention at Syracuse," *Frederick Douglass Paper*, September 17, 1852; Lucy Stone to Henry Blackwell, 1854, Tremont House (Boston?), BFP.

46. *New York Times*, May 14, 1853 (clipped from the *Syracuse Weekly Chronicle* with no title).

47. Lucy Stone to Samuel May, Westfield, MA, April 1849, and Wendell Phillips to Lucy Stone, n.p., October 8, 1853, both in BFP. Parker Pillsbury often suffered from health issues and the grueling demands of lecturing. See Robertson, *Parker Pillsbury*, 76–90.

48. Susan B. Anthony to Lucy Stone, Rochester, NY, May 1, 1853, BFP.

49. Alice Stone Blackwell, "Journal—Reminiscences," April 7, 1884, BFP.

50. Lucy Stone to Alice Stone Blackwell, Reminiscences, October 5, 1891, BFP.

51. Alice Stone Blackwell, "Journal—Reminiscences," April 7, 1884, and Lucy Stone to Samuel May Jr., Westfield, MA, April 14, 1850, both in BFP.

52. Lucy Stone to Henry Blackwell, n.p., n.d., BFP.

53. "Anti-Slavery Society," *Pennsylvania Freeman*, August 10, 1848; Robertson, *Parker Pillsbury*, 90; "Pioneer Experiences," Lucy Stone File, Oberlin; and Lucy Stone to Alice Stone Blackwell, Reminiscences, September 22, 1893, BFP.

54. Nellie Blessing Eyster, "An Evening with Lucy Stone," October 10, 1896, BFP; "Lucy Stone's Presence of Mind," Lucy Stone File, Oberlin; Lucy Stone to Alice Stone Blackwell, Reminiscences, April 15, 1893, BFP; "Mob on Cape Cod," the *Liberator*, September 1, 1848.

55. "Anti-Slavery Convention," *New York Times*, September 5, 1853.

56. Lucy Stone to Susan B. Anthony, Boston, MA, March 22, 1853, BFP.

57. Lucy Stone to Susan B. Anthony, West Brookfield, MA, February 2, 1854, BFP.

58. Lucy Stone to Susan B. Anthony, New York City, January 25, 1854, BFP.

59. "Rights and Wrongs," *New York Times*, April 26, 1853.

60. Lucy Stone, "Speech," April 4, 1849, BFPS. Many of Lucy's speeches were extemporaneous and are known today only if a scribe or reporter was present and took detailed notes or if Lucy later wrote down her words on paper. An early address to the Salem (MA) Female Anti-Slavery Society on November 5, 1848 is in full in BFP.

61. "Latest Intelligence," *New York Times*, September 9, 1852.

62. "Woman's Rights Convention Second Day," *New York Times*, September 10, 1852 and "Latest Intelligence," *New York Times*, September 11, 1852.

63. Lucy Stone, "Speech," *Proceedings of the National Woman's Rights Convention Held at Cleveland, Ohio, October 5–7, 1853*, American Memory.

64. Lucy Stone, "Disappointment Is the Lot of Woman," in *Standing Before Us: Unitarian Universalist Women and Social Reform, 1776–1935*, ed. Dorothy May Emerson (Boston: Skinner House Books, 2000), 54–56; "National Convention in Cincinnati," *New York Daily Times*, October 23, 1855.

65. Lucy Stone, "The Province of Woman," BFP.

66. "Speech of Miss Lucy Stone," the *Liberator*, May 27, 1853.

67. Susan B. Anthony to Lucy Stone, Albany, NY, March 12, 1854, BFP.

68. Quote in Elizabeth R. Varon, *Disunion!: The Coming of the American Civil War, 1789–1859* (Chapel Hill: University of North Carolina Press, 2008), 150.

69. Mayer, *All on Fire*, 313, 328; Varon, *Disunion!*, 152–53; and David F. Ericson, *The Debate over Slavery: Antislavery and Proslavery Liberalism in Antebellum America* (New York and London: New York University, 2000), 63–68. This message intensified with the passage of the Compromise of 1850 and the Supreme Court's 1857 Dred Scott decision. Some abolitionists feared this extreme idea might cause abolitionists to abandon slaves, not free them. Many Americans felt the issue was alienating the public rather than drawing them to the cause. See Mayer, *All on Fire*, 452.

70. Lucy Stone to Hannah Stone, Oberlin, OH, March 14, 1847, BFP.

71. "Speech at New York Anti-Slavery Convention," *National Anti-Slavery Standard*, September 10, 1853.

72. "Speech of Lucy Stone," New England Anti-Slavery Convention, the *Liberator*, June 16, 1854.

73. W. D. Gallagher to Henry Blackwell, Louisville, KY, October 19, 1853, BFPS.

74. Lucy Stone to Henry Blackwell, December 1, 1853, Lafayette, IN, BFP; and Lucy Stone to Alice Stone Blackwell, Reminiscences, September 22, 1893, BFP.

75. Lucy Stone to Henry Blackwell, Indianapolis, IN, November 7, 1853, BFP.

76. Lucy Stone to Susan B. Anthony, Pittsburg, PA, January 10, 1854, BFP. Apparently a couple of Lucy's hosts in southern cities urged her not to wear bloomers, but she ignored them.

77. See "Lucy Stone at St. Louis," *St. Louis Republican*, December 20, 1853, and "Woman's Rights," *St. Louis Intelligencer*, December 20, 1853. Other newspapers in the city were also favorably impressed.

78. Lucy Stone to Susan B. Anthony, Pittsburgh, PA, January 10, 1854, BFP.

CHAPTER 4

1. Lucy Stone to Alice Stone Blackwell, Reminiscences October 8, 1893, BFP; Harriet H. Robinson, *Massachusetts in the Woman Suffrage Movement: A General Political, Legal, and Legislative History, from 1774 to 1881*, 2nd ed. (Boston: Roberts Brothers, 1883).

2. Blackwell, *Lucy Stone*, 96.

3. Sarah Grimké and Angelina Weld Grimké to Lucy Stone, July 15, 1850, BFP; Lucy Stone to Antoinette Brown, June 9, 1850, West Brookfield, MA, in Lasser and Merrill, *Friends and Sisters*, 72–73. For background on Davis, see "Kellogg, Paulina Wright Davis," s.v., *American National Biography*. In her pamphlet, "History of the National Woman's Rights Movement" (New York: Journeymen Printers' Cooperative Association, 1871), 13, Davis incorrectly gave herself total credit for organizing the Worcester convention, claiming that all the work fell to her.

4. This was the second major cholera epidemic to hit the nation, beginning in 1848 and lasting until the early 1850s. It affected residents in the North and South, as well as many of those traveling west to Oregon and to California. Cholera is a bacterial infection, not contagious, but caught by drinking water or food infected by those who have had it. The mortality rate was high, and no one at the time knew the cause or how to cure the disease. For more information, see Charles Rosenberg, *The Cholera Years: The United States in 1832, 1849, and 1866* (Chicago: University of Chicago Press, 1962, 1987).

5. Lucy Stone to Samuel May Jr., West Brookfield, MA, October 13, 1850, BFP.

6. Lucy wrote that there had been three fatal cases of cholera in Hutsonville as well as outbreaks of smallpox, measles, mumps, and whooping cough, and the water was miserable. Lucy Stone to Samuel May, Hutsonville, IL, July 25, 1850, and Lucy Stone to Samuel May, West Brookfield, MA, October 13, 1850, both in BFP. In August 1853, Henry Blackwell visited Ann and Jemmy Egen in Bellville, IL, who well remembered two women who stayed with them, one of

whom (Lucy) "was so sick." They related details of Lucy's illness, "taking great credit . . . for their excellent nursing and attention." Henry Blackwell to Lucy Stone, Walnut Hills, OH, August 24, 1853, in Wheeler, *Loving Warriors*, 53.

7. Lucy Stone to Samuel May Jr., West Brookfield, MA, October 13, 1850, BFP.

8. J. G. Forman, "Woman's Rights Convention at Worcester, Massachusetts," *New York Daily Tribune*, October 24, 1850. The *Boston Daily Chronotype* called the weather "the finest possible." See *Boston Daily Chronotype*, October 24, 1850. Several accounts list the total number of attendees as a thousand. For background on the convention, see *The Proceedings of the Woman's Rights Convention Held at Worcester, 1850* (Boston: Prentiss & Sawyer, 1851); and John McClymer, *This High and Holy Moment: The First National Woman's Rights Convention* (New York: Harcourt Brace, 1999).

9. "Grand Demonstration of Petticoatdom at Worcester," *Boston Daily Mail*, October 24, 1850.

10. *Boston Daily Mail*, October 25, 1850. Ernestine Rose became actively involved in the women's rights movement and was a strong presence at many women's rights conventions. She sought to make others aware of European efforts to advance women. She left for Europe in 1869 and died in London in 1892. See "Rose, Ernestine," s.v., *American National Biography*; and Paula Doress-Worters, *Speeches and Letters of Ernestine Rose, Early Women's Rights Leader* (New York: Feminist Press, 2008), 1–54 (introduction).

11. *Proceedings of the Woman's Rights Meeting, Held at Worcester, 1850*, http://www.wwhp.org/Resources/WomansRights/proceedings.html.

12. "Woman's Rights Convention," *New York Herald*, October 25, 1850.

13. J. G. Forman, "Lucy Stone at National Woman's Rights Convention," *New York Daily Tribune*, October 26, 1850.

14. Ibid. The *New York Herald*, the chief rival of Horace Greeley's *New York Tribune*, was far less charitable toward the event. The reporter called Lucy "very ambitious. She wanted woman put ahead, so that when she died, it should not be written upon her grave-stone that she was the 'relict' [widow] of somebody." The "Woman's Rights Convention," *New York Herald*, October 28, 1850.

15. "Woman's Rights Convention, Awful Combination of Socialism, Abolitionism, and Infidelity," *New York Herald*, October 25, 1850.

16. Ibid.

17. The *Liberator*, November 1, 1850.

18. Horace Greeley, *New York Tribune*, November 2, 1850.

19. Paulina Wright Davis, "The First Annual Woman's Rights Convention."

20. Elizabeth Blackwell to "M," December 24, 1850, http://www.wwhp.org/Resources/WomansRights/proceedings.html.

21. Anonymous reader to *New York Tribune*, November 2, 1850.

22. Jane Swisshelm, *The Saturday Visiter*, November 2, 1850; Parker Pillsbury, "Women's Rights Convention and People of Color," *The North Star*, December 5, 1850.

23. Harriet Taylor Mill, "Enfranchisement of Women," *Westminster Review* (1851), http://womhist.alexanderstreet.com/awrm/doc15.htm.

24. "Proceedings of the National Woman's Rights Convention, Worcester, 1851," in Stanton, Anthony, and Gage, eds., *History of Woman Suffrage*, 1:234–36, 229–30 and McMillen, *Seneca Falls*, 115–16.

25. Lucy Stone to Alice Stone Blackwell, Reminiscences, October 10, 1892, BFP.

26. For background on Anthony, see, "Anthony, Susan Brownell," s.v., *American National Biography* and McMillen, *Seneca Falls*, 54–55.

27. Lucy Stone to Anna Parsons, Cleveland, OH, September 7, 1853, BFP.

28. Lucy Stone to Henry Blackwell, Philadelphia, PA, October 22, 1854, in Wheeler, *Loving Warriors*, 103.

29. *New York Tribune*, October 20, 1854, in Million, *Woman's Voice*, 173.

30. Antoinette Brown to Lucy Stone, Rochester, NY, April 14, 1852, BFPS.

31. Wendell Phillips to Lucy Stone, n.p., August 20, 1852, BFP.

32. "The Syracuse National Convention," in Stanton, Anthony, and Gage, eds., *History of Woman Suffrage*, 1:527, 529.

33. "Woman's Rights Amendment to Massachusetts Constitution," the *Liberator*, February 4, 1853, and Susan Zaeske, *Signatures of Citizenship: Petitioning, Antislavery, and Women's Political Identity* (Chapel Hill and London: University of North Carolina Press, 2003), 128–29, 179–81.

34. "Speech of Miss Lucy Stone," the *Liberator*, May 27, 1853, and "The New England A.S. Convention," the *Liberator*, June 3, 1853.

35. "Equal Political Rights," the *Liberator*, June 3, 1853; "Weekly Summary," *Boston Recorder*, June 9, 1853; and Million, *Woman's Voice*, 134–36.

36. Commonwealth of Massachusetts, "Official Report of the Debates and Proceedings in the State Convention, May 4, 1853" (Boston: White & Porter, 1853), 43. Historian Dr. Drew Gilpin Faust became the first female president of Harvard University in 2007.

37. Lucy Stone to Elizabeth Cady Stanton, n.p., August 14, 1853, in Stanton and Anthony, *Selected Papers*, 1:224–25; McMillen, *Seneca Falls*, 124.

38. L. Sampson to Lucy Stone, West Brookfield, June 16, 1851, and Lucy Stone to L. Sampson, West Brookfield, MA, June 20, 1851, BFP.

39. Lucy had already given up on the Orthodox Congregational Church and declared herself a Unitarian.

40. James Fairchild to Lucy Stone, Oberlin, OH, June 15, 1852, Lucy Stone to I. H Fairchild, West Brookfield, MA, June 22, 1852, and Lucy Stone to William Lloyd Garrison, West Brookfield, MA, June 22, 1852, all in BFP. This appeared in the *Liberator*, June 25, 1852. Fairchild taught mathematics, languages, natural philosophy, and theology. He served as president of Oberlin from 1866 to 1889. See also Lasser and Merrill, *Friends and Sisters*, 33 n. 9.

41. Lucy Stone to Lydia Mott, Damariscotta, ME, March 5, 1854, BFP.

42. "Lucy Stone at Musical Fund Hall, Philadelphia," *Frederick Douglass Paper*, February 17, 1854; and James Mott to Lucy Stone, Philadelphia, December 9, 1856, BFP.

43. Erwin Palmer, "A Partnership in the Abolition Movement," *University of Rochester Library Bulletin* 26 (Autumn/Winter 1970-71); James Mott to Lucy Stone, Philadelphia, PA, February 18, 1854, BFP. See also Tyrone Tillery, "The Inevitability of the Douglass-Garrison Conflict," *Phylon* 37, no. 2 (1976): 137-49; and Million, *Women's Voice,* 166-68.

44. Lydia Mott to Lucy Stone, Albany, NY, February 19, 1854; and Lucy Stone to Lydia Mott, Damariscotta, ME, March 5, 1854, BFP. Lydia Mott lived in Albany, New York, was an ardent abolitionist, and regarded by Garrison as principled and courageous. Three years later, Lucy was asked to speak in Philadelphia for the "People's Literary Institute," and shortly before the event, learned that the lectures were to be held in the Musical Fund Hall. She wrote the man who had invited her, saying that she could only speak there on condition that "colored people" be allowed to attend or that he find another hall. In defense of Richardson, apparently he had sent Lucy a circular announcing her lecture and its location, but she failed to examine it carefully, claiming she received many circulars every year. Richardson was able to change the location and the date. Lucy spoke on December 29 at National Hall. See Lucy Stone to Mr. W. H. Richardson, December 7, 12, and 16, 1854, New York, BPF.

45. Anne C. Coon, "The Bloomer Costume," *Rochester History* 57, no. 3 (1995): 18-24; and Jennifer Ladd Nelson, "Dress Reform and the Bloomer," *Journal of American Culture* 23, no. 1 (Spring 2000): 21-25.

46. Sarah Grimké, Letter 11, "Dress of Women," in Sarah Grimké and Angelina Grimké, *Letters on the Equality of the Sexes,* in *The Public Years of Sarah and Angelina Grimké: Selected Writings, 1835–1839,* ed. Larry Ceplair (New York: Columbia University Press, 1989), 230. See also McMillen, *Seneca Falls,* 129-130; Mary Curtis, "Amelia Bloomer's Curious Costume," *American History Illustrated* (June 1978): 11-15; Gayle V. Fischer, *Pantaloons and Power: A Nineteenth-Century Dress Reform in the United States* (Kent, OH: Kent State University Press, 2001); and Million, *Woman's Voices,* 114-15.

47. "Mrs. Livermore on Lucy Stone," Lucy Stone File, Oberlin.

48. Elizabeth Cady Stanton to Lucretia Mott, Seneca Falls, NY, October 22, 1852, in Stanton and Anthony, *Selected Papers,* 1:213, 214.

49. Susan B. Anthony to Lucy Stone, Rochester, NY, May 23, 1852, BFP. See also Isenberg, *Sex and Citizenship,* 48-55.

50. Lucy Stone to Susan B. Anthony, West Brookfield, MA, February 13, 1854, and Lucy Stone to Susan B. Anthony, Hallowell, ME, March 3, 1854, both in BFP.

51. Nette never adopted the costume. See Cazden, *Antoinette Brown Blackwell,* 68-69.

52. *Harper's New Monthly Magazine* 4, no. 20 (January 1852); "Full Dress for Home," *Harper's New Monthly Magazine* 4, no. 21 (February 1852); McMillen, *Seneca Falls* 132; "The Bloomer Dress," *Woman's Journal,* October 12, 1889; *Harper's,* August 1851; and Antoinette Brown to Lucy Stone, n.p., January 30, 1851, BFP.

53. Susan B. Anthony to Lucy Stone, Albany, NY, February 9, 1854, BFP.

54. Susan B. Anthony and Elizabeth Cady Stanton to Lucy Stone, Albany, NY, February 16, 1854, BFP.

55. "Mrs. Livermore on Lucy Stone," Lucy Stone File, Oberlin.

56. Lucy Stone to Ednah Cheney, Boston, August 17, 1885, in Florence Hazard Papers, Smith College. James Mott assumed that Lucy gave up bloomers because Henry Blackwell, who was courting Lucy at the time, asked her to do so. According to Mott, that proved "thee will be an obedient wife." That comment no doubt offended Lucy. See James Mott to Lucy Stone, Philadelphia, March 15, 1854, BFP.

57. "World's Temperance Convention," *New York Times*, May 13, 1853; "Woman, to the Breach!," May 14, 1853, *New York Times*; McMillen, *Seneca Falls*, 56; "New York Correspondence," *National Era*, September 22, 1853; Ian Tyrrell, "Women and Temperance in Antebellum America, 1830-1860," *Civil War History* 28 (1982): 147; Cazden, *Antoinette Brown Blackwell*, 78-80.

58. "Men and Women," *New York Times*, September 6, 1853; Anna May Wells, *Dear Preceptor: The Life and Times of Thomas Wentworth Higginson* (Boston: Houghton Mifflin, 1963), 82-83; and "The Whole World's Temperance Convention," New York, September 1 and 2, 1853, 23-26, quotes, 25, http://www1.assumption.edu/ahc/1853TemperanceConvention.html. Lucy named both men and women as drunkards, though she admitted that far more men fell victim to excessive drinking. See also Lucy Stone to Anna Parsons, West Brookfield, MA, July 8, 1853, BFP.

59. "The Women Pests," *New York Times*, September 8, 1853.

60. "Phillips, Wendell," s.v., *American National Biography*; Irving H. Bartlett, *Wendell and Ann Phillips: The Community of Reform, 1840-1880* (New York: Norton, 1979), 24; and James Brewer Stewart, *Wendell Phillips: Liberty's Hero* (Baton Rouge: Louisiana State University Press, 1986), 84-96.

61. Quoted in Wells, *Dear Preceptor*, 62. Higginson's wife Mary became an invalid after they married. According to Wells, she became more infirm as Higginson became increasingly famous as a Unitarian minister and ardent advocate for abolition and women's rights. Certainly neurasthenia comes to mind as her problem. See Wells, *Dear Preceptor*, 81.

62. Thomas Wentworth Higginson, "Ought Women to Learn the Alphabet," in Michael S. Kimmel and Thomas E. Mosmiller, eds., *Against the Tide: Pro-Feminist Men in the United States, 1776–1990, a Documentary History* (Boston: Beacon Press, 1992), 111-14, 105. Higginson's *Women and the Alphabet: A Series of Essays* (Cambridge, MA: Riverside, 1859) articulated his devotion to the cause.

63. Preface by Lucy Stone, "Woman's Rights Tracts," Massachusetts Historical Society, Boston; Theodore Parker, "A Sermon: Of the Public Function of Woman" (Boston: Robert I. Wallcut, 1853).

64. Lucy Stone to Susan B. Anthony, Pittsburg, PA, January 10, 1854, BFL. The Young Men's Mercantile Library Association and Mechanical Institute in Pittsburg was founded in 1848. A number of cities claimed these organizations

of young men who created subscription libraries and often organized lyceums or sponsored lecturers.

65. "Prospectus," *Una*, February 1, 1843.

66. Sterling, *Ahead of Her Time*, 301 n.

67. Letter in the *Liberator*, October 29, 1852, in Million, *Woman's Voices*, 123–24; and Antoinette Brown to Lucy Stone, Henrietta, NY, December 16, 1852, BFPS.

68. McMillen, *Seneca Falls*, 134–35; Isenberg, *Sex and Citizenship*, 73; Million, *Woman's Voices*, 125-26; and Lucy Stone to Antoinette Brown, Walnut Hills, OH, July 11, 1855, in Lasser and Merrill, *Friends and Sisters*, 144. Lucy raised the point of a woman's right to her body with Stanton in August 1853, upset by laws that defended a husband's right to his wife's body, but she felt it was too soon to raise that issue. See Lucy Stone to Elizabeth Cady Stanton, August 14, 1853, in Stanton and Anthony, *Selected Papers*, 1:223. At this point, Lucy was no doubt doing lots of soul searching about marital issues while Henry Blackwell courted her.

69. Lucy Stone to Susan B. Anthony, Racine, WI, November 2, 1855, BFPS.

70. Lucy Stone to Susan B. Anthony, Racine, WI, November 25, 1856, BFPS.

71. Lucy Stone to Alice Stone Blackwell, Reminiscences, March 3, 1893, BFP.

72. Susan B. Anthony to Lucy Stone, Rochester, NY, May 25, 1852, BFP.

73. Lucy Stone to Susan B. Anthony, Hollidayburg, PA, January 9, 1857, BFP.

74. Lucy Stone to Susan B. Anthony, Cincinnati, OH, January 16, 1856, in Stanton and Anthony, *Selected Papers*, 1:313; and Susan B. Anthony to Lucy Stone, Rochester, NY, July 18, 1853, BFP.

75. Susan B. Anthony to Lucy Stone, Rochester, NY, May 1, 1853, BFP.

76. Susan B. Anthony to Lucy Stone, Rochester, NY, July 18, 1853, BFP.

77. Lucy Stone, "Remarks," National Woman Suffrage Association, *Report of the International Council of Women, March 25 to April 1, 1888* (Washington, DC: Rufus H. Darby, 1888), 334. Accounts of when the women first met differ. According to Elisabeth Griffith's biography of Stanton, the women first met in Seneca Falls with Susan B. Anthony to discuss the idea of a progressive women's college. Stone's memory years later offered a different view. See Griffith, *In Her Own Right*, 76.

78. Lucy Stone to Elizabeth Cady Stanton, n.p., August 14, 1853, in Stanton and Anthony, *Selected Papers*, 1:224; Lucy Stone to Susan B. Anthony, n.p., October 22, 1856, BFP; Ginzberg, *Elizabeth Cady Stanton*, 169.

79. She described a legislative session in Massachusetts when politicians discussed the gypsy moth and woodchuck, analyzed the length of trout and lobsters suitable for sale, compared butter to margarine, and set a price for chickens. But those same men avoided the topic of female suffrage and refused to pass a law that would force a husband to repay a wife when he borrowed money from her. Lucy Stone, "Some Things the Massachusetts Legislature of 1889 and 1890 Did for Men, Who Have Votes, Contrasted with What It Did for Women, Who Have no Votes," BFP.

80. Ginzberg, *Elizabeth Cady Stanton*, 27.

81. Stone, "Workers for the Cause."

82. Antoinette Brown to Lucy Stone, Henrietta, NY, March 28, 1848, BFPS. See also Carroll Smith-Rosenberg, "Female World of Love and Ritual: Relations between Women in Nineteenth-Century America," *Signs* 1, no. 1 (Autumn 1975): 1–29.

83. Antoinette Brown to Lucy Stone, Henrietta, NY, March 18, 1848, Oberlin, OH, and June 2, 1850, BFP; Antoinette Brown to Lucy Stone, Henrietta, NY, April 15, 1852, BFPS.

84. Antoinette Brown to Lucy Stone, Rochester, NY, April 14, 1852, BFPS.

85. Lucy Stone to Alice Stone Blackwell, Reminiscences, September 25, 1893, BFP.

86. Lucy Stone to Henry Blackwell, n.d., 1854, n.p.

CHAPTER 5

1. Lucy Stone to Antoinette Brown, West Brookfield, MA, August 1849, in Lasser and Merrill, *Friends and Sisters*, 56.

2. Apparently Lucy's check was drawn up by the treasurer of the Ohio Anti-Slavery Society; the draft was on the hardware store's previous owner. Henry's abolitionist sentiments made him sympathetic to Lucy's situation and her need for money to complete the journey home. See Wheeler, *Loving Warriors*, 33. Henry later claimed that he was instantly attracted to Lucy on their very first meeting.

3. Henry's siblings (in birth order) were Anna, Marian, Elizabeth, Samuel, Henry, Emily, Ellen, Howard, and George. Anna moved to Paris as a newspaper correspondent; Ellen became a writer and artist; Elizabeth and Emily were physicians; and Marian was an invalid and lived with her mother. George became the wealthiest of the brothers. Howard journeyed to India and died young. See Wheeler, *Loving Warriors*, 27.

4. "Blackwell, Elizabeth," *Notable American Women, 1607–1950*, vol. 1 (Cambridge, MA: Belknap Press of Harvard University Press, 1971), 161–62.

5. "Blackwell, Henry Browne," s.v., *American National Biography*; Elinor Rice Hays, *Those Extraordinary Blackwells: The Story of a Journey to a Better World* (New York: Harcourt, Brace & World, 1967), 34 and Wheeler, *Loving Warriors*, 23–24. Henry mentioned the calomel treatment, which was a common cure-all at this time for numerous diseases. Calomel is a mercury chloride and usually did more harm than good. See Henry Blackwell to Lucy Stone, Cincinnati, OH, September 9, 1853, in Wheeler, *Loving Warriors*, 59.

6. Marian Blackwell to Henry Blackwell, Walnut Hills, Cincinnati, OH, November 5, 1848, BFPS; and Wheeler, *Loving Warriors*, 22–25. While his family and Lucy called him Harry, for the sake of consistency, this author is calling him Henry. Today, psychologists might diagnose Henry as bipolar or suffering from ADHD.

7. Wheeler, *Loving Warriors*, 28.

8. Sam Blackwell to Elizabeth Blackwell, New York, February 18, 1870, BFPS.

9. Alice Stone Blackwell to Kitty Blackwell, Dorchester, MA, October 13, 1889, BFP.

10. Marian Blackwell to Henry Blackwell, n.p., 1850, BFP and Hays, *Those Extraordinary Blackwells*, 35. Hays writes aptly that the Blackwell family "overflowed with unsolicited advice." See Hays, *Those Extraordinary Blackwells*, 189.

11. Hannah Blackwell to Henry Blackwell, Walnut Hills, Cincinnati, OH, February 12, 1849, BFP.

12. The hardware store claimed to be "Importers and Dealers in Staples & Fancy Hardware, Cutlery Tools." It was located at 90 Main Street, Cincinnati. Hays, *Those Extraordinary Blackwells*, 72, 76 and Wheeler, *Loving Warriors*, 28.

13. Marian Blackwell to Harry Blackwell, Walnut Hills, Cincinnati, OH, November 5, 1848, BFPS.

14. Thomas Wentworth Higginson to his mother, Worcester, MA, May 1, 1855, in *Letters and Journals of Thomas Wentworth Higginson, 1846–1906*, ed. Mary Thacher Higginson (Boston and New York: Houghton Mifflin Company, 1921), 60; Wheeler, *Loving Warriors*, 29; and Leslie Wheeler, "Lucy Stone, Wife of Henry Blackwell," *American History Illustrated* 16, no. 8 (December 1981), 40.

15. Henry Blackwell to George Blackwell, Cincinnati, OH, October 19, 1855, BFPS. Henry wrote younger brother George "Do not drink, chew, smoke, nor loaf." On March 9, 1856, he also urged him to "bathe frequently."

16. "The New England A.S. Convention," the *Liberator*, June 3, 1853.

17. Henry Blackwell to Sam Blackwell, in Wheeler, *Loving Warriors*, 34.

18. Henry Blackwell to Lucy Stone, n.p., June 13, 1853, BFP.

19. Lucy Stone to Henry Blackwell, West Brookfield, MA, July 27, 1853, BFP.

20. Henry Blackwell to Sam Blackwell, in Wheeler, *Loving Warriors*, 34. These letters are amazing to read. Most literally go on for pages, in beautiful, small cursive writing, lines close together. One wonders how Henry had time for anything other than to correspond with Lucy. Writing to her seemed to be his primary occupation.

21. Henry Blackwell to Lucy Stone, New York, June 13, 1853, BFP; and Henry Blackwell to Lucy Stone, Walnut Hills, Cincinnati, OH, July 2, 1853, in Wheeler, *Loving Warriors*, 45.

22. Henry Blackwell to Lucy Stone, New York, June 13, 1853, and Walnut Hills, Cincinnati, OH, July 2, 1853, both in BFP. In 1839 Angelina married abolitionist Theodore Wright Weld, and they moved with Sarah to New Jersey. Angelina gave birth to three children and suffered bouts of ill health. To many in the women's rights and antislavery movement, their situation was not one to copy.

23. Henry Blackwell to Lucy Stone, Walnut Hills, OH, July 2, June 13, and August 24, 1853, BFP.

24. Henry Blackwell to Lucy Stone, Walnut Hills, OH, Augusts 24, 1853, BFP.

25. Lucy Stone to Henry Blackwell, Boston, MA, June 21, 1853, BFP.

26. Henry Blackwell to Lucy Stone, Cincinnati, OH, July 2 and August 20, 1853, BFP; and Lucy Stone to Henry Blackwell, July 27, 1853, West Brookfield, MA, BFP.

27. Henry Blackwell to Lucy Stone, Cincinnati, OH, August 20, 1853, BFP.

28. Henry Blackwell and Lucy Stone, quoted in Wheeler, *Loving Warriors*, 62–63.

29. Henry Blackwell, "Speech," "Cleveland National Convention, October 5, 6, 7, 1853," in Stanton, Anthony, and Gage, eds., *History of Woman Suffrage*, 1:126–27 and *Proceedings of the National Woman's Rights Convention Held at Cleveland, Ohio*.

30. Lucy Stone to Anna Parsons, Pittsburgh, PA, January 12, 1854, BFP.

31. Lucy Stone to Hannah Blackwell, Chicago, IL, December 18, 1853; and Lucy Stone to Henry Blackwell, Chicago, IL, December 30, 1853, both in BFP.

32. Lucy Stone to Henry Blackwell, Lafayette, IN, December 1, 1853, BFP.

33. Henry Blackwell to Lucy Stone, Cincinnati, OH, January 3, 1854, BFP.

34. Lucy Stone to Henry Blackwell, n.p., n.d. 1854, BFP.

35. Henry Blackwell to Lucy Stone, OH, January 22, 1854, in Wheeler, *Loving Warriors*, 69.

36. Henry Blackwell to Lucy Stone, Cincinnati, OH, April 25, 1854, in Wheeler, *Loving Warriors*, 80.

37. Henry Blackwell to Lucy Stone, Cincinnati, OH, May 2, 1854, BFP.

38. Henry Blackwell to Lucy Stone, New York, NY, May 12, 1854, BFP.

39. Lucy Stone to Henry Blackwell, Gardner, MA, July 23, 1854, BFP.

40. Henry Blackwell to Lucy Stone, Cincinnati, OH, September 1, 1854, BFP. The Supreme Court of Ohio had ruled that any slave brought to Ohio could be freed if the slave stated he or she wanted to be free. See Wheeler, *Loving Warriors*, 92. A local family adopted the girl, whom abolitionists named Abby Kelley Salem. Henry was indicted on kidnapping but the lawyer handling the case was a friend of Henry's and the case never came to trial. See Wheeler, *Loving Warriors*, 95. For a full description of the event, see Stacey M. Robertson, *Hearts Beating for Liberty: Women Abolitionists in the Old Northwest* (Chapel Hill: University of North Carolina Press, 2010), 162–64.

41. Lucy Stone to Henry Blackwell, West Brookfield, MA, September 10, 1854, BFP. It was suffragist Elizabeth Buffum Chace who heard Henry admit the importance of his rescuing the slave girl. See Lillie Buffum Chace Wyman and Arthur Crawford Wyman, *Elizabeth Buffum Chace, 1806–1899: Her Life and Its Environment*, vol. 2 (Boston: W. B. Clarke Co., 1914), 220. These volumes contain many actual letters.

42. Geneva Medical School in upstate New York accepted Elizabeth. Only later did she discover that school administrators had turned over her unusual application to the student body for consideration. The young men decided to accept "her," assuming it was a joke played by another school. Elizabeth showed up and spent two years studying medicine, the normal program at the time. Despite discrimination by schoolmates and townspeople, she graduated in

1849 as the first woman in America to earn a medical degree. Henry was present for her graduation.

43. "Blackwell, Elizabeth" and "Blackwell, Emily," s.v., *American National Biography*; Margo Horn, "Sisters Worthy of Respect," *Journal of Family History* (Winter 1983): 367–82; and Nancy Ann Sahli, *Elizabeth Blackwell (1821–1910): A Biography* (New York: Arno Press, 1982).

44. Anna Blackwell to Henry Blackwell, in Wheeler, *Loving Warriors*, 114. Apparently Henry let Lucy read this letter, despite its negative tone, feeling that because Anna had not met Lucy and knew little about her, Lucy would not be offended by her words. She was hurt.

45. Elizabeth Blackwell to Lucy Stone, New York, NY, June 1, 1854, BFP.

46. Ibid. Elizabeth had expressed her distaste in December 1850, feeling that women would win their rights in a far better way than by haranguing and holding conventions. Elizabeth Blackwell to "M," n.p., December 24, 1850, North American Women's Letters and Diaries online, http://www.alexander-street.com/products/north-american'womens-letters-and-diaries.

47. Lucy Stone to Elizabeth Blackwell, Gardner, MA, June 10, 1854, BFP.

48. Henry Blackwell to Theodore Parker, Walnut Hills, Cincinnati, OH, April 16, 1853, BFPS.

49. Wisconsin Historical Society, "19th-Century Immigration," http://www.wisconsinhistory.org/turningpoints.

50. Henry Blackwell to Lucy Stone, Milwaukee, WI, June 18, 1854, BFP; and Elizabeth Blackwell to George Blackwell, New York, August 16, 1856, BFPS.

51. Henry Blackwell to Lucy Stone, Philadelphia, PA, July 12, 1854, BFP; and Elizabeth Blackwell to George Blackwell, New York, NY, August 16, 1856, BFPS.

52. Lucy Stone to Henry Blackwell, Philadelphia, PA, October 22, 1854, BFP.

53. Ibid.; and Henry Blackwell to Lucy Stone, n.p., November 8, 1854, BFP.

54. Antoinette Brown to Elizabeth Cady Stanton, Andover, MA, December 28, 1854, in Stanton and Anthony, *Selected Papers*, 1:290.

55. Henry Blackwell to Lucy Stone, Cincinnati, OH, December 22, 1854, in Wheeler, *Loving Warriors*, 110–11.

56. Lucy Stone to Henry Blackwell, Boston, MA, December 25, 1854, BFP.

57. Emily Blackwell to Elizabeth Blackwell, Edinburgh, January 2–5, 1855, BFPS.

58. Elizabeth Blackwell to Emily Blackwell, London, January 19, 1855, BFPS.

59. Elizabeth Blackwell to Henry Blackwell, London, December 29, 1854, BFPS.

60. Emily Blackwell to Elizabeth Blackwell, Edinburgh, January 2–5, 1855, BFPS.

61. Henry Blackwell to Emily Blackwell, n.p., March 3, 1855, BFPS.

62. Henry C. Wright, *Marriage and Parentage: The Reproductive Element in Man, as a Means to his Elevation and Happiness* (Boston: 1858), 252.

63. Antoinette Brown to Susan B. Anthony, Dover, NH, January 8, 1855, BFPS.

64. Henry Blackwell to Lucy Stone, Cincinnati, OH, March 18, 1855, in Wheeler, *Loving Warriors*, 124–25.

65. Marian was ill, and Elizabeth chose not to come alone. Sarah and her family were living in Cincinnati at the time, and Frank lived too far away to attend. Bo had given up his Gardner church in 1850 for health reasons, and he and his family now lived in the Stone farmhouse. Henry also did not want Lucy to travel because her recent migraines had caused her to become seriously ill.

66. Thomas Wentworth Higginson to his mother, May 1, 1855, in *Letters and Journals of Thomas Wentworth Higginson*, 60. Lucy had wanted Nette to perform the ceremony, but she was not qualified to do it. Although Mary Higginson was an invalid, she apparently rallied and made the train trip with her husband. See Wells, *Dear Preceptor*, 91.

67. Henry Blackwell to Emily Blackwell, Cincinnati, OH, May 9, 1855, BFPS.

68. Apparently Elizabeth felt the "Protest" was in bad taste by dragging personal matters into public. See Sahli, *Elizabeth Blackwell*, 127.

69. "Marriage of Lucy Stone under Protest, 1855," in Stanton, Anthony, and Gage, eds., *History of Woman Suffrage*, 1:260–61; Lucy Stone and Henry B. Blackwell, "Protest," in Wheeler, *Loving Warriors*, 135–36; McMillen, *Seneca Falls*, 142; and Lerner, *The Grimké Sisters*, 242. The socialist reformer Dale Owen, when he married Mary Robins, wrote a statement denouncing the law that gave him control of her property and renounced that right. See Una Stannard, *Mrs. Man* (San Francisco, CA: Germain Books, 1977), 96.

70. "A Marriage under Protest," *New York Times*, May 4, 1855.

71. F.D. Gage, "Lucy Stone," *Lily*, June 1855.

72. "A Marriage under Protest," *New York Times*, May 4, 1855.

73. "Fol-de-rol," *New Albany Daily Ledger*, May 15, 1855.

74. For this brief comment, see the *St. Paul Daily Pioneer*, June 6, 1855; *Chicago Times*, June 7, 1855; *New Albany Daily Ledger* (Indiana), June 7, 1855; and the *Weekly Wisconsin Patriot*, Madison, June 16, 1855.

75. "Lucy Stone No More," *Springfield Republican* in the *National Aegis*, Worcester, MA, May 9, 1855.

76. Elizabeth Blackwell to Emily Blackwell, September 15, 1855, New York, BFP.

77. Stannard, *Mrs. Man*, 98. A few sources, including Stannard, claim that Lucy was the first married woman to retain her maiden name throughout her long marriage—a claim that is hard to prove or disprove. See Stannard, *Mrs. Man*, 131. French feminists as early as the 1830s argued for women to keep their own names when marrying. See Carolyn J. Eichner, "'In the Name of the Mother': Feminist Opposition to the Patronym in Nineteenth-Century France," *Signs: Journal of Women in Culture and Society* 39, no. 3 (Spring 2014): 659–83. Certainly because of her fame, Lucy's decision made an impact.

78. Lasser and Merrill, *Friends and Sisters*, 92; Stannard, *Mrs. Man*, 98, 103. Higginson could not understand why women did not feel indignant that they had to merge their individuality with their husbands. Stannard, *Mrs. Man*, 99.

79. Martha Fullam Blair, "Reminiscences," Frank Warren Blair Autograph Collection, Massachusetts Historical Society.

80. Lucy Stone to Mr. Cobb, New York, NY, October 21, 1856, BFP. She added, "In justice, a wife should not take her husband's name." Lucy may never have known how often newspapers and books referred to her as Lucy Stone Blackwell but researching periodicals and publications of the time show this was often the case.

81. Lucy Stone to Susan B. Anthony West Brookfield, MA, September 7 and 21, 1856, BFP; and Million, *Woman's Voice*, 225–26. Lucy may have been particularly emotional because brother Bo's wife had just died, and Lucy was collecting her possessions from her parents' home to move to the home she and Henry had purchased in Orange, NJ. As she wrote in the September 7 letter, "Weary and half sad with the thought that this old home of my childhood will be mine no longer."

82. Henry Blackwell to Lucy Stone, Cincinnati, OH, September 12, 1855, and Lucy Stone to Henry Blackwell, Dayton, OH, January 30, 1855 and Richmond, IN, February 3, 1856, in Wheeler, *Loving Warriors*, 145, 151.

83. Lucy Stone to Susan B. Anthony, Cincinnati, OH, May 30, 1855, BFP.

84. Lucy Stone to Hannah Stone, Cincinnati, OH, January 8, 1856, BFP.

85. Lucy Stone to Francis Stone, WI, November 12, 1856; and Lucy Stone to Susan B. Anthony, Racine, WI, November 25, 1856, both in BFPS.

86. Lucy Stone to Anna Parsons, Cincinnati, OH, March 11, 1856, BFP. Margaret Garner was the inspiration for Toni Morrison's novel *Beloved* and the heroine of the opera, "Margaret Garner," music by Richard Danielpour, libretto by Toni Morrison.

87. For the speech and details of the Garner trial, see Lucy Stone "Lucy Stone Blackwell's Speech," in Mark Reinhardt, ed., *Who Speaks for Margaret Garner?* (Minneapolis and London: University of Minnesota Press, 2010), 110–12; Lucy Stone to Alice Stone Blackwell, Reminiscences, September 30, 1893, BFP; and "Ohio Fugitive Slave Case—Eloquent Speech from Lucy Stone," *The National Era* (Washington, DC), February 28, 1856. Lucy used the tale of Margaret Garner in her speech delivered at the twenty-third anniversary of the American Anti-Slavery Society as carried in the *Anti-Slavery Bugle*, May 24, 1856, in Reinhardt, *Who Speaks for Margaret Garner*, 219–24.

88. "The Cincinnati Fugitive Slave Case," *Alexandria Gazette*, February 19, 1856.

89. Lucy Stone to Susan B. Anthony, Racine, WI, November 25, 1856, BFP.

90. Sam Blackwell to George Blackwell, n.p., January 1856, BFP; Lucy Stone to Susan B. Anthony, n.p., November 8, 1855, BFP.

91. Lucy Stone to Susan B. Anthony, n.p., May 25, 1856, BFP.

92. Lucy Stone to Sarah Lawrence, Bridgeville, IL, June 7, 1856, BFP. Lucy was traveling with Henry while he was examining his properties.

93. Lucy Stone to George Blackwell, Waukegan, WI, November 30, 1855, BFPS; and Hays, *Morning Star*, 127.

94. Henry Blackwell to George Blackwell, Dunleith, IL, August 17, 1856, BFPS; Lucy Stone to Henry Blackwell, Cincinnati, OH, April 26, 1856, in Wheeler, *Loving Warriors*, 159.

95. Lucy Stone to Antoinette Brown Blackwell, n.p. January 20, 1856, BFP. Nette and Sam were to stay in Lucy and Henry's home, and Lucy was glad they would be away so the newlyweds could enjoy "solitude," which Lucy claimed "becomes so imperative a necessity."

96. Henry Blackwell to George Blackwell, New York, NY, September 29, 1856, BFPS.

97. James McPherson, *Battle Cry of Freedom: The Civil War Era* (Oxford and New York: Oxford University Press, 1988), 145.

98. Lucy Stone to Susan B. Anthony, Viroqua, WI, July 22, 1856, BFP.

99. Lucy Stone to Susan B. Anthony, West Brookfield, MA, September 11, 1856, BFP.

100. Lucy Stone "Speech," *Proceedings of the Seventh National Woman's Rights Convention* (New York: Edward O. Jenkins, Printer, 1856).

101. Ibid.

102. Henry Blackwell to George Blackwell, New York, NY, March 27, 1857, and Emily Blackwell to George Blackwell, New York, NY, April 16, 1857, both in BFPS.

103. Lucy Stone to Hannah Stone, Orange, NJ, June 11, 1857, BFP.

104. Emily Blackwell to George Blackwell, New York, NY, June 7, 1857, and Henry Blackwell to George Blackwell, n.p., March 27, 1857, both in BFPS.

105. Henry Blackwell to George Blackwell, Cincinnati, OH, April 12, 1856, and Sam Blackwell to George Blackwell, New York, NY, December 21, 1856, BFPS.

106. Sam Blackwell to George Blackwell, New York, NY, December 21, 1856, and Henry Blackwell to George Blackwell, Orange, NJ, July 27, 1857, both in BFPS. The recession began when many people lost confidence in the nation's banks and railroads. Recovery was not complete until the Civil War began.

107. Lucy Stone to George Blackwell, n.p., November 12, 1855, BFPS.

108. See Lucy Stone to George Blackwell, Madison, WI, November 12, 1855; Hench, WI, November 21, 1855; and Waukegan, IL, November 30, 1855, all in BFPS.

109. Henry Blackwell to George Blackwell, New York, NY July 27, 1857, and Orange, NJ, May 9, 1857, BFPS.

110. Antoinette Brown to Susan B. Anthony, Newark, NJ, March 12, 1856, in Stanton and Anthony, *Selected Papers*, 1:318. At least one historian feels that Lucy was afraid to have intercourse. That may have been so, but it was not unusual for a 38-year-old woman to have problems conceiving. Lucy had expressed a strong desire to have children.

111. Lucy Stone to Susan B. Anthony, Racine, WI, November 2, 1855, BFPS.

112. Lucy Stone to Antoinette Brown Blackwell, n.s., in Sarah Gilson Memoirs, BFPS in Cazden, *Antoinette Brown Blackwell*, 114.

113. Susan B. Anthony to Lucy Stone, Rochester, NY, August 2, 1857, BFP.

114. Lucretia Mott to Lucy Stone, Philadelphia, PA, July 1, 1857, BFP.

115. Henry Blackwell to George Blackwell, New York, NY, September 3, 1857, and Orange, NJ, September 16, 1857, both in BFPS.

116. For the sake of inconsistency, I call the baby Alice, even though at this time her parents called her "baby" and "Sarah."

117. Henry Blackwell to George Blackwell, Orange, NJ, November 23, 1857, BFPS.

118. Lucy Stone, "Protest of Taxation without Representation," *Orange (NJ) Journal*, January 18, 1858, http://www.scc.rutgers.edu/njwomenshistory; "Lucy Stone and the Collector," *New York Times*, January 25, 1858; and McMillen, *Seneca Falls*, 128. I am grateful to Rich Newman for reminding me of the parallels between these two acts. There is no evidence that Lucy continued to refuse to pay taxes.

119. *New York Times*, January 29, 1858; "Is She Married or Not?" *New York Times*, January 27, 1858; and *New York Times*, February 15, 1858.

120. Lucy Stone to Susan B. Anthony, n.p., March 16, 1858, BFP.

121. Lucy Stone to Hannah Stone, Orange, NJ, March 16, 1858, BFP.

122. Stanton and Anthony, *Selected Papers*, 1:361 n 2. The Shirt Sewers' Cooperative Union formed in 1851. See also "Appeal on Behalf of the Shirt-Sewers," *The Lily* 3, no. 10 (October 1851), in Cherise Kramarae and Ann Russo, eds., *The Radical Women's Press of the 1850s* (New York and London: Routledge, 1991), 121; Jonathan A. Glickstein, *American Exceptionalism, American Anxiety: Wages, Competition, and Degraded Labor in the Antebellum United States* (Charlottesville and London: University of Virginia Press, 2002); and Edwin P. Burrows and Mike Wallace, *Gotham: A History of New York City to 1898* (New York and London: Oxford University Press, 1999), 666.

123. Susan B. Anthony to Antoinette Brown Blackwell, at home, April 22, 1858, in Stanton and Anthony, *Selected Papers*, 1:462; "Lucy Stone on the Right of Women to the Elective Franchise," *New York Times*, April 23, 1858; and "Rights and Wrongs," *New York Times*, April 28, 1858. Anthony expressed similar impatience with Stanton and Antoinette Blackwell when they gave birth, feeling their commitment to the women's movement would wane.

124. Susan B. Anthony to Lucy Stone, at home, April 22, 1858, in Stanton and Anthony, *Selected Letters*, 1:360; and Lucy Stone to Susan B. Anthony, Orange, NJ, April 1, 1858, BFP.

125. Henry Blackwell to George Blackwell, Chicago, IL, April 5, 1858, BFPS.

126. Lucy Stone to Henry Blackwell, Orange, NJ, April 1, 1858, BFP.

127. Henry Blackwell to Lucy Stone, Chicago, IL, May 1, 1858, BFP.

128. Henry Blackwell to Lucy Stone, Janesville, WI, March 25, 1858, in Wheeler, *Loving Warriors*, 176, and Henry Blackwell to Lucy Stone, Chicago, IL, May 1, 1858, BFP.

129. Lucy Stone to Henry Blackwell, Orange, NJ, May 21, 1858, BFP.

130. Henry Blackwell to Lucy Stone, Chicago, IL, May 7, 1858, BFP.

131. Henry Blackwell to Lucy Stone, Chicago, IL, June 10, 1858, and Henry Blackwell to Lucy Stone, Chicago, IL, May 1, 1858, both in BFP.

132. Lucy Stone to Henry Blackwell, Gardner, MA, June 2, 1858, BFP.
133. Henry Blackwell to Lucy Stone, Chicago, IL, June 23, 1858, BFP.
134. Henry Blackwell to Lucy Stone, Chicago, IL, July 8, 1858, BFP.
135. Sam Blackwell to George Blackwell, New York, NY, August 18, 1858, BFPS. West Bloomfield became Montclair in 1868. Emily reported that they saved $100 on their mortgage.
136. Lucy Stone to Francis Stone, New York, NY, August 27, 1858, BFP.
137. Sam Blackwell to George Blackwell, n.p., September 18, 1858, BFPS.
138. Lucy Stone to Antoinette Brown Blackwell, Chicago, IL, February 20, 1859, BFP.
139. Henry Blackwell to George Blackwell, Chicago, IL, February 18 and July 18, 1859, BFPS; Lucy Stone to Antoinette Brown Blackwell, in Hays, *Morning Star*, 142.
140. Antoinette Brown Blackwell to Lucy Stone, Westport, NY, August 29, 1859, in Lasser and Merrill, *Friends and Sisters*, 158. Cholera infantum was not a definable disease in today's medical terminology but a catch-all term used at that time to explain babies' early deaths. Death might have been caused by any number of medical issues that babies confronted in their first two years of life, including teething. See Sally G. McMillen, *Motherhood in the Old South: Pregnancy, Childbirth and Infant Rearing* (Baton Rouge: Louisiana State University Press, 1990), 165–79.
141. "Clippings," BFPS.
142. Antoinette Blackwell, "Lucy Stone at Oberlin," *Woman's Journal*, February 10, 1894, in Lasser and Merrill, *Friends and Sisters*, 94.
143. Foner, *Fiery Trial*, 136–38.
144. "The Woman's Rights Meeting," *New York Times*, February 3, 1860; "The Question of Woman's Rights," *New York Herald*, February 4, 1860; and "Lucy Stone as Maid and Wife," *Providence Evening Press* (RI), February 22, 1860.
145. Lucy Stone to Henry Blackwell, West Brookfield, MA, September 20, 1860, BFP.
146. Lucy Stone to Alice Stone Blackwell, Dorchester, MA, August 12, 1888, in Wheeler, *Loving Warriors*, 313.
147. Million, *Woman's Voice*, 267 and Foner, *Fiery Trial*, 140–44. The three other candidates were Illinois Senator Stephen A. Douglas, John Breckinridge of Kentucky, and John C. Bell, who represented the newly created Union Party.
148. Stanton and Anthony, *Selected Papers*, 1:346 n. 2; Wendell Phillips to Lucy Stone and Susan B. Anthony, Boston, MA, November 6, 1858, BFP; and McMillen, *Seneca Falls*, 147.
149. "Will of the Late Francis Jackson," the *Liberator*, December 6, 1860; Stanton, Anthony, and Gage, eds., *History of Woman Suffrage*, 3:311; and "Will of the Late Francis Jackson," *Testimonials to the Life and Character of Francis Jackson* (Boston: R. F. Wallcut, 1861), 35. Reflecting the esteem with which Jackson was held

among abolitionists, those giving testimonials at his funeral were William Lloyd Garrison, Wendell Phillips, and Samuel May Jr.

150. Susan B. Anthony to Lucy Stone, n.p., June 16, 1857, in Stanton and Anthony, *Selected Papers*, 1:345–46; and Lucy Stone to Susan B. Anthony, Chicago, IL, February 28, 1859, BFP.

151. Anna Raymond, "Musings," *Mystic Pioneer*, March 3, 1860.

152. "National Convention in Philadelphia," October 18, 1854, in Stanton, Anthony, and Gage, eds., *History of Woman Suffrage*, 1:380; Elizabeth Cady Stanton, "To the Women of the State of New York," *Frederick Douglass Paper*, December 22, 1854; and Stanton, "Paper for the Yearly Meeting of the Friends of Human Progress," June 6, 1857, in Stanton and Anthony, *Selected Papers*, 1:344.

CHAPTER 6

1. Susan B. Anthony to Lydia Mott, Rochester, NY, after April 10, 1862, in Stanton and Anthony, *Selected Papers*, 1:475.

2. Lucy Stone to Antoinette Brown Blackwell, n.p., January 19, 1861, BFP; and Henry B. Stanton to Elizabeth Cady Stanton, Washington, DC, January 12, 1861, in Stanton and Anthony, *Selected Papers*, 1:454–55.

3. Lucy Stone to Henry Blackwell, Dayton, OH, January 30, 1861, BFP; and Kerr, *Lucy Stone*, 113.

4. See Jeannie Attie, *Patriotic Toil: Northern Women and the American Civil War* (Ithaca and London: Cornell University Press, 1998), 38–43.

5. David Williams, *A People's History of the Civil War: Struggles for the Meaning of Freedom* (New York and London: The New Press, 2005) in Ginzberg, 141; and Frederick Law Olmsted to Henry Whitney Bellows, August 16, 1861, in Olmsted, *The Papers of Frederick Law Olmsted*, ed. Charles E. Beveridge, vol. 4 (Baltimore, MD: Johns Hopkins University Press, 1977–90), 148, in Attie, *Patriotic Toil*, 55.

6. Nina Silber, *Daughters of the Union: Northern Women Fight the Civil War* (Cambridge, MA: Harvard University Press, 2005), 177.

7. Ibid., 185.

8. They were called sanitary fairs because they raised money for the USSC and other soldiers' aid organizations. See Kerry Bryan, "Civil War Sanitary Fairs," *The Encyclopedia of Greater Philadelphia*, http://philadelphiaencyclopedia.org/archive/civil-war-sanitary-fairs.

9. "The Soldiers' Aid Society Last Evening," *The Cleveland Plain Dealer*, March 4, 1863.

10. Attie, *Patriotic Toil*, 82–83. For background on sanitary fairs, see Melinda Lawson, *Patriot Fires: Forging a New American Nationalism in the Civil War North* (Lawrence: University Press of Kansas, 2002), 14–39.

11. For personal insights into this experience, see Sarah Rosetta Wakeman, *An Uncommon Soldier: The Civil War Letters of Sarah Rosetta Wakeman, Alias Pvt.*

Lyons Wakeman, 153rd Regiment, New York State Volunteers, 1862–1864, ed. Lauren Cook Burgess (Oxford and New York: Oxford University Press, 1994).

12. This organization is often called the Woman's National Loyal League, but its official name when founded, as noted on its stationery, was the WLNL.

13. Elizabeth Cady Stanton, "To the Women of the Republic," New York, April 24, 1863, in Stanton and Anthony, *Selected Papers*, 1:483.

14. Silber, *Daughters of the Union*, 153–54.

15. "Loyal Women's League," *Evening Post* (NY), May 15, 1863, and *Boston Daily Advertiser*, May 16, 1863.

16. McMillen, *Seneca Falls*, 156–57.

17. Lucy Stone in "Resolutions and Debate," Woman's Loyal National League Meeting, May 14, 1863, http://www.sscnet.ucla.edu/history/dubois/classes/995/98/F/doc21.html; and "The Ladies League," *New York Times*, May 1, 1863.

18. McMillen, *Seneca Falls*, 156; Ginzberg, *Elizabeth Cady Stanton*, 109. The Emancipation Proclamation was a war measure, and it selectively sought to abolish slavery throughout most of the Confederacy but protect it in areas occupied by Union soldiers.

19. William Lloyd Garrison to his wife in *Letters* 5:154, as quoted in Stanton and Anthony, *Selected Papers*, ed. Gordon, 1:488. Anthony's salary of $12 a month came from Hovey funds.

20. "Meeting of the Women's Loyal National League," May 29, 1863, and Susan B. Anthony to Elizabeth Cady Stanton, Worcester, MA, October 10, 1863, both in Stanton and Anthony, *Selected Papers*, 1:494, 502–3.

21. Stanton and Anthony, *Selected Papers*, 1:503 n. 1.

22. Charles Sumner, "The Prayer of One Hundred Thousand," February 9, 1863, American Memory. (This brief speech's year is misdated, since the organization began in May 1863.) See also Elizabeth Cady Stanton, "To the Women of the Republic," January 25, 1864, http://www.pbs.org/wnet/slavery/experience/gender/docs2.html.

23. Wendy F. Hamond, "The Woman's National Loyal League: Feminist Abolitionists and the Civil War," *Civil War History* 35, no. 1 (March 1989): 30–58; Julie Roy Jeffrey, *The Great Silent Army of Abolitionists: Ordinary Women in the Antislavery Movement* (Chapel Hill and London: University of North Carolina Press, 1998), 216–17; Eric Foner, "Letter to the Editor," *New York Times*, November 27, 2012, and *The Fiery Trial*, 291. Foner only names Anthony and Stanton as leading the WLNL, leaving out Lucy.

24. "The Abolition Convention," *The Daily Age*, Philadelphia, PA, December 4, 1863, and "The American Anti-Slavery Convention," *The Liberator*, December 25, 1863.

25. Million, *Woman's Voices*, 269. Andrea Kerr sees all these separations as evidence of a very troubled marriage, though that interpretation is hard to believe since their letters to one another expressed deep affection. See also Kerr, *Lucy Stone*, 114–16.

26. Henry Blackwell to George Blackwell, New York, NY, May 29, 1862, and Lucy Stone to George Blackwell, New York, NY, May 29, 1862, both in BFPS.

27. Henry Blackwell to George Blackwell, West Brookfield, MA, July 1862, BFPS.

28. Kerr, *Lucy Stone*, 114.

29. Emily Blackwell to George Blackwell, New York, NY, September 1–3, 1862, BFPS. Slavery was no longer legal in Washington, DC, by spring 1862.

30. Lucy Stone to Henry Blackwell, West Brookfield, MA, June 7, 1861, BFP.

31. Henry Blackwell to Lucy Stone, New York, NY, June 22, 1863, BFP.

32. Henry Blackwell to Lucy Stone, New York, NY, June 20, 1863, BFP.

33. Lucy Stone to Henry Blackwell, West Brookfield, MA, June 21, 1864, BFP.

34. Lucy Stone to Susan B. Anthony, West Brookfield, MA, July 12, 1864, in Wheeler, *Loving Warriors*, 194. Bo had left the ministry, and he and his family now lived in the Stone farmhouse.

35. On menopause in the nineteenth century, see Carroll Smith-Rosenberg, "Puberty to Menopause: The Cycle of Femininity in Nineteenth-Century America," in *Clio's Consciousness Raised: New Perspectives on the History of Women*, ed. Marty S. Hartman and Lois Banner (New York: Octagon Books, 1976), 23–37; and "Menopause" Mayo Clinic, Family Physician website: http://www.mayoclinic.org/diseases-coditions/menopause/basics/symptoms/com.

36. Lucy Stone to Susan B. Anthony, West Brookfield, MA, July 12, 1864, in Wheeler, *Loving Warriors*, 194.

37. Lucy Stone to Henry Blackwell, Gardner, MA, July 22, 1864, BFP.

38. Lucy Stone to Henry Blackwell, West Brookfield, MA, July 22, 1864, in Wheeler, *Loving Warriors*, 196; and Kerr, *Lucy Stone*, 117.

39. McPherson, *Battle Cry of Freedom*, 758; and Lucy Stone to Henry Blackwell, West Brookfield, MA, June 14, 1864, in Wheeler, *Loving Warriors*, 192.

40. Lucy Stone to Henry Blackwell, Gardner, MA, September 4, 1864, in Wheeler, *Loving Warriors*, 199–200.

41. Lucy Stone to Henry Blackwell, Gardner, MA, September 20, 1864, in Wheeler, *Loving Warriors*, 201. Lucy often referred to Henry as "little boy."

42. Lucy Stone to Henry Blackwell, Gardner, MA, December 4, 1864, in Wheeler, *Loving Warriors*, 205.

43. See Kerr, *Lucy Stone*, 143–45 and Jean H. Baker, *Sisters: The Lives of American Suffragists* (New York: Hill and Wang, 2005), 35–36.

44. Lucy Stone to Henry Blackwell, West Brookfield, MA, June 21, 1864, BFP.

45. Henry Blackwell to George Blackwell, West Brookfield, MA, July 1862, BFPS.

46. Lucy Stone to Francis Stone, n.p., December 31, 1862, BFP.

47. Lucy Stone to Susan B. Anthony, West Brookfield, MA, July 12, 1864, BFP.

48. Lucy Stone to Alice Stone Blackwell, Grand Rapids, MI, November 30, 1869, BFP.

49. Lucy Stone to Emma Lawrence, New York, NY, March 28, 1865, BFPS. Alice later wrote of her mother's affection for Emma, calling her "Mamma's baby—her first, I believe, and slept with her the first night of her life." Alice Stone

Blackwell to Kitty Barry Blackwell, December 21, 1897, quoted in Blackwell, *Growing up in Boston's Gilded Age*, 49.

50. Lucy Stone to Hannah Blackwell, West Brookfield, MA, October 23, 1864, BFP. For a discussion of burial customs at this time, see Drew Gilpin Faust, *This Republic of Suffering: Death and the American Civil War* (New York: Alfred A. Knopf, 2008), 61–63. A "decent" burial, she argues, required proper preparations of the body and certain rituals.

51. Lucy Stone to Henry Blackwell, Gardner, MA, December 4, 1864, in Wheeler, *Loving Warriors*, 205–6.

52. Lucy Stone to Henry Blackwell, Gardner, MA, December 17, 1864, in Wheeler, *Loving Warriors*, 206.

53. Lucy Stone to Henry Blackwell, Gardner, MA, Sept. 20, 1864, in Wheeler, *Loving Warriors*, 201.

54. Lucy Stone to Henry Blackwell, West Brookfield, MA, August 9, 1864, in Wheeler, *Loving Warriors*, 198.

55. Lucy Stone to Hannah Blackwell, West Brookfield, MA, October 23, 1864, BFP.

56. Dorothea McClain Moore, "Reclaiming Lucy Stone: A Literary and Historical Appraisal," PhD dissertation, University of Texas, Arlington, 1996.

57. Lucy Stone to Henry Blackwell, Gardner, MA, December 1, 1864, BFP. This was the Thirteenth Amendment.

58. Foner, *Fiery Trial*, 291–94, 299, 312–13.

59. Lucy Stone to Henry Blackwell, Gardner, MA, December 4, 1864, BFP.

60. Henry Blackwell to George Blackwell, Boston, MA, January 6 and 13, 1865, BFPS; Wheeler, *Loving Warriors*, 211. Apparently it was not all that unusual to adopt an orphan. What was unusual was that both Elizabeth and Emily Blackwell, though single women, adopted female orphans. Elizabeth adopted Katherine Barry (Kitty) in 1854 when Kitty was only 5 years old, and they spent the rest of their lives together as family and companions. When Emily was 50 years old, she adopted a girl in 1871.

61. Lucy Stone to Mrs. Field, Newark, NJ, March 24, 1869, BFP.

62. "Extension of Suffrage," *Daily Constitutional Union*, Washington, DC, December 28, 1865; and "Woman's Rights," *Newport Mercury*, January 13, 1866. See also Faye E. Dudden, *Fighting Chance: The Struggle over Woman Suffrage and Black Suffrage in Reconstruction America* (Oxford and New York: Oxford University Press, 2011).

63. Cholera broke out in New York City on May 2, 1866, after affecting European cities several months earlier. One can imagine Lucy was frightened for Alice. See G. F. Pyle, "The Diffusion of Cholera in the United States in the Nineteenth Century," *Geographical Analysis* 1, no. 1 (September 2010): 13 and Rosenberg, *The Cholera Years*.

64. Wheeler, *Loving Warriors*, 212 and Blackwell, *Growing up in Boston's Gilded Age*, 230. Lucy later commented when Sumner died, "I don't know that Woman's

Suffrage owes much to Mr. Sumner." He proved a champion of black men but not of women.

65. Silber, *Daughters of the Union*, 264.

66. Ginzberg, *Elizabeth Cady Stanton*, 118; Alexander Keyssar, *The Right to Vote: The Contested History of Democracy in the United States* (New York: Basic Books, 2000), 89.

67. Emily Blackwell to Elizabeth Blackwell, New York, NY, 1866, BFP.

68. Henry Blackwell to Lucy Stone, n.p., May 7, 1866, BFP.

69. Flyer, BFPS.

70. Lucy Stone to Abby Kelley Foster, New York, NY,, January 24, 1867, BFP. In her letter, Lucy addressed her as "Mrs. Foster," suggesting a chill in their relationship.

71. Henry Browne Blackwell, "What the South Can Do: How the Southern States Can Make Themselves Masters of the Situation" (New York: Robert J. Johnson, 1867), 1–4 (quote p. 1). Henry calculated that the South had 1.6 million white men and 1.6 million white women voters while there were 800,000 black men and an equal number of black women who could vote (p. 3). This same argument was used later in the century.

72. Marjorie Spruill Wheeler, *New Women of the New South: The Leaders of the Woman Suffrage Movement in the Southern States* (New York and Oxford: Oxford University Press, 1993), 113–14. After Lucy's death, Henry campaigned in southern states on this issue, using white supremacy and educated white female voters as the best means to gain suffrage for women. See Wheeler, *New Women of the New South*, 122–25.

73. Lucy Stone, "Woman Suffrage in New Jersey," March 6, 1867, American Memory. See also Elizabeth Cady Stanton and Susan B. Anthony, *The Selected Papers of Elizabeth Cady Stanton and Susan B. Anthony*, vol. 2: *Against an Aristocracy of Sex, 1866 to 1873*, ed. Ann D. Gordon (New Brunswick, NJ: Rutgers University Press, 2000), 70 n. 5. Voting irregularities led New Jersey officials to confine voters to white males.

74. Emily Blackwell to Elizabeth Blackwell, New York, July 21–23, 1866, BFPS.

75. Henry Blackwell to George Blackwell, Gardner, MA, May 17, 1866, and Henry Blackwell to Emily Blackwell, West Tisbury, MA, July 8, 1866, both in BFPS; and Samuel Blackwell to Elizabeth Blackwell, New York, NY, July 21, 1866, BFP.

76. Emily Blackwell to Elizabeth Blackwell, West Tisbury, MA, August 26, 1866, BFPS. As Emily wrote in that letter, "When any one wants service, they 'go to Gay Head.'"

77. Elizabeth Cazden, *Antoinette Brown Blackwell: A Biography* (Old Westbury, NY: The Feminist Press, 1983), 135.

78. Susan B. Anthony to Wendell Phillips, New York, NY, November 4, 1866, in Stanton and Anthony, *Selected Papers*, 1:597.

79. Lucy Stone to Elizabeth Buffum Chace, n.d., n.p. and Lucy Stone to Elizabeth Buffum Chace, New York, NY, March 20, 1867, both in Wyman and Wyman,

Elizabeth Buffum Chace, 1:288–89, 291. Lucy reassured Chace that they also would "cheerfully apply" Jackson funds to help pay for the campaign, but that money was nearly depleted.

80. Lucy Stone to Emma Lawrence, n.p., January 14, 1867, BFPS.

81. Samuel Wood, "Proceedings of the First Anniversary of the American Equal Rights Association," May 9 and 10, 1867 (New York: Robert J. Johnston, 1867), 62.

82. Henry Blackwell to "Friends, E.C. Stanton, Susan B. Anthony," Junction City, KA, April 12, 1867, in Wheeler, *Loving Warriors*, 217. Probably it was this campaign that drew Henry fully into the women's rights movement, for from this point on, Lucy often asked him to carry out several tasks, such as printing tracts, arranging speaking engagements, and so on.

83. Lucy Stone to Susan B. Anthony, Fort Scott, KA, May 1, 1867, in Wheeler, *Loving Warriors*, 219. See also Lucy Stone to Elizabeth Cady Stanton, Leavenworth, KA, April 10, 1867, in Stanton and Anthony, *Selected Papers*, 2:48–49.

84. "Proceedings of the First Anniversary of the Equal Rights Association," 6.

85. Lucy Stone to Friends, Elizabeth Cady Stanton and Susan B. Anthony, Junction City, KA, April 21, 1867, in Wheeler, *Loving Warriors*, 217; Lucy Stone to Susan B. Anthony, Atchison, KA, May 9, 1867, BFP.

86. In her authorized three-volume biography, Anthony claimed that Train, who was in Omaha when they went west, wrote to ask if he could help their campaign in Kansas. She also referred to Train as "brilliant," "courtly," "handsome," and "erratic." See Ida Husted Harper, *The Life and Work of Susan B. Anthony* (Indianapolis, IN: Hollenbeck Press, 1898), 282, 292.

87. See George Francis Train, "Championship of Woman," the *Revolution* (Leavenworth, KA: Prescott and Hume Daily Commercial Office, 1867), 52.

88. Lucy Stone to William Lloyd Garrison, March 6, 1868, New York, NY, in archives, Boston Public Library, http://archive.org/details/; William Lloyd Garrison, "Letter to Susan B. Anthony," the *Revolution*, January 29, 1868; and McMillen, *Seneca Falls*, 167–68.

89. Elizabeth Cady Stanton to Edwin A. Studwell, Buffalo, NY, November 30, 1867, in Stanton and Anthony, *Selected Papers*, 2:116; and "Who Are Our Friends?" *Revolution*, January 15, 1868.

90. Ibid.

91. E.C.S., "Women and Black Men," the *Revolution*, February 4, 1869.

92. Ginzberg, *Elizabeth Cady Stanton*, 122, 123.

93. Henry Blackwell to Lucy Stone, Lawrence, KA, October 25, 1867, BFP.

94. McMillen, *Seneca Falls*, 170.

95. "Woman's Right to Vote," *New York Times*, December 27, 1867.

96. Henry Blackwell to Lucy Stone, Park Row, October 12, 1867, and Lucy Stone to Henry Blackwell, Newark, NJ, October 13, 1867, both in BFP.

97. McMillen, *Seneca Falls*, 171–72.

98. Fenians were a revolutionary group in Ireland and the United States, bent upon ending British rule over Ireland and creating an independent nation.

99. See Rodger Streitmatter, *Voices of Revolution: The Dissident Press in America* (New York: Columbia University Press, 2001), 36–53; Lynne Masel-Walters, "Their Rights and Nothing More: A History of the *Revolution*, 1868–70," *Journalism Quarterly* 53 no. 2 (summer 1976): 242–51; and McMillen, *Seneca Falls*, 171–72. Stanton anticipated a circulation of 100,000; the number was 3,000. See Streitmatter, *Voices of Revolution*, 37. Stanton and Pillsbury never paid Anthony their share of the $10,000. Anthony was able to pay back every dollar by lecturing for the next six years. For part of this time, Stanton was in England visiting daughter Harriot. McMillen, *Seneca Falls*, 172.

100. Lucy Stone to Henry Blackwell, Plymouth, MA, April 1868, and April 11, 1868, BFP.

101. Deborah Bickman Clifford, *Mine Eyes Have Seen the Glory: A Biography of Julia Ward Howe* (Boston: Little, Brown, 1978), 174–75; and "Ward, Julia Ward," s.v., *American National Biography*.

102. Julia Ward Howe, *Reminiscences* (Boston and New York: Houghton, Mifflin and Company, 1899), 372–77. See also Blackwell, *Lucy Stone*, 204.

103. Howe, *Reminiscences*, 372–88, quotes 373, 376; Blackwell, *Lucy Stone*, 267. See also Clifford, *Mine Eyes Have Seen the Glory*.

104. See "Meeting of the American Equal Rights Association in New York, 1868," Stanton and Anthony, *Selected Papers*, 2:135–38.

105. Susan B. Anthony to Thomas W. Higginson, New York, NY, May 20, 1868; Stanton and Anthony, *Selected Papers*, 2:141–42. Two months later, three-fourths of the states ratified the Fourteenth Amendment.

106. "Female Suffrage," *Flake's Galveston (Texas) Bulletin*, November 28, 1868.

107. "Woman Suffrage," *New York Times*, December 4, 1868.

108. Lucy Stone to Antoinette Brown Blackwell, Newark, NJ, February 10, 1869, BFP.

109. Lucy Stone to Samuel May Jr., Newark, NJ, April 9, 1869, BFP.

110. Munroe, "Woman Suffrage," *New York Times*, March 31, 1869; and Lucy Stone to Antoinette Brown Blackwell, Newark, NJ, February 10, 1869, BFP.

111. "Commonwealth of Massachusetts, Joint Special Committee on Woman's Suffrage," May 24, 1869, American Memory.

112. Stanton and Anthony, *Selected Papers*, 2:120 n. 3.

113. Frederick Douglass, "The May Anniversaries in New York and Brooklyn"; Stanton, Anthony, and Gage, eds., *History of Woman Suffrage*, 2:382.

114. Ginzberg, *Elizabeth Cady Stanton*, 127.

115. "Annual Meeting of the American Equal Rights Association," *The Revolution*, May 20, 1869. For background on violence in the Reconstruction South, see Stephen Budiansky, *The Bloody Shirt: Terror after the Civil War* (New York and London: Penguin, 2008) and Hannah Rosen, *Terror in the Heart of Freedom: Citizenship, Sexual Violence, and the Meaning of Race in the Post-emancipation South* (Chapel Hill: University of North Carolina Press, 2009).

116. "Equal Rights," *New York Times*, May 13, 1869.

117. Elizabeth Cady Stanton in *History of Woman Suffrage*, 1:681, in Griffith, *In Her Own Right*, 111.

118. Lucy Stone to Elizabeth Buffum Chace, July 11, 1869, in Wyman and Wyman, *Elizabeth Buffum Chace*, 1:316.

119. Susan B. Anthony to Anna Dickinson, New York, NY, July 10, 1868, in Stanton and Anthony, *Selected Papers*, 2:153.

120. Harper, *Susan B. Anthony*, 1:182.

121. In her biography of Anthony, Harper (with Anthony's approving every word) writes that it was women from nineteen states at the AERA meeting who requested the founding of a new organization. In an exaggeration, she also claimed that the meeting held the following week took place before "an immense audience." See Harper, *Susan B. Anthony*, 1:326–27. See also Dudden, *Fighting Chance*, 176–83.

122. Henry Blackwell to George Blackwell, Pomfret, CT, July 21, 1869, BFPS.

123. Emily Blackwell to George Blackwell, Kennebunkport, ME, August 8, 1869, BFPS.

124. See Kerr, *Lucy Stone*, 143–44, quotation at 144 and Baker, *Sisters*, 35–36. Kerr feels that the marriage was deeply troubled and that Henry and Lucy discussed a permanent separation. This author has found little to suggest the relationship reached that point. See Kerr, *Lucy Stone*, 116.

125. Emily Blackwell to Elizabeth Blackwell, New York, NY, September 14, 1869, BFPS.

126. Lucy Stone to Emily Blackwell, Boston, MA, April 15, 1870, BFPS.

127. Emily Blackwell to Elizabeth Blackwell, New York, NY, March 15, 1870, BFPS. See also Lucy Stone to George Blackwell, Boston, MA, December 1869, BFPS. For background on the Pattons, see "Ludlow Patton Dead," *New York Times*, September 6, 1906, and Henry Whittemore, *The Founders and Builders of the Oranges* (Newark, NJ: L. J. Hardman, 1896), 271–74.

128. Marian Blackwell to Elizabeth Blackwell, Somerville, NJ, December 3–8, 1871, and Marian to Emily Blackwell, Boston, MA, June 10, 1872, both in BFPS.

129. Henry Blackwell to Lucy Stone, New York, NY, November 1, 1869, in Wheeler, *Loving Warriors*, 230–31 and New York, NY, November 6, 1869, BFP.

130. Samuel May to Richard Davis Webb, June 28, 1869, Leicester, MA, Boston Public Library archives; http://archive.org/details/lettertodearfrie00mays-93; "Remarks by Susan B. Anthony to the Western Woman Suffrage Association in Chicago," in Stanton and Anthony, *Selected Papers*, 2:265–68.

131. Lucy Stone to Esther Pugh, n.p., 1869, BFP.

132. "Woman Suffrage Call: A Genuine National Association," *New York Herald-Tribune*, October 20, 1869; and *Boston Daily Advertiser*, October 20, 1869.

133. Lucy Stone to the Rev. James Freeman Clarke, Newark, NJ, October 6, 1869, BFP.

134. Lucy Stone to the Rev. James Freeman Clarke, New York, NY, November 17, 1869, BFP.

135. Lucy Stone to Elizabeth Cady Stanton, Newark, NJ, October 19, 1869, BFP.

136. Elizabeth Cady Stanton, "The Cleveland Convention," October 28, 1869, *The Revolution* in Stanton and Anthony, *Selected Papers*, 2:276–78.

137. Martha Wright to Lucy Stone, Auburn, NY, August 22, 1869, Garrison Family Papers, Smith College Archives.

138. Lucy Stone to Esther Pugh, Boston, MA, c. 1869, BFP.

139. Lucy Stone to John Hooker, Boston, MA, April 16, 1883, BFP.

140. Wendell Phillips to Lucy Stone, Northampton, MA, August 20, 1852, BFP.

141. Ellen DuBois feels the two organizations energized the movement and encouraged the growth of feminism. Such conflict pushed the movement forward, "liberated it from its subservience to abolitionism" and made it more independent. See DuBois, *Feminism and Suffrage*, 200–201. Eleanor Flexner in *Century of Struggle* feels it had a negative impact. This historian tends to side with those who feel it had a negative effect. See McMillen, *Seneca Falls*, 183.

142. Lucy had first asked Wendell Phillips to serve as the AWSA's first president, but he turned her down, claiming that he never accepted any official position in organizations he joined. See Wendell Phillips to Lucy Stone, Boston, MA, n.d., c. 1869, BFP.

143. "Woman Suffrage: The National Convention," *Plain Dealer* (Cleveland), November 26, 1869.

144. McMillen, *Seneca Falls*, 175–76; "Conventions," *New York Times*, November 25, 1869; Lucy Stone to Antoinette Brown Blackwell, Eastport, ME, October 31, 1869, BFP; and Ellen Carol DuBois, *Feminism and Suffrage: The Emergence of an Independent Women's Movement in America, 1848–1869* (Ithaca and London: Cornell University Press, 1978), 197–98. There is some disagreement about the number of states represented, varying from sixteen to twenty-one.

145. McMillen, *Seneca Falls*, 176–77.

146. "Constitution of the American Woman Suffrage Association and the History of Its Formation" (Boston: George H. Ellis, 1881), 3.

147. Lucy Stone to Mrs. Sargent, Boston, MA, July 12, 1877, BFP.

148. After a few years the NWSA eliminated a by-law limiting officeholders to women, but Anthony said, "We have not elected any men to office simply because no men have offered us much help. We have treated them as they treat us." See "Minutes of Informal Conference between Lucy Stone and Susan B. Anthony," December 21, 1887, in Elizabeth Cady Stanton and Susan B. Anthony, *The Selected Papers of Elizabeth Cady Stanton and Susan B. Anthony*, vol. 5: *Their Place Inside the Body-Politic*, ed. Ann D. Gordon (New Brunswick, NJ: Rutgers University Press, 2009), 61. See also Gaylynn Welch, "Local and National Forces Shaping the American Woman Suffrage Movement, 1870–1890," PhD dissertation, SUNY Binghamton, 2009, 7.

149. Stanton had presented the divorce issue at the 1860 National Woman's Rights Convention in New York City. Phillips opposed this issue as irrelevant to the

movement, saying that divorce affected men as well as women. Stanton felt divorce had greater meaning to women than to men. See Lucy Stone to Elizabeth Buffum Chace, n.p., August 17, 1869, in Wyman and Wyman, *Elizabeth Buffum Chace*, 1:318. Chace ultimately joined the AWSA.

150. According to biographer Carol Faulkner, although Mott supported the Fifteenth Amendment, she became uncomfortable with the AWSA's concern with morality. See Faulkner, *Lucretia Mott's Heresy*, 196, 215.

151. Faulkner, *Lucretia Mott's Heresy*, 205.

152. Martha Wright to Lucy Stone, Roxbury, MA, December 21, 1874, Garrison Family Papers, Smith College.

153. Lucy Stone to Emma Lawrence, n.p., September 26, 1869, BFPS; Lucy Stone to Antoinette Brown Blackwell, Eastport, ME, October 31, 1869, in Wheeler, *Loving Warriors*, 230. Apparently the time Alice spent there was happy, for she later visited her former school and teacher and admitted, "I do love Miss Andrews." See Blackwell, *Growing Up in Boston's Gilded Age*, 228–29.

154. Sam Blackwell to Elizabeth Blackwell, New York, NY, February 18, 1870, BFPS.

155. Lucy Stone to "Dear Friend," n.p., c. 1869, BFP.

156. Stanton and Anthony, *Selected Papers*, 2:292 n. 1 and Lynne Masel-Walters, "A Burning Cloud by Day: The History and Content of the 'Woman's Journal,'" *Journalism History* 3, no. 4 (Winter 1976–77): 103–10. The *Woman's Journal* endured until 1920 when the Nineteenth Amendment giving women the right to vote became part of the Constitution. It changed names in 1917 and became the *Woman Citizen*.

157. "Our Office," *Woman's Journal*, January 15, 1870.

158. Robert Morris to *The Revolution* in Tom Rea, "Right Choice, Wrong Reasons: Wyoming Women Win the Right to Vote," http://www.wyohistory.org/essays/right-choice-wrong-reasons.

159. H.B.B., "Governor Campbell and Wyoming," *Woman's Journal*, December 23, 1871; and T. A. Larson, "Woman Suffrage in Wyoming," *Pacific Northwest Quarterly* 16 (April 1965): 57–63.

160. Both quotes from E.C.M., "Wyoming and Women," *The Revolution*, January 6, 1870. Two years later, the Wyoming legislature had second thoughts and tried to pass a law overturning women's suffrage. The governor vetoed the bill.

161. Beverly Beeton, *Women Vote in the West: The Woman Suffrage Movement, 1869–1896* (New York and London: Garland Publishing, Inc., 1986), 1–17.

162. Committee of the Judiciary, "Suffrage in Utah: Memorial of the New York Woman Suffrage Society," 42nd Congress, 3rd Session, 1872; Beeton, *Women Vote in the West*, 23–37; Carol Cornwall Aadsen, ed., *Battle for the Ballot: Essays on Woman Suffrage in Utah, 1870–1896* (Logan: Utah State University Press, 1997) and McMillen, *Seneca Falls*, 182–83. Utah women enjoyed universal suffrage until 1887 when their right to vote was nullified as Utah prepared for statehood.

CHAPTER 7

1. Lucy Stone to Antoinette Blackwell, Eastport, ME, October 31, 1869, in Lasser and Merrill, *Friends and Sisters*, 175.

2. "The Woman's Journal," *Boston Daily Journal*, January 8, 1870; "The Woman's Journal," *St. Albans Daily Messenger* (VT), January 14, 1870; and "What the Papers Say of Us," *Woman's Journal*, March 23, 1872. Two papers, quoting verbatim of one another, were the *Richmond State Journal* (VA) and the *Detroit New World*.

3. "What the Papers Say of Us," *Woman's Journal*, March 23, 1872.

4. Emily Blackwell to Elizabeth Blackwell, New York, NY, August 29, 1871, BFPS.

5. Lucy Stone to George Blackwell, Boston, MA, December 16, 1870, and September 10, 1871, BFPS. Information gathered by the author's visit to the home site at 43 Boutwell Street; Anthony Sammarco, "Nineteenth-Century Pope's Hill Home to Wealthy Merchants, Famous Families," Dorchester Community News (June 1990); and http://www.dorchesterhistoricalsociety.org. The rambling house was destroyed in 1971. Today, houses sit on some of the property where Lucy's house formerly stood. See also "Lucy Stone House" souvenir program, June 14, 1950, and Blackwell, *Growing up in Boston's Gilded Age*, 8.

6. Henry Blackwell to George Blackwell, Boston, MA, March 9, 1870, BFPS.

7. Wendy Hamand Venet, *A Strong-Minded Woman: The Life of Mary A. Livermore* (Amherst and London: University of Massachusetts Press, 2005); Livermore, *The Story of My Life*; and "Livermore, Mary," s.v., *American National Biography*.

8. Higginson also wrote weekly editorials and essays for the paper, which were later collected into two volumes, *Common Sense about Women* (Boston: Lee and Shepard, 1882) and *Women and Men* (New York: Harper & Bros., 1888).

9. Henry Blackwell to George Blackwell, Dorchester, MA, January 28, 1872, BFPS.

10. Lucy Stone to Henry Blackwell, Boston, MA, April 11, 1872, and Lucy Stone to Rebecca Smith Janney, Boston, MA, April 17, 1871, both in BFP.

11. Catt quote in Blackwell, *Lucy Stone*, 243.

12. "Another Year," *Woman's Journal*, January 3, 1874; Lucy Stone to Margaret Campbell, Dorchester, MA, December 8, 1874, BFP.

13. Lucy Stone to Margaret Campbell, Boston, MA, December 8, 1874, November 9, 1875, and January 8, 1876, BFP. Lucy Stone to Margaret Campbell, Boston, MA, April 12, 1877, BFP; and "Lucy Stone, 1818–93," Florence Hazard Papers, Sophia Smith Collection, Smith College.

14. Stanton, Anthony, and Gage, eds., *History of Woman Suffrage*, 3:312; "Lucy Stone and Miss Anthony in Luck," *New York Times*, June 4, 1883; Lucy Stone to Ednah Cheney, Dorchester, MA, September 1, 1888, and Lucy Stone to Ednah Cheney, Gardner, MA, July 20, 1882, both in New England Hospital Records, Sophia Smith Collection, Smith College Library. During the four years when the will was being contested, Lucy often mentioned her hope that they would

soon receive the money. Even newspapers carried brief accounts of the contesting of the Eddy will.

15. Lucy Stone to Margaret Campbell, Dorchester, MA, October 20, 1878, BFP; Lucy Stone to Mrs. John L. Whiting, Dorchester, MA, September 16, 1892, John L. Whiting Collection, Massachusetts Historical Society, Boston.

16. Lucy Stone to Margaret Campbell, Dorchester, MA, October 20, 1878, BFP.

17. "Foreign Correspondence," "What Women are Doing," and "Editorial Correspondence," *Woman's Journal,* January 8 and February 19, 1870.

18. "Parliamentary Progress in England," "Our English Letter," "Women Enslaved in San Francisco," and "Suffrage Debate at Harvard College," *Woman's Journal,* August 11 and 18, 1888, June 2, 1888, and January 5, 1889.

19. See "A Woman's Cows Sold to Pay Her Taxes," January 10, 1874; "News from Glastonbury," January 17, 1874; "To Miss Abby Smith, Greetings," February 7, 1874; L.S., "Ku Klux in Connecticut," November 18, 1874 (quote); and "Protest of Julia E. Smith," May 7, 1881, all in *Woman's Journal.*

20. "Progress among Colored Women," *Woman's Journal,* July 6, 1889.

21. Amie M. Hale, "The 'Poor White' Women of N.C.," *Woman's Journal,* August 10, 1889.

22. "Ennoble Domestic Work," *Woman's Journal,* April 16, 1870; Lucy Stone to Margaret Campbell, Boston, MA, January 24, 1874, BFP. Myra Bradwell sued the state of Illinois in 1873 in *Bradwell v. Illinois* for not allowing her to practice law, a case which went all the way to the US Supreme Court. She lost her suit on two counts: she was a woman and a married woman.

23. Edward H. Clarke, *Sex in Education; or, a Fair Chance for the Girls* (Boston: James R. Osgood and Co., 1873); "Harvard and Oberlin," *Woman's Journal,* March 24, 1873.

24. Lydia Maria Child, "Physical Strength of Women," March 15, 1873; T.W.H, "Sex in Education," November 8, 1873; Frances D. Gage, "Sex in Education," November 29, 1873; Mary, "What We Think of Dr. Clarke's Book in California," November 29, 1873; T.W.H., "Sex in Education Again," December 6, 1873; "Sex in Education, Once Again," January 3, 1874; and Mercy N. Jackson, M.D., "Sex in Education," all in *Woman's Journal.*

25. Lucy Stone to Margaret Campbell, Boston, MA, February 8, 1875, BFP.

26. "Burned Out," *Woman's Journal,* December 16, 1871; Emily Blackwell to Henry Blackwell, New York, NY, December 13, 1871, and to Lucy Stone, New York, NY, December 7, 1871, both in BFP.

27. Blackwell, *Growing up in Boston's Gilded Age,* 9; Lucy Stone to Margaret Campbell, Dorchester, MA, August 1, 1875, BFP; Hattie E. Turner, "Reminiscences," June 12, 1922, BFP; and Lucy Stone to Margaret Campbell, Dorchester, MA, June 2, 1881, BFP.

28. His office was on Bromfield Street, and Alice and her friends sometimes helped mail copies of the *Journal.* See Blackwell, *Growing Up in Boston's Gilded Age,* 53 n. 28. For information on the "servant problem," see Carol Lasser, "The

Domestic Balance of Power: Relations between Mistress and Maid in Nineteenth-Century New England," *Labor History* 28, no. 1 (winter 1987): 5–22; Faye E. Dudden, *Serving Women: Household Service in Nineteenth-Century America* (Middletown, CT: Wesleyan University Press, 1983); Andrew Urban, "Irish Domestic Servants, 'Biddy' and Rebellion in the American Home, 1850–1900," *Gender & History* 21, no. 2 (August 2009): 263–286; and Diane M. Hostten-Somers, "Relinquishing and Reclaiming Independence: Irish Domestic Servants, American Middle-Class Mistresses, and Assimilation, 1850–1920," *Eire-Ireland* 36, no. 1/2 (Spring 2001): 185–201.

29. Lucy Stone to Emma Lawrence Blackwell, Dorchester, MA, October 12, 1888, BFPS.

30. "Lucy Stone, 1818–93," in Florence Hazard Papers, Sophia Smith Collection, Smith College.

31. Lucy Stone to Margaret Campbell, Dorchester, MA, April 22, 1871, BFP.

32. Blackwell, *Growing Up in Boston's Gilded Age*, 1; Lucy Stone to Margaret Campbell, Dorchester, MA, September 19, 1871, June 16, 1873, and August 1, 1875, BFP.

33. Mary Flynn Head, "Reminiscences of Lucy Stone," n.p., December 25, 1914, BFP.

34. Lucy Stone to Margaret Campbell, Boston, MA, November 9, 1875, and "Margaret W. Campbell," Iowa Biographies Project, http://www.rootsweb.ancestry.com/~iabios/hi1903c. The New England Woman Suffrage Association contributed $100 monthly for Campbell to conduct her work in 1875.

35. "Woman Suffrage," *Cleveland Herald*, November 24, 1870, as carried in the *New York Herald*, November 26, 1870. See also "The Woman Suffrage Fight," *New York Tribune*, December 2, 1870.

36. "Remarks" (Susan B. Anthony to the AWSA), Cleveland, OH, November 23, 1870, *Woman's Journal*, December 3, 1870; Blackwell, *Lucy Stone*, 218–20.

37. "The Cleveland Meeting," *The Revolution*, December 1, 1870; and "Remarks by Susan B. Anthony to the American Woman Suffrage Association in Cleveland," Stanton and Anthony, *Selected Papers*, 2:377; Lucy Stone to Margaret Campbell, Boston, MA, December 16, 1878, BFP.

38. "National Convention in Philadelphia," October 18, 1854, in Stanton, Anthony, and Gage, eds., *History of Woman Suffrage*, 1:380; and Susan B. Anthony, "The Woman's Rights Convention, Penn Yan, NY," *Yates County Whig*, January 10, 1855, Papers of Elizabeth Cady Stanton and Susan B. Anthony, microfilm.

39. "Miss Alcott on Woman Suffrage," *New York Times*, January 29, 1883. The letter's appearance in the *New York Times* was likely at Lucy's instigation.

40. Susan B. Anthony to Laura De Force Gordon, Williamsport, PA, November 17, 1870, in Stanton and Anthony, *Selected Papers*, 2:373.

41. Susan B. Anthony to Elizabeth Boynton Harbert, Rochester, NY, August 5, 1880, Papers of Elizabeth Cady Stanton and Susan B. Anthony, microfilm; *Woman's Journal*, November 5, 1870, and *New York Tribune*, November 11, 1870, in Stanton and Anthony, *Selected Papers*, 2:374 n. 5. The Decade Celebration

commemorated the second decade since the first national women's rights convention met at Worcester

42. Susan B. Anthony to Elizabeth Boynton Harbert, Rochester, New York, NY, August 5, 1880, Papers of Elizabeth Cady Stanton and Susan B. Anthony, microfilm.

43. Lucy Stone to Margaret Campbell, Boston, MA, April 18, 1876, BFP.

44. Antoinette Brown Blackwell to Elizabeth Cady Stanton, Somerville, NJ, December 21, 1874, Papers of Elizabeth Cady Stanton and Susan B. Anthony, microfilm; and Martha Coffin Wright to Ellen Wright Garrison, n.p., May 14, 1873, quoted in Sherry H. Penney and James D. Livingston, *A Very Dangerous Woman: Martha Wright and Women's Rights* (Amherst: University of Massachusetts Press, 2004), 207..

45. Susan B. Anthony to Harriet Jane Hanson Robinson, Tenafly, NJ, October 24, 1880, Papers of Elizabeth Cady Stanton and Susan B. Anthony, microfilm.

46. Ibid.

47. Henry B. Blackwell to Elizabeth Cady Stanton, Boston, MA, June 8, 1872, in Stanton and Anthony, *Selected Papers*, 2: 503–5.

48. Blackwell, November 11, 1872, *Growing up in Boston's Gilded Age*, 121.

49. Elizabeth Cady Stanton to Lucy Stone, Tenafly, NJ, December 28, 1873, Papers of Stanton and Anthony, microfilm. See also "Why There Are Two National Woman Suffrage Associations," *Woman's Journal*, December 3, 1870; and McMillen, *Seneca Falls*, 197–98.

50. For background on Woodhull, see "Woodhull, Victoria Claflin," s.v., *American National Biography*; Lois Beachy Underhill, *The Woman Who Would Be President: The Many Lives of Victoria Woodhull* (Bridgehampton, NY: Bridge Works, 1995); Rodger Streitmatter, *Voices of Revolution: The Dissident Press in America* (New York: Columbia University Press, 2001), 61–79; and Barbara Goldsmith, *Other Powers: The Age of Suffrage, Spiritualism, and the Scandalous Victoria Woodhull* (New York: Knopf, 1998), 139, 149.

51. McMillen, *Seneca Falls*, 191–92.

52. Elizabeth Cady Stanton to Lucretia Mott, New Castle, DE, April 1, 1871, in Stanton and Anthony, *Selected Papers*, 2:427–29; Ginzberg, *Elizabeth Cady Stanton*, 144–45; and McMillen, *Seneca Falls*, 189–92.

53. Henry Blackwell to Lucy Stone, New York, NY, March 20, 1872, BFP.

54. Margaret Campbell to Lucy Stone, n.p., November 1874, BFP; and Lucy Stone to Margaret Campbell, Boston, MA, July 6, 1874, BFP; Lucy Stone to Mr. Wildman, Boston, MA, October 21, 1871, BFP.

55. Lucy Stone to Rebecca Smith Janney, Boston, MA, July 8, 1874, BFP.

56. "Letter by Mr. Beecher," Brooklyn, NY, June 30, 1873, *Brooklyn Eagle* printed in *Woman's Journal*, July 5, 1873.

57. See Ginzberg, *Elizabeth Cady Stanton*, 145; McMillen, *Seneca Falls*, 192; Debbie Applegate, *The Most Famous Man in America: The Biography of Henry Ward Beecher* (New York: Doubleday, 2006), 395–454 passim; Goldsmith, *Other Powers*.

58. Lucy Stone to Margaret Campbell, Dorchester, MA, August 15 and August 8, 1874, BFP; and Lucy Stone to Henry Blackwell, Gardner, MA, August 22, 1876, BFP.

59. Lucy Stone to Mrs. Field, Boston, MA, September 8, 1874, BFP. The Woodhull sisters eventually went to England where both married well. Victoria lived her final years as a lady.

60. "The Tilton-Woodhull Conspiracy," and editorial in *Woman's Journal*, August 29, 1874, in Wheeler, *Loving Warriors*, 248.

61. See Underhill, *The Woman Who Would Be President* and Goldsmith, *Other Powers*.

62. "New England Woman's Tea Party," *Woman's Journal*, December 20, 1873, and Blackwell, *Growing up in Boston's Gilded Age*, 211–12. See also Linda K. Kerber, *No Constitutional Right to Be Ladies: Women and the Obligations of Citizenship* (New York: Hill and Wang, 1998), 100.

63. "Speech by Susan B. Anthony to the Centennial of the Boston Tea Party in New York City," December 16, 1873, in Elizabeth Cady Stanton and Susan B. Anthony, *The Selected Papers of Elizabeth Cady Stanton and Susan B. Anthony*, vol. 3: *National Protection for National Citizens, 1873 to 1880*, ed. Ann D. Gordon (New Brunswick, NJ: Rutgers University Press, 2003), 22–25. This society seemed to be a state organization affiliated with the NWSA.

64. Lucy Stone to Antoinette Brown Blackwell, Dorchester, MA, September 18, 1890, in Lasser and Merrill, *Friends and Sisters*, 260. See also Lisa Tetrault, *The Myth of Seneca Falls: Memory and the Women's Suffrage Movement* (Chapel Hill: University of North Carolina Press, 2014).

65. Lucy Stone to Margaret Campbell, Philadelphia, PA, July 19, 1876, BFP; "American Woman Suffrage Association Fourth Anniversary and Fifth Annual Meeting," *Woman's Journal*, October 18, 1873.

66. *Memorial of the International Exhibition at Philadelphia, 1876* (Philadelphia: Thomas Hunter, n.d.).

67. L.S. "Not Exhibited at the Centennial," *Woman's Journal*, November 18, 1876; and Lucy Stone to Cornelia Hussey, Boston, MA, November 29, 1876, BFP.

68. Ibid.; L.S., "Women's Work at the Centennial," *Woman's Journal*, December 23, 1876. A letter to Cornelia Hussey said that Mrs. James T. Field had asked Lucy to prepare the exhibit.

69. Lucy Stone to Margaret Campbell, Dorchester, MA, July 19, 1876, BFP; McMillen, *Seneca Falls*, 193–94. As Lucy's correspondence shows, planning this AWSA meeting proved extremely stressful.

70. In 1869 Parliament passed the Municipal Corporations (Franchise) Act, which granted women the right to vote in local elections, though they had to be single women ratepayers. Married women could not vote because their husbands legally were the ratepayers. See Harold L. Smith, *The British Women's Suffrage Campaign, 1866–1928* (London and New York: Longman, 1998), 6.

71. "Declaration of Rights of the Women of the United States," July 4, 1876, American Memory; Lucy Stone to Margaret Campbell, Philadelphia, PA, July 19, 1876, BFP; Susan B. Anthony to Laura De Force Gordon, New York, NY, May 15, 1876, in Stanton and Anthony, *Selected Papers*, 3:224–25; McMillen, *Seneca Falls*, 193–94; and Tetrault, *Myth of Seneca Falls*, 98–101.

72. For background on Willard, see "Willard, Frances Elizabeth Carolina," s.v., *American National Biography*; and Ruth B. A. Bordin, *Frances Willard: A Biography* (Chapel Hill: University of North Carolina Press, 1986).

73. Lucy Stone to Cornelia Hussey, Boston, MA, November 29, 1876, BFP; Tetrault, *Myth of Seneca Falls*, 87–89.

74. Lucy Stone to Margaret Campbell, Boston, MA, August 9, 1877, BFP; Lucy Stone to Alice Stone Blackwell, Central Colorado, September 21, 1877, in Wheeler, *Loving Warriors*, 266–67.

75. Henry Blackwell to Emily Blackwell, Pueblo, CO, July 21, 1877, BFP; Henry Blackwell, "The Lessons of Colorado," *Woman's Journal*, October 20, 1877. At this time, political parties rather than the government printed ballots and supervised elections. Ballots were cast in public. For the vote, see Stanton and Anthony, *Selected Papers*, 3:326 n. 3.

76. Susan B. Anthony to Elizabeth Cady Stanton, Denver, CO, October 5, and Susan B. Anthony to Nancy Hall Allen and the Iowa Woman Suffrage Association, Denver, CO, October 14, 1877, in Stanton and Anthony, *Selected Papers*, 3:325, 327–29. Not until November 1893, a few weeks after Lucy died, did Colorado women win universal suffrage, becoming the second state after Wyoming to gain that right.

77. Elizabeth Cady Stanton and Susan B. Anthony, *The Selected Papers of Elizabeth Cady Stanton and Susan B. Anthony*, vol. 4: *When Clowns Make Laws for Queens*, ed. Ann D. Gordon (New Brunswick, NJ: Rutgers University Press, 2006), 61 n. 2; Lucy Stone to Margaret Campbell, Dorchester, MA, June 22, July 15, and August 30, 1882, BFP; Lucy Stone to Margaret Campbell, June 30, 1882, Dorchester, MA, BFP. For background on the Nebraska campaign, see Kristin Mapel Bloomberg, "'Striving for Equal Rights for All': Woman Suffrage in Nebraska, 1855–1882," *Nebraska History* 90 (2009): 84–103.

78. Susan B. Anthony, "Remarks to the American Woman Suffrage Association," Omaha, NE, September 13, 1882, in Stanton and Anthony, *Selected Papers*, 4:176; and Lucy Stone to Margaret Campbell, Boston, MA, August 30, 1882, BFP.

79. Lucy Stone to Alice Stone Blackwell, in Nebraska, September 24, 1882; and Henry Blackwell to Alice Stone Blackwell, Wisner, NE, September 24, 1882, both in Wheeler, *Loving Warriors*, 283.

80. Lucy Stone to Alice Stone Blackwell, Wahoo, NE, September 7, 1882, and Schuyler, NE, September 21, 1882, BFP. See also Carmen Heider, "Adversaries and Allies: Rival National Suffrage Groups and the 1882 Nebraska Woman Suffrage Campaign," *Great Plains Quarterly* 25 (Spring 2005): 87–103.

81. Henry Blackwell to Alice Stone Blackwell, Wisner, NE, September 24, 1882, BFP.

82. Lucy Stone to Alice Stone Blackwell, Schuyler, NE, September 21, 1882 and Grand Island, NE, October 12, 1882, BFP; Henry Blackwell to Alice Stone Blackwell, Wisner, NE, September 24, 1882, in Wheeler, *Loving Warriors*, 282; Lucy Stone to Alice Stone Blackwell, Wisner, NE, September 24, 1882, BFP.

83. Stanton and Anthony, *Selected Papers*, 4:202 n. 2.

84. Lucy Stone to Alice Stone Blackwell, Wisner, NE, September 24, 1882, and Henry Blackwell to Lucy Stone, Boston, MA, March 15, 1880, both in Wheeler, *Loving Warriors*, 283, 274; and Lucy Stone to Mr. James Freeman Clarke, Boston, MA, February 11, 1885, BFP.

85. Lucy Stone to Mrs. Smith, Dorchester, MA, July 22, 1892, BFP.

86. Lasser and Merrill, *Friends and Sisters*, 170–71; Lucy Stone to Henry Blackwell, Boston, MA, April 11, 1872, BFP. Slavery ended in Puerto Rico in 1873 and in Cuba, not until 1886. Henry did benefit from his Santo Domingo travels by lecturing on his adventures, "Two Months in Santo Domingo," to which he charged fifty cents admission. See "Santo Domingo" flyer, February 11, 1873, BFPS.

87. Henry Blackwell to Lucy Stone, Portland, ME, October 28, 1876; Blackwell, *Lucy Stone*, 269; Lasser and Merrill, *Friends and Sisters*, 171, 201; Kerr, *Lucy Stone*, 201; Henry Blackwell to Lucy Stone, Portland, ME, April 12, 1880, in Wheeler, *Loving Warriors*, 278; and Lucy Stone to Margaret Campbell, Boston, MA, February 4, 1881, BFP. Henry estimated that he had lost $35,000 in this venture.

88. Henry Blackwell to Lucy Stone, Portland, ME, October 26, 1878; and Lucy Stone to Henry Blackwell, Boston, MA, September 16, 1880, BFP.

89. Alice Stone Blackwell to Kitty Blackwell, Dorchester, MA, April 14, 1889, BFP.

90. Henry Blackwell to Lucy Stone, Sebago Lake, ME, April 30, 1878, BFP.

91. Henry Blackwell to Elizabeth Blackwell, Boston, MA, January 13, 1874; Henry Blackwell to Lucy Stone, Portland, ME, April 28, 1878; Lucy Stone to Henry Blackwell, Boston, MA, April 30, 1879; Henry Blackwell to Lucy Stone, Portland, ME, April 5, 1880, all in BFP; and Turner, "Reminiscences."

92. Alice Stone Blackwell to Kitty Blackwell, October 29, 1872, in Blackwell, *Growing Up in Boston's Gilded Age*, 239; Thomas Cushing, *Historical Sketch of Chauncey-Hall School, 1828–1894* (Boston: Press of David Clapp and Son, 1895), 91 and "Higher Education for Women," *Woman's Journal*, August 23, 1873. Alice is listed as '74—the date she started. Initially Chancey Hall was all-male, with the express purpose of preparing young men for Harvard. Apparently Alice and Henry did not feel the best girls' schools did enough to prepare students for college. See Blackwell, *Growing up in Boston's Gilded Age*, 19, 190. Here Lucy wrote "I wont I wont I wont—unless I have to." When she visited Chancey Hall with her mother, she was "appalled by the sight of a great hall full of boys." September 15, 1873, 192.

93. Henry Blackwell to Elizabeth Blackwell, Boston, January 13, 1874, BFPS. Lucy felt that women's colleges were not as rigorous as men's colleges, offered a

different curriculum, and upheld different standards for women. What she most wanted was for the top men's colleges to open their doors to women. See "Female Colleges," August 5, 1871, *Woman's Journal*. Alice had two women and twenty-six men in her college class. See Blackwell, *Growing Up in Boston's Gilded Age*, 237.

94. Blackwell, *Growing Up in Boston's Gilded Age*, 237–38.

95. Henry Blackwell to George Blackwell, Boston, MA, August 20, 1877, BFPS.

96. Lucy Stone to Rev. Dr. William F. Warren, Boston, MA, August 21, 1878, BFP.

97. Alice Stone Blackwell to Kitty Blackwell, September 28, 1879, in Blackwell, *Growing Up in Boston's Gilded Age*, 237.

98. Lori Bogle, "Paradox of Opportunities: Lucy Stone, Alice Stone Blackwell, and the Tragedy of Reform," *Historical Journal of Massachusetts* 22, no. 1 (winter 1994): 17–33. Lucy constantly worried about Alice's working too hard, often commenting that she was "brain dead" and needed a vacation. In the spring of 1883, Alice took a two-month trip to California with friends.

99. Lucy Stone to Margaret Campbell, Boston, MA, March 25, 1883, BFP.

100. Lucy Stone to Margaret Campbell, Dorchester, MA, February 5, 1887, BFP; Alice Stone Blackwell to Kitty Blackwell, Dorchester, MA, April 14, 1889, BFP.

101. Henry Blackwell to Lucy Stone, Portland, ME, July 8, 1879, in Wheeler, *Loving Warriors*, 270–71.

102. J. M. Wightman to Lucy Stone, Boston, MA, November 25, 1879; Lucy Stone to J. M. Wightman, Boston, MA, December 4; J. M. Wightman to Lucy Stone, Boston, MA, December 5, 1879, BFP.

103. Stanton and Anthony, *Selected Papers*, 4:158 n. 2; "The Work in Massachusetts— Shoulder to Shoulder," *Woman's Journal*, March 4, 1882. For much stronger language, see also Lucy Stone to Margaret Campbell, Boston, MA, February 5, 1882, and February 7, 1882, BFP.

104. "The Wars of the Amazons," *Macon Weekly Telegraph*, February 2, 1870; David Plumb, "Mrs. General Sherman and 1000 Other Ladies Against Us," *Woman's Journal*, January 28, 1871; and "The Anti-Suffrage Effort," March 11, 1871, *Woman's Journal*. Elmira Phelps urged her pupils and students of her late sister's to oppose women's suffrage. For a study of Remonstrants' efforts in New York, see Susan Goodier, *No Votes for Women: The New York State Anti-Suffrage Movement* (Urbana and Chicago: University of Illinois Press, 2013).

105. "The Obstacles to Woman's Advancement," *Woman's Journal*, July 5, 1873.

106. "Harvard and Oberlin," *Woman's Journal*, March 24, 1873.

107. William Lloyd Garrison Jr., "Address of Mr. Garrison," March 1885, Garrison Family Papers, Smith College Suffrage Collection, Smith College Library. William Jr. was as dedicated to woman suffrage as his father had been.

108. Lucy Stone to Margaret Campbell, Boston, MA, March 11, 1883, BFP; Lucy Stone to Charles A. Stott, Boston, MA, July 10, 1882, BFP. Those three states did not approve women's suffrage.

109. Lucy Stone to Margaret Campbell, Newark, NJ, April 9, 1869, BFP. Margaret W. Campbell and her husband John became stalwart supporters of Lucy and the AWSA; Wells, *Dear Preceptor,* 203.

110. Lucy Stone to Margaret Campbell, Dorchester, MA, March 30, 1874; Wheeler, *Loving Warriors,* 249; Henry Blackwell to Lucy Stone, Portland, ME, March 10, 1880, BFP. Henry's sugar beet efforts in Maine ended in the winter of 1881.

111. Emily Blackwell to Henry Blackwell, New York, NY, March 6 and March 30, 1880, BFP.

112. Lucy Stone to Margaret Campbell, Wilmington, DE, July 4, 1880; Emily Blackwell to Lucy Stone, New York, NY, April 15, 1880, BFP; Lucy Stone to Margaret Campbell, Boston, MA, August 19, 1883, BFP.

113. Turner, "Reminiscences."

114. Lucy Stone, "Oberlin and Woman," *The Oberlin Jubilee, 1833–1883,* ed. W. G. Ballantine (Oberlin, OH: Oberlin College, 1884), 316–17, 320–21.

115. Lucy Stone to Alice Stone Blackwell, Oberlin, OH, June 30, 1883, and Painesville, OH, June 22, 1883, BFP.

116. Jack Wilson, "Belva Lockwood for President," *The Keynoter* 2008, no. 2–4 (2008): 10. Lockwood received over 4,000 votes in the six states where her name was on the ballot.

117. "Victory," *Woman's Journal,* November 24, 1883; T. A. Larson, "The Case in Washington Territory," *Woman's Journal,* June 9, 1888; "The Columbia Annex," *Woman's Journal,* October 5, 1889; Lucy Stone to Margaret Campbell, Dorchester, MA, March 3, 1878, BFP; and "Women's College in Mississippi," *Woman's Journal,* June 9, 1888. Radcliffe College was founded in 1894 as a coordinate college to Harvard. By 1977, women became well integrated into Harvard. In 1999 Radcliffe closed its doors to become the Radcliffe Center for Advanced Study.

118. "Birthday Celebrations," BFP; "Her Seventieth Birthday," *New York Times,* August 14, 1888; "Lucy Stone's Seventieth Birthday," *Springfield Republican,* August 19, 1888.

119. Savage, "Lucy Stone," in *Sermons of M. J. Savage,* 18–19.

120. Elizabeth Cady Stanton, "Lucy Stone," 392–94, in James Parton et al., *Eminent Women of the Age* (Hartford, CT: S. M. Betts & Co., 1868), 392. See also Tetrault, *Myth of Seneca Falls.*

121. Elizabeth Cady Stanton to Lucy Stone, Tenafly, NJ, July 30, 1876, and Lucy Stone to Elizabeth Cady Stanton, Dorchester, MA, August 3 and 30, 1876, BFP.

122. Antoinette Brown Blackwell to Susan B. Anthony, Somerville, NJ, August 14, 1876, in Papers of Elizabeth Cady Stanton and Susan B. Anthony, microfilm.

123. Susan B. Anthony to Harriet Hanson Robinson, Rochester, NY, August 12, 1879, in Stanton and Anthony, *Selected Papers,* 3:469. The essay on Lucy is only two and a half pages long, one of the shortest ones in the encyclopedia.

124. Ginzberg, *Elizabeth Cady Stanton,* 156; Lucy Stone to Mrs. H. R. Robinson, Boston, MA, March 4, 1879, BFP; and Elizabeth Cady Stanton to Harriet Hanson Robinson, Tenafly, NJ, October 26, 1881, Stanton and Anthony Papers,

microfilm. Lisa Tetrault shows how contentious and often unpleasant the writing and editing of these three volumes proved to be. See Tetrault, *Myth of Seneca Falls*, 119–20, 135–37.

125. L.S., "The History of Woman Suffrage," June 11, 1881, *Woman's Journal*. Tetrault feels that Stone may have refused to participate "presumably—if ineffectively— hoping to limit its influence." See Tetrault, *Myth of Seneca Falls*, 170.

126. Lucy Stone to Rebecca Smith Janney, Boston, MA, April 27, 1882. For other comments on Mormons, see Lucy Stone to Frances Willard, Dorchester, MA, August 23, 1888, in Wheeler, *Loving Warriors*, 315.

127. L.S., "The History of Woman Suffrage," *Woman's Journal*, June 11, 1881; Julie Des Jardins, *Women and the Historical Enterprise in America: Gender, Race, and the Politics of Memory, 1880–1945* (Chapel Hill and London: University of North Carolina Press, 2003), 179–81; Tetrault, *Myth of Seneca Falls*, 119–20, 135–37. In addition to what Stanton and Anthony had written, Paulina Wright Davis had produced an account of the 1850 Worcester Convention.

128. Harriot received only mention in a footnote that she was the editor of this long, final chapter. See Des Jardins, *Women and the Historical Enterprise in America*, 181, quote 182.

129. "Woman Suffrage History," *Woman's Journal*, March 10, 1883.

130. "New York Nation," *Woman's Journal*, October 12, 1880.

131. Lucy Stone to Margaret Campbell, Boston, MA, November 26, 1886, BFP. Ultimately there were six volumes in this set, though the last three cover the years up to the passage of the Nineteenth Amendment. See also Tetrault, *Myth of Seneca Falls*.

132. Lucy Stone to Mr. Wildman, Dorchester, MA, February 10, 1887, BFP.

133. "In Memorium," *Woman's Journal*, July 8, 1876.

134. Mary Grew, "Lucretia Mott," *Woman's Journal*, November 20, 1880; Elizabeth Buffum Chace, Boston, MA, March 1, 1884, in Wyman and Wyman, *Elizabeth Buffum Chace*, 2:180; Lucy Stone to "Friends," Boston, March 11, 1884, BFP; and "Wendell Phillips Buried," *New York Times*, February 7, 1884.

135. Lucy Stone to Samuel May Jr. Boston, MA, February 12, 1884, BFP.

136. Lucy Stone to Margret Campbell, Boston, MA, February 5, 1887, BFP; "Abby Kelley Foster Dead," *New York Times,* January 15, 1887.

137. Lucy Stone to Alice Stone Blackwell, Reminiscences, February 9, 1890, and p. 34, BFP.

138. Lucy Stone to Cornelia Hussey, Boston, MA, November 28, 1884, in Wheeler, *Loving Warriors*, 287–88.

139. See T.W.H., "Many Women, Many Minds" and L.S., "More Facts against Cleveland," *Woman's Journal*, October 4, 1884; T.W.H., "Impartial Justice," *Woman's Journal*, October 18, 1884; W.T.H., "On the Eve of Election Day"; and H.B.B., "Loaded Dice for Cleveland," *Woman's Journal*, November 1, 1884.

140. Lucy Stone to Cornelia Hussey, Boston, MA, November 28, 1884, in Wheeler, *Loving Warriors*, 287–88.

141. Lucy Stone to Thomas Wentworth Higginson, Boston, MA, December 18, 1884, BFP.

142. Lucy Stone to Alice Stone Blackwell, Minneapolis, MN, October 12, 1885, BFP.

143. Lucy Stone to Alice Stone Blackwell, Warsaw, IN, October 27, 1885, BFP.

144. Lucy Stone to Alice Stone Blackwell, Reminiscences, November 20, 1885, BFP.

145. Lucy Stone to New Hampshire Chairman of the Committee on Statues, Boston, MA, 1885, BFP.

146. Lucy Stone to Dr. Gleason, Boston, MA, March 2, 1886, BFP.

147. Lucy Stone, "Address to the New England Woman's Club," 1887, BFP.

148. Lucy Stone to Elizabeth Chace, March 9, 1886, in Wyman and Wyman, *Elizabeth Buffum Chace*, 2:218.

149. Lucy Stone to Margaret Campbell, Boston, March 24, 1886; and Lucy Stone to Mrs. Smith, Dorchester, MA, October 16, 1886, BFP.

150. Lucy Stone to Margaret Campbell, Dorchester, MA, November 12, 1888, BFP.

151. Lucy Stone to Frank and Harriet Stone, Thomasville, GA, March 12, 1887, BFPS; Lucy Stone to Mrs. Wilde, Thomasville, GA, April 14, 1887, BFP; Lucy Stone to Mr. Killian, Thomasville, GA, April 15, 1887, BFP.

152. Lucy Stone to Margaret Campbell, Thomasville, GA, March 15, 1887, BFP; Lucy Stone to Henry Blackwell, Thomasville, GA, May 1, 1887. The first suffrage organization in Georgia was formed in 1890, the Georgia Woman Suffrage Association, as a branch of the National American Woman Suffrage Association. Whether any of these women in Lucy's group became suffragists is unknown.

153. "Eastern Massachusetts," *Springfield Republican*, May 17, 1887.

154. Lucy Stone to Margaret Campbell, Thomasville, GA, March 15, 1887, BFP; Alice Stone Blackwell to Lucy Stone, Boston, MA, March 12, 1887, BFP.

155. Lucy Stone to Alice Stone Blackwell, Thomasville, GA, May 31, 1887, BFP; Alice Stone Blackwell to Lucy Stone, Dorchester, MA, March 30 and 31, 1887, BFP.

156. Lucy Stone to Susan B. Anthony, Boston, MA, March 18, 1884, and January 2, 1885, BFP.

157. Lucy Stone to Antoinette Brown Blackwell, Boston, MA, January 19, 1886, in Wheeler, *Loving Warriors*, 293.

158. Henry Blackwell to Alice Stone Blackwell, Dorchester, MA, August 7, 1887, BFP.

CHAPTER 8

1. Lucy Stone to Alice Stone Blackwell, Thomasville, GA, April 12, 1887; and Lucy Stone to Antoinette Brown Blackwell, Dorchester, MA, July 23, 1887, BFP.

2. Lucy Stone to Susan B. Anthony with Enclosure, Boston, November 7, 1887, in Stanton and Anthony, *Selected Papers*, 5:52–53.

3. Susan B. Anthony to Lucy Stone, Philadelphia, PA, December 13, 1887, in Stanton and Anthony, *Selected Papers*, 5:57; and Susan B. Anthony to Lucy Stone, Philadelphia, PA, December 20, 1887, BFP.

4. "Minutes of Informal Conference between Lucy Stone and Susan B. Anthony," December 21, 1887, in Stanton and Anthony, *Selected Papers*, 5:60–64. No stenographer was present. Alice and Rachel took notes.

5. Lucy Stone to Margaret Campbell, Boston, MA, March 17, 1888, BFP. See Rheta Childe Dorr, *Susan B. Anthony: The Woman Who Changed the Mind of a Nation* (New York: Frederick A. Stokes Company, 1928), 295–96.

6. Lucy Stone to Margaret Campbell, Dorchester, MA, March 13, 1888, BFP. Stanton disliked leading organizations and had become impatient with attending conventions. Susan knew her friend well, and she may have sensed that Stanton might accept the presidency but want to have little to do with running the organization.

7. "Executive Sessions of the National Woman Suffrage Association," Washington, DC, April 3, 1888, in Stanton and Anthony, *Selected Papers*, 5:110–17, quote 116.

8. Susan B. Anthony to Olivia Bigelow Hall, Rochester, NY, January 6, 1889, in Stanton and Anthony, *Selected Papers*, 5:165. Lisa Tetrault claims that Anthony totally ignored the democratic process and forced unification upon members, despite some strong opposition. Some of her former supporters accused her of "underhanded" tactics and violating procedure. See Tetrault, *Myth of Seneca Falls*, 160–62.

9. Susan B. Anthony to Olympia Brown, Leavenworth, KA, March 11, 1889, in Stanton and Anthony, *Selected Papers*, 5:179.

10. Lucy Stone to Margaret Campbell, Dorchester, MA, January 8 and 11, 1889, BFP.

11. Blackwell, *Growing up in Boston's Gilded Age*, 216.

12. Lucy Stone to Margaret Campbell, Dorchester, MA, June 8, 1888, BFP.

13. Lucy Stone to Margaret Campbell, Dorchester, MA, July 2, 1888, BFP.

14. Lucy Stone to Margaret Campbell, Boston, MA, October 19, 1888, BFP.

15. Lucy Stone to Antoinette Brown Blackwell, Dorchester, Winter 1888; and Antoinette Brown Blackwell to Lucy Stone, Elizabeth, NJ, February 10, 1888, both in Lasser and Merrill, *Friends and Sisters*, 255, 256. See also Tetrault, *Myth of Seneca Falls*, 145–180 passim.

16. Alice Stone Blackwell to Kitty Blackwell, Dorchester, MA, August 10, 1890; Henry Blackwell to Lucy Stone, Bismarck, ND, July 9, 1889, BFP.

17. Henry Blackwell to Lucy Stone, Home, SD, September 11, 1890, in Wheeler, *Loving Warriors*, 339; Henry Blackwell to Lucy Stone, Bismarck, ND, July 10, 1889, BFP.

18. Lucy Stone to Mrs. Chapman and to Margaret Campbell, Dorchester, MA, November 26, 1890, BFP.

19. Henry Blackwell to Lucy Stone, Helena, MT, July 14, 1889, BFP. For background on Henry's efforts in Montana, see Leslie Wheeler, "Woman Suffrage's

Gray-Bearded Champion Comes to Montana," *The Magazine of Western History* 31, no. 3 (September 1981): 2–13.

20. Henry Blackwell to Lucy Stone, Helena, MT, July 18, and Olympia, WA, July 22, 1889, BFP.

21. Henry Blackwell to Lucy Stone, Tacoma, WA, July 20, 1889. See T. A. Larson, "The Woman's Movement in Washington," *Pacific Northwest Quarterly* 67, no. 2 (1975): 49–62. Some good did ensue from the agitation over women's rights in these states and territories. North Dakota gave women school suffrage. Montana did the same and also gave taxpaying women the right to vote on all issues that related to taxes. Washington gave women school suffrage in 1890. See Wheeler, *Loving Warriors*, 329.

22. Henry Blackwell to Lucy Stone, Olympia, WA, July 21, 22, 1889.

23. Susan B. Anthony to Lillie Devereux Blake, Washington, DC, February 27, 1888, in Stanton and Anthony, *Selected Papers*, 5: 86–87.

24. "Conference of the Pioneers," National Woman Suffrage Association, "Report of the International Council of Women," 322, 331, speech, 331–35.

25. Ibid.

26. Ibid., 331.

27. Alice Stone Blackwell to Kitty Blackwell, Dorchester, MA, April 8, 1888, BFP; McMillen, *Seneca Falls*, 227.

28. Alice Stone Blackwell to Kitty Blackwell, Dorchester, MA, April 8, 1888, BFP; "Received at the White House," *Washington Post*, March 31, 1888; and Lucy Stone to Margaret Campbell, Washington, DC, April 7, 1888, BFP. According to Lisa Tetrault, a number of NWSA members did not want to create a new organization. Anthony stood firm in wanting this to happen and therefore, unlike the procedure in the AWSA, no proposal was ever submitted to NWSA members to approve or disapprove the measure to unite. Only the Executive Committee of the NWSA voted, and Anthony had a good deal of control over those women. See Tetrault, *Myth of Seneca Falls*, 160–63.

29. "Open Letter to the Women of America," February 18, 1889; and Lucy Stone to Susan B. Anthony, Boston, MA, December 11, 1890, both in BFP.

30. Elizabeth Cady Stanton to Susan B. Anthony and Clara Bewick Colby, Basingstoke Hants, England, June 6, 1890, in Stanton and Anthony, *Selected Papers*, 5:297–99.

31. Elizabeth Cady Stanton to Clara Bewick Colby, Basingstoke, England, March 6, 1891, in Stanton and Anthony, *Selected Papers*, 5: 371.

32. Ibid.

33. Elizabeth Cady Stanton, "Solitude of Self," delivered to the US Congress, Committee of the Judiciary, January 8, 1892, in McMillen, 242–50, quote, 243.

34. McMillen, *Seneca Falls*, 232–33.

35. Lucy Stone to Alice Stone Blackwell, Reminiscences, March 13, 1892, BFP.

36. Ibid. and Alice Stone Blackwell, "Birthday Celebrations," BFP.

37. Alice Stone Blackwell, "Birthday Celebrations," BFP.

38. Lucy Stone to Francis Stone, Dorchester, MA, February 11, 1893, BFP. The bust was completed in the fall of 1892 and then sent to Italy to be perfected in marble. The plan was to send it to the Woman's Department of the Chicago's World's Columbian Exposition to display it there. See Blackwell, "Journal," September 3, 1892, 287, BFP. Alice was both "half vexed and half-pleased" at the tribute to her mother, feeling that since other suffragists had busts sculptured of them, her mother definitely deserved the same attention. She knew Whitney would create a "beautiful" bust but she worried because once Lucy agreed to the idea, many might accuse her of being inconsistent after protesting so long. See Alice Stone Blackwell letter excerpt, February 21, 1892, BFP. After being exhibited in Chicago, the bust returned to Boston where it was offered to the State House. Officials showed no interest, so today the bust sits high on a shelf in the reading room at the Boston Public Library. Two plaster replicas were also made, one of which is in a Boston public school; the other at Oberlin College. See Boston Public Library, "Information about bust of Lucy Stone," BFP. Obtaining a photo of this beautiful bust proved an impossible task.

39. Lucy Stone to Alice Stone Blackwell, Reminiscences, March 3, 1893, BFP.

40. Wanda M. Corn, *Women Building History: Public Art at the 1893 Columbian Exposition* (Berkeley: University of California Press, 2011), 1–6; "Woman's Congress in Chicago," *New York Herald*, May 15, 1893; and Hubert Howe Bancroft, *The Book of the Fair* (Chicago and San Francisco: Bancroft Company, 1893), ch. 11.

41. "Dress Reform Costumes," *New York Herald*, May 17, 1893.

42. Annelise K. Madsen, "Women Speak Out," in Corn, *Women Building History*, 82–83.

43. "Progress of Women," *Daily Inter Ocean* (Chicago), May 25, 1893.

44. Lucy Stone to Henry Blackwell, Chicago, IL, May 1893, BFP.

45. Henry Blackwell to Lucy Stone, Boston, MA, May 17, 1893, BFP. Calomel totally flushed out the body. Many Americans, as late as the early twentieth century, still believed that if you rid the body of "poisons" that allegedly caused a disease or health problem, you would improve. This is an interesting comment from Henry since his father had taken calomel to try to cure his bout of malaria and died (see ch. 3).

46. Henry Blackwell to Lucy Stone, Boston, MA, May 15 and 19, 1893, BFP.

47. Lucy Stone to Ednah Cheney, Dorchester, MA, August 17, 1888, New England Hospital Records, Sophia Smith Collection, Smith College.

48. Lucy Stone to Henry Blackwell, n.p., May 1, 1893, BFP.

49. James T. Patterson, *The Dread Disease: Cancer and Modern American Culture* (Cambridge, MA: Harvard University Press, 1987), 12–18. He writes that "the topic of cancer was riddled with controversy and bewilderment in the 1880s and 1890s." Patterson, *The Dread Disease*, 21.

50. Lucy Stone to Henry Blackwell, Gardner, MA, August 15, 1893, BFP.

51. Henry Blackwell to Lucy Stone, Boston, MA, August 16, 1893, BFP.

52. "Closing Days," Henry Blackwell to Julia Ward Howe, Dorchester, MA, n.d.; and Julia Ward Howe to Lucy Stone, Boston, MA, n.d., BFP.

53. Ada Bowles to Lucy Stone, Gloucester, MA, October 2, 1893, BFP.

54. Antoinette Brown Blackwell to Lucy Stone and Thomas Wentworth Higginson to Lucy Stone, "Closing Days," BFP.

55. "Closing Days," Samuel May Jr. to Lucy Stone, n.d., n.p., BFP.

56. "Closing Days," 1893, BFP.

57. Alice Stone Blackwell Diary, p. 52, BFP.

58. Lucy Stone to Alice Stone Blackwell, Reminiscences, February 9, 1890, BFP.

59. Many of Lucy's tracts, pamphlets, and books were given to the Library of Congress and to the Massachusetts Historical Society.

60. "Mrs. Lucy Stone's Will," New York Times, October 31, 1893.

61. Lucy Stone Reminiscences told to Alice Stone Blackwell, September 25, 1893; and Lucy Stone to Mr. Garrison, Gardner, MA, August 14, 1892, both in BFP.

62. Alice Stone Blackwell Journal, September 25, 1893, BFP; and Savage, "Lucy Stone," 19.

63. "Closing Days," compiled by Alice Stone Blackwell, and Blackwell, "Journal—Reminiscences," October 7, 1893, BFP.

64. Lucy Stone to Mrs. John R. Hanna, Dorchester, MA, September 19, 1893, in Lucy Stone to Alice Stone Blackwell, Reminiscences, September 19, 1893.

65. Lucy Stone to Alice Stone Blackwell, Reminiscences, October 9, 1893, BFP.

66. Hattie E. Turner, "Reminiscences," June 12, 1922, BFP.

67. Henry Blackwell to George Blackwell, Dorchester, MA, October 4, 6, 10, 1893, BFPS; William Lloyd Garrison Jr., "Address of Mr. Garrison," Woman's Journal, 1893, Smith College. The New Zealand vote took place on September 19, 1893.

68. "Memorial Service," October 28, 1893, Woman's Journal; and Wheeler, Loving Warriors, 355. The Church of the Disciples included among its members the Peabody sisters and Julia Ward Howe. Its most famous minister was James Freeman Clarke, an ardent abolitionist who founded the church along with a group of Unitarian dissenters. He died five years before Lucy.

69. William Lloyd Garrison Jr., "At Lucy Stone's Funeral, October 21, 1893," Lucy Stone file, Massachusetts Historical Society, Boston, MA.

70. William Lloyd Garrison Jr., "At Lucy Stone's Funeral"; "Lucy Stone Blackwell Dead," Washington Post, October 19, 1893; "Mrs. Lucy Stone Blackwell Dead," New York Times, October 19, 1893; "Lucy Stone Buried," New York Times, October 23, 1893; Garrison, "Address of Mr. Garrison."

71. Laura Ormiston Chant, letter to Lucy Stone's funeral, Lucy Stone file, Massachusetts Historical Society, Boston.

72. Savage, "Lucy Stone," 18. Savage had been a Congregational minister but left in 1872 to become a Unitarian. He was called to the Church of the Unity where he served until 1891.

73. "Lucy Stone Blackwell Dead," *Washington Post*, October 19, 1893. Lucy would have been upset that the *Post* used a last name she never did. A similar account appeared in "Mrs. Lucy Stone Blackwell Dead," *New York Times*, October 19, 1893.

74. "Make the World Better," *Washington Post*, October 22, 1893.

75. Mrs. Laura Ormiston Chant, letter in "At Lucy Stone's Funeral, October 21, 1893," Massachusetts Historical Society, Boston; Ednah D. Cheney in "Lucy Stone, 1818–1893" biography in Florence Hazzard Papers, Sophia Smith Collection, Smith College.

76. "Lucy Stone's Body Cremated," *Washington Post*, December 31, 1893. For information on the history of cremation, see Stephen R. Prothero, *Purified by Fire: A History of Cremation in America* (Berkeley: University of California Press, 2001), 15–23.

77. Henry Blackwell to Sarah and Henry Lawrence, Dorchester, Boston, MA, December 31, 1893, BFPS.

78. Ibid.

79. Lucy Stone to Henry Blackwell, West Brookfield, MA, July 27, 1853, in Wheeler, *Loving Warriors*, 51.

80. Emily Blackwell to Henry Blackwell, New York, NY, October 27, 1893, BFP.

81. Wheeler, *Loving Warriors*, 356, 358–59.

82. Ibid., 357.

83. Frederick Douglass, "Eulogy to Lucy Stone," *Proceedings of the Twentieth-Sixth Annual Convention of the National Woman's Suffrage Association*, February 15–20, 1894, Washington, DC (Warren, Ohio: Chronicle Print, 1894), 81–84.

84. Quoted in Wheeler, *Loving Warriors*, 356.

85. Henry B. Blackwell, "Address to the NAWSA Convention, 1895," http://www.sscnet.ucla/edu/history/dubois/classes.

86. Wheeler, *Loving Warriors*, 357–59. The Armenian Massacre was the systematic extermination of the Armenian population from the Ottoman Empire (current-day Turkey) beginning in 1895. Estimates are that over a million people were killed.

87. "Blackwell, Alice Stone," s.v., *American National Biography*; Blackwell, Alice Stone, s.v., *Notable American Women*, 1:156–58; Wheeler, *Loving Warriors*, 359; "Alice Blackwell, Noted Suffragist," *New York Times*, March 16, 1950.

88. Apparently Catt uttered racist remarks similar to what Stanton and Henry had said years earlier. To gain support in the South for the Nineteenth Amendment, Catt commented that women's suffrage would strengthen white supremacy. She also said that uneducated immigrants should not be allowed to vote. See "Suffragette's Remarks Haunts College," *New York Times*, May 5, 1986.

89. The states were Wyoming in 1890, Colorado in 1893, Utah and Idaho in 1896, Washington in 1910, California in 1911, Arizona, Kansas, and Oregon in 1912,

Montana and Nevada in 1914, New York in 1917, and Michigan, Oklahoma, and South Dakota in 1918.

90. See Pamela Paul, "The Problem That Has Two Names," *New York Times*, August 24, 2013 and letters to the editor, *New York Times*, September 1, 2103.

91. Ida Husted Harper, *The Life and Work of Susan B. Anthony . . . in Two Volumes* (Indianapolis, IN: The Hollenbeck Press, 1898–1908). The subtitle of volume 3 published in 1908 reads, *In Three Volumes*. Harper went on to complete the next three volumes of *History of Woman Suffrage*. This is an amazing biography to peruse or read. However one feels about Anthony, there is no doubt it is self-serving and exhaustingly laudatory.

92. See Des Jardin, *Women and the Historical Enterprise in America*, 184–202.

93. "Comments on Alice Stone Blackwell Biography," in Garrison Family Papers, Smith College Archives.

94. "Lucy Stone: Lost and Found," *Oberlin Alumni Magazine* 99, no. 4 (Spring 2004), http://www.oberlin.edu/alummag/spring2004/feat_Lucy_02.html.

95. "Suffragist's Home Doomed in New Jersey," *New York Times*, March 18, 1956. One can, of course, visit Elizabeth Cady Stanton's home in Seneca Falls, New York, and Susan B. Anthony's home in Rochester, New York.

96. "Lucy Stone Home," Souvenir Program for Morgan Memorials, June 14, 1950, BFP.

97. "Blackwell, Alice Stone," s.v., *American National Biography*; Donald R. McKay, "Press Release," Morgan Memorial, August 13, 1957, Boston, MA, BFP.

98. Lucy Stone to Henry Blackwell, West Brookfield, MA, July 27, 1853, in Wheeler, *Loving Warriors*, 51.

99. Lucy Stone to Ednah Cheney, Dorchester, MA, August 17, 1885, Florence Hazzard papers, Smith College Archives.

Index